CASE STUDIES OF FAMOUS TRIALS AND THE CONSTRUCTION OF GUILT AND INNOCENCE

Caroline Gorden and Christopher Birkbeck

T0355631

BRISTOL
UNIVERSITY
PRESS

First published in Great Britain in 2022 by

Bristol University Press
University of Bristol
1–9 Old Park Hill
Bristol
BS2 8BB
UK
t: +44 (0)117 954 5940
e: bup-info@bristol.ac.uk

Details of international sales and distribution partners are available at bristoluniversitypress.co.uk

Cover design by blu inc
Front cover image: 2A25YHF World History Archive / Alamy Stock photo;
B4R47P Trinity Mirror / Mirrorpix / Alamy Stock Photo; BYBF24 Pictorial
Press Ltd / Alamy Stock Photo; M1PAAC GL Arichive / Alamy Stock Photo;
P19HWB MIKE WALKER / Alamy Stock Photo
Bristol University Press uses environmentally responsible print partners
Printed and bound in Great Britain by CMP, Poole

Our book is dedicated to Paul Firth
(1951–2021) who contributed so much to
the early development of this project.

Contents

List of Tables

List of Abbreviations

ALI   American Law Institute
ATF   Alcohol, Tobacco and Firearms
DEA   Drug Enforcement Administration
LAPD   Los Angeles Police Department
MHLG   Music Hall Ladies Guild
NGRI   Not Guilty by Reason of Insanity
PACE   Police and Criminal Evidence Act 1984
PEACE   Prepare & Plan; Engage & Explain; Account;
            Closure; Evaluation

Introduction

On 5 December 2009, US citizen Amanda Knox and Italian citizen Raffaele Sollecito were convicted of the murder of British student Meredith Kercher in the Italian city of Perugia – a crime which had happened on 1 November 2007, and which soon attracted worldwide attention. They were convicted by two professional judges and six lay judges in the Corte d'Assise in Perugia. On 3 October 2011, they were acquitted by the Appeals Court in Perugia, comprising a different team of two professional and six lay judges. On 26 March 2013, those acquittals were overturned and a retrial ordered by the Italian Supreme Court. Finally, on 27 March 2015, Knox and Sollecito were acquitted for a second time by the Supreme Court in Rome.

The procedural principles and routines of the Italian legal system meant that this case could be heard four times. Like most other European countries, Italy has what is known as a 'continental' or 'inquisitorial' system in which judges, sometimes accompanied by 'lay judges', decide on guilt and innocence: there are no jurors as we would understand them in the UK. A complementary feature is a strong appeals system in which higher courts can reconsider cases heard at a lower level, affirming, overturning or reversing previous decisions. By contrast, in 'adversarial' criminal justice systems, such as are found in most English-speaking countries, juries decide on guilt or innocence while judges oversee due process. Adversarial systems usually produce definitive decisions at the first sitting, rarely admit appeals about them and, if they do, more often than not uphold the original decision. Those who followed the Knox/Sollecito case in the UK or US, and who did not understand the principles and practices of the criminal justice system in Italy, easily became critical of the shifting decisions – convict, acquit, convict, acquit – and were tempted to see in them the failings of the continental legal system. But the august figures sitting in the Italian courts, the time they took to hear and decide on the case, the extensive and public transcripts of their decision-making, and the fierce international scrutiny of their judgments, belie any easy criticisms of their work. It seems safer to conclude that a convincing case could be made for Knox and Sollecito's guilt *or* for their innocence.

If so, the Italian courts had simply illustrated the nature of truth as a social artefact: the truth is not *what is*, but *what is agreed on*. We are so accustomed to the words of the courtroom oath, which invoke 'the truth, the whole truth, and nothing but the truth', that it is easy to operate with the assumption that the truth has an existence which is independent of all inquiries about it. The opposite perspective has been well expressed by philosopher Richard Rorty (1989: 3) who wrote that 'the truth is made, not found'. Applied to criminal cases, we would say that although the courts – and almost everyone else – usually operate as if the truth is found, they are actually constructing it. Two courts concluded that Knox and Sollecito were guilty and two concluded that they were not. Thus, perhaps we need to question if there is any point in clinging to some notion of an ultimate truth about the case that could somehow be 'found'. As Nobles and Schiff (2000) observe, justice is always contested and uncertain.

To work with a vision of the truth as made is not to abandon a commitment to standards. Indeed, so much of the work that goes into the methods for collecting, handling and analysing evidence is designed precisely to aim for the highest standards possible, which is why courts in the legal domain – just like scientists in the research domain – can make legitimate, authoritative and convincing claims about the nature of events. Even for truths that are made there are better and worse standards of manufacture. The 'best' truths are those that are constructed with the best methods and, hopefully, subscribed to by the great majority of observers. But of course, they are always provisional, in the sense that new information or a new way of looking at the information might lead to a different conclusion. In criminal cases, the 'facts' are only those bits of information that people agree about, or at least do not choose to question. And what the facts of a case will be, what is accepted rather than challenged, depends on the positions taken up by accuser and accused. In one case, all may agree that the defendant shot the victim but disagree about whether or not the defendant intended to do it; in another case, the accused and the accuser may lock horns over whether or not the accused is the shooter.

Viewing the truth as made, not found, leads to a different perspective on criminal cases, both for those directly involved and those who are not. For those directly involved, it implies that the truth is actively constructed, and indeed the chapters in this book are concerned with the process of manufacture, sometimes conscious and explicit, at other times imperceptible or nearly so. For those who are not directly involved, despite the temptation it does not make much sense to ask if the accused was guilty or innocent but *why they were judged to be guilty or innocent*. For example, in the Knox/ Sollecito case, the key question for the uninvolved observer should not be whether they committed the crime of which they were accused, but why they were declared guilty at the first trial. And because there were three subsequent decisions (not guilty, guilty, not guilty), for each we can ask what explains it. There are plenty of studies undertaken by researchers in sociology, psychology, law, criminology and associated fields that offer interesting hypotheses in this regard, and these are the foundation to each of the chapters that follow.

But this is not a book about what might broadly be termed the sociology of law. Its focus and objective are rather different. Each chapter takes a well-known case from the annals of criminal trials and uses it to illustrate some of the processes at work in the construction of guilt or innocence. This case-study approach brings with it one great advantage and two important limitations. First, case studies provide a rich description of the processes at work in the construction of guilt and innocence, even if they are not immediately evident, and help to illuminate the otherwise abstract – although invaluable – concepts and theories that are of relevance in explaining outcomes. Second, however, a single case can never conclusively demonstrate that the explanation proposed for its outcome is valid. Confirmation of explanations requires a sample of cases with varied outcomes (in this case, judgments of both guilt and innocence) in order to demonstrate that a particular cause is associated with a particular effect. Third, a single case will generally combine a number of processes that lead to its outcome. Our answer to the first limitation is already stated: we believe the cases chosen illustrate, sometimes quite vividly, the abstract hypotheses proposed by researchers, even as they fail to constitute proof that the hypothesised process was at work. For example, the portrayal of Amanda Knox by the prosecution and a significant portion of the media as a sexually deviant and violent female fits the feminist theory that women who kill are judged by harsh patriarchal standards. Our answer to the second limitation is that although we select and review each case in relation to a specific process in the construction of guilt and innocence, in subsequent chapters we identify additional processes at work in some of the cases already reviewed. We do not subscribe to a monocausal view of the construction of truths. For example, in addition to patriarchal values that might have influenced the court which first convicted Knox, it is also likely that her 'confession' – produced under duress and soon retracted – contributed to the perception of her guilt.

Our defence of the use of cases is also based on the widespread attention that they have attracted. From a practical perspective, this means that there is a lot more material available with which to approach them. But more than that, these cases have attracted attention because they have involved significant, often highly fraught, disputes about guilt and innocence. As such, the counterposed strategies for arguing one side or the other bring the manufactured quality of 'truth' to the fore. The Knox/Sollecito trials made worldwide headlines and have already provided abundant material for the 'true crime' industry. The case will continue to resurface from time to time in the media as some newsworthy development is picked up by reporters: significant events in the lives of Knox or Sollecito, or of Meredith Kercher's family, a new 'revelation' about what 'really happened', or a new book or film about the case. And, as happened from almost the day on which Meredith's body was discovered, people who have never known any of the key figures in this case, have never lived in Perugia, may not have visited Italy, will debate and judge Knox's and Sollecito's guilt or innocence. We argue that they do so not because of some morbid fascination with violent crime, but because of a deep-seated anxiety, probably unrecognised, about the status of truth. The truth must, they would hope, be ultimately *found* and with that will come a secure judgement about the moral or immoral character of Amanda Knox and Raffaele Sollecito. For, in the absence of certainty, when truths are made rather than found, morality's place in human experience becomes considerably more precarious.

The content of this book

The chapters that follow explore different aspects of the construction of guilt and innocence, most of which have been the focus of considerable attention among researchers in law, criminology, sociology or psychology. The first half of the book is based on a perspective that sees guilt and innocence as broadly narrative and rhetorical accomplishments. We begin with the Florida trial of Casey Anthony in Chapter 1, using it to review and apply the influential work of Bennett and Feldman, who interpret the legal requisites for establishing guilt in terms of a dramatistic framework involving the accused's presence at the scene of the crime, the act of committing the crime, and the intent to commit the crime. This 'storytelling' approach emerged in part to challenge the long-held view that guilt and innocence are decided only on the basis of evidence. We believe that it helps to understand why Casey Anthony was acquitted. In Chapter 2 we use the 1960s case of Londoner James Hanratty, executed for murder, to look at the comparative merits of the evidentiary and storytelling approaches as they arguably played out, not only in his conviction but also in the public debate during the next 40 years about whether or not this was a case of miscarriage of justice. In Chapter 3, we take the famous case of H.H. Crippen, convicted and executed for murder in London in 1910, to focus on the problems of changing the story as the investigation or trial develops. Such changes are perceived to reflect inconsistency and signal a lack of credibility, a factor that was also present in the Hanratty case. In Chapter 4, we use the case of Rosemary West, convicted in the 1990s of ten murders in the city of Gloucester, to broaden the focus by exploring the psychological and sociological research bearing on the perception of credibility. In Chapter 5, we review the case of Timothy McVeigh, convicted and executed for the 1995 bombing of a federal building in Oklahoma City, to explore the role of techniques of neutralisation and other narrative accounts that offenders may use to deny or mitigate their guilt. And in Chapter 6, we use the case of O.J. Simpson to look at guilt and innocence as rhetorical accomplishments, arguing that one of the factors that contributed to his acquittal was the superior courtroom oratory of his defence team.

The next three chapters examine the impact of the defendant's status on the construction of guilt and innocence. Chapter 7 takes the case of Michael Jackson, acquitted of child molestation charges in 2005, to explore the widely researched topic of social status and case outcomes. The argument, fairly evidently, is that Jackson's celebrity status and wealth contributed to his acquittal. In Chapter 8, we take the case of Brendan Dassey, convicted of murder in Wisconsin (in a case made famous by the documentary *Making a Murderer*), to look at the research on vulnerability and its impact on interviews with the police and on forced confessions. And in Chapter 9, we use the case of Peter Sutcliffe (popularly known as 'The Yorkshire Ripper') to explore the legal concept of diminished responsibility and the social constructions that are made of it. It is these social constructions (and Sutcliffe's diminished credibility), we argue, that led to his conviction for murder.

The final two chapters address the topic of judging guilt and innocence, for – after all – judgments represent completed constructions of guilt and innocence (even though subject to possible change) that are influenced by the sorts of process discussed in earlier chapters. But judgments also entail additional factors which merit consideration in their own right. In Chapter 10, we take the case of South African Oscar Pistorius, convicted for the death of his girlfriend, to examine the role played by common sense and reasonableness in judicial decisions about guilt and innocence. Finally, in Chapter 11, we use the case of Amanda Knox to explore constructions of guilt and innocence in the media and the wider social domain.

We conclude with an Afterword about what we believe is the significance of the approach taken in this book for the understanding of criminal case outcomes, not only those receding into the past but also those yet to come.

1

Failing to Establish Guilt in the Trial of Casey Anthony

We truly don't know what happened. Somebody knows, but we don't know.[1]

The death of Caylee Marie Anthony

On 11 December 2008, the Orange County Emergency Dispatch in Florida received a call from utility worker Roy Kronk. He explained to the operator that he had found a skull that he believed to be human. This and other skeletal remains were in a wooded area close to a residential neighbourhood approximately ten miles south-east of downtown Orlando. Duct tape was found on the skull, covering the area where the nose and mouth had been. The body had been wrapped in a blanket, a plastic bag and a laundry bag. The Orange County Medical Examiner, Dr Jan Garavaglia, confirmed that the remains were those of two-year-old Caylee Marie Anthony and that the cause of death was 'homicide by undetermined means' (Ashton, 2012: 313). Her body was found not very far from where she had lived with her mother, Casey Anthony, and grandparents, Cindy and George Anthony.

Caylee had not been seen by her grandparents since 16 June 2008, but the alarm about her disappearance was only raised a month later on 15 July. On 16 June Casey had gone out with Caylee but they did not return that day or for the next 31 days. During that time, in the first phone calls with her mother Casey claimed that she had taken Caylee with her to a work conference at Busch Gardens, in Tampa, Florida. Because Casey had for some time told her parents that she worked at Universal Studios as an event planner, Cindy accepted this account of their whereabouts. Casey further explained that, to help her with Caylee, she was with her nanny, Zenaida Fernández ('Zanny'), as well as the nanny's friend and her children. She later offered various explanations to her mother about her own and Caylee's whereabouts, including having to stay away for longer because of a car accident that led to Zanny being hospitalised. Days later, Casey explained to her mother that her return home with Caylee was further delayed because she would be staying in another hotel with a friend who was visiting the area. Later still, she told her mother that she was staying in Jacksonville with the same friend.

Casey's parents only realised that there might be a problem when, on 15 July 2008, they were informed that their car, which Casey had borrowed, had been taken to the local towing garage in Orlando after it was found abandoned. When Cindy Anthony went to retrieve the car, she found a phone number inside belonging to Casey's friend, Amy Huizenga. Cindy telephoned Amy, who told her that Casey was staying at the home of her boyfriend, Tony Lazzaro. Cindy went to Tony's apartment and found Casey but not Caylee. Casey told her that Zanny had kidnapped Caylee.

Taking Casey home with her, Cindy immediately called the police to report that her granddaughter was missing (Ashton, 2012) and repeated Casey's story that Caylee had been kidnapped by Zanny. Casey also spoke to the operator and, when asked why she had not called 31 days ago when the child first went missing, she replied, 'I've been looking for her and have gone through other resources to try to find her – which is stupid' (Casey Anthony, 911 call, 15 July 2008 cited in Ashton, 2012: 24). One of the first actions by the police was to take Casey to what she said was Zanny's apartment, but Zenaida Fernández did not live there and, when she was subsequently located and questioned by the police, it was established that she had never been a nanny to Caylee – in fact, there was no nanny. Beginning to suspect Casey's story, the police also took her to Universal Studios on 16 July 2008 so that she could show them her office, but once there she admitted that she had not worked at the studios for a long time. On the same day, she was arrested for child neglect, providing false information to law enforcement and obstruction of a criminal investigation. Some months later and based on initial forensic evidence, on 14 October 2008 Casey was indicted by a grand jury, charged with first-degree murder, aggravated manslaughter, aggravated child abuse and four counts of providing false information to police. These charges were filed even before Caylee's remains had been found and the prosecution also announced that if Casey were convicted of first-degree murder they would seek the death penalty. When arraigned in court, she pleaded not guilty to all charges (Ashton, 2012).

Florida law allows the information discovered by the prosecution to be released not only to the defence but also to the media. Cameras are also allowed inside courtrooms. Because of the great demand for what, in this case, turned out to be a large amount of information, the prosecution created its own website so that the media could access the latest information provided to the defence (Ashton, 2012). Given the volume of pretrial publicity, it was considered that an impartial jury could not be found in Orange County (where the alleged crime had occurred), so a jury was selected from nearby Pinellas County instead. The jurors were taken to Orlando for the trial and 'sequestered' (isolated from the public and the media) for its duration. The trial began on 24 May 2011 and lasted for six weeks (Ashton, 2012).

Establishing guilt: the prosecution's strategy

In criminal cases, the prosecution is under a legal obligation to prove the defendant's guilt beyond a reasonable doubt. Social scientists Bennett and Feldman (1981) argued that the prosecution's strategy is underpinned by presenting the evidence in the form of a story (see Chapter 2). That is, the jury compare and contrast the competing stories of the defence and the prosecution, and the story that is judged to be true or truer depends on how well organised, coherent and believable it is. The present chapter, however, is concerned not so much with the story as with the underlying strategies that support the prosecution's story. We utilise the trial of Casey Anthony to illustrate how these strategies are employed, and importantly, how the manner in which they are employed may strengthen or weaken the prosecution's case. The prosecution's strategy focuses on a small set of categories that are the requisites for establishing guilt: *presence, state of mind* and *action. Presence* refers to the scene of the crime (thus showing that the defendant was *situated* at the scene of the crime at the time that the offence took place); *state of mind* refers to the defendant's *intention* to commit the crime and in law is known as *mens rea* (the mental intent to carry out the crime); and *action* refers to the *execution* of the act that constituted the crime, and in law this is known as *actus reus* (whereby the prosecution must prove that the accused carried out the act) (Clarkson, 2005).

Ideally, these requisites must be established by direct evidence: 'Evidence which requires no mental process on the part of the tribunal of fact [the jury] in order to draw the conclusion sought by the proponent of the evidence' (Murphy and Glover, 2009: 17). For example, the accused being chosen from an identity parade by someone who witnessed the crime, or the testimony of a witness claiming to have first-hand knowledge of the accused committing the crime both represent direct evidence. However, direct evidence may not be available in all cases and the law also accepts circumstantial evidence which 'helps us indirectly establish a criminal intent or criminal act' (Lippman, 2013: 117), or presence at the scene of the crime. Circumstantial evidence supports an inference. For example, a fingerprint of the accused found at a crime scene or the testimony of a witness claiming to have seen the accused near the scene of the crime (Murphy and Glover, 2009) are circumstantial indicators of presence, showing that the accused had the *opportunity* to

Table 1.1: Criteria for direct and circumstantial evidence to establish guilt

Dimension of the crime	Direct evidence	Circumstantial evidence
Presence	Situatedness	Opportunity
State of mind	Intention	Motive
Action	Execution	Capability

commit the crime. And just as *opportunity* is the circumstantial equivalent of *situatedness, motive* and *capability* are the circumstantial equivalents of *intention* and *execution* (see Table 1.1).

To avoid confusion, we will hereafter refer to *presence, state of mind* and *action* in the circumstantial form of *opportunity, motive* and *capability*. For example, in order to convict Casey Anthony of first-degree murder, the prosecution needed to prove that:

- Casey Anthony **(actor)**
- had the *opportunity*
- and was *motivated* to murder
- and had the *capability*
- to cause the death of Caylee Anthony **(act)**

However, the strategy further requires that opportunity, motivation and capability be specified in sufficient detail so that a clear link between the actor and the act are established. For example:

1. *Actor–motive–act*: Casey Anthony was motivated and did wilfully and knowingly intend to murder Caylee Anthony.
2. *Actor–capability–act*: Casey Anthony had the capability and means to accomplish this and chloroformed and suffocated the victim, Caylee Anthony.
3. *Actor–opportunity–act*: Casey Anthony had the opportunity and committed the said act on or after 16 June 2008 in Orlando, Florida.

Exercise 1:

Imagine you are the lead prosecutor in the trial of Casey Anthony. Remember that your goal is to secure a conviction. Using Bennett and Feldman's model of the three requisites for establishing guilt, how would you attempt to:

1. Construct an argument for establishing that Casey had the *motive* to murder Caylee?
2. Construct an argument for establishing that Casey had the *opportunity* to murder Caylee?
3. Construct an argument for establishing that Casey had the *capability/means* to murder Caylee?

The prosecution's case for premeditated murder in the trial of Casey Anthony

We will now analyse how the prosecution attempted to establish that Casey was guilty of premeditated murder using the three circumstantial requisites for establishing guilt (*opportunity*, *motivation* and *capability*). For their part, in any criminal case the defence team are under no obligation to prove their client's innocence because the burden is on the prosecution to prove the defendant's guilt beyond a reasonable doubt. In order to create reasonable doubt, the defence need only show the omission of one of the requisites in the prosecution's case (for example, that *motivation* has not been demonstrated), or inconsistencies between the requisites for establishing guilt (for example, that the alleged *opportunity* would not have allowed the defendant to deploy their specific *capability* for committing the crime). According to Bennett and Feldman (1981), the defence can *challenge*, *redefine* or *reconstruct* the prosecution's *story*. Interestingly, as we will see, Casey's defence pursued all three of these strategies to weaken the prosecution's case and strengthen theirs. We will examine how the prosecution's theory of *motive* was *challenged* and their evidence for *capability* was *redefined*. We will explore in detail how the defence capitalised on the unknown cause of Caylee's death which ultimately enabled them to *reconstruct the story*. Thus, the defence attempted to redirect the jury from the scenario of Caylee's premeditated murder to that of a drowning accident that 'snowballed out of control' (Baez, 2011: defence closing statement).

Opportunity and motive

It might be argued that, because Casey was Caylee's mother, there would have been many instances in which the two of them were together, therefore providing Casey with the *opportunity* to murder Caylee. Indeed, the prosecution began their closing statements by explaining the 'point' of the story, which connected the mother and daughter in a conflicted way: the responsibility-free life which Casey allegedly wanted to live, and the burden that was her daughter, Caylee. This enabled the prosecution to link the *opportunity* with a *motive* for the crime:

It's easy to be a parent. Sometimes. It's easy to be a parent when you're playing with your children. It's easy to be a parent when children are a joy, when children are fun. But we all know that being a parent is so much more than just playing with your children. Being a parent is about sacrifice. Being a parent is about sacrificing your time. About sacrificing your love and about sacrificing your dreams and sacrificing your life. When you have a child, that child becomes your life. This case is about the clash between that responsibility and the expectations that go with it and the life that Casey Anthony wanted to have. When Caylee was born, Casey was saddled with expectations and responsibilities. (Ashton, 2011: prosecution closing statement)

The prosecution and defence both acknowledged that Casey was aware of her daughter's death during her month's stay with her boyfriend Tony. They also agreed that Casey behaved as though nothing had happened following the death of her daughter. The prosecution argued that this could be understood in the context of Casey's *motive* to murder her daughter; she appeared to be living a life that was free of parental responsibility. Indeed, within three weeks of Caylee's disappearance, Casey had the words 'Bella Vita' (Italian for 'beautiful life') tattooed on her left shoulder (Ashton, 2012). However, after the trial alternate juror[2] Russell Huekler told NBC's *Today* show 'Just because Casey was a party girl it did not show why she would possibly kill Caylee' (NDTV, 2011), suggesting that the prosecution could not establish the motive convincingly enough. For their part, the defence argued that Casey's behaviour could be understood in the context of what they alleged was her sexual victimisation at the hands of her father. They claimed that this experience taught Casey to lie and thus, knowing that Caylee had drowned in an accident, she was able to behave in a way that concealed this fact from everyone else (Baez, 2011: defence closing statement).

Exercise 2:

Now, imagine that you are the lead defence attorney for Casey. Your goal is to achieve an acquittal. How would you challenge the prosecution's argument that Casey had the *motive* and *opportunity* to murder Caylee?

Challenging opportunity and motive

The jury might have accepted that Casey had the *opportunity* to murder Caylee but the defence argued that the prosecution was not able to offer a clear explanation of *where* and *when* the murder took place. Defence attorney

Baez said in closing statements, 'They want to give you the "who" without the "where," "when" and "how"' (Baez, 2011: defence closing statement). This dilemma was echoed in a post-trial interview with Juror No. 2 who said, 'We don't know *when* she died. Technically, we didn't even know *where* she died' (Thalji and LaPeter, 2011).

The defence also challenged the prosecution's explanation for *motive*. During his closing statement, Baez reminded the jury that witnesses testified to Casey's good parenting behaviour and claimed that the loving mother could never kill her own child in cold blood. In addition, Baez referred to the charge that Casey had subjected Caylee to child abuse, emphasising that no evidence could be found to support it (Baez, 2011: defence closing statement). Furthermore, photographs made public of Casey and Caylee and descriptions by friends and family gave the impression of a healthy and happy relationship between the two. For example, Casey's boyfriend Tony appeared to accept Casey's child in his life (direct examination of Tony Lazzaro: Lazzaro, 2011). No evidence was presented to show that there was any previous child abuse or neglect or any other indication that Casey was a bad mother. Although Casey's mother called the police to report her granddaughter missing, it appears that she did not suspect her daughter of any wrongdoing at the time. Rather, it appears that she believed Casey's kidnapping story. In his book written after the trial, prosecutor Jeff Ashton (2012) suggested that once Casey was suspected of being involved in Caylee's death, Cindy chose her daughter over her granddaughter, perhaps to protect her daughter who was, after all, going on trial for capital murder. Thus, Cindy would not testify against Casey. Ashton (2012) argued that interviews with Cindy's co-workers revealed that Cindy had her doubts about Casey's parenting, but the evidence was not admissible in court because it was considered hearsay. Therefore, Ashton argued, without Cindy's testimony, the *motive* for Caylee's murder was more difficult to establish.

Capability

The prosecution presented forensic evidence to the jury to support the theory that Caylee's death was the result of premeditated murder and that Casey had the *capability* of carry out the killing. The results from a forensic test revealed a high level of a chemical in a piece of carpet from the car that Casey had been driving. The FBI later confirmed that the substance was chloroform, although the source of the chloroform could not be established (Ashton, 2012). Computer forensics determined that on two afternoons three months prior to Caylee's death, someone had used the family computer at the Anthony home and searched on Google for 'chloroform' and 'how to make chloroform'. Work records showed that Cindy and George Anthony were not at home when these searches were conducted (Drane-Burdick, 2011: prosecution rebuttal), making Casey the prime suspect.

Other evidence that supported the prosecution's theory of premeditated murder and that Casey had the *capability* to carry out the crime included:

- A witness for the prosecution, Dr Arpad Vass, forensic anthropologist and an expert in the field of odour mortis, used a gas chromatograph to test the odour coming from the trunk (boot) of the car that Casey had been driving. He testified that the results were consistent with the odour of a decomposing body. In addition, a specially trained dog detected the scent of human remains in the car.
- Two days after leaving the house with Caylee on 16 June, Casey returned and asked a neighbour, Brian Burner, if she could borrow a shovel. She returned it an hour later and the shovel appeared not to have been used. The prosecution hypothesised that Caylee's body was in the trunk of the car and it was Casey's intention to bury her in the back garden of the Anthony home. However, the prosecution argued that she changed her mind, returned the shovel and later disposed of the body in the local woods, which was where Roy Kronk would later find Caylee's remains.
- Karen Lowe, senior analyst in the Trace Analysis Unit of the FBI Crime Laboratory Division, analysed a nine-inch light brown hair found in the trunk of the car. Although it could not be conclusively proved, evidence showed that the hair was most likely from Caylee. The hair had an unusual dark band near the root and although it is not understood why this banding occurs, it has only been found in hairs taken from decomposing bodies.
- Dr Haskell, forensic entomology expert, testified that 'coffin flies' (flies that live on decaying matter) were found in the trunk of the car.
- Caylee's skeletal remains were found with an unusual make of duct tape over her nose and mouth, a Winnie the Pooh blanket and laundry bag. The prosecution argued that all of these items belonged to the Anthony household (Ashton, 2012).

Exercise 3:

As the lead defence attorney, how might you question this evidence and *reinterpret* it so that the jury might have reasonable doubts about the prosecution's case? Also, imagine that you are able to *reconstruct* an entirely different story about what happened to Caylee, such as the accident claimed by the defence. What sort of story might you tell to the jury?

Redefining capability

As well as disputing much of the evidence that the prosecution presented, the defence also offered a different interpretation for some of it. For example, Baez offered an alternative explanation for the search for chloroform on the Anthony's home computer. He argued that Casey was curious to find out what chloroform was after she had visited her previous boyfriend's (Ricardo Morales') Myspace page where he had posted an icon about chloroforming women. The defence also had to contend with the issue of the duct tape found with Caylee's skeletal remains. It was not a piece of evidence that they could dispute was there (unlike their insistence that the trunk of the car was not emitting any sort of odour). Thus, another explanation for the duct tape was required. In fact, two alternative explanations were offered. First, Baez suggested that, when he found the skull, Roy Kronk took it home and later returned it with the duct tape (although Baez did not explain how Roy Kronk might have gained access to duct tape that was the same as that found at the Anthony's house). Second, it was argued that George Anthony had put the duct tape there when *he* allegedly disposed of Caylee's body. Baez further argued that George had deliberately used the duct tape to stick up 'missing' posters for his granddaughter and did this so that he could later frame Casey for the death (Baez, 2011: defence closing statement).

Reconstructing the story

The specific cause of Caylee's death could not be determined primarily because she was skeletonised by the time she was discovered. Having charged Casey with first-degree murder, the prosecution set itself the task of proving that Caylee's death was a homicide. They were helped by Dr Garavaglia's opinion that the cause of Caylee's death was 'homicide by undetermined means' but hindered by the absence of evidence regarding those means. Failing to establish the cause of death meant that they were vulnerable to the defence constructing an entirely new and different story: that Caylee's death was caused by an accidental drowning. The defence claimed that Caylee had drowned in the family swimming pool while at home with Casey and her grandfather, George. Casey was woken in the morning by George telling her that Caylee had drowned, that it was her fault and that he would cover up the accident because otherwise 'you'll go to jail for the rest of your frickin' life' (Baez, 2011: defence closing statement). For the next 31 days, the defence argued, Casey was in a 'fog', not knowing really what she was doing or why. The 'Bella Vita' tattoo, suggested the defence, was meant to represent the irony that her life had been anything but beautiful. The reason that Casey had been persistently dishonest during the 31 days, the defence

CASEY ANTHONY: FAILING TO ESTABLISH GUILT

claimed, was because her father had sexually abused her as a child and so she was trained to deceive others (Baez, 2011: defence closing statement).

In order to support the new and different story, the defence questioned Casey's *capability* for committing murder by principally attacking the prosecution on their forensic evidence, referring to it as 'fantasy forensics' which reflected their 'level of desperation' (Baez, 2011: defence closing statement). In addition, Baez argued that the forensic evidence was irrelevant since it did not reveal *how* Caylee had died. Spotting the weakness in the prosecution's case enabled the defence to emphasise their theme of an 'accident that snowballed out of control'. The gap in the prosecution's story appeared in other critiques developed by the defence. For instance, Baez accused the prosecution of trying to make the jury angry and emotional, arguing that 'Casey's character has nothing to do with *how* she [Caylee] died' and that the prosecution's evidence relating to the trunk of the car also did not reveal *how* Caylee died (Baez, 2011: defence closing statement).

Closing statements: was it premeditated murder or not?

Inability to offer an irrefutable cause of Caylee's death appears to be at the heart of the prosecution's failure to establish guilt. For instance, the prosecutors vigorously argued that Casey was guilty of premeditated murder but this was at odds with their filing of three different charges. Casey was charged with *first-degree murder, aggravated manslaughter* and *aggravated child abuse*. However, even the charge of first-degree murder proved problematic because in Florida there are two ways in which a person can be convicted of this crime: premeditated murder and felony murder (2015 Florida Statutes). To prove premeditated murder, the State had to prove beyond a reasonable doubt that Casey murdered Caylee after consciously deciding to do so. To prove felony murder, the State needed to prove beyond a reasonable doubt that Caylee's death occurred as a consequence of committing a felony, in this case, aggravated child abuse or attempted aggravated child abuse by Casey. Thus, the prosecution explained to the jury that they could find Casey guilty of either premeditated murder or felony murder. More than one version of *motive* and *capability* was offered and we would argue that this strategy was detrimental to the prosecution's case. The point is illustrated in Jeff Ashton's closing statement:

> Our position is that this was a pre-meditated murder of a young child but we know that you can reconstruct the events in any way that you want. So you also need to know what felony murder is. ... The reason that we talk about this is that you can postulate a number of different hypotheses in this case. Some might say well maybe Casey put the duct

tape on Caylee to keep her quiet. Maybe she was being loud. Maybe she put it on to keep her quiet and she put it on too tight and Caylee died by accident. I would submit it's not really consistent with what we have here but you know, someone could think that. The reason I bring that out is because if that is what you think happened, that is felony murder. That's also first degree murder. Or if you think she used the chloroform to sedate Caylee so that she could spend time with her boyfriend – as bizarre as that seems. Let's say that she used the chloroform in the trunk of the car to sedate Caylee so that she could go have a good time with Tony on the 16th and that Caylee accidentally died. It's still first degree murder. (Ashton, 2011: prosecution closing statement)

These comments made it seem as if the prosecution were trying to offer different versions about what happened and they did not fit together very well: that Casey deliberately killed her daughter, and that Casey seriously harmed Caylee through aggravated child abuse leading to her death. Multiple charges meant that the prosecution offered the jury different possibilities, but they revealed a tactical weakness because they showed that the prosecution could not be sure of what happened. It gave the jury the message that the prosecution *thought* that the act was murder but if they did not 'buy' it then it could have been manslaughter because Casey had the intent to harm her daughter while not exactly intending to kill her. Indeed, if the jury did not 'buy' that, it would not be a problem because the prosecution had offered them the charge of aggravated child abuse, that is, there must at least have been child abuse because Casey neglected her daughter and allowed her to die. The prosecution's argument would have been more consistent if they had focused on one argument only, and they appeared to lower their probabilities of success by offering more than one version of *opportunity*, *motive* and *capability*. Multiple charges and possibilities meant offering three separate constructions of events for the same crime (the death of Caylee).

To prove the charge of aggravated child abuse, the State needed to establish that Casey knowingly or wilfully committed child abuse upon Caylee and in doing so caused great bodily harm, permanent disability or permanent disfigurement. To prove aggravated manslaughter of a child, the State needed to establish that Casey's act(s) caused the death of Caylee, or that the death of Caylee was caused by Casey's culpable negligence. Judge Perry instructed the jury that culpable negligence 'is a course of conduct showing reckless disregard of human life … culpable negligence is consciously doing an act or following a course of conduct that the defendant must have known, or reasonably should have known, was likely to cause death or great bodily injury' (Perry, 2011). The judge further instructed that, for the jury to find Casey guilty of aggravated manslaughter of a child, then it must determine if the State had proved that Caylee was a child whose death was caused by the neglect of Casey, a caregiver. The judge instructed that 'caregiver' 'means a parent, adult household member, or other person responsible for a child's welfare' (Perry, 2011).

In fact, the lesser charges encountered the same problems as the charge of first-degree murder because there were still gaps in the evidence relating to *opportunity*, *motive*, *capability* and the cause of death. If the prosecution had tried to prove the charge of aggravated manslaughter, it would remain difficult for them to establish *opportunity* (when and where the act took place). It would also be difficult to show *motive* in the absence of compelling evidence to indicate previous child abuse. Indeed, proving *capability* would present the same problems and issues as those presented in the case for proving first-degree murder. The forensic evidence would be disputed in the same way. Again, the charge of aggravated child abuse also presented the same problems and issues, particularly in relation to *motive* given the absence of evidence that there was similar behaviour in the past. Capitalising on these problems, the defence began their closing statements by emphasising that the prosecution could not prove *how* Caylee had died. Baez argued that this problem was also relevant to the aggravated manslaughter and aggravated child abuse charges:

> Here we are at the end of our journey and I have to tell you that I think you probably have more questions than you have answers. And if you recall at Opening Statements, the final thing that I told you, at the end of the day with everything said and done, the one question that will never be answered, the key question in this case will never be answered … it can never be proven … and that is how did Caylee die? That's why we're all here. Really, there's no dispute that Caylee has passed on. There's no dispute whatsoever about that. So really, the key question as it relates to all manslaughter, child abuse, and murder charges that you're going to be presented with is how did she die? What happened to her? What is proven beyond and to the exclusion of every reasonable doubt? Not just some but every single one and those questions were never answered [by the prosecution]. That evidence was never presented to you. (Baez, 2011: defence closing statement)

To add weight to the defence's emphasis on the problematic issue concerning the unknown cause of death, Baez introduced his own expert to criticise the autopsy carried out by Medical Examiner Dr Garavaglia and during closing statements Baez described the autopsy as 'botched'. Furthermore, he offered an example of courtroom rhetoric employed in the art of persuasion (see Chapter 6) by focusing on and criticising the prosecution's choice of words:

> Mr Ashton gets up here and says 'we can only *hope* she issued the chloroform'. '*Hope?*' They're *hoping* they're going to get a conviction

now? They're *hoping* that you'll buy the chloroform. They're *hoping*? You're not supposed to '*hope*'! You're supposed to prove cases beyond and to the exclusion of every reasonable doubt! (Baez, 2011: defence closing statement).

As we have seen, during closing statements the prosecution had acknowledged and developed more than one version of what happened to Caylee. Later, use of the word 'hope' in connection with how Caylee *may* have died underlined the same uncertainty about what happened to Caylee and why.

The verdict

On 5 July 2011, Casey Anthony was found not guilty of first-degree murder, not guilty of aggravated manslaughter and not guilty of aggravated child abuse of her two-year-old daughter, Caylee Marie Anthony. She was, however, found guilty on four counts of providing false information to law enforcement, although two of those counts were overturned in 2013. Casey was sentenced to four years' imprisonment and fined $1,000 for each count. She was released on 17 July 2011 for time served and good behaviour (Morgenstein, 2013).

A number of talk shows covered the case each evening, but in particular American television host, journalist and former prosecutor Nancy Grace followed and scrutinised the case from Caylee's reported disappearance through to the prosecution, trial and acquittal of Casey. Details about the case were aired every evening on the *Nancy Grace Show* and her belief in the defendant's guilt was apparent throughout the coverage. The talk shows capitalised on the 'novel-like' intrigue (Shaw, 2011) that the case presented and, because Florida law allows cameras in the courtroom, the trial of Casey Anthony has been compared to that of a reality show. Trial by media refers to the influence of media outlets on public perceptions of a court case, even before the trial has begun (Hantler et al, 2004). Indeed, because of the extensive commentary about the case on Twitter and Facebook, *Time* magazine described Anthony's trial as 'The Social Media Trial of the Century' (Cloud, 2011). Two iPhone apps were even developed that enabled users to receive constant updates about the trial. However, to say that it was 'The Social Media Trial of the Century' strictly meant 'of the century so far', because there will doubtless be even higher profile cases during the coming decades. Nevertheless, the trial publicity in Anthony's case doubtlessly shaped public perceptions of her guilt and according to Moran (2019), social media did have some influence on the construction of Casey Anthony's guilt. Moran argued that in the age of social media, the defendant's right to a fair trial stands in direct conflict with the media's right to free speech. Importantly, unlike traditional media, social media outlets are not held to a *sub judice* standard which legally suppresses the publication of certain information such as previous convictions and other information that can elicit bias. Furthermore, 'flash mobs' of people coming together on social media (Brown, 2012) can very quickly generate opinions, unfounded on fact, for all potential jurors to access and review.

Pretrial publicity is at the heart of the discussion in Chapter 11 where we examine the effect of pretrial publicity on the construction of Amanda Knox's guilt (and innocence). Indeed, traditional media platforms delivered prolific coverage of Casey Anthony's case from the moment she was arrested in 2008, even though the trial itself did not take place until 2011. Incentivised to increase ratings, aspects of the story were sensationalised (Ashton, 2012; Moran, 2019). Narratives about her life and character as well as interpretations of the evidence were expressed via various media platforms. Despite the trial verdict of 'not guilty', the court of public opinion found her guilty of murder and she and her family were subjected to social punishment (Moran, 2019). For example, in September 2008, before Caylee's body was found, YouTube clips were uploaded of protesters outside the Anthony home. They held up placards affirming Casey Anthony's guilt with one sign declaring 'Casey is a baby eater' (YouTube Clip, 2008). Because she was found guilty in the court of public opinion, the punishment has been both social and economic. She has been ostracised in the community (Moran, 2019) and has apparently struggled to maintain a living with several failed business ventures (Hernandez, 2021).

Conclusion

In this chapter we have aimed to highlight the weakness of the prosecution strategy in the Casey Anthony trial within the framework of establishing the requisites for proving guilt. We have further learned how Bennett and Feldman (1981) help us to understand that, with circumstantial evidence, a person's guilt or innocence is judged by the three dimensions of *opportunity*, *motive* and *capability*. If the defendant (actor) and the act cannot be connected to each of the requisites, then the defence is provided with a more realistic prospect of raising reasonable doubt. Additionally, if, in a murder trial, the prosecution cannot determine the cause of a victim's death conclusively, then they succumb to the possibility of the defence reconstructing the story entirely. This is what happened in Casey Anthony's trial. In this chapter we have built on Bennett and Feldman's framework to show that the prosecution and defence will have far lower probabilities of success if they offer more than one version of *presence*, *action* and *state of mind*. Ultimately, the prosecution presented three separate constructions of events for the same event (death of Caylee) although, interestingly, this strategy did not feature in Ashton's (2012) explanations for the acquittal of Casey. Finally, it is much more likely that the defence was successful because they argued that the prosecution had not made its own case rather than because they reconstructed the story as an accidental death.

The strategies used by the prosecution and the defence is one explanation for the not guilty verdicts in the trial of Casey Anthony. However, a full explanation for the outcome of this case, and indeed any other, is unlikely to involve only one factor. Several other possible explanations have been offered by commentators. For example, Judge Strickland (the original judge in the trial who removed himself following the defence's claim that he was biased against Casey Anthony (Cuevas–Nazario and Karas, 2010)) said, 'I try to think of why it occurred and I'm still not sure' (Strickland, 2012). Both he and Judge Perry praised the prosecution attorneys for the case they made against her. Explanations for what allegedly 'went wrong' for the prosecution range from jurors' misunderstanding of the nature of circumstantial evidence and reasonable doubt (Strickland, 2012) through to the effect of pretrial publicity (Moran, 2019) to the defendant's life being at stake because of the possible imposition of the death penalty if found guilty of first-degree murder (Ashton, 2012). Judge Perry stated, 'All the defence had to do was create that reasonable doubt and that's what they did' (Perry, 2013), although he could not precisely know what reasonable doubt the jurors would have identified. Finally, other sociological perspectives discussed in this book may shine a light on other explanations for Anthony's acquittal. In Chapter 2 we will draw on the perspective of storytelling in the courtroom and its influence on trial outcomes. Perhaps one explanation for Anthony's acquittal is that the prosecution were not able to tell a good story that aligned with their version of events. That is, the prosecution's argument that Anthony murdered her daughter was not well supported by their narrative that she was a poor and negligent mother because they did not have the evidence to suggest she was such a parent. Additionally, in Chapter 6 we will discuss the influence on case outcomes of the persuasive skills of the prosecution and defence. For example, Anthony's defence lawyer Baez was perhaps a more skilled orator than Ashton; that is, his style and use of language were more persuasive to the jury. As you read those and other chapters in this book, you may also identify other factors of possible significance for understanding the outcome of Casey Anthony's trial.

Recommended reading

Bennett and Feldman's 1981 book *Reconstructing Reality in the Courtroom* has recently come back into print and you can buy it easily and quite cheaply. As well as reading more about the requisites for establishing guilt, the book is also useful for Chapter 2 when we cover *storytelling in the courtroom* and Chapter 6 when we examine *rhetoric* and *persuasion in the courtroom*. Both

Jeff Ashton (prosecutor) and Jose Baez (defence attorney) have written books about the case and they are useful to compare and contrast because one constructs Casey's guilt (Ashton, 2012) and the other constructs her innocence (Baez and Golenbock, 2013).

Notes

[1] Juror number 2 during an interview with *Tampa Bay Times* following the verdict (Thalji, 2011).

[2] An alternate juror is an additional member of the public selected to sit on the jury for a trial, who listens to the evidence just as the jurors do. If a member of the jury cannot continue in the trial (because of illness, for instance) the alternate juror is substituted in order to maintain a total of 12 members.

2

The Tension Between Evidence and Storytelling in the Trial of James Hanratty

I am not a man the court can approve of, but I am not a maniac of any kind.[1]

The crime

At about 6.30 am on 23 August 1961, John Kerr, a student arriving to work on a traffic census on the A6 south of Bedford, saw the bodies of a man and a woman in a lay-by. When he got nearer, he found that the man was dead with two shots to the head; but the woman was still alive, although she had been shot five times, including once in the spine, which paralysed her for life. She identified herself as Valerie Storie and the dead man as Michael Gregsten. Kerr flagged down a car to ask the driver to call the emergency services. Once the police arrived, and given that Gregsten was dead, it fell to Storie to narrate – briefly at the scene and much more fully after she was recovering in hospital – what had happened and how she and Gregsten came to be in this lay-by.

Gregsten (36) and Storie (22) both worked at the Road Research Laboratory in Slough (then in Buckinghamshire), some 60 miles from where they were found. They were having an affair (Gregsten was estranged from his wife) and on the previous evening they had driven a few miles from work for a drink in a pub at Taplow and from there to nearby Dorney Reach where they had parked in a cornfield. They were in Gregsten's car, a grey Morris Minor (possibly having sexual intercourse, as forensic analysis 40 years later would suggest [*Hanratty v Regina*, 2002]), when at around 9.30 pm, a man approached their car, tapped on the window with a gun and said:

> This is a hold up, I am a desperate man. I have been on the run for four months. If you do as I tell you, you will be all right. (Miller, 2001: 90)

According to Storie, he was immaculately dressed, wearing a dark suit and had tied a handkerchief over his face. He got into the back of the car, telling them that he had been living rough for a couple of days, and asked questions about them. He demanded that they hand over their wristwatches, but after seeing that they had little value, he eventually returned them to Storie. He also asked them to hand over their wallet and purse. He carried on with small talk, saying that he was hungry, but also said some more significant things, such as that he had never had a chance in life. Storie recalled him saying that he had done 'CT' (corrective training); that he had 'done the lot'[2] and that next time he would get 'PD' (preventive detention). On his instruction, Gregsten drove towards Slough. They stopped for petrol, headed towards Hayes, and again stopped in Harrow for cigarettes. Storie and Gregsten spoke to each other in quiet voices and occasionally the man would tell them 'Be quiet will you, I am finking' (Miller, 2001: 102).

They continued their journey through north-west London, turning for Watford on the A6, later heading towards St Albans and then Bedford. By this time, the gunman was complaining of being tired and said that he needed 'a kip' (Miller, 2001: 103). Looking for somewhere they would not be disturbed, as they neared Bedford he told Gregsten to pull the car into a lay-by where the assailant tied Storie's wrists to the door handle. The gunman then asked Gregsten to pass him a duffel bag that was on the floor by the front passenger seat. As Gregsten picked up the bag and turned to hand it over to the back seat, the assailant shot him twice in the head at point blank range, killing him instantly. Storie shouted, 'You shot him, you bastard! Why did you do that?' The gunman replied, 'He frightened me. He moved too quick, I got frightened' (Miller, 2001: 106). The time was somewhere between 2 am and 4 am, and while Storie and her assailant argued she attempted to seize his gun. The man eventually forced her into the back seat of the car where he raped her. Storie commented later how the assailant grew anxious about the time and as they continued to talk she told him, 'Well, look, I must call you something … What shall I call you?' According to Storie: 'He sort of said, "Jim". That's the only name, obviously not his proper name I shouldn't think' (Miller, 2001: 117).

At almost daybreak, the assailant ordered Storie to remove Gregsten's body from the car. Having dragged his body to the edge of the concrete strip, the gunman then ordered her to show him how to work the gears in the car. She urged him to leave but he expressed his concern that she would go for help once he left. Out of the car again, he walked two or three metres back towards it, then turned and shot Storie five times. She lay still, pretending to be dead as he kicked and prodded her body. Finally, he got into the Morris Minor and drove away.

The investigation

From the first information that Storie gave to the police, they were able to issue the following description of the offender:

> man aged about 25 years, smooth face, big eyes, smartly dressed in a dark grey or black suit. When speaking says 'fings' instead of 'things'. (Miller, 2001: 108)

The Morris Minor was found abandoned later that evening near Redbridge underground station in Ilford, East London. Previously, two sightings of the car had also been made because of the way it was being erratically driven. John Skillett and Edward Blackhall were travelling in their car when a Morris Minor almost collided with them; they wound down the window and Skillett shouted at the driver who, they said, smiled back. They noted that the driver was heading in the direction of Redbridge underground station. Another witness, James Trower, said that he saw the car pass him close to where it was found abandoned in Avondale Crescent. He said that it caught his attention because he could hear the crunching of the gears. He claimed to have looked briefly at the driver (Miller, 2001).

On the evening of 24 August, the day after the crimes, a bus cleaner found a fully loaded .38 revolver, wrapped in a handkerchief under the back seat on the top of a 36A London bus. The Metropolitan Police's Forensic Science Laboratory identified it as the murder weapon. Two identikit pictures of the suspect were released, one based on Storie's impressions, and the other on the information from the witnesses who saw the Morris Minor being driven erratically on the morning of 23 August. After that, the investigation largely stalled,[3] until a couple of weeks later when two empty cartridge cases, identified as being from the murder weapon, were found in a room at the Vienna Hotel in Maida Vale, London. It was discovered that a man named Peter Alphon had stayed at the hotel on the night of the murder. Unemployed Alphon had already been interviewed by the police about the crimes when the manager of another London hotel, Alexandra Court, reported suspicious behaviour by a man resembling the photofit who was staying in the hotel. The manager said that the man had locked himself in his room for five days after the murder (Woffinden, 1997). However, this promising lead came to an end when Storie did not pick out Alphon in an identification parade (Miller, 2001).

The police then discovered that a person by the name of 'J Ryan' had stayed at the Vienna Hotel on the night of 21/22 August. It was quickly found that the name was false and that the guest's real name was James Hanratty. The officer in charge of the case, Detective Superintendent Basil Acott, also found that there were only five men in Britain who had recently 'done the lot' of a corrective training sentence and one of them was James Hanratty. Indeed, Hanratty was a known petty criminal who had previously been convicted of housebreaking, theft and car theft. He had spent time in prison for these offences, including three years of corrective training (Miller, 2001). The police put out a call for information on Hanratty's whereabouts and, when he realised that he was a suspect, he telephoned Acott from Liverpool to claim his innocence, saying that he had stayed with three men in Liverpool on the night of the crime. He said that he could not reveal the names of those who could support his alibi because they were criminals who did not want to get involved. Subsequently, on 11 October, Hanratty was arrested in Blackpool. Three days later, he was placed in an identity parade during which each person was directed to repeat the phrase that had been used by the assailant, 'Be quiet, will you, I'm thinking'. Storie identified Hanratty, and in a separate identity parade two of the witnesses to the erratic driving in the Morris Minor, Trower and Skillett, identified Hanratty although Blackhall did not. Hanratty was charged with the murder of Gregsten, which he continued to deny and, on 22 January 1962, his trial began at Bedfordshire Assizes[4] before Mr Justice Gorman (Foot, 1971). Eighty-three witnesses were called for the prosecution and 15, including Hanratty, for the defence. The trial lasted for 21 days, which at that time was the longest trial in British history (Moles and Sangha, 2002).

The prosecution's case

The lead prosecutor, Graham Swanwick, QC, focused particularly on Storie's evidence, which described the appearance of her assailant, including his smart dress, his accent, pronunciation and use of the word 'kip', and his indication that his name was 'Jim' (which was often how Hanratty was referred to). Additionally, the assailant had offered her a quite detailed account of his criminal history. Swanwick argued that these descriptions were all consistent with the characteristics of Hanratty (Moles and Sangha, 2002):

> He told her he had been to prison, he told her that since he was eight he had been to a remand home and to Borstal, and to CT, corrective training, and that the next one coming up was PD, preventive detention. That might well follow after a sentence of corrective training, but not in a man of the age of the accused. He told her he had done five years for housebreaking, and done the lot, meaning, you may think, that he had served the whole sentence without remission; that he had been on the run for four months and every police force in Britain was looking

for him. ... It will be true of James Hanratty to say that he had been to prison. It would not be true to say he had been to remand home or Borstal. It would be true to say he had done corrective training. It would not be true to say he had done five years for housebreaking but he had in fact been sentenced to imprisonment for housebreaking, to two years for housebreaking. He had 'done the lot' not on that occasion, but when serving the sentence of corrective training. (Swanwick, opening statement, cited in Woffinden, 1997: 175)

Arguably the strongest evidence for the prosecution was Storie's identification of Hanratty. Although still recovering from her injuries in hospital, Storie attended court to give evidence and verify the positive identification she had made of Hanratty at the identity parade. Swanwick asked Storie if she had any doubt that Hanratty was the man who she picked out as the person who shot her and Gregsten:

Storie:	I had no doubt at all that this was the man who shot Mike and myself.
Swanwick:	Have you any doubt now?
Storie:	I have no doubt whatsoever. (Direct examination of Storie, cited in Woffinden, 1997: 183)

Then Storie was asked when she was first sure that Hanratty was her assailant:

| Storie: | I was absolutely certain as soon as I heard him speak. (Direct re-examination of Storie, cited in Moles and Sangha, 2002) |

Swanwick put to the jury that it was suspicious that Hanratty had removed dye from his hair once he realised the police were looking for him (Woffinden, 1997). He drew on the identifications that Skillett and Trower made of Hanratty, testifying that they witnessed him driving the Morris Minor erratically at around 7 am on 23 August heading in the direction towards where the car was eventually found. Trower testified that he had no doubt that Hanratty was the man he saw driving the Morris Minor. Swanwick also introduced evidence from friends of Hanratty who testified that his driving was erratic (Woffinden, 1997).

In relation to the murder weapon found on the bus, the prosecution argued that it must have been put there on the morning of 24 August. The 36A route passed Sussex Gardens, which was very close to the home of one of Hanratty's friends with whom he occasionally stayed. Furthermore, the route also passed along the bottom of Sutherland Avenue, Maida Vale, which was very close to the Vienna Hotel. This evidence was combined with Hanratty's comment to a friend, Charles France, that the back seat of a bus was a good place to dispose of unwanted stolen goods, to suggest that it must have been Hanratty who placed it there (Moles and Sangha, 2002). Furthermore, the two cartridge cases from the gun were found in room 24 at the Vienna Hotel which Hanratty had occupied on the night of 21/22 August. Not only had he used the name 'J Ryan', but he had also given a false address. Moreover, the room had been occupied only once between Hanratty's stay and the discovery of the two empty cartridge cases, and that occupant had been eliminated from the list of suspects. Additionally, prior to the trial, a prison officer claimed to have heard Roy Langdale, a prisoner, telling another inmate that Hanratty had admitted that he was the gunman responsible for the crime. Langdale said that he exercised with Hanratty, who was in custody awaiting trial, and they became friendly. According to Langdale, during one of their conversations in the exercise yard Hanratty admitted that he was the murderer (Moles and Sangha, 2002).

The prosecution also brought in evidence from Storie describing how, at one point during the long drive, the assailant warned Gregsten about some roadworks round the next corner. This was in Harrow, not far from where Hanratty's parents lived in Kingsbury, and could be used to infer that he was the assailant because of his familiarity with the roadworks. The prosecution also pointed out that Hanratty had admitted that he was making inquiries about obtaining a gun and wanting to be a 'stick-up' man. Following his release from a previous prison sentence in 1961, he had contacted a man called Fisher about a gun: 'a shooter to do some stick-ups' (*Hanratty v Regina*, 2002: para 52). Hanratty acknowledged that he knew where to get a gun if he wanted one, but said that he had never owned one and that the whole thing was 'just talk'.

Hanratty's original alibi was that he was in Liverpool at the time of the murder and had been staying with three men on the nights of 22 and 23 August, who he refused to name because of their criminal activities. In his opening statement, Swanwick expressed strong doubts about the men's existence. Hanratty had previously claimed that the men would not come forward because their flat contained stolen jewellery and gelignite (an explosive material), and that they were wanted for non-payment of a fine for having televisions on hire purchase. Swanwick argued that those circumstances were not sufficiently serious to prevent the men from coming forward to support Hanratty's alibi as witnesses in a murder case (Woffinden, 1997). He added:

> All warrants outstanding in the Liverpool area (something over 3,000) were checked, including around Scotland Road, which is an area that abounds in thieves. No trace was found of a man who had a warrant outstanding to do with television or hire purchase. So there was

no trace of the three men. (Swanwick, opening statement, cited in Woffinden, 1997: 174)

The prosecution's doubts proved correct when, halfway through the trial, Hanratty admitted to lying about staying in Liverpool and changed his alibi to claim that he was staying at a guesthouse in Rhyl, North Wales, on the night of 22 August. His explanation for the lie about Liverpool was that he did not think he would be able to remember the exact location of the guesthouse in Rhyl. The prosecution countered that this explanation was implausible (Miller, 2001).

To summarise, the prosecution's evidence against Hanratty included Storie's identification of him; the details the gunman offered about himself while in the Morris Minor; Skillett and Trower's identification; the discovery of the murder weapon on the bus in the precise location where Hanratty admitted to telling an acquaintance that he liked to discard unwanted objects from burglaries; the cartridge cases from the murder weapon found in the hotel room in which Hanratty had stayed; Hanratty's admission to a fellow inmate, Roy Langdale, that he had committed the murder; and the lack of a solid alibi for the night on which the crime occurred. Swanwick argued that by a process of elimination, all the evidence pointed to Hanratty's guilt (Woffinden, 1997). To this, he added claims about Hanratty's motivations for committing the crimes:

> Gregsten was shot through the head – twice, deliberately and in cold blood, for no better reason than that man wished to possess himself of Gregsten's companion in that car, Valerie Storie. (Swanwick, opening statement, cited in Woffinden, 1997: 175)

Referring to the assailant's demand for the victims' wristwatches and then returning them, Swanwick posited:

> That, you may think, possibly supports the view that the principle motive for this crime was perhaps sex rather than money. (Swanwick, opening statement, cited in Woffinden, 1997: 176)

Finally, Swanwick suggested other motives for Hanratty's shooting of Gregsten:

> The gunman said that he had got scared because Gregsten had moved too quickly. I suppose that might be true. Or was he lusting after Miss Storie at this time and did he want Gregsten out of the way? Or was the urge to use his new and exciting toy to shoot someone for the first time too much for him? Or did he think that Gregsten had seen him and might recognise him? (Swanwick, opening statement, cited in Woffinden, 1997: 176)

The defence

It is useful to remind ourselves here that the defence's task is not to prove innocence. The primary task of the defence is to create sufficient doubt about the evidence which the prosecution puts to the jury ('agreed facts') plus 'facts to be determined by the jury' plus 'inferences to be drawn from all the facts', so that the jury cannot be satisfied beyond a reasonable doubt, that the prosecution has indeed demonstrated the guilt of the accused (Firth, 2016).

Hanratty denied his *presence* at the crime scene and his defence counsel, Michael Sherrard, QC, argued that, other than the testimony of Storie, there was no evidence to suggest he was in or around the vicinity of Dorney Reach on the evening of 22 August. The defence sought to challenge the prosecution's evidence, arguing that Storie had only a very limited opportunity to see her assailant and that, at a first identity parade which did not include Hanratty, she had picked out another man. Furthermore, although some of the description of the assailant's history was consistent with Hanratty's, some of it was not and also his accent was not unique (Moles and Sangha, 2002). Similarly, Sherrard contended that Skillett and Trower had only a limited opportunity to see the driver of the Morris Minor and, moreover, Blackhall (Skillett's passenger) had picked out another man who was an innocent volunteer in the identity parade (Woffinden, 1997). The defence further submitted that the description of the assailant's erratic driving was inconsistent with Hanratty's knowledge and experience of driving cars (Moles and Sangha, 2002).

The discovery of the gun, Sherrard argued, was not meaningful evidence against Hanratty because the back seat of a bus was not an uncommon place to discard unwanted items. Furthermore, it was argued that it did not make sense for two empty cartridge cases to be discarded in the Vienna Hotel prior to the murder (meaning that the bullets were fired beforehand). A more likely scenario, it was suggested, was that the cartridges were discarded after the murder. This pointed to someone else having placed them there (Moles and Sangha, 2002). It was also argued that fellow inmate Roy Langdale's evidence was inconsistent with Hanratty's repeated protestations of his innocence. Under cross-examination, Langdale admitted that he had been paid by two newspapers to sell his story about the case (Woffinden, 1997). Hanratty admitted to having a conversation with someone about becoming a stick-up man but it was simply 'talk' and merely an example of him being boastful (Moles and Sangha, 2002).

Having changed his alibi midway through the trial, when he took the stand Hanratty explained that on 22 August, he left the Vienna Hotel at approximately 9.30 am and walked to Paddington train station by mistake. He took a taxi to Euston Station and caught a train to Liverpool, arriving at about 4.30 pm. He said that he intended to meet a man called Aspinall, whom he had met in prison some three to four years previously, in order to sell him a stolen ring worth £350. According to Hanratty, Aspinall was in the greengrocery business and although he could not quite recall the exact name of the road where he lived in Liverpool, he was sure it was called Carlton, Tarelton or Talbot Road. Upon arriving at Lime Street Station, he said that he had had a wash and deposited his suitcase in the left luggage office with a man whose hand, he remembered, was deformed. Outside the station, he caught a bus and got off in Scotland Road and walked into a sweetshop asking for directions. A helpful woman told him to go back into town because he had come too far. Unable to find the road, he ate a meal and then talked to a man on the steps of a billiard hall and tried to sell him a watch. After giving up his search for Aspinall, he travelled to Rhyl to look for a man named Terry Evans. Evans was a man he had met only once before, but Hanratty thought that he might be able to sell him some stolen jewellery. Based on his description of the boarding house at which he claimed to stay, the defence team were able to find it in Rhyl and the owner, Grace Jones, was called to the stand. However, she could only say that she was sure that Hanratty had stayed at the guesthouse sometime between 19 and 26 August. His stay was not registered in her guest book, perhaps because he said he stayed in a room that was actually a bathroom and regulations would not permit a guest to stay in such a room (Foot, 1971).

Finally, the defence contended that the jury was aware of Hanratty's previous criminal record and that the crimes committed on 22 and 23 August against Storie and Gregsten were inconsistent with his character, for he did not have any previous convictions or alleged offences relating to violence or sexual assault (Moles and Sangha, 2002).

Exercise 1:

1. Which pieces of evidence, if any, make a persuasive case for Hanratty's conviction or acquittal? Or does a story need to be told?
2. Did the prosecution establish that Hanratty had the *opportunity, motive* and *capability/means* to commit the crime?
3. How and why do you think the jury arrived at a guilty verdict?

Verdict and aftermath

On 17 February 1961 the jury began deliberations on the case. At one point, the judge was asked to clarify what is meant by 'reasonable doubt', suggesting that some jurors might have had doubts about Hanratty's guilt. Nevertheless, the jury unanimously found Hanratty guilty of Gregsten's murder and he was sentenced to death. His defence team filed an appeal on the grounds that the jury's verdict was unreasonable or could not be supported by the evidence; that the judge failed to properly put the defence to the jury; and that the judge misdirected the jury in relation to the evidence and failed to summarise the issues raised by the defence. The appeal was rejected and the Lord Chief Justice Parker observed:

> The summing up was clear, it was impartial, it was not only fair but favourable to the prisoner and contained no misdirections of law and no misdirections in fact on any of the important issues in the case. The court is of the opinion that this was a clear case. (Cited in Moles and Sangha, 2002)

Reflecting growing opposition to the death penalty, and perhaps some doubts among the public about Hanratty's guilt, after the conviction and sentence his father handed in a petition to the Home Office with more than 90,000 names of British citizens calling for a reprieve of his death sentence. The Hanratty family received a reply stating that the Home Secretary was 'unable to find any sufficient ground to justify him in recommending Her Majesty to interfere with the due course of the law' (Foot, 1971: 294) and, on 4 April 1962, Hanratty was executed by hanging. He was one of the last offenders to be executed in the UK and, in 1965, the death penalty was permanently abolished under the Murder (Abolition of Death Penalty) Act 1965 (Moles and Sangha, 2002).

Hanratty's conviction and subsequent execution caused outrage among some sectors of the public and an A6 Murder Committee was established, comprising a group of campaigners and activists. Among them was journalist Paul Foot, politicians, and even John Lennon and Yoko Ono. Their aim was to try and disprove Hanratty's guilt and get his conviction overturned posthumously (Foot, 1971). In particular, his supporters contended that he did not have a plausible motivation for the crime and that the prosecution had great difficulty in properly establishing this requisite for his guilt. Indeed, Woffinden (1997: 176) observed that the various suggestions put forward by the prosecution (outlined earlier in this chapter) only served to highlight 'a black hole at the centre of the case'. He added:

> For all the individual pieces of evidence, there was no coherent framework. The Crown simply had no viable explanation as to why this man had ambushed those two people, or this extraordinary crime had ever taken place.

Thus, a long-standing tension developed between the prosecution's evidence and an understanding of what happened on the night of the crime. We argue that this tension arose because the prosecution did not, and perhaps could not, construct a story that organised and linked the available evidence to 'the black hole': a putative description of Hanratty the man, his motivation and his intentions. It was this tension that fuelled the nearly 40-year posthumous campaign to overturn his conviction and which, as we would see it, reflected the importance of storytelling in constructions of guilt and innocence. To understand this better, we need to examine the story model of juror decision-making.

The story model of juror decision-making

The law does not often instruct jurors to think about stories (but see Griffin, 2013: 295–8 for some counter examples from the US); rather, it directs them to focus on the evidence and to weigh up each item in terms of its contribution to establishing, beyond a reasonable doubt, the defendant's guilt. Jurors are not told how to do this, but legal scholars have expended considerable effort to develop models of how it does or should work, based on the use of logic and inferences to link items of evidence to a decision about conviction or acquittal (Wigmore, 1931; Anderson et al, 2005). This evidence-based model sees the role of evidence as 'any tendency to make a fact more or less probable than it would be without the evidence' (Federal Rules of Evidence, cited by Griffin, 2013: 293). Thus, jurors are hypothesised to assess whether the prosecution or defence has the strongest evidence overall. The perspective might also be called the 'mathematical approach' because it usually involves statistical or algebraic computations; however, a key difficulty is that jurors are unlikely to process information and evidence in this way (Devine, 2012).

Over the last 40 years, an alternative perspective on jury decision-making has been developed which focuses on stories. In their influential 1981 book, *Reconstructing Reality in the Courtroom*, Bennett and Feldman set out to answer the question, how do lawyers present cases in a way that makes sense to judges, jurors, witnesses and other observers? They analysed data from more than 60 trials covering a wide range of offences and concluded that criminal trials are organised around storytelling. That is, the jury compares and contrasts the competing stories of the defence and the prosecution and the story that is judged to be true or truer is that which is better organised, more coherent and more believable. The results of an experiment they conducted are particularly interesting. They asked college students to tell others a story about themselves, with some being instructed to make up a story while others were instructed to tell a truthful story. They found that a truthful story was no more likely to be accepted than a false one. Rather, what mattered was the coherence and structure of the story; that is, the more each element of the story connected with others in a clear and unambiguous way, the more likely the story would be judged to be true regardless of whether it was in fact true or false. Thus, they argued, the more coherent a story that is presented at a criminal trial, the more likely it is to be accepted. Conversely, if jurors are presented with a jumble of information and isolated facts, they are likely to become confused and less accepting of the evidence.

We can think of two ways in which stories may be introduced in a trial (Griffin, 2013). First, a witness may be led to develop a narrative through the questions they are asked by whichever side (prosecution or defence) has called them to testify. Of course, this narrative may be questioned or partly disassembled in cross-examination, making it harder to identify a clear story from everything that was said. Second, because the evidence in a trial is introduced by calling witnesses to the stand, the cumulative testimony does not make a story. Rather, it falls to the prosecution and defence advocates to use opening and closing statements to weave the evidence into a story. It is this second type of story, about the whole case rather than the evidence of a single witness, which is of most importance if jurors do indeed focus more on the story rather than specific parts of the evidence.

Pennington and Hastie (1988) conducted some important research about how jurors make sense of evidence in a criminal trial. In a mock jury study, they presented college students with stories and evidence relating to a crime. Some participants received the evidence in a story order that was chronological; that is, it had a beginning, a middle and an end. The other participants received the same information but this time it was given in witness order meaning that the jurors read each witness's testimony about everything that happened regardless of where the information fitted into the actual chronological order of events. The study found that the participants were more likely to vote in favour of the prosecution's case if their evidence was presented in story order and the defence's evidence was presented in witness order, and vice versa. Pennington and Hastie's (1991, 1992) research also indicated that factfinders compare stories about what happened and choose the one they find the most believable. For a story to approximate the standard of legal proof, a good narrative is dependent on three components: consistency, plausibility and completeness. A consistent story does not have any internal contradictions; plausibility concerns how well the story fits with juror's knowledge of the world; and completeness ensures that the story includes most or all of the evidence. When a story contains all three elements then it becomes a coherent one.

Griffin (2013: 286) noted that each element of the story interacts in ways that 'alter their individual significance: each merges with what came before and flows into what comes after'. Thus, a single piece of evidence cannot be evaluated or understood in isolation. As Bruner (1990: 43) noted, individual elements of a story do not mean anything on their own, and rather, meaning arises from 'their overall configuration of the sequence as a whole – its plot or *fabula*'. Burns (1999: 222) suggested that each event must correspond to the 'beginning, middle, [or] end of a well-constructed story'. Indeed, Wesson (2006: 343) observed that 'every lawsuit begins and ends as a story'. As Griffin (2013: 297) suggested, most trial lawyers, at least in the US, begin their opening statements with 'This is a case about ... lies, greed' and so on. For example, in the case of O.J. Simpson discussed in Chapter 6, we shall see that the theme the prosecution advanced throughout was a story about the defendant as 'a burning fuse' and domestic violence that ultimately led to murder. Indeed, the notion that domestic abuse can lead to murder is possibly a view that resonates with a juror's knowledge, common sense and world view. As Pennington and Hastie (1991: 528) suggested, jurors evaluate facts based on their 'knowledge about what typically happens in the world'.

Importantly, Griffin (2013) argued that juror decision-making is not exclusively grounded in identifying with stories or in applying an evidence-based model. Rather, she argued that a story offers structure, enabling jurors to build hypotheses and then the evidence-based model is utilised when jurors weigh up and assess those hypotheses. To this end, jurors not only consider which is the most compelling narrative and how it fits with familiar stories, but they also assess the plausibility of each account and interpret evidence according to which provides the most coherent theory (Pardo and Allen, 2008). Stories are constructed and then jurors logically evaluate 'which version was more likely to yield the evidence that has been presented in court, and by how much' (Friedman, 1991: 667). Developed by Pardo and Allen (2008), the 'explanation-based account' means that, rather than simply making decisions based on the probability of guilt as each piece of evidence is presented, jurors make inferences based on how well each piece of evidence, if true, would explain what happened (Griffin, 2013). Explanationist theorists view criminal evidence in a trial as 'a competition between stories, scenarios or explanations of what happened' (Jellema, 2020: 2) and Griffin (2013) argued that this perspective helps to overcome a simple reliance on either the story model or evidence-based model. Other explanationists include Wagenaar et al (1993), Josephson (2000), van Koppen (2011) and Bex (2011).

Although very influential as a *description* of juror decision-making, it is important to note that some legal scholars have criticised the story model as a *prescription* for what should happen. For example, Laudan (2006) argued that it is unclear at what point the prosecution have succeeded in demonstrating that their story implies the defendant's guilt. Although criminal courts use the standard of 'beyond a reasonable doubt', Laudan (2006: 295–6) argued that the standard is 'obscure, incoherent, and muddled' and therefore encourages jurors to draw on their subjective intuitions. Griffin also noted that jurors may fill in the 'gaps' in the stories told by the prosecution or the defence and thereby compromise the integrity of decision-making. If jurors process information in terms of stories rather than logic, then they risk being misled by following familiar story lines: 'The implicit invitation for jurors to participate in constructing facts, combined with the missing narrative components, can introduce bias and lead to error' (Griffin, 2013: 302). The story model is further critiqued because jurors may rely on pieces of evidence to offer meaning where there may not be any. Griffin referred to Dershowitz (1996), who drew on the example of a man accused of murdering his wife having taken out a life insurance policy prior to her death. Although on the face of it, such an action appears incriminating, Dershowitz (1996: 100) pointed out that many people take out such policies and what has a mundane explanation can result in a prejudicial assessment of the facts: 'Events are often simply meaningless, irrelevant to what comes next; events can be out of sequence, random, purely accidental, without purpose'. In other words, stories impose order on events, an order which may not have existed when they occurred. Indeed, Griffin (2013) observed that each detail mentioned in a story has salience, but that real life is not like that and people often do not know the reasons for their actions nor are able to articulate their motives clearly. As a result, Griffin argued, the integrity of juror decision-making may be compromised by their expectations that all evidence given at the trial will hold meaning when in fact it may not. In turn, 'confirmation bias' may occur because jurors interpret evidence based on their existing beliefs and the juror's 'belief perseverance' may occur when evidence is cast in doubt because it does not align with a juror's pre-existing beliefs and expectations. Overall, then, while there is ample evidence that stories play an important role in trials and jurors' decisions, they may work against the strict evaluation of evidence which is often proclaimed as an ideal.

Stories about the A6 murder

Griffin (2013: 296) cited an opinion from a US judge about a murder trial in which the defendant was found to be 'guilty but mentally ill'. The judge commented that 'a narrative richer than the "bare facts of his bizarre behavior" was necessary to effective representation' for the defendant. This comment underscores the importance of providing contextual information through narrative which helps to explain the alleged actions of the defendant and make sense of the crime itself, whether it be a narrative of guilt or of innocence. What is interesting about Hanratty's case is that he was convicted in the absence of a narrative which went beyond 'the bare facts' of his identification as the murderer and the circumstantial evidence in support of that – in other words, in the absence of a narrative that would fill the 'black hole' identified by Woffinden (1997: 176).

Indeed, part of the public concern caused by Hanratty's conviction was that he had no violent history; by his own admission, he was a thief, *not* a rapist and murderer. There was simply no contextual information to demonstrate how and why he turned into a 'ruthless' (Foot, 1971: 275) murderer. In cross-examination, Swanwick submitted to Hanratty that it was his ambition to be a stick-up man, that he 'went to the Vienna Hotel to play with it [the gun] like a new toy', and went out to use it for the first time on 22 August (Foot, 1971: 284). Hanratty replied:

> Well, is it not quite obvious if I did that I would not be looking for a car in a cornfield, as you put it to the court. I will be looking for some cash, a bank, a shop, something to that effect. I would not be looking for a car in a cornfield for some cash for a stick up. (Cross-examination of Hanratty, cited in Foot, 1971: 284)

Hanratty's response appears to provide a much more plausible view that makes sense of his traditional criminal activities and motivations. He underscored this further when Swanwick attempted to elicit evidence for his lack of regard for the homeowners he burgled:

> Sir, I must put this point quite clear. I ain't a man the court approved of as of good character, but I am not a murderer. This is a murder trial, not a housebreaking trial. (Cross-examination of Hanratty, cited in Foot, 1971: 285)

Swanwick put other possible motives to Hanratty:

Swanwick: It may be that the predominant motive was that you wanted the girl; it may be that you wanted to practise a stick-up; it may be that you did not mind the money and the car?

Hanratty: I had all the money I wanted. I give Mrs France £15 that day. If I wanted a woman I could have gone in the West End and had a woman for a fortnight. If I wanted a woman I could get one for a fortnight. (Cross-examination of Hanratty, cited in Foot, 1971: 285)

Here, Hanratty highlighted the absence of the story connections required to make sense of the crime he was on trial for. If there had been behaviours preceding the crime, for example, sexual offences such as voyeurism, indecent exposure or indecent assault, it might have provided a plausible connection to the later and more serious sexual offence against Storie. To this end, Swanwick referred again to his desire to be a stick-up man, seemingly in an attempt to connect the pieces of evidence into a coherent story:

Swanwick:	But is the difference this, that then you would not have had the thrill of holding them up with a gun?
Hanratty:	The man who committed this is a maniac and a savage. I know what you have proved here. I am not a man the court can approve of, but I am not a maniac of any kind. (Cross-examination of Hanratty, cited in Foot, 1971: 285)

Again, Hanratty's reply highlighted the absence of the connections between pieces of evidence that, when added together, would create a compelling story to make sense of how he could come to commit a crime that appeared to diverge so greatly from his traditional criminal activities.

For his part, as we have seen, Hanratty did not provide a credible story about his activities and whereabouts on 22 and 23 August, and his integrity was doubtlessly undermined by his inconsistency in the Liverpool/Rhyl alibi. The failure of both the prosecution and defence to tell a credible story adding context to the evidence led some of Hanratty's key supporters to offer narratives themselves, narratives that converted to a readily 'recognizable plot' (Griffin, 2013: 311). An incomplete and implausible story about Hanratty suddenly appearing in a cornfield out of nowhere and randomly deciding to attack the victims spurred his supporters to *reconstruct* the story. They based it on a 'confession' by Peter Alphon in 1967 that he was the murderer, even though Alphon had been eliminated as a suspect during the police investigation.

It is important to read the alternative and reconstructed stories about what happened in the context of Alphon's dubious confession to the crime. There was no compelling evidence to link Alphon to the crime and his confession was probably false. In Chapter 8 we will be examining the nature of false confessions in more depth and exploring the different reasons for why they can and do occur. For example, some suspects, like Alphon, will falsely confess voluntarily, often to gain fame in a high-profile case or because of mental illness (Kassin and Gudjonsson, 2004). The study of false confessions is a relatively new area of research and the notion that a person could confess to a crime they did not commit has been deemed so counter-intuitive that this is perhaps why Alphon's admissions were accepted as truth. Viewing Alphon as the person responsible for Gregsten's murder implies a story in which he played the central character with a motivation for the crime, enabling the preceding and subsequent elements in the story to connect to one another in a plausible way. For example, the context of Alphon's drifter lifestyle, unemployment and, indeed, his confession, makes subsequent events in the story more convincing, such as accepting payment to commit a crime and following Hanratty for the purposes of framing him. Added to this was Storie's admission during cross-examination that she told a doctor and Acott that there was a resemblance between Alphon and the man who attacked her (Woffinden, 1997).

Journalist Paul Foot focused on the relationship between Michael Gregsten and Valerie Storie. As Griffin (2013: 311) commented, a story containing an extramarital affair provides a 'recognizable plot' that could serve as a likely motive for murder. Foot noted that Gregsten's wife, Janet, was 'irritated and depressed' by his affair with Storie (Foot, 1971: 25). Although Foot did not explicitly outline his theory (for risk of a libel claim), Miller (2001) submitted that the inference was clear: Janet Gregsten knew and paid Peter Alphon to threaten her husband and Storie so that their relationship would end. Foot constructed a story to demonstrate how Janet Gregsten and her brother-in-law, William Ewer, were directly involved in framing Hanratty for the crime. To support this claim, Foot referred to a newspaper article that was published two days after Hanratty's conviction, reporting that Janet Gregsten claimed to have seen Hanratty walking into a launderette in the Swiss Cottage area of London eight days after her husband's murder. She was with Ewer when she pointed out Hanratty and said that he matched the murderer's description. At the time, Hanratty was not a suspect and, although Gregsten claimed she did not know who he was, she said she felt intuitively that it was him:

> That's the man. He fits the description. But it's more than that. I've got an overpowering feeling that it's him. (Foot, 1971: 50)

Foot (1971: 51) drew on another newspaper article that referred to Ewer's 'miracle' encounter with Hanratty in a café the following day. It is clear from Foot's comments that he did not believe either Janet Gregsten or Ewer's stories, arguing:

> The articles presented a series of coincidences which would strain the credulity of the most gullible mystic. (Foot, 1971: 51)

Foot pointed out that, after speaking to the manager at the launderette, Janet Gregsten and Ewer learned that the man was called J. Ryan, which was the alias Hanratty often used. Ewer then saw Hanratty the next day in a café and followed him into a florist's shop. The manager there told Ewer that the man had bought some flowers for his mother: a Mrs Hanratty of 12 Sycamore Grove, Kingsbury. Foot theorised that both Janet Gregsten and Ewer knew precisely who Hanratty was and because the police had initially failed to identify him as a suspect, she intervened and pointed them in his direction. This, Foot suggested, was proof that Janet Gregsten and/or Ewer were directly involved in framing Hanratty for the crime. For Foot

(1971: 51), this meant that 'Scotland Yard had Hanratty's name and his alias long before they started to hunt him as the murderer'.

Jean Justice, who wrote *Murder vs. Murder* in 1964, suggested that the motive for the crime was not robbery but sex. Justice also theorised that Alphon was in fact the murderer and that he knew Hanratty. Like Foot, Justice came to believe that Alphon was the person responsible for the crime and in 1967 Alphon publicly confessed saying that he had been paid £5,000 by Janet Gregsten's brother-in-law William Ewer to confront the victims in the cornfield:

> Let's say the mission was to see that they were separated. ... The mission was to see that the affair was finished. (Miller, 2001: 69)

Alphon said that this could be proved by looking at his bank account, although he rapidly retracted his confession (Miller, 2001).

In his book *Hanratty: The Final Verdict*, journalist Bob Woffinden (1997) also argued that Alphon was the man responsible for the crime. However, he suggested that the theory that the crime was the result of trying to separate Gregsten and Storie was untenable because, for Woffinden, the story was incomplete in the absence of the couple not having received warnings prior to being taken hostage and, therefore, a story about a family plot to end the relationship was not plausible. Instead, he referred to a conversation Alphon had with Jean Justice in which he advised him to seek a more banal motivation for the murder. To this end, Woffinden's narrative was one of love and passion that appeared to emerge following Janet Gregsten's admission of an affair after her husband's death (Miller, 2001). Although he did not name the man who was in love with Janet Gregsten, it seems that Woffinden was referring to Ewer, her brother-in-law:

> The motive in this case was the most 'mundane' and time honoured of all: the passion of a man for Janet Gregsten. He became more and more obsessed with her. She was demure, delightful, intelligent, articulate and wonderfully attractive. He yearned for her. Yet not only was she married, she resolutely refused to leave her husband, even though he treated her despicably. How unbearably frustrating for a would-be lover. (Woffinden, 1997: 436)

According to Woffinden's theory, Janet Gregsten's would-be lover got in touch with Alphon and gave him the gun. Woffinden further theorised that Alphon was instructed to pretend to be Hanratty[5] but amid the confusion, Alphon, who was unstable anyway, became confused and that is why the intended crime went wrong. According to Woffinden, the coincidence of

Alphon having stayed at the same hotel as Hanratty can be explained by the theory that Alphon followed him there.

Exercise 2:

What problems do you see with the stories presented by Foot, Justice and Woffinden? How plausible do you think their narratives are? Consider the reasons for your answer.

Perhaps one of the more compelling narratives to explain the A6 murder can be found in Miller's (2001) book *Shadows of Deadman's Hill: A New Analysis of the A6 Murder*. Miller told a story that fills the gaps between pieces of evidence in a more coherent, consistent, plausible manner, consistent with jurors' common sense and world knowledge. Miller began with presence (one of Bennett and Feldman's (1981) requisites for establishing guilt), offering an explanation as to why Hanratty might have feasibly placed himself in an unlikely location. For example, contrary to the popular conception that the cornfield was miles away from civilisation, it was in fact within walking distance to two railway stations. The cornfield was also near a small village where domestic burglaries had occurred previously. Miller therefore immediately provided the context to the crime by outlining Hanratty's career as a professional housebreaker and other convictions for vehicle theft. He pointed out that Hanratty had spent time in several different prisons and in the build-up to the crime he had burgled several houses. He referred to Woffinden's comments quoting Hanratty as saying 'I always work on my own. I often change my area. I usually do night jobs. ... All my jobs are big ones' (Woffinden, 1997: 89). Thus, for Miller, Hanratty wandering around Dorney Reach late at night was consistent with his previous criminal activities, especially since he had committed housebreakings in the Ruislip and Northwood areas nearby. Although there was no independent evidence that he was in the area around Dorney Reach, Miller argued that his whereabouts after his release from prison in March 1961 were often a mystery. He described Hanratty as 'essentially a loner and an enigma' and observed that 'He wasn't a member of a criminal gang. He came and went as he pleased. He emerged out of nowhere, socialised, then disappeared again. He was a solitary criminal. No one really knew what he was up to, where he was, how he spent his time' (Miller, 2001: 85).

To explain Hanratty's possession of a gun, Miller argued that he moved in criminal circles where it was easy to acquire such a weapon. He theorised that Hanratty reloaded the gun in the hotel room, perhaps test shooting beforehand, and that leaving the cartridges was symptomatic of his carelessness. He explained that Hanratty's motive for possessing a gun was his desire to move up from housebreaking to something bigger, such as armed robbery. In the past, Hanratty had either caught the bus or walked to carry out his housebreaking; however, to get away quickly after an armed robbery, a bus service would be too slow and thus, a train would be more effective, thereby explaining his *presence* in Dorney Reach, which was within walking distance of a mainline railway station (Miller, 2001).

Far from being a premeditated crime, the abduction in the cornfield was a random event. He could not have known that the couple were in the cornfield; rather, he was walking down the lane when he suddenly came across them. Miller (2001: 91; emphasis in the original) theorised:

> The crime was the consequence of two unrelated, arbitrary events – Hanratty being on Marsh Lane at ten o'clock at night with a gun in his pocket, and Gregsten and Storie sitting in the Morris in the field. The gunman acted on *impulse*.

Providing the context for the crime, Miller speculated that Hanratty did not have rape and murder on his mind, but 'what followed all stemmed from Hanratty's own damaged life and impoverished personality' (Miller, 2001: 91). The randomness of the crime was reflected in, and similar to, the random nature of Hanratty's previous crimes, which were characterised by impulsiveness and short-term thinking. Miller (2001: 93) thought that the crime began with no 'rhyme or reason' and that even Hanratty himself did not know what he wanted, but he was probably enjoying the new power of possessing a gun and using it to threaten his victims. Miller argued that Gregsten was shot because Hanratty felt threatened and reacted instinctively, again situating this within the landscape of his character – his 'learning disabilities, not very bright, impulsive, indecisive, unable to think through the consequences of his actions' (Miller, 2001: 107). Additionally, Miller proposed that the rape of Storie was motivated by his need to punish his victim for her continuous displays of defiance while being held hostage. He argued that the rape could not have been planned since he could have committed it in the cornfield where they were isolated instead of on the lay-by. Similarly, Miller argued that, as well as silencing his victim, her shooting was also motivated by the desire to punish a woman who was not compliant – something Hanratty was not accustomed to.

We can see that, of the four stories that we have reviewed, three (those by Foot, Justice and Woffinden) were developed to support the claim that there had been a miscarriage of justice and that Hanratty had been wrongfully convicted. They relied on information, such as Janet Gregsten's depression and Alphon's confession, and on speculation about Janet Gregsten's and William Ewer's amorous motivations, which were not introduced as evidence during the trial because Hanratty's defence strategy was focused solely on denying that he was the murderer and not on reconstructing the story with new participants. Indeed, given that Alphon had been eliminated as a suspect by the police, and that his 'confession' only emerged after Hanratty had been convicted and executed, it would have been very difficult – if not impossible – for Hanratty's defence team to have called him as a witness. Nevertheless, the story of Alphon as the murderer sustained public concern about Hanratty's conviction for a very long time and, as we see, added a clear motive for the crime in comparison to the prosecution's tentative explorations for Hanratty's motivation in their cross-examination of him.

The fourth story, by Miller, was developed in support of Hanratty's conviction. It is worth noting that Miller's book was published just as DNA evidence was pointing to Hanratty as the murderer (see later), so that he probably knew that he was on strong ground in developing his narrative. His account was speculative in that it follows Hanratty's movements on the day the crime began, and even his thoughts, none of which can be independently verified, showing how stories may, as Griffin (2013) commented, fill in the gaps in the evidence and provide a context for the central action. Nevertheless, his story builds a plausible picture of a petty criminal who one day toys with violence, leading to a horrendous outcome.[6] If the prosecution at Hanratty's trial had built this kind of account into their closing statements, it is possible that more 'sense' – for the public – would have been made of the crime and fewer reservations about his conviction would have emerged.

The DNA evidence

In 1997, after continued public pressure and following developments in DNA analysis and evidence, the Criminal Cases Review Commission investigated the Hanratty case, and Storie's underwear (containing semen from the rapist) and the handkerchief (that was found wrapped around the gun) were examined for DNA and compared to DNA donated by Hanratty's family. Expecting the new evidence to finally exonerate him, they were told that the results indicated a strong match (two and a half million times more likely to belong to Hanratty than anyone else) (Gould, 2000). Subsequently, Lord Chief Justice Woolf permitted the exhumation of Hanratty's body and in 2001 his DNA was extracted. DNA samples from both the underwear and handkerchief matched Hanratty's DNA exactly. Only Hanratty's DNA profile was found on the handkerchief and two profiles were found on Storie's underwear – one was Hanratty's and the other was considered to be most likely Gregsten's. The possibility of contamination was considered by the Court of Appeal but was dismissed and it noted that 'DNA evidence, standing alone, is certain proof of guilt' (England and Wales Court of Appeal (Criminal Division Decisions), 2002).[7]

Exercise 3:

Consider for a moment that the DNA evidence had been available in the 1962 trial.

1. What story might the prosecution have told?
2. What story, or stories, might Hanratty and his defence team have told?

Conclusion

In this chapter we have sought to show that the vigorous and sustained campaigning for Hanratty's innocence may be partly understood by turning to the storytelling model of adjudication. The lack of a coherent story to explain Hanratty's motivation and guilt was for a long time (at least up until the results of the DNA evidence in 2001) argued to reflect a gross miscarriage of justice. Indeed, even in the face of the DNA evidence, Hanratty's supporters continued to believe in his innocence and argued that the newly discovered evidence was a result of cross-contamination (Milmo, 2014). This perhaps tells us something important: despite the DNA evidence, a man who seemingly had none of the requisites to make a behavioural progression from theft and burglary to abduction, rape and murder simply could not be understood in the absence of a plausible story. However, it is more than this. The A6 murder was fraught with complexities arising from contradictions and coincidences throughout the investigation, not least the discovery that Alphon had stayed in the same hotel where the empty cartridge cases were found, that Storie admitted he bore a resemblance to her assailant, and that he confessed to the crime. Indeed, the strong belief in Alphon's guilt was further fuelled by his visit to the Hanratty family asking if he could compensate them for what had happened to their son (Foot, 1971). The Hanratty case is exceptionally unique in that the absence of motive and a plausible story in the prosecution's case was accompanied by another person's confession. For Hanratty's defenders, Alphon's confession ultimately made sense of the lack of a story to explain Hanratty's guilt. However, as Griffin (2013) argued, a juror's construction of a story that fills in the gaps in the evidence may lead to bias and erroneous judgments and, indeed, not all isolated pieces of evidence can fit neatly into a story or necessarily be connected in a way that arrives at the truth. Perhaps when it comes to the case of Hanratty, Malcolm's (1999: 26) observation about the truth may be particularly relevant: 'truth is messy, incoherent, aimless, boring, absurd ... [it] does not make a good story; that's why we have art'.

However, despite the lack of a good story in the prosecution's case, Hanratty was found guilty and we observed in this chapter that it was perhaps because jurors considered that the isolated pieces of evidence proved his guilt beyond a reasonable doubt. Nevertheless, like with every other case we examine in this book, there are other factors that could have contributed to his conviction. One explanation may be found in comparing the lower social status of Hanratty in relation to the higher social status of his victims, Gregsten and Storie. In Chapter 7, we will be learning about how the law can behave differently depending on the relative social positions of the defendant and victim. Additionally, Hanratty's guilty verdict may have been powerfully influenced by the inconsistency in his testimony, that is, his frank admission halfway through his trial that he had lied about his initial alibi. In the next chapter, we will explore the nature and impact of inconsistencies in testimony.

Recommended reading

Pennington and Hastie's (1991) 'A cognitive theory of juror decision making: the story model' and their 1992 article 'Explaining the evidence: tests of the story model for juror decision making' both offer a comprehensive analysis and overview of the story-telling model. For a critique and alternative models, see Griffin's (2013) article 'Narrative, truth, and trial' and also Jellema's (2020) 'The reasonable doubt standard as inference to the best explanation'. Perhaps the most comprehensive overview of the Hanratty case is Woffinden's (1997) book *Hanratty: The Final Verdict* and, as you have seen in this chapter, Woffinden seeks to argue throughout for Hanratty's innocence. Unfortunately, Miller's (2001) book *Shadows of Deadman's Hill* is not widely available (or is very expensive). However, for an account that depicts Hanratty's guilt, we recommend Louis Blom-Cooper's (1963) book *The A6 Murder, Regina v. James Hanratty: The Semblance of Truth*.

Notes

[1] Hanratty's testimony during cross-examination at his trial for murder (Foot, 1971: 285).

[2] 'Done the lot' was a slang term for serving the whole of a sentence with no remission (Miller, 2001).

[3] It is important to bear in mind that, although the police found traces of semen on Valerie Storie's underwear, it could only be used to determine blood type and not to identify DNA, because DNA testing had not been invented in 1961.

[4] The charges of rape and attempted murder of Valerie Storie were dropped in favour of prosecuting Hanratty for the more serious charge of murdering Michael Gregsten.

[5] Miller (2001) argued that there is no evidence that Hanratty and Alphon knew each other.

[6] Similar to Miller's speculation, sociologist Jack Katz (1988: 276) analysed some high profile crimes in the US which looked 'senseless' and noted that they could have reflected the 'dizzying emotions of deviance' as the situation unfolded.

7   Despite the Court of Appeal's opinion that the DNA evidence 'standing alone' was certain proof of guilt, it is important to remember that even DNA evidence needs a story to support its interpretation. The story to support conviction needed to include information about where the evidence had been found, how it had been preserved, how it had been tested and with what result. A story questioning conviction might focus on how the evidence had been badly preserved (for example, with the possibility of contamination) or tested. Indeed, Hanratty's family introduced a new appeal against his conviction based on their claim that the DNA evidence had been contaminated (BBC, 2010). In Chapter 6, we will see how O. J. Simpson's defence team successfully raised doubts about the reliability of the DNA evidence collected by the police and introduced by the prosecution at his trial.

3

Consistency and Inconsistency in Stories: The Case of Dr Crippen

Sheer hypocrisy? It is already admitted, sir.[1]

Dinner with the Crippens

On the evening of Monday, 31 January 1910, Clara and Paul Martinetti were invited for dinner at the home of Peter Crippen and Belle Elmore at 39 Hilldrop Crescent, in Holloway, North London. They had got to know each other through the music hall business: Clara and Belle were both members of the Music Hall Ladies Guild (MHLG), and Belle was also its treasurer. 'Belle Elmore' was a stage name, used for her (not very successful) singing career. Like Crippen, she hailed from the United States, and when he married her in 1892 she was called Cora Turner. But 'Cora Turner' was not her real name either, for she was born Kunigunde Mackamotzki, the daughter of European immigrants. For that matter, 'Peter' was not Crippen's real name; he was born Hawley Harvey Crippen in Coldwater, Michigan, in 1862. And although he generally signed himself as H.H. Crippen, among those associated with the MHLG he went by the name of Peter (Smith, 2005).

According to the Martinettis, they had a pleasant evening with the Crippens. Belle was a lively person and something of a socialite, while Peter was quiet but very courteous and hospitable. When they left the house at about 1 am (1 February), this would be the last time that anyone, except Crippen, saw Belle. On 2 February, Crippen sent notes, apparently dictated by Belle, to the MHLG, one of which was addressed to its president:

39, Hilldrop Crescent, N.
Feb 2/1910
Dear Miss May,

46

Illness of a near relative has called me to America on only a few hours' notice, so I must ask you to bring my resignation as treasurer before the meeting to-day so that a new treasurer can be elected at once. You will appreciate my haste when I tell you I have not been to bed all night packing, and getting ready to go. I shall hope to see you again a few months later, but cannot spare a moment to call on you before I go. I wish you everything nice until I return to London again.

Now, good-bye, with love hastily,

Yours,

BELLE ELMORE

p.p. H.H.C. (Young, 1920: 23)

These messages served not only to announce Belle's departure but also to explain why, during dinner with the Martinettis, nothing had been said about it, for the news from America had arrived 'on only a few hours' notice', which implied sometime on 1 February. Afterwards, Crippen told Clara Martinetti that the 'news' had arrived late on that evening.

At Belle's suggestion, the MHLG had earlier rented an office in Crippen's suite in Albion House, New Oxford Street. Although he had trained in medicine in the US, in London he worked in various capacities, mainly as a vendor and manager for Munyon's Remedies and most recently with the Yale Tooth Specialists. Thus, it was hard for him to avoid contact with members of the MHLG, who naturally expressed surprise at Belle's hasty departure. Surprise turned to worry when, in mid-February, Crippen reported that Belle had fallen ill with a lung problem and was in California. Then, on 20 March, he wrote that:

> I have been really upset by very bad news from Belle that I did not feel equal to talking about anything, and now I have just had a cable saying she is so dangerously ill with double pleuro-pneumonia. (Young, 1920: 14)

And on 24 March, he sent the following telegram to the Martinettis:

> 24 March. Victoria Station. Belle died yesterday at 6 o'clock. Please phone Annie [another member of the MHLG]. Shall be away a week. Peter. (Young, 1920: 14)

To announce her death publicly, on 26 March Crippen paid for an obituary notice to appear in *The Era*, a weekly newspaper popular with theatregoers.

But even before the announcement of Belle's death, worry among her friends had been accompanied by rising suspicion. Her complete silence after 1 February was seen as very strange, because she was a frequent letter writer and her friends could not understand why she had not been in touch. Then, on 20 February, Crippen and Ethel Le Neve were seen together at an MHLG charity dinner. Le Neve also worked in Albion House as a typist and bookkeeper and, like Crippen, had worked for Munyon's and most recently with the Yale Tooth Specialists. It was she who delivered to the MHLG the messages purportedly dictated by Belle. What struck the members of the MHLG was that Le Neve was wearing jewellery which friends were certain belonged to Belle. At some point in February, she began staying overnight at Hilldrop Crescent and on 12 March, she moved in. She was increasingly seen with Crippen in public, often wearing dresses that belonged to Belle. A member of the MHLG, Lilian Hawthorn, was travelling to the US with her husband John Nash and they were asked by others to make inquiries there. They were unable to find any record of a 'Belle Elmore', 'Cora Crippen' or Cora Mackamotzki having died in California, and when they returned on 30 June, John Nash went to Scotland Yard to suggest that they make inquiries (Young, 1920).

Detective Chief Inspector Walter Dew, assigned to the case, interviewed Crippen at his office on 8 July. It was a long meeting, interrupted by Crippen's occasional disappearances to the dental practice to extract teeth and included lunch at the Holborn Restaurant. In his meeting with Dew, Crippen told a very different story about Belle's disappearance. He said: 'I suppose I had better tell the truth. The stories I have told … about her death are untrue. As far as I know, she is still alive' (Young, 1920: 34). He then went on to make a signed statement, from which the following excerpts are relevant:

> It is quite four years since she ever went out at all to sing, and, although we apparently lived very happily together, as a matter of fact there were very frequent occasions when she got into most violent tempers, and often threatened she would leave me, saying she had a man she could go to, and she would end it all. …
>
> In consequence of these frequent outbursts, I discontinued sleeping with her, and have never cohabited with her since. …
>
> On the Monday night, the day before I wrote the letter to the Guild resigning her position as treasurer, Mr. and Mrs. Paul Martinetti came to our place to dinner, and during the evening Mr. Martinetti wanted to go to the lavatory. As he had been to our house several times, I did not take the trouble to go and show him where it was. After they had left my wife blamed me for not taking him to the lavatory, and abused me, and said, 'This is the finish of it. I won't stand it any longer. I shall leave you tomorrow, and you will never hear of me again.' She had said this so often that I did not take much notice of it, but she did say one thing which she had never said before, viz., that I was to arrange

to cover up any scandal with our mutual friends and the Guild the best way I could. ...

I afterwards realised that [the illness of a near relative] would not be a sufficient explanation for her not coming back, and later on I told people that she was ill with bronchitis and pneumonia, and afterwards I told them she was dead from this ailment. ...

Miss Le Neve has been in my employ, and known to me through being employed by the firms I have worked for, for the past eight years, and she is now living with me as my wife at Hilldrop Crescent. I have been intimate with her during the past three years, and have frequently stayed with her at hotels, but was never from home at nights. ...

My belief is that my wife has gone to Chicago to join Bruce Miller, whose business on the music hall stage is a musical instrument turn, but I think he has now gone into another business, and has speculated and made money. (Young, 1920: 34–9)

Dew returned with Crippen to Hilldrop Crescent and looked around the house and the garden but found nothing suspicious. The next day, 9 July, he returned to Crippen's office only to find that the doctor had been and gone, leaving instructions with one of his assistants to pay for the remaining months' rent on his house. It quickly transpired that Le Neve was missing as well.

On 13 July, Dew went back to Hilldrop Crescent and made a thorough search of the house. In the cellar he noticed that some bricks were loose and after a bit of digging he uncovered what looked to be human remains. A warrant was issued for the arrest of Crippen and Le Neve and a poster with photographs and samples of their handwriting was widely circulated in the press. It turned out that they had first travelled from London to Belgium, and on 22 July the captain of the SS *Montrose*, on its way from Antwerp to Quebec, telegraphed Dew to say that the suspects were aboard, travelling under the name of Robinson with Le Neve disguised as a young man. Presumably fearing that if Crippen and Le Neve reached Canada they would slip across the border to the United States and disappear, Dew went to Liverpool and took a faster ship across the Atlantic in order to arrive ahead of the *Montrose*. As he made his way towards Canada, Dew kept Scotland Yard informed of this progress and the Yard relayed messages to him from the *Montrose*. The British press reported these developments in great detail because the Crippen case and the pursuit across the Atlantic had gripped the attention of the public. Meanwhile, Crippen apparently suspected that the couple were going to be arrested in Quebec and he was making arrangements to make it look as if he had killed himself by jumping overboard, while actually hiding in the crew's quarters and smuggling himself into Canada unnoticed. However, on 31 July, Dew boarded the *Montrose* before it reached Quebec; Crippen and Le Neve were arrested for Belle's murder and taken back to London. During the return trip, Crippen protested his innocence of the charges and insisted that he had never told Le Neve anything about the circumstances of Belle's disappearance. Crippen and Le Neve were taken to a first hearing at Bow Street Magistrates' Court, where they said nothing, and were sent for separate trials at the Old Bailey. Crippen was the first to be put in the dock on 18 October in what, at the time, was declared to be 'the trial of the century'.

At the start of proceedings, the clerk of the court read out the charge of 'wilful murder of Cora Crippen[2] on the 1st February last', against which Crippen entered a plea of not guilty. It was then for the prosecution to make an opening statement setting out the case against him. The lead prosecution barrister was Richard Muir, known for being 'ferocious and daunting … thorough, grim and remorseless' (Connell, 2005: 120). He developed the prosecution's case through a narrative of events leading up to and following the disappearance of Belle.[3] Given Crippen's insistence that she had travelled to the United States, it was necessary to establish that the remains found at Hilldrop Crescent were hers. Although those remains were headless, limbless and boneless, Muir explained that hair and scar tissue would identify them as Belle's and that a pyjama top buried with them had only been manufactured after the Crippens began renting the house and therefore the remains could not have been buried by previous occupants. Forensic analysis of the remains also revealed that they contained lethal levels of hyoscine hydrobromide,[4] suggesting death by poisoning, and it was known that Crippen had purchased five grains of this substance on 17 January.

If Belle Elmore had been killed, dismembered and buried in this way, no one other than the murderer had witnessed the events, and Muir's narrative needed to demonstrate that there was *circumstantial evidence* to indicate that Crippen had the *motive, opportunity* and *capability* for committing the crime.[5] Crippen's *motive*, Muir argued, was to remove Belle Elmore from the scene so that he could continue his relationship with Ethel Le Neve and also take possession of Belle's savings and jewellery. The *opportunity* to commit the crime was ever present, as Crippen and Belle lived together and there was no one else in the house; and *capability* was evidenced by his knowledge of, and access to, hyoscine hydrobromide and also by his training in medicine which could have facilitated the dismemberment of the body. Following this opening statement, numerous witnesses were called to establish the prosecution's case, including members of the MHLG, Inspector Dew and several medical and forensic experts (Young, 1920).

Crippen was represented by 'the clever, industrious, experienced' barrister Arthur Tobin (Connell, 2005: 122). He had not done a great deal to cross-examine many of the prosecution's witnesses, except the medical and forensic experts whom he pressed about the certainty with which the remains could be identified as Belle's, the length of time they had been buried, and whether the hyoscine hydrobromide could have been generated through burial and decomposition. In his opening statement for the defence, Tobin began by arguing that the prosecution had not proved beyond a reasonable doubt that the remains were of a female, and specifically of Belle Elmore. He noted that Crippen was universally recognised by witnesses as a 'good-hearted' and 'good tempered' person – someone who could not commit murder – and he challenged the prosecution's claims about *motive* (Crippen did not need to murder Belle to continue in his relationship with Le Neve; he did not need money) and *capability* (Crippen had not trained as a surgeon and could not have dismembered the body in the way that it had been). He also told the story already put forward by Crippen, that Belle had left him and returned to the US and that he had told lies about her illness and death in order to cover up any scandal. Crippen had fled after the interview with Inspector Dew, said Tobin, because he did not know where Belle was and felt that there was a 'high mountain of prejudice' against him (Young, 1920: 83).

Crippen then took the stand in his own defence. Following a lengthy set of questions from Tobin's assistant barrister Huntley Jenkins, which were designed to allow Crippen to set out his side of the story and refute the prosecution's claims, he was cross-examined by Richard Muir. The latter focused particularly on Crippen's decision to tell a story about his wife's death, pointing out that he could only have said this if his wife really was dead and therefore unable to contact any of her friends and family (and show his story to be a lie). He also called attention more than once to Crippen's self-admitted lies:

Muir:	You got a letter from Dr. Burroughs and his wife; two of your wife's oldest friends?
Crippen:	Yes.
Muir:	And you wrote to him?
Crippen:	I did.
Muir:	Take exhibit 31. [Letter handed to witness.] It is on black-edged paper?
Crippen:	Yes.
Muir:	In keeping with your mourning?
Crippen:	Yes.
Muir:	And the letter in keeping with your role of bereaved husband?
Crippen:	Yes.
Muir:	'Albion House, 5th April. My Dear Doctor, I feel sure you will forgive me for my apparent neglect, but really I have been nearly out of my mind with poor Belle's death, so far away from me.' Sheer hypocrisy?
Crippen:	It is already admitted, sir.

Muir:	Sheer hypocrisy?
Crippen:	I am not denying any of this.
Muir:	'She would keep up when she should have been in bed, with the consequence that pleuro-pneumonia terminated fatally. Almost to the last she refused to let me know there was any danger, so the cable that she had gone came as a most awful shock to me.' Your imagination was equal to the shock?
Crippen:	I do not see why you keep on with these questions, because I am willing to admit and tell you that they were all lies right through.
Lord Chief Justice:[6]	That may be quite true, Dr. Crippen, but it is a very serious part of the case, and you must really answer the questions, lies or no lies.
Crippen:	I beg your pardon, my lord.
Muir:	That was pure imagination this awful shock?
Crippen:	All imagination entirely.
Muir:	You are telling lies, which you hope will be believed?
Crippen:	Yes.
Muir:	And you think they will be believed?
Crippen:	I believed they would be.
Muir:	How were you saving yourself from anything by telling those lies?
Crippen:	I was saving myself from the scandal of my friends.
Muir:	What scandal were you covering up?
Crippen:	The scandal of the separation from my wife. (Cross-examination of Crippen, cited in Young, 1920: 103–4)

Further lies were also revealed in Muir's cross-examination. Crippen claimed that he had first told Le Neve that his wife had left him (the story that he told to Inspector Dew and at the trial), but later told her that Belle was dead (just as he had said to the MHLG). Additionally, having become suspicious that the *Montrose*'s captain had identified them as the fleeing couple, he wrote a card to Le Neve saying that he could not stand the pressure and was going to jump overboard, when in fact he had arranged with a quartermaster to be hidden in the ship until it docked in Quebec from where he hoped to get ashore incognito and reunite with Le Neve after arrival.

Muir:	'I have made up my mind to jump overboard to-night. I know I have spoilt your life, but hope some day you will learn to forgive me; the last word, Love, your H.' That was all pretence?
Crippen:	Certainly.
Muir:	And the horrors [of arrest] were the horrors of your imagination entirely?
Crippen:	Yes.
Muir:	You had arranged this with Miss Le Neve?
Crippen:	Yes.
Muir:	That she was to remain on board and carry on the pretence?
Crippen:	Yes. (Cross-examination of Crippen, cited in Young, 1920: 118)

Tobin also produced three medical witnesses to rebut the claims made by the prosecution's experts, who were extensively cross-examined by Muir, and with that the presentation of evidence for the defence came to an end. In his closing statement to the court, Tobin largely repeated the arguments from his opening statement and again described Crippen's self-acknowledged lies as a strategy to cover up the scandal of Belle's departure. These lies, said Tobin, fed Crippen's fear of arrest 'until this woman is found', which led to his decision to flee with Le Neve. But, said Tobin, the law did not require Crippen to locate his wife and he had not attempted to do so. Moreover, 'His disappearance, his lies, his flight were no proof whatever that he committed murder' (Young, 1920: 148). In effect, Tobin was *reconstructing* the story told by the prosecution: the remains in the cellar were not those of Belle, who was still alive somewhere. And in his final appeal to the jurors he said:

> You need all the will power a man[7] could have to enable you to expel the poison or prejudice which must have been instilled into your minds by reason of his lies, by reason of his folly, and beyond that by reason of so much that has appeared in the columns of the papers. You need the will power to expel all that prejudice. (Tobin, defence closing statement, cited in Young, 1920: 150)

In closing for the prosecution, Muir rebutted all of the defence's arguments. He took particular aim at the description of Crippen as too kind-hearted to be a murderer. In contrast:

> The prisoner had admitted that over a long series of months he led a life of studied hypocrisy, utterly regardless of the pain which the lies which he was telling and was acting would inflict upon friend or sister of his wife. ... What were they [the jurors] to say of all that hypocrisy

and of all those lies? (Muir, prosecution closing statement, cited in Young, 1920: 154)

Crucially, in a passing mention of Crippen's claim in the witness box that Le Neve had spent the night at Hilldrop Crescent on 2 February, he commented that 'It was for the jury to say what weight, if any, they attached to any statement of Crippen's uncorroborated' (Young, 1920: 156). The implication was clear: if Crippen had openly acknowledged lying about some things, why would he not lie about other things as well?

Finally, as in all jury trials in England, the judge summed up the case and relevant issues for the jurors. Among other things, he noted the lies that Crippen had told and the implications to be drawn from them:

> You cannot have sat in that box long in the course of this case without probably coming to the conclusion that if it is a simple question of oath against oath, or statement against statement, you cannot rely upon the mere statement made by Dr. Crippen. He has on his own confession lied for his own purpose, and was prepared to lie, if necessary, for the purpose of his own advantage. Even when he was purporting to tell the truth, certain things were false, and false to his own knowledge, though he was asserting the truth.
>
> It is quite obvious, from the speeches both of Mr. Tobin and of Mr. Muir, that the fact that Dr. Crippen has lied on material points in this case is a very important matter for your consideration. (Lord Chief Justice's charge to the jury, 22 October 1910, cited in Young, 1920: 165)

And the judge also gave examples of Crippen's inconsistent statements:

> The evidence given by Dr. Crippen yesterday I do not think is much worthwhile calling attention to, because in the box, as out of it, he certainly was ready to make statements which he afterwards had to admit not to be true. He at first said with great confidence that his wife never bought pyjamas, that he always preferred to buy them himself. He then said with equal confidence that those sets were part of two which he bought in September of last year, 1909, and that the trousers were part of an old set which he bought some time back. When he was further pressed by Mr. Muir, who put it to him distinctly that they were bought by his wife at a sale at Jones in January, 1909, he said it might be so; and when I pointed out to him that he had sworn exactly the contrary, and that his wife had never bought pyjamas for him, he said he had been too confident in answering the first question. You must judge him, you have heard him, and I can say no more. (Lord Chief Justice's charge to the jury, 22 October 1910, cited in Young, 1920: 172–3)

After the judge's summing up, the jury retired for just 27 minutes and returned with a unanimous verdict of guilty. Asked if he had anything to say, Crippen replied 'I am innocent'. He was sentenced to death and executed by hanging on 23 November 1910.[8] As we will outline at the end of this chapter, several factors probably contributed to his conviction, but the one that we wish to focus on here is Crippen's failure to tell a consistent story, not only about what he claimed had happened to his wife but also about more minor aspects of the case, such as who purchased his pyjamas. Inconsistencies can significantly weaken the perceived reliability of testimony given by defendants and witnesses.

Exercise 1:

Now that you have read our overview of the case and trial, it should be clear that Crippen created significant problems for himself by changing the story about Belle's disappearance, from one in which she had died to one in which she had left him for another man. It did not need the prosecution to accuse him of lying about Belle's death, because he readily admitted that he had lied. Therefore, an important question to consider is: why did Crippen change his story when interviewed by Inspector Dew? When thinking about answers, it is also interesting to reflect on why lawyers advise their clients to tell one story and 'stick to it'. (Pardieck, 2006)

Inconsistency, reliability and credibility

When Richard Muir and the Lord Chief Justice pointed to Crippen's lies and inconsistencies as indicators of his lack of credibility, they were echoing both common sense and the views of legal scholars. For example, in 1904 the American legal scholar John H. Wigmore had written a very influential text about evidence (reprinted in 1970) in which he stated 'a prior self-contradiction shows a defect either in the memory or in the honesty of the witness'[9] (1970: 993; cited in Fisher et al, 2009: 123). And this opinion has persisted. For example, Fisher et al (2009: 123) noted that instructions to the jury in many contemporary US trials include a guideline about inconsistency such as the following in New York State Courts: 'You may consider whether a witness made statements at this trial that are inconsistent with each other. You may also consider whether a witness made previous statements that are inconsistent with his or her testimony at trial' (New York Criminal Jury Instructions 2d, Credibility of Witnesses-Inconsistent Statements, 2007; cited in Fisher et al, 2009: 123). Similarly, legal practitioners recommend focusing on inconsistencies in testimony. For example, Australian barrister

James Glissan (1991: 108; cited in Brewer et al, 1999: 208) wrote that 'A true inconsistency can effectively destroy a witness, and sometimes a whole case', and American lawyer Thomas Mauet (2017) suggested that raising prior inconsistent statements can be a significant tactic for discrediting a witness.

Fisher et al (2009) argued that the focus on inconsistencies in testimony reflects and reinforces beliefs among potential jurors and criminal justice personnel about the reliability and credibility of witnesses. In this regard, Potter and Brewer (1999) found that police officers, lawyers and mock jurors all rated inconsistent statements by witnesses as the strongest indicator of doubts about the accuracy of what they say. Eades (2008) described this belief as 'the ideology of inconsistency', and Fisher et al (2009) proposed that it represents a 'courtroom theory' of memory based on assumptions that are often not supported by psychological studies. For example, questions asked in one interview may differ in format to those asked in another, just as questions asked in examination may differ from those asked in cross-examination, and each may lead to different answers. Additionally, crimes can often be a complex set of events, for which memory is clearer on some dimensions than others; thus, inconsistency in recalling some events does not necessarily indicate that the whole testimony is inconsistent and unreliable. Overall, Fisher et al argued that 'contrary to two centuries of accepted legal folklore, an inconsistent witness may not be an inaccurate witness' (2009: 132).

Nevertheless, as implied by Fisher et al's conclusion, it may be a long time before psychological research breaks down commonly held beliefs about inconsistency. This is partly because more research needs to be done in order to demonstrate the generality of psychological models of memory; and such research would need to be introduced in the courtroom (for example, by expert witnesses) when matters of inconsistency are at stake. But it is also because inconsistencies in testimony, if they exist, are expressed in words and documented through transcripts or records of successive interviews and statements in court. Thus, they can easily be assembled for the court's attention. We will see in Chapter 4 that there are other beliefs about the credibility of witnesses that focus on non-verbal communication such as whether they make eye contact with the person interrogating them and whether they look nervous, raise their voice or speak hesitantly. Once again, psychological research has strongly questioned these beliefs but they continue to hold sway among criminal justice personnel and the public (Strömwall and Granhag, 2003). However, even though non-verbal cues may influence perceptions of credibility, they are difficult to use as arguments against the accuracy or honesty of testimony because non-verbal behaviour is not recorded, except in some trials in the US where recording is allowed. An advocate in court would probably find it hard to sustain a claim that, for example, the witness avoided all eye contact or spoke hesitantly, but is on much firmer ground when referring to inconsistencies in what was said. Thus, identifying inconsistencies is likely to continue as a strategy for questioning the accuracy and honesty of witnesses' accounts. Indeed, such is the power wielded by claims of inconsistency that this term has been used to denote several different things. We explore each meaning and give examples, including from the Crippen case.

Inconsistent with common sense (implausibility)

In this type of inconsistency, it is argued that something the suspect claims to have done, or not done, is contrary to what 'common sense' would dictate or expect them to do: the claim is just not plausible. Matoesian (1997) identified the construction of this kind of inconsistency in the trial of William Kennedy Smith for the rape of Patricia Bowman in 1991. Smith, a nephew of former President John F. Kennedy, met Bowman at a bar in Palm Beach, Florida, asked her for a ride back to the house he was staying at and invited her for a walk on the beach. While on the beach, Bowman claimed that Smith raped her, but Smith claimed that the sex was consensual. Matoesian analysed the tactics used by Smith's lawyer at the trial to suggest an inconsistency between Bowman's actions and her claim that she was raped. That inconsistency was succinctly expressed after the trial by Diane Sawyer an ABC News journalist who said that Bowman's story did not 'fit the logic' of sexual indifference in the encounter because of 'the victim's statement that she had no sexual interest in the defendant, on the one hand, and the fact that she went to his home, walked on the beach, and exchanged kisses with him, on the other' (Matoesian, 1997: 56). Although Smith was acquitted, Matoesian argued that the 'logic' invoked by Sawyer was not neutral but represented a patriarchal view of the interactions between men and women and of the indicators of sexual interest which are applied to the latter. Bowman's claim that she did not want sex did not fit the patriarchal model. This case shows how 'common sense', while always a social construction, can be used effectively to question the consistency or plausibility of a person's claims (something we will explore in detail in Chapter 10).

A similar tactic for identifying this type of inconsistency was used by Richard Muir in Crippen's trial. He focused on the fact that, after his arrest, Crippen made no attempt to locate his wife:

Muir:	Of course, you understand that if your wife is alive there is no foundation for this charge at all?
Crippen:	Decidedly not.
Muir:	And that if she could be found you would at once be acquitted of it?
Crippen:	Oh, rather.

Muir:	What steps have been taken by you to find your wife?
Crippen:	I have not taken any steps.
Muir:	So far as you know, has anybody else taken any steps to find your wife?
Crippen:	Not that I know. I have left myself entirely in my solicitor's hands. I have made no efforts of any kind in fact, I could not. (Cross-examination of Crippen, cited in Young, 1920: 119)

And Muir returned to Crippen's inaction in his closing statement:

> There was something to be said for the proposition, why should he inquire after his arrest? The most obvious inquiries neglected the tradesmen who would come to the door, the neighbours who would see her, or the cabman who would take her luggage. Here was a man defended by a London solicitor whose defence was that his wife was alive, and, as far as the defendant knew, not a tradesman, cabman, or steamship owner questioned to find what had become of her. Was that fact explicable upon any hypothesis except one, that Crippen knew her remains were buried in that cellar, and that any inquiries for her would be absolutely fruitless and futile? She had friends at home in England, friends in America, relatives in America. Any inquiry made at them? None, either before or after the flight. (Muir, prosecution closing statement, cited in Young, 1920: 159)

Similarly, in his summing up the judge mentioned this 'extraordinary' situation:

> Of course, one most extraordinary thing will probably strike you [the jurors] – that if Crippen honestly believed that the woman had gone to Bruce Miller at Chicago when he made that suggestion ... to Mr. Dew on 8th July you would have thought that there was one channel at least whereby inquiries might be made of a most important character; and probably the thought has occurred to you, if Dr. Crippen believed that his wife had gone, either for a moral or immoral purpose, to visit Bruce Miller, among her own friends, how is it that no inquiry was made by Dr. Crippen of Bruce Miller? (Lord Chief Justice's charge to the jury, 22 October 1910, cited in Young, 1920: 167)

As Richard Muir and Judge Alverstone implied, Crippen was on trial for his life, and common sense dictated that if, as he alleged, she had left him, he would have attempted to locate his wife in order to prove that she was still alive. Yet he did nothing. The judge also commented that if Belle Elmore were still alive she would surely have heard about the case, and the trial, and that she would have been 'abominably wicked' (Young, 1920: 170) not to come forward and save him from the gallows, despite the tensions that Crippen described in their relationship. In other words, these things rendered his story implausible.

Inconsistent narratives

Ghetti et al (2002) defined consistent testimony as the narration of exactly the same information on repeated occasions. On this definition, then, when the information varies between tellings (whether by a little or a lot), witnesses are perceived as inconsistent in their version of events. Ghetti et al (2002) cited prior research which reports that jurors are less likely to believe witnesses whose narratives vary from one occasion to another, a finding that has also been confirmed in subsequent studies (for example, Oeberst, 2012; Krix et al, 2015). But, as these and other researchers point out, varied narratives do not necessarily mean that any of them are inaccurate. Thus, in one statement a witness might report that the suspect wore a brown jacket and in another that the suspect wore black trainers. Not mentioning the brown jacket in the second statement is what researchers call a 'forgotten detail' while the mention of the black trainers is a 'reminiscent detail'. However, there is every possibility that the two statements are compatible – the suspect wore a brown jacket *and* black trainers – and accurate.

To test whether forgotten and reminiscent details are less accurate than consistent (that is, repeated) details, Fisher et al (2009) conducted 19 experiments in which subjects observed simulated events and were questioned about them twice – after about 30 minutes, and after two weeks. Comparing the two accounts, they found that forgotten details were almost as accurate as consistent details and reminiscent details were only slightly less accurate. Overall, second accounts with forgotten or reminiscent details were no less accurate than accounts with only consistent details. Similarly, Krix et al (2015) showed a short video of a (staged) wallet theft to a group of students and measured their recall accuracy immediately after seeing the video and one week later. Forgotten and reminiscent details were observed – separately or jointly – in about a quarter of the second accounts, and by comparing this information with the video Krix et al found that those details were no less accurate than details which were reported in both the first and second accounts.

Interestingly, Krix et al also found that the frequency of forgotten and reminiscent details was significantly influenced by the type of recall that the students were directed to use. One group filled out a questionnaire about the incident, while the other was simply asked to describe it. Perhaps unsurprisingly, the first group gave more consistent accounts on both occasions, whereas the second group had higher proportions of forgotten and reminiscent details. Other studies have focused on additional factors which can cause accounts to vary between one telling and another. For example, Brönimann et al (2013) found that the characteristics of the interviewer (for example, male/female; prosecutor/defence) significantly affected the content of an interview, meaning that the narrative given by the interviewee changed somewhat from one interviewer to another. Thus, in their questioning, female interviewers tend to use more cognitive process words denoting insights (think, know and so on) or causation (because, effect and so on) which leads to these words appearing more frequently in interviewees' replies.

In contrast to these research findings, forgotten and reminiscent details are generally perceived as indicating less accurate statements. Thus, Krix et al (2015) also showed their video to a sample of police detectives and asked them to rate the likely accuracy of accounts with forgotten and reminiscent details. The detectives significantly underestimated the accuracy of those accounts, perceiving them as hardly more accurate than contradictory statements appearing in the first and second account. This is further evidence that the 'courtroom theory' of memory, accuracy and credibility prevails among criminal justice personnel, even though it is negated by careful psychological research.

For example, using a fictional case widely employed in training for trial lawyers in the US, in which the defendant is charged with knowingly selling alcohol to an inebriated person, Kerper (1997) identified a forgotten detail and evaluated its significance for the cross-examination of the witness. In his first report on the incident, the arresting officer wrote that 'he observed Mr. Watkins stagger and weave across the street, stumble at the curb, pause for a moment at the entrance of the Cut-Rate Liquor store, enter the store and later exit the store carrying a paper bag containing wine' (Kerper, 1997: 85). However, when he took the stand the officer gave a very similar account but did not mention that Mr Watkins paused at the entrance to the store. Kerper argued that this forgotten detail is significant because a pause before entering the store would mean that Mr Watkins was trying to gather himself and appear sober before going in to buy alcohol. A defence lawyer could raise this forgotten detail, not only to support the defendant's claim that Mr Watkins looked sober when he entered the store but also to question the accuracy of the officer's testimony. Kerper also used a separate example, from a real case, in which a reminiscent detail was made to look like a contradiction, although the witness was partially successful in integrating both the previous and current accounts:

Prosecutor:	You pretty much hate the defendant though, don't you?
Witness:	No, not really. I just think he is a crazy kid. That's all.
Prosecutor:	Didn't you describe him before as a punk, liar, thief, cheat and murderer and the lowest form of life that you know? [Implying a contradiction]

Witness:	Yeah. That pretty well sums him up. But he is a crazy kid on top of that. [Making the new information a reminiscent detail] (Kerper, 1997: 84)

Returning to Crippen's case, once he became a person of interest to the criminal justice system, he gave two narratives of events and associated circumstances, first to Inspector Dew and then at his trial. Both were exactly the same in their main story: Belle had left him and presumably gone to America to join Bruce Miller. However, the first account was very general, being given in a police interview when Belle's disappearance – but not murder – was being investigated, while the second was much more detailed being developed through his examination by Huntley Jenkins and cross-examination by Richard Muir, who both asked him about many things of relevance to the murder trial – his use of the cellar at Hilldrop Crescent, his use of hyoscine hydrobromide, his pyjamas, what he told Le Neve, and so on. Given that this second account was not a spontaneous narrative from the defendant, it would have been difficult for Muir to claim that Crippen had forgotten details from his first account or added reminiscent details in his second account, both of which could have been used to cast doubt on the accuracy and honesty of his testimony. Therefore, this kind of inconsistency is of least relevance to understanding Crippen's case. Nevertheless, both Muir and the judge noted minor narrative inconsistencies during Crippen's testimony on the stand. In cross-examination about when and why he pawned his wife's jewellery, Muir pointed out a forgotten detail:

Muir:	Were those two occasions, the 2nd and 9th February of this year, the only two occasions on which you had ever pawned jewellery of your wife's?
Crippen:	Those were the only two occasions.
Muir:	Had you forgotten that you had pawned that jewellery on the 8th July?
Crippen:	No. [Forgotten detail]
Muir:	You remember it quite well?
Crippen:	Quite well. (Cross-examination of Crippen, cited in Young, 1920: 99)

For his part, in trying to clarify Crippen's testimony, the judge identified a reminiscent detail:

Judge:	Two minutes ago you said to Mr. Muir that your wife never bought you pyjamas, but that you always bought them yourself?
Crippen:	Yes.

Judge:	Now, you have said, 'My wife did buy me some, but I do not know whether these are they?' [A reminiscent detail]
Crippen:	Perhaps I should not have put it so positively.
Muir:	Which is true?
Crippen:	Perhaps I should not have said so positively; I said she may have bought some. (Cross-examination of Crippen, cited in Young, 1920: 109)

In his reply, Crippen opted to make the reminiscent detail ambiguous: 'I said she may have bought some'. Overall, however, inconsistent narratives did not play a large role in eroding Crippen's credibility; it was contradictory narratives which had the largest impact on his case.

Contradictory statements

Contradictory statements are identified when two statements made by the same person cannot both be true.[10] For example, if a witness says that the suspect wore a blue jacket, and later says that the suspect wore a red jacket, only one of these statements might be true: the jacket was either blue or it was red, but not both. Common sense suggests that contradictory statements will reduce the accuracy of a witness's account, and research largely supports this. Thus, in their study Fisher et al (2009) found that only 49 per cent of contradictory statements were accurate, meaning that one of the two statements correctly described what had happened whereas the other did not. Similarly, Krix et al (2015) found that only 40 per cent of contradictory statements were accurate, indicating that some subjects actually made contradictory statements which were *both* inaccurate (for example, saying the jacket was red, then blue, when it was actually purple). Interestingly, when looking at the accuracy of the whole statement, Fisher et al found that witnesses who made many contradictory statements were not much less accurate overall than witnesses who made few contradictory statements, suggesting that the 'courtroom theory', which equates contradictions with inaccurate testimony, is incorrect. Fisher et al recommended that the accuracy of testimony should be judged in relation to specific details, and that contradictions should not be used to discredit the witness and their whole testimony.

However, as to the effect of contradictory statements on judgements of witnesses' accuracy and credibility, studies have found that the 'courtroom theory' is commonly held among mock jurors (who are usually university students recruited as participants for the research projects). In these projects, subjects watch, or listen to, a simulated cross-examination in which witnesses are either consistent with what they said before or contradict themselves on one or more details. While an early study by Lindsay et al (1986) found that contradictory testimony from a key prosecution witness did not affect mock jurors' decisions to convict or acquit the defendant, Berman et al (1995) found the opposite: contradictory testimony by prosecution witnesses, particularly on details which were central to the case, was perceived as less credible and defendants were judged to be less culpable. In a later study, Brewer and Burke (2002) found that contradictory testimony lowered the likelihood of conviction, but that a stronger influence came from the level of confidence shown by the witness. When the witness was presented to mock jurors as confident, the frequency of conviction was almost the same for both consistent and contradictory testimony. In another study, Brewer and Hupfeld (2004) found that contradictory testimony for the prosecution lowered the likelihood of conviction and was not affected by similarities or differences in identity and beliefs between jurors and the witness. Overall, a remark by Brewer et al in 1999 summarised the research in a way that is still valid: 'Although the methodologies of these studies differed, and the results were mixed, the balance of evidence seems to indicate that jurors' assessments of witness credibility and defendant culpability/guilt were diminished by inconsistent or contradictory testimony' (1999: 298).

It is important to note that these studies focused on two versions of single pieces of testimony (one consistent, one with contradictions) and their possible effects on mock jurors' perceptions of credibility and decisions to convict. However, while the second versions included contradictions in testimony, these projects did not study their *significance*, by which we mean the ways in which contradictions were, or might have been, handled both within and beyond the testimony itself. Thus, some advocates might make a great deal of contradictions and their negative implications for the witness, while others may not. Witnesses may try to repair the contradictions, with more or less success. Finally, in their closing statements both prosecution and defence may highlight contradictions in witness testimony as part of their case for conviction or acquittal. All of these strategies can arguably influence the effect that contradictions will have on jurors' decisions.

Although the conventions of legal strategy recommend exploiting contradictions as a means to weaken the testimony for the opposing case, little has been written about how lawyers should, or do, deal with this. Which contradictions are worth pursuing and why? Kerper (1997), cited previously, is one of the few legal scholars to have considered this question, making some interesting recommendations. Thus, she advised focusing on contradictions that do not look as if they can be resolved by the witness. For example, in commenting on the witness who was challenged about his attitude towards the defendant (he previously had called him a punk, liar and so on, whereas on the stand he simply referred to him as a crazy kid), she noted that this was not a strong example of a contradiction because the witness was able to resolve it by adding the previous and current statements together as a general description of the defendant. (We have described this as treating the current statement as a reminiscent detail.) One can think of other examples; thus, while a first account may describe the suspect's jacket as red, and the second may describe it as blue, the contradiction may only be apparent and would disappear if, on further questioning, it emerges that the jacket was red at the front and blue at the back. Kerper also recommended ignoring contradictions which are not central to the advocate's case. For example, if the arresting officer's report described Mr Watkins as 'stumbling at the curb' as he approached the store but on the stand he described Mr Watkins as 'slipping', this might be exploited by the defence as a contradiction that shows the unreliability of the officer's evidence. However 'slipping' and 'stumbling' are not absolute opposites and this potential contradiction is less important than the forgotten detail in the officer's testimony on the stand (Mr Watkins paused before entering the store). Contradictions are best pursued if they have a central bearing on the case. This recommendation is supported by Berman et al's (1995) finding that contradictions in 'central details', such as those referring to the identity of the suspect, more strongly lower the credibility of a witness than contradictions in 'peripheral details', such as those referring to the crime scene.

If a contradiction is identified in cross-examination, the advocate will almost certainly seek clarification on which version is the witness's 'correct' statement in order to confirm or deny particular pieces of evidence. In many cases, the advocate may also challenge the witness about the reason for the contradiction: was it a mistake, or a matter of lying?[11] While mistakes and lies both weaken or even nullify the accuracy of a specific part of the evidence, the moral difference between them is great: mistakes are unintentional misrepresentations, but lies are intentional. A witness who makes mistakes can be seen, and will present themself, as someone who is making a sincere effort to be accurate even if they sometimes get things wrong. A witness who lies is actively trying to change the evidence so as to favour whichever side they are representing, be it the prosecution or defence. While a mistake can weaken the credibility of a witness, a lie can destroy it.

Thus, when challenged about a contradiction, a witness will save moral face and at least some of their credibility if they can present it as a mistake rather than a lie. Brewer and Hupfeld (2004) developed an example of this strategy where a witness is asked about a contradiction between something said in examination and, now, in cross-examination:

[The witness told the defence attorney that they were four metres away from the attacker] ... the defence attorney asked, 'You said before in your evidence to my learned friend that you were only 2 meters away from the attacker when the assault took place. Which is it?' The witness answered, 'Sorry. I meant about 4 meters. I don't know what made me say 2 meters'. (Brewer and Hupfeld, 2004: 500)

As we can see, the defence advocate was looking to clarify the evidence relating to the distance between the witness and the attacker – was it two metres or four? The witness provided the clarification but also went on to say something about how the contradiction arose. The apology and clarification ('Sorry. I meant about 4 meters') were followed by a claim that the origin of the contradiction was a mystery ('I don't know what made me say 2 meters'), but importantly, the mystery made the contradiction unintentional. It was a mistake, not a lie.[12]

Although there have been no studies of the frequency with which, if challenged about contradictions, witnesses portray them as either mistakes or lies, the general desire to 'save moral face' (and credibility) almost certainly means that their portrayal as lies is comparatively rare. Stated more simply, witnesses rarely say that they have been lying. And if they do, the only way in which they can hope to save some moral face is by giving purportedly acceptable reasons for lying. As we will see in Chapter 5, the presentation of reasons for doing something deemed objectionable – whether committing a crime or telling a lie – is what sociologists call an 'account' (Scott and Lyman, 1968). Thus, witnesses who say they have lied will probably feel compelled to account for the lie(s) in ways that – hopefully for them – maintain their moral face.

As Scott and Lyman (1968) and others (for example, Schönbach, 1990) have observed, accounts can include many different kinds of reason for doing something (which we will review in Chapter 5), but what is also important is whether or not the accounts are accepted by those to whom they are given. This is what Blumstein et al (1974) termed the 'honouring' of accounts, and when accounts are 'honoured' the moral worth of the transgressor is re-established. In their study, Blumstein et al found that a number of things affect the likelihood that an account will be accepted, including the moral status of the 'accounter' and the offensiveness of the violation, but particularly important is what they called the 'adequacy' of the account (see also Shapiro, 1991). Relatedly, Riordan et al (1983) found that the plausibility of an account – the extent to which it reflected what 'everyone knows' could be true – was the most important predictor of its acceptance.

It is likely that a lack of adequacy undermined Crippen's attempt to account for his lying. The key contradiction in his narratives lay between what he first told the members of the MHLG and what he later told Inspector Dew when interviewed on 8 July. To the former, he had said that Belle had been taken ill and died in the US, while to the latter he said that Belle had travelled to the US, presumably to be with Bruce Miller, and was still alive. Rather than trying to present this contradiction as a mistake, and without prompting from Inspector Dew, he called the first story a lie ('the stories I have told them about her death are untrue') and claimed that the second story was true. He accounted for the lie by saying that, before she left, Belle had directed him to 'cover up any scandal with our mutual friends and the Guild the best way I could' (Young, 1920: 37). He repeated this account when he took the stand at trial and Huntley Jenkins from his defence team asked him if his story of Belle's illness and death was true. Finally, when cross-examined by Richard Muir, he said the same thing:

Muir:	How were you saving yourself from anything by telling those lies?
Crippen:	I was saving myself from the scandal of my friends.
Muir:	What scandal were you covering up?
Crippen:	The scandal of the separation from my wife. (Cross-examination of Crippen, cited in Young, 1920: 106)

When he returned to this claim in his closing statement, Muir was sceptical about the plausibility of Crippen's account of his reason for lying:

What were they [the jurors] to say of all that hypocrisy and of all those lies? They were told to cover up a scandal. For whose sake? For the sake of the wife who had betrayed him, who put on a fair face to the world and made her most intimate friends believe she was a bright, happy-natured woman, but to him indifferent, bad-tempered, extravagant, a person having no affection towards him at all. A living lie he would have them believe his wife was; deserted him for another man; and it was to cover up the scandal attaching to her name when she deserted him without cause that he told all those lies and acted all that hypocrisy. (Muir, prosecution closing statement, cited in Young, 1920: 154)

As the judge commented in closing remarks to the jury: 'what the scandal was it is difficult to see' (Young, 1920: 169). This latter comment is particularly significant because both Muir and the judge had also mentioned what they saw as different standards of morality in the music hall world. If relationships were more fluid and free than in conventional middle-class England, why would Belle or Crippen think that her leaving him would be a scandal in the circles that they moved in? And because Crippen's account for the lie was framed as loyalty to Belle's final instructions, he needed to explain why he sought to follow them and cover up the scandal, both for himself and for her. Why was he still interested in defending her moral status? Why would Belle leaving him for another man reflect badly on Crippen? Without this further information, his account looked inadequate, and the prosecution alleged an alternative reason for lying about Belle's death in the US: Crippen knew that she was already dead because he had murdered her.

Conclusion

As with all the cases we review in this book, a single explanation for Crippen's conviction is unlikely to be sufficient. Apart from inconsistencies in his testimony, there are other aspects of his case which also need to be considered. First, the forensic evidence that we have mentioned only in passing – the identity of the remains in the cellar and the presence of hyoscine hydrobromide in them – occupied quite a large part of the trial proceedings as expert witnesses were examined and cross-examined by both the prosecution and the defence. Among the experts for the prosecution was Bernard Spilsbury, who went on to achieve national fame as 'the people's pathologist' and who was in the vanguard of forensic pathologists' efforts 'to secure its expertise over the evidentiary centrepiece of murder investigations – the dead body' (Burney and Pemberton, 2011: 44). If the presentational strategies of the experts for the prosecution were persuasive, jurors would most likely have concluded that the remains in the cellar at Hilldrop Crescent were those of Belle Elmore and this piece of evidence would have had a strong influence on the decision to convict Crippen.

Second, Crippen was perhaps not best served by the lawyers he sought for assistance. After his arrest off the coast of Canada and before arriving back in England he accepted the services of Arthur Newton, a solicitor from London who had sent him a telegram saying that 'Your friends desire me to defend you and will pay all necessary expenses' (*The Fargo Forum*, 1910). However, Newton did not have a good reputation – he was subsequently suspended from practice in 1911[13] – and he was thought to have advised Crippen wrongly by telling him to say nothing in his first appearance at Bow Street Magistrates' Court prior to the trial at the Old Bailey. This, at least, was the opinion of Sir Edward Marshall Hall, the most famous defence barrister of the time (Marjoribanks, 1929), who later gave a talk on the case in which he put forward an alternative defence strategy. Belle, he would have argued, was sexually demanding of Crippen (an appalling way to demonise the victim) and to pacify her appetite Crippen gave her hyoscine hydrobromide but got the dose wrong. When she died from the overdose, he panicked and disposed of her body, rather than tell the authorities. If this defence were successful, Crippen might have avoided execution.[14] However, Marshall Hall said that he declined to take the case because Crippen had already appeared at the Magistrates' Court, represented by Newton, and had said nothing to alter his story about Belle's disappearance. In Marshall Hall's view, this made the defence of accidental death more difficult to put forward (Young, 1920).[15]

As it was, Newton contracted with Arthur Tobin to represent Crippen at the Old Bailey, and Tobin and his team had no option but to continue with Crippen's story that Belle had gone to the US.

Third, as we will see in Chapter 7, the social geometry of a case has been theorised to affect its outcome. It looks as if Crippen underestimated the strength and resources of Belle's social network, whose members were able to make inquiries in the US about her purported death and also to make effective representations to Scotland Yard expressing their concern about her disappearance. If, rather than throwing herself into the music hall world, Belle had lived the isolated life of a foreigner in England, married to a foreign man, would her disappearance have been noticed, or caused concern, or led to a persuasive request to get the police involved? If Crippen had been English rather than American, would *he* have had an active social network to aid in his defence; and would his social standing as a citizen rather than a foreigner lead him to have been judged less severely?

However, alongside these factors that probably played a part in his conviction, the inconsistencies in his testimony – which we have explored in this chapter and which were exploited by the prosecution – were arguably an additional contributing influence. In particular, his admission that he had lied and his failure to provide an adequate account for his lying destroyed his credibility. In Chapter 2, we saw how James Hanratty changed his alibi midway through his trial, to say that he had spent the night of 22 August in Rhyl, not Liverpool. When cross-examined about why he had first claimed he had been in Liverpool, he admitted lying:

Hanratty: Because at this stage when I spoke to Mr. Acott over the phone I know I had already told Mr. Acott a lie about Liverpool and it was quite obvious to me inside that I never committed this crime and I had nothing at all to fear. (Cross-examination of Hanratty, cited in Foot, 1971: 272)

As we can see, Hanratty was even less clear than Crippen in accounting for his lying, something which surely contributed to his conviction.

In the next chapter, we will look at other ways in which credibility is challenged.

Exercise 2:

What do you think about Marshall Hall's proposed defence for Crippen? At trial, Crippen would have had to acknowledge that the stories he told to the MHLG and to Inspector Dew were *both* lies. How might he have accounted for this?

In 1910, there were no rules governing the interviewing of potential suspects by the police; they did not have to be cautioned, and there was no obligation on the part of the police to offer a suspect the opportunity to be assisted by a lawyer (St. Johnston, 1966). When Crippen gave his statement to Inspector Dew, he had not been cautioned or arrested, and he did not have a solicitor present during the interview. If Crippen had been assisted by a solicitor, might his narrative to Inspector Dew have been different? What conclusion can we draw about the impact that the first statement to the police has on the way in which a case develops and concludes?

Recommended reading

Undoubtedly the best account of Crippen's trial is in Filson Young's book *Hawley Harvey Crippen* published in 1920 as part of William Hodge's Notable Trials series. It includes the transcript of the trial prepared by shorthand note takers at the Old Bailey which, while not including every word that was said, captured almost everything. A digital copy of the book is available at: https://archive.org/details/trialofhawleyhar00cripiala. For a useful overview of types of inconsistency in testimony and their effects on judgements of witness accuracy by police, lawyers and mock jurors, see Potter and Brewer (1999).

Notes

1   Hawley Harvey Crippen, quoted in Young, 1920: 103.
2   Although in court the victim was always named as 'Cora Crippen', for consistency with our preceding narrative we will continue to refer to her as 'Belle Elmore'.
3   This was an example of using a story to present the evidence (see Chapter 2).
4   In very small doses, hyoscine hydrobromide is used to prevent travel sickness.
5   See Chapter 1 and the overview of Bennett and Feldman's (1981) model of the requirements for establishing guilt. Like many lawyers, Muir did not explicitly refer to that framework, but his narrative covered all of the elements in the model.
6   The judge in this case was Richard Webster (Lord Alverstone) who was the Lord Chief Justice of England. He directed the proceedings and also intervened from time to time to clarify the information being given by witnesses.
7   In 1910, juries were still all male. Women were only allowed to serve as jurors after 1919 (Crosby, 2017).
8   Ethel Le Neve was put on trial at the Old Bailey on 25 October 1910, one week later than Crippen, for 'being an accessory after the fact in the murder of Cora Crippen'. Lord Alverstone and Richard Muir reprised their roles as judge and prosecution barrister, respectively, while Le Neve was defended by Frederick Smith. Le Neve did not take the stand, and in fact the defence called no witnesses. In less than a day, Le Neve was acquitted of the charge and released (see Young (1920) for a transcript of the proceedings). After Crippen's execution, she moved to Canada for three years, returned to London as 'Ethel Harvey' and in 1915 married Stanley Smith. As Ethel Smith, she lived in anonymity in East Croydon for the rest of her life, dying at the age of 84 in 1967. See: https://web.archive.org/web/20131029210448/http://www.drcrippen.co.uk/whoswho/ethel_le_neve.html

[9] It is important to note that the term 'witness' describes everybody who takes the stand in a trial, including defendants – such as Crippen – who choose to give evidence in support of their cases.

[10] The other meaning of contradiction is when one witness 'contradicts' another by affirming something different (Schum and Martin, 1982: 112). For example, Smith – a prosecution witness – might state that the defendant threatened to hit the victim, but Jones – a defence witness – might state that the defendant never threatened the victim. This kind of contradiction is not relevant to the topic of inconsistency, which relates to the incompatibility of two statements made by the same person.

[11] This is probably particularly likely to happen when the witness is the defendant who has taken the stand on their own behalf and is cross-examined by the prosecution.

[12] From the world of sales and business, Llewellyn and Whittle (2019) provided three good examples of the way in which contradictions were portrayed as mistakes rather than lies. Crucially, the success of the strategy depended on the cooperation of the other party, who was willing to accept the claim that it was a mistake in order to complete the transaction. In trials, the adversarial relationship between advocates and witnesses during cross-examination might make claims of mistakes more difficult to sustain if the advocate is trying to portray the witness as a liar.

[13] The 'friends' that Newton mentioned in his telegram were apparently not friends at all, but the editor of the newspaper *John Bull*, Horatio Bottomley, who was interested in obtaining exclusive information about the case. In November 2010, Newton gave Bottomley a letter supposedly written by Crippen just before his execution, saying that he had an accomplice in the murder of Belle. However, Newton later admitted that the letter was false, and for that he was suspended from practice. Some years later Newton was convicted of fraud and imprisoned for three years (Symons, 2001).

[14] It would have been an example of telling a story to fit the forensic evidence (see Chapter 2 on stories in the courtroom).

[15] Years after the famous barrister's death in 1927, his clerk, Archibald Bowker, gave a different reason for declining to accept the case, which was that Newton had approached Bowker to see if Marshall Hall would represent Crippen but only collect his fee after the trial had ended. Bowker rejected this offer, and Marshall Hall later agreed that he had made the correct decision (Bowker, 1949).

4

The Role of Credibility and Believability in the Trial of Rosemary West

A woman who is, among many other odd things, a bumpkin.[1]

Just after midday on 1 January 1995, officers at Winson Green Prison in Birmingham found Frederick Walter Stephen West dead in his cell. He had killed himself by hanging. Fred, as he was always referred to, had been charged with 11 murders and was being held before appearing at Winchester Crown Court. He had already admitted the killings, albeit with frustrating changes of focus and detail, during various interviews with the police after his arrest in February 1994. The case had quickly attracted extensive national and international media coverage, not only because of the number of victims, determined to have died over an extended period of time between 1967 and 1987, but also because most of them had been sexually assaulted before being murdered. Most of the remains were buried under the patio or cellar at Fred's home at 25 Cromwell Street, Gloucester (soon to be christened by the press as the 'Gloucester House of Horrors'). It had also emerged that his wife, Rosemary West (hereafter Rose) had a history of promiscuity, bisexual relations and a documented case of sexual assault on a young woman carried out with Fred in 1972. Particularly shocking was the record of serious physical abuse of Fred and Rose's eight children and repeated serious sexual abuse against their daughters.

While Fred had confessed to the murders and said that Rose knew nothing about them, the police and prosecutors were not convinced. She was arrested in April 1994 and questioned about the murders, always claiming that she was innocent. Nevertheless, she was charged with nine of the murders, which were thought to have occurred after she and Fred began living together in 1970. And in late 1994, Fred changed his earlier confessions and blamed Rose for the death of their daughter Heather.[2] The Wests were due to appear at a hearing at Winchester Crown Court in February 1995 during which their pleas to the charges would be taken. With Fred's suicide, seen by much of public opinion as a means to 'cheat justice' (for example, Birmingham Live, 2012), attention now focused fully on Rose. The prosecution added a tenth murder charge against her and at the February hearing she entered a plea of not guilty to all charges. The trial was set for October 1995. With Fred deceased and no other witnesses to the killings, the task for the prosecution was to assemble sufficient circumstantial evidence to prove beyond a reasonable doubt that Rose was a murderer. Details of each death help to illustrate some of the challenges involved.

Two of the victims were family members. Charmaine West was eight years old when she died. She was the daughter of Fred's previous wife 'Rena' West (also a murder victim) and at the time of her disappearance was living with Fred and Rose in their home, which was then on Midland Road, Gloucester. The last evidence that Charmaine was alive dated from early June 1971, when she appeared in a school photograph. Her body was found buried in the garden at Midland Road in 1994. Heather West was 16 years old when she died. She was the daughter of Fred and Rose and last seen alive on 19 June 1987. Fred told the family that Heather's friend had picked her up and she had left to take up a job several miles away (Masters, 1997). It was her disappearance that ultimately raised concerns about her welfare among social workers and police officers, fuelled by cryptic remarks from her brothers and sisters that 'Heather was buried beneath the patio' (Masters, 1997: 177), and led to Fred's arrest in February 1994. Hers was the first set of remains to be recovered by the police from the property at Gloucester Road.

Seven of the other victims were girls and young women aged between 15 and 21 who were murdered sometime between 1973 and 1977: Linda Gough, Lucy Partington, Carol Ann Cooper, Juanita Mott, Shirley Hubbard, Therese Siegenthaler, and Alison Chambers. They were either known to Fred and Rose or had been abducted from the street; although, with the exception of Lynda Gough, Rose insisted that she had never met any of the other victims. Their dismembered bodies were found buried at Gloucester Road, along with gags, tapes and ligatures, indicating that they had been raped and tortured prior to being murdered. The tenth victim was Shirley Robinson, who was 18 years old and eight months pregnant when she was murdered. In 1977, she became a lodger at 25 Cromwell Street and Fred soon began an affair with her. According to Masters (1997), it was common knowledge that Fred was the father of Shirley's unborn child.

Although the victims had been located and Fred had admitted to killing them, his sparse and changing accounts meant that the police were unable to construct a detailed picture of each murder. It was impossible to specify the day, time and precise location of each killing, to reconstruct its gruesome progress, and to establish whether anyone other than Fred was also present and involved. Therefore, at Rose's trial the prosecution had to try and establish sufficient circumstantial evidence that she was a murderer. They sought to do this in three ways.

First, they argued that Rose, on her own, killed Charmaine. Comparisons between the skull found at Midland Road and the school photograph from 1971 confirmed that it was Charmaine's because her two front teeth had not yet descended. And if it could be determined *when* she died, it might help determine *who* murdered her. A dental examination conducted for the prosecution concluded that Charmaine had died between late June and the end of July 1971, although a second examination, not given in evidence at the trial, suggested that death could have occurred between August and October (Masters, 1997). Although Fred was in prison (for petty crimes) at least until early June of that year, his release date was not known. Thus, between the lack of certainty surrounding the date of his release and the date of Charmaine's death, it was impossible to establish whether he would have had the opportunity to kill her. To incriminate Rose, the prosecution therefore relied on the testimony of a neighbour who claimed she had seen Charmaine being made to stand on a chair with her hands behind her back while Rose stood there with a wooden spoon (suggesting that Rose had been hitting, or was about to hit, the child). The same witness also testified that she visited Rose while Fred was in prison and did not see Charmaine in the house which, as Masters (1997) observed, strengthened the circumstantial case against Rose. We saw in Chapter 2 that evidence presented in the form of a story is more persuasive to a jury than pieces of evidence that are presented in isolation. Here, the prosecution's story about Rose was one of a 'wicked stepmother' who wanted to be rid of Charmaine and, in a fit of anger, murdered her and dumped her body in the coal cellar of the house until Fred disposed of it in the garden (Masters, 1997). However, the defence argued that Fred had admitted to murdering Charmaine alone and that during one of Rose's prison visits she had told him that Charmaine was yearning to return to her mother. Fred reassured Rose that he would 'sort it out' (Masters, 1997: 22–3).

Second, in relation to the seven victims showing signs of sexual assault and torture, the prosecution requested, and was granted, the opportunity to introduce 'similar fact evidence'. Similar fact evidence is 'Evidence that a party, especially the accused, has on previous occasions misconducted himself in a way similar to the misconduct being alleged against him in the proceedings before the court' (Oxford Reference, 2021). In this case, the prosecution introduced as 'similar facts' evidence that Rose had participated with Fred in sexual assaults on several young women, although they had not been killed. The use of similar fact evidence is rare (Winter, 2004) because of the safeguarding principle of the presumption of innocence

(Goatley, 2019). Thus, introducing evidence that points to the defendant as having the *propensity* to commit the crime may be prejudicial because of its suggestion that the defendant is most likely guilty based on their previous behaviour. In the case of Rose West, this is precisely what happened – several women provided testimonies of sexual abuse perpetrated against them by the Wests during the period in which the murders were thought to have taken place (1967–87). A key witness was Caroline Owens, a previous lodger at 25 Cromwell Street. In 1972, Fred and Rose pleaded guilty to indecently assaulting her and causing actual bodily harm and were fined £100. According to Masters (1997), Caroline Owens's testimony indicated similarities with the experiences of the murder victims (the use of ties and gags) and it was the prosecution's case that, because Rose was present for the assault on Owens, she must also have been present when the seven victims were murdered. Thus, the prosecution argued that these 'similar' cases showed Rose's propensity to commit sexually motivated offences, providing a link to the sexual assaults on the murder victims. Rose's defence barrister Richard Ferguson described this as a 'superficially attractive theory' (Masters, 1997: 328) rather than being evidence that could prove her guilt beyond a reasonable doubt. Winter (2004) pointed out that the use of similar fact evidence meant that Rose was effectively on trial for previous behaviours of sexual assault and that one reason for the general exclusion of similar fact evidence is its potential to confuse jurors and, indeed, cause great anger among them, provoking a desire for punishment.

Third, in relation to Shirley Robinson, the prosecution sought to present a compelling motive for Rose to murder her. It was argued that, as Rose was also pregnant at the time, she was intensely jealous of Fred's relationship with Shirley. However, the defence countered that Rose was under the impression that her husband was covering as the father of Shirley's baby until she established a more stable situation. Additionally, Fred's confession to the police corroborated Rose's story when he explained that he needed to conceal from Rose that he was in fact the father of the baby. A witness testified at the trial that Shirley became increasingly afraid of Fred and that he himself was panicking about the situation. Fred admitted to the police that, when Shirley started threatening to tell Rose about their relationship, he hit her and then strangled her. Notwithstanding his confession, the prosecution argued that, given the considerable mess Fred would have made after murdering Shirley (and removing the foetus that was found next to her remains), Rose must have at least served as his accomplice (Masters, 1997).

It is interesting to note that the prosecution did not develop a clear line of argument in relation to the remaining victim, Heather West. Fred had admitted to murdering her (although he later said that Rose had led him to do it), and Rose had become very distressed when first told by the police that Heather was dead. To her claim that she did not murder Heather, the prosecution's response appeared to be that 'she must have known', in other words, that she must have at least witnessed the killing or its aftermath. Indeed, such were the identities of all the victims, the method of killing and dismemberment, and the locations of their remains that it would not be far-fetched to claim that 'she must have known' about all the murders (Masters, 1977).

It was perhaps to counter this general claim that Rose decided to take the stand in her own defence. With no details about the dates, times and locations of the murders, it would have been self-defeating to try and present an alibi for each – her alibis would have had to specify times, dates and locations, thereby indicating that she *did* know about the murders. Rather, her objective appeared to be denial of all knowledge of them. As is well known, the accused does not have to testify at the trial, because it is for the prosecution to prove the charges beyond a reasonable doubt. Additionally, when defendants take the stand, they can expect a searching cross-examination from the prosecution. Thus, it is crucial for the accused to appear as credible as possible in what they say. As Wilson (2006) argued, because there were no witnesses to any of the murders, Rose's appearance and demeanour in the courtroom became vitally important for the construction of her guilt or innocence. According to her daughter Mae, the family considered it very important that she give a positive impression to the jury and, to this end, bought her smart clothes for the trial (West, 2018). Despite this, Rose's credibility in her denials of guilt was arguably weakened by her courtroom demeanour and by her social characteristics such as having little education and the evidence of her sexual deviancy and cruelty towards her children. Although there is no published transcript of her appearance on the stand, we draw mainly on the work of two journalists who observed Rose's trial, Brian Masters and A.N. Wilson, to examine how credible *they* perceived her to be.

What is credibility?

Think for a moment about a recent occasion where you met someone for the first time. Did you decide quickly whether you liked or disliked that person? According to Rieke and Stutman (1995), we rapidly form an impression about a new person in order to judge their character. Because we possess limited information about the person, we must rely on stereotypes. Hastie (1980) suggested that these first impressions are used when making later judgements. For example, we might actually recall false information about the person so that we remain consistent with our first impression. The personal characteristics of an individual become important to us when we are trying to make sense of their motivations for the way they behave. Depending on the person's characteristics, they will be judged as either having low or high credibility and, in turn, this will determine whether we accept or doubt what they say. In fact, it was the Greek philosopher Aristotle who first defined credibility when he used the term *ethos*, referring to the image and character of the person speaking. Aristotle suggested that if we hold a positive perception of the speaker then we are more likely to accept their argument. For an individual to possess *ethos* is, for Aristotle, to possess good sense, moral character and goodwill (Rieke and Stutman, 1995).

Research on the effects of a person's credibility, that is, whether the more credible he or she is perceived, the more likely the message will be accepted by the listener, was conducted predominantly in the 1970s (see Pornpitakpan, 2004, for a review of the empirical evidence up to the early 2000s). Much of the research has focused on the source credibility[3] of speakers in commercial settings, celebrity-endorsed advertisements and consumers' attitudes. These studies indicate that a speaker with attributes associated with high credibility will have more influence on a listener's attitude and behaviour than a speaker with low credibility. Since the 1990s, research on credibility and persuasion appears to have petered out although some resurgence can be observed in areas related to sports reporters (see Hahn and Cummins, 2014); athletes (see Dix, 2015); teachers (Ramos and McCullick, 2015); online product reviews (Shan, 2016); climate change (Dong et al, 2018); social media information quality (Zha et al, 2018); and mobile news stories (Wei and Lo, 2021). Additionally, communication scholars such as Rieke and Stutman (1995), Ganer (1999) and Rieke and Sillars (2001) have written about the credibility of advocates and defendants in a legal context.

Fairly obviously, perceived credibility is the 'largest determinant of a deception judgement' (Bond and DePaulo, 2008: 487) and is a crucial determinant of whether or not testimony is accepted by jurors and others. Denault and Dunbar (2019) reviewed the extensive research showing that adversarial justice systems have consistently emphasised the demeanour of witnesses as a way of assessing their credibility (for example, Imwinkelried, 1985; Wellborn, 1990; Blumenthal, 1993; Timony, 2000; Morrison et al, 2007; Minzner, 2008; O'Regan, 2017). Denault and Dunbar also referred to several laboratory experiments that evidenced this influence (for example, Pryor and Buchanan, 1984; Bodenhausen, 1988; Winkel and Koppelaar, 1991; Bothwell and Jalil, 1992; Rogers et al, 2015). Usefully, Rieke and Stutman (1995) separated credibility according to its intrinsic and extrinsic dimensions.

Intrinsic credibility

Rieke and Sillars (2001: 220) defined intrinsic credibility as:

> the support for a claim that is developed by the decision makers' perception that the arguer reveals competence, trustworthiness, good will, and dynamism.

Thus, if a person is perceived as speaking with *competence*, their message is more likely to be perceived as credible. In this regard, when Rose took the stand to give testimony at the trial, Wilson (2006: 502) observed her attempt to speak with competence when she said, 'Sir, as I should like to emphasise'. However, Wilson commented:

> These were the phrases which would have seemed more natural on the lips of a lawyer than a woman who is – among many other odd things – a bumpkin.

Wilson (2006: 501) was suggesting that a 'bumpkin' like Rose could not possess the linguistic skills to utilise the powerful language with the competence that she appeared to speak with. Thus, 'one felt she was giving rehearsed answers'. Similarly, Rose's eagerness to get her point across to the jury was interpreted by Masters as an indication that her answers were rehearsed, insinuating that the truth of her statements should be treated with caution. Relatedly, he commented that Rose referred to counsel as 'sir' and it 'did not come across as a word she had used very often' (Masters, 1997: 331).

If a person speaking is perceived to be *trustworthy*, then their message is perceived to be valid (Hovland et al, 1953). As we have seen, Masters (1997) observed that the theory of the prosecution was that Rose 'must have known' about the murders, suggesting that the alternative to this is inconceivable. Accordingly, Rose, and anything she said in her defence (to support her claim that she did not know), could not be trusted because she *must* have known. One strategy the prosecution used to prove this point was to offer a detailed description of the dimensions of 25 Cromwell Street to demonstrate to the jury that it would have been impossible for Fred to torture, murder and dismember the bodies found there while going undetected by Rose. This supported the prosecution's theme that 'they were in it together' (Masters, 1997: 296). Of course, the jury's knowledge of Rose's sexual abuse of Caroline Owens and other witnesses as well as the cruelty towards her children, coupled with her denial of these accusations, further underscored her lack of trustworthiness.

When a speaker conveys signs of *goodwill*, they are more likely to be perceived as kind, friendly and impartial (Rieke and Sillars, 2001). Another journalist who observed the trial reflected that, because Rose took the witness stand and was cross-examined by the prosecution, the jury were able to observe at first-hand her 'petty, spiteful character' where her temper manifested with 'flashes of anger' (Summers, 2005). Masters (1997: 331) described her decision to take the stand as 'her undoing' because she frequently switched between answering the questions respectfully to becoming defiant or 'stroppy' (Masters, 1997: 337) and this, Masters argued, was 'to mirror, in the jury's mind, the switches they had already heard concerning her moods and behaviours'. Masters further commented that on some occasions Rose made uninvited statements, including some that related to legal argument and therefore her 'belligerence kept bursting through' (Masters, 1997: 331). For example, in relation to Miss A's evidence of abuse by the Wests, Rose retorted, 'Why didn't she tell someone if it was so terrible?' Masters reflected that she was not a naturally 'meek' person. With Rose appearing to lack empathy and kindness, Brian Leveson, prosecuting, was content to allow her to interrupt him for it further demonstrated these qualities (Masters, 1997). If the members of the jury perceived Rose in a similar way, it may have served to show that she was indeed not a kind or caring person, which made it easier to imagine her cruel nature. By extension then, if she could not maintain a gentle demeanour towards the individuals judging her guilt or innocence, what could she be capable of outside a courtroom? Her apparent lack of goodwill was inextricably attached to her trustworthiness. A person who shows themself to be hostile cannot be trusted and although a person's character defects cannot be equated with being guilty of murder, it was the absence of these strands in Rose's intrinsic credibility that might have gone some way towards helping to explain her failure to convince the jurors of her innocence, hence leading to her conviction.

A speaker's *dynamism* refers to their energy, enthusiasm and boldness (Berlo et al, 1969) and increases their credibility and believability (Schweitzer, 1970). In Chapter 6 we will be examining the trial of O.J. Simpson, about whom commentators made repeated references to his charisma and ability to command attention when he walked into the courtroom (Ganer, 1999). Although Simpson did not take the stand, his perceived dynamism and charisma might even have been bolstered when he stood up to plead 'Absolutely one hundred percent not guilty' to the charges against him (Drummond Ayres, 1994). This is in stark contrast to Rose who was described by observers in a sexist fashion as 'matronly' (Masters, 1997; Wilson, 2006), who walked with a 'managerial, school matron sort of march, her right hand swinging mannishly' (Wilson, 2006: 500). Wilson further underscored Rose's 'otherness' when he suggested that she did not 'do herself any good' by taking the stand, seeing it as an attempt to 'ingratiate' herself with the jury when they 'were clearly appalled by her lifestyle as well as by her crimes'. Wilson (2006: 504) also wrote that 'She did not come over as a sympathetic figure; one did not find her loveable' and 'certainly if there is a case for hanging anyone, there would be a case for hanging Mrs West' (Wilson, 2006: 513).

Although Rieke and Sillars (2001) did not mention it, *consistency* in testimony could also be considered as a dimension of intrinsic credibility, something we discussed in detail in Chapter 3. In this regard, Masters (1997) thought that Rose was not a convincing witness because of inconsistencies in her testimony. For example, she claimed to recall an incident clearly at one moment and then could not remember in the next moment:

Leveson (prosecuting counsel):	Are you saying it didn't happen [the sexual assault against Caroline Owens], you can't remember or what?
Rose:	I can't say either way. (Cross-examination of West, cited in Masters, 1997: 336)

According to Masters, perhaps the most damaging example of Rose's inconsistency was her denial of child abuse. By conveying some truthfulness, Rose might have been able to evidence some credibility and believability. As Masters (1997: 337) suggested, 'if she could not be believed on this, then it was easier to disbelieve her on the rest'. Similarly, Wilson (2006: 502) suggested that her 'transparent lies' during cross-examination by Mr Leveson were such that he did not think any of the jurors believed a word that she said.

Extrinsic credibility

Extrinsic credibility refers to a person's *status, physical appearance, age* and *general reputation* (Rieke and Stutman, 1995) and Rose's status and physical appearance were often the subject of comment among observers at the trial. Kraus and Mendes (2014) argued that, because of increasing social inequality, clothing has become a symbol of class. In their study, they found that a person's *social status* can be quickly judged just by the clothes they are wearing. Their research measured physiological responses and perceptions of participants dressed in either upper-class clothing (business suit) or in lower-class clothing (tracksuit). The results demonstrated that perceiving a person as upper class increased participants' sense of vigilance and reduced their sense of power. Interestingly, those participants wearing lower-class clothing showed decreased levels of testosterone following their interaction with other participants, demonstrating a reduction of feelings of dominance. Sounes (1995) and Woodrow (2012) have written journalistic profiles of Fred and Rose and both described accounts given by their children that Rose's dress sense and behaviour were odd; for example, she wore a bobble hat and white socks when she went shopping, using a pram as a shopping cart. We noted earlier that Wilson (2006) referred to Rose as a 'bumpkin' when he made a direct comparison between how someone like a lawyer (a middle/upper-class person) and someone like unsophisticated Rose (a lower-class person) would speak. Similarly, Wilson (2006: 507) attributed the Wests' lack of detection for so long to their 'low peasant cunning', which was to say that, despite their allegedly immoral and uneducated characters which lacked 'intelligent introspection' (Wilson, 2006: 504), they remained clever in concealing their crimes.

In relation to the dimension of *physical appearance*, Masters (1997) described Rose as wearing the same outfit every day throughout the trial, that is, a black jacket with a white shirt underneath. This would have been the outfit bought for her by her family in a bid to present her as respectable. Unfortunately, she was described by both Masters (1997) and Wilson (2006: 499) as looking like a 'school matron' and Wilson highlighted aspects of her unattractiveness, describing her as a 'plump, bespectacled woman'. Indeed, Wilson's negative descriptions of Rose's appearance were excessive. He described her attire as reminiscent of a 'battledress of some female Gestapo officer'. He wrote that he imagined her as a prison guard in a Nazi concentration camp 'using her victims … for pleasure', thereby making Rose's alleged offences akin to war crimes. Wilson (2006: 500) also used Rose's physical features to portray her as a figure of distrust when he suggested that there was something 'very strange about the upper part of her face' because of the presence of a ghostly 'darkness' and 'shadow'. Furthermore, when she cried, he did not believe Rose's tears to be genuine because he described them as theatrical (Wilson, 2006: 503):

> She would produce the handkerchief and then weep ostentatiously as if she had taken out an onion and decided that she should appear vulnerable to the jury.

Shoemaker et al (1973) found that the physical appearance of a defendant can influence the way jurors perceive them. If, for example, the defendant is perceived as having odd or deviant features, the jurors are more likely to take the view that there is something abnormal about them (Secord, 1958, cited in Rieke and Stutman, 1995). Wilson (2006: 500), observing Rose's trial, drew attention to the defendant's seemingly unconscious habit of moving her tongue that 'snaked in and out of her lips' while she listened to the 'hideous memories' of witnesses, as though underscoring her deviance. Wilson (2006: 499) also mentioned Rose's 'f-ing and blinding' to the police when she was first arrested. Highlighting Rose's swearing to figures of authority further underscored her generally poor reputation and low social status.

Although not mentioned by Rieke and Stutman (1995), an individual's accent can also affect their extrinsic credibility. For example, Dixon et al (2002) examined the effects of a regional accent (in this case a 'Brummie'[4] accent) on perceptions of guilt. One hundred and nineteen students listened to a brief recording of a mock police interrogation and rated the 'suspect' as guilty or innocent. A 'matched-guise' technique was used meaning that the characteristics of the 'suspect' changed in each interview; so, for example, in some he spoke with a Brummie accent and in others with a standard accent; in some, he identified himself as Black and in others as White; and finally, the crime type varied between a 'blue-collar' and a 'white-collar' offence. The results were interesting in that the Brummie 'suspect' was more frequently judged as guilty, while the highest rate of guilt attribution was found for the Brummie accent/Black suspect/blue-collar crime. The authors concluded that innocence is associated with the perceived superiority and social attractiveness of the suspect. In a later study, Dixon and Mahoney (2004) used another 'matched-guise' technique through which, similar to their previous project, the 'suspect' spoke with an English regional/ standard accent, and the crime type was blue collar/white collar; but this time evidence was introduced as either strong or weak. The authors found that when evidence was also in consideration, the 'suspect's' accent did not significantly influence attributions of guilt. However, what is interesting to note is that when the 'suspect' spoke with a regional accent, he was perceived to be typically more criminal and more likely to be accused again of a crime than the 'suspect' who spoke with a standard accent. A more recent study in the US also demonstrated the effect of stereotypical accents on decisions about guilt and innocence. Although there is a wealth of research demonstrating the influence of race and ethnicity on legal decision-making (Colon et al, 2018), as far as we are aware, Cantone et al's (2019) is the only study that has examined how stereotypical accents may also play a role in criminal case processing of minority defendants. Their study found that Black defendants were judged more negatively than White and Mexican American defendants, but even more so when the Black defendant spoke with a stereotypical accent (Cantone et al, 2019).

Kalven and Zeisel (1966) undertook an early large study on juror decision-making and found that when the evidence in a case is clear and strong, the verdict will reflect this accordingly. However, when the evidence is weak or vague, the authors found that jurors become 'liberated' from basing their decisions on the evidence and, rather, rely upon what are known as 'extralegal' factors to help them reach a verdict.[5] A defendant's accent and mode of speech would be one such extralegal factor.

Exercise 1:

What do you think made Rose's lies appear 'transparent', as Wilson suggests? Do you think you could detect a liar? Let's have a go at this exercise and see if you are correct!

1. Do liars decrease eye contact?
2. Do liars raise the pitch of their voice?
3. Do liars increase their body movements?
4. Are liars less likely to be consistent in what they say?

The reliability of behavioural cues to deception

So, just how reliable are behavioural cues of deception? Do liars decrease eye contact? No, they don't. In fact, according to research by Vrij (1995), liars are more likely to maintain the same level of eye contact with others, or actually increase it. How about the raised pitch in their voice? Yes, according to Vrij (2000) it seems they do. Do liars increase their body movements? No, they don't (Mann et al, 2002). Are liars less likely to be consistent in what they say? Again, you may be surprised to learn that the answer is no (Strömwall and Granhag, 2003).[6] The problem is that there is a widely shared set of stereotypes about how people behave when they lie, but these behaviours are not indicators of deception. In their review of over 200 studies, Bond and DePaulo (2006) found that people are no more accurate at detecting lies than judgements made by pure chance (for example, on the toss of a coin). This finding is true for all types of people – whether they are a student or indeed (and you might find this surprising) a police officer or other types of criminal justice practitioner! One interesting study by Strömwall and Granhag (2003) found that many legal professionals, that is, police officers, prosecutors and judges, held inaccurate beliefs about indicators of deception. We do not know whether Wilson (2006) was referring to Rose's body language when he suggested that her lies were 'transparent'. However, what is evident here are Masters's and Wilson's judgements of Rose's low credibility, which reflect Rieke and Sillars's (2001) definition of intrinsic credibility and Rieke and Stutman's (1995) definition of extrinsic credibility. These observers of the trial referred to Rose's status, her physical appearance, her poor reputation and her lack of trustworthiness, goodwill, dynamism and competence, and it is perhaps their comments on Rose's low credibility that made her lies appear 'transparent'.

Incorrect stereotyping and beliefs about the meaning of a defendant or witness's demeanour, then, can have an adverse influence on the outcome of a trial (Denault and Dunbar, 2019). Denault and Dunbar offered some interesting anecdotal examples to illustrate the influence of credibility on decision-making, and importantly, the perils of doing so. Drawing on the case of Ronald Cotton, a man who served ten years in prison for a rape he was not guilty of,[7] Denault and Dunbar (2019) referred to one of the jurors' comments that Cotton's facial expressions during the trial contributed to his conviction:

> He had no change of emotions for eight days. He never changed his facial expression. This was extremely strange to me and, as time went by, I expected to see him react and I never did. And so he seemed more guilty and guiltier and guiltier as time went by. (Loeterman, 1997, cited in Denault and Dunbar, 2019: 921)

As Denault and Dunbar (2019: 922) critically underscored, 'the assumption that demeanor is a window to the soul of witnesses to reliably identify remorse is not only baseless, but also highly problematic'. Denault and Dunbar cited another case where a judge declared a defendant in a drugs case dishonest because of his confused testimony and 'body language':

> Here it appears that the way the defender testifies is such that his version cannot be believed from the outset; his body language as well as his confused explanations have, in some respect, cast doubt on his sincerity. (*R. c. Pinard*, 2014: 7, cited in Denault and Dunbar, 2019: 922)

Another example given by Denault and Dunbar concerned the influence of a nervous and hesitant demeanour where the defendant averted his gaze. The presiding judge commented:

> Having carefully observed the accused during his testimony and noted his great nervousness, his fleeting glare and his numerous hesitations in cross-examination, the court is convinced that [the defendant] has simply forged his version of the facts according to the evidence disclosed, and that he thereby lied to the court in a shameless manner. (*R. c. Martin*, 2017: 27, cited in Denault and Dunbar, 2019: 923)

However, Denault and Dunbar pointed out that both liars and truth-tellers can present as nervous and hesitant. As we have already seen, gaze aversion is not an indicator of deception (DePaulo et al, 2003; Vrij, 2008). As Vrij (2008) emphasised, bodily movements, eloquence, and physiological responses may be indicative of an individual's character but they are not reliable deception cues.

Because it has been found that the detection of deception through non-verbal behaviours is not reliable, interest in studying this area has decreased (Denault and Dunbar, 2019) and instead the focus has turned to verbal cues of deception (Hauch et al, 2015; Denault and Dunbar, 2019). However, verbal cues of deception have been found to be equally unreliable and Denault and Dunbar report that scholars have now turned their attention to interviewing techniques that serve to elicit deceit. These include the Cognitive Credibility Assessment, the Strategic Use of Evidence technique, the Assessment Criteria Indicative of Deception technique and the Comparable Truth Baseline technique.

The *Cognitive Credibility Assessment* is based on the premise that people find it more mentally taxing to lie than to tell the truth and uses three approaches to look for deception (Vrij et al, 2017). The first involves imposing 'cognitive load' on the person, for example by instructing the suspect to tell their story in reverse order. The second approach involves encouraging interviewees to say more because, when liars are asked to do this, their answers may be less plausible and there may be a lack of willingness to do so in the knowledge that their answers may be checked (Vrij et al, 2017). The third approach includes asking unexpected questions based on the premise that liars will rehearse answers to questions they anticipate being asked. To this end, rehearsed answers will feature less deception cues than spontaneous ones (DePaulo et al, 2003; Vrij et al, 2017) and this process is cognitively demanding which could result in the liar answering 'I don't know' or 'I can't remember', therefore raising the suspicions of the interviewer (Vrij et al, 2017). Vrij et al's (2017) overview of the research using the Cognitive Credibility Assessment approach revealed its superior ability to help interviewers accurately detect deception.

The *Strategic Use of Evidence* technique requires the interviewer to use the available evidence in a strategic manner in such a way that a liar will produce inconsistencies in their statements. The idea is to ask simple and indirect questions such as 'We have information that you went to ...', followed by more questions that indicate possession of strong evidence, for example, 'CCTV footage shows you ...'. In sequencing questions like this, stronger cues of deception (by changing the story) are more likely than if presenting the interviewee with the most direct question first (Vrij, 2014).

The *Assessment Criteria Indicative of Deception* technique is based on the premise that truth-tellers will provide longer, more vivid and spontaneous answers compared to liars, whose answers are shorter, less vivid, more rigid, and carefully worded (Colwell et al, 2009). The technique aims to increase the cognitive effort for the interviewee by introducing memory enhancement techniques such as asking them to recall the events from another perspective (Suckle-Nelson et al, 2010). Research indicates that it is successful in enabling accurate deception detection (Vrij and Fisher, 2016; Vrij, 2018).

The *Comparable Truth Baseline* (CTB) is based on the premise that if the interviewer holds previous knowledge about the interviewee's truthful behaviour, it can be used as a baseline to help the interviewer detect deception. The more familiar a listener is with the speaker's truthful behaviour, the more they are able to accurately detect deception because of a change in behaviour observed when the interviewee lies. Although there is some research to support the CTB approach (see Palena et al, 2018 and Caso et al, 2019a), Caso et al's (2019b) study demonstrated little support for it and pointed out that because investigators and suspects are typically unknown to one another, the familiarity baseline is difficult, if not impossible, to obtain.

The credibility of victims is important too

Whether they are aware of it or not, jurors, judges, prosecution and defence lawyers, and everyone who follows a trial assess the credibility of all the witnesses who give evidence. Some witnesses may always be treated as credible because of commonly held beliefs about them, such as, 'Most ballistic experts tell the truth' (Wagenaar, 1995: 268), or 'police officers "in the line of duty never lie"' (den Boer, 1995: 327). At the opposite end of the spectrum are defendants who take the stand, where assessments of their credibility are often crucial to case outcomes. Research has also shown that the credibility of victims may come under scrutiny, particularly in relation to sexual offences. O'Neal and Hayes (2020) pointed out that it is well documented in the literature that reports of sexual offences in the US do not often lead to arrest. In England and Wales, despite an increase in reporting, just 3.2 per cent of all sexual offences result in a charge, often the result of evidential difficulties such as the victim not supporting further police action (Home Office, 2020). Campbell et al (2015) highlighted the research demonstrating the role and importance of victim credibility in sexual assault cases (for example, see Frohmann, 1991, 1997; Horney and Spohn, 1996; O'Donohue et al, 1998; Spohn et al, 2001; Alderden and Ullman, 2012; O'Neal, 2017; O'Neal and Hayes, 2020). They further noted that prosecutors perceive convictability based on legal (seriousness of the assault and strength of evidence) and extralegal characteristics (victim behaviour at the time of offence and the victim's moral character). It is the latter characteristics, Campbell et al argued, that determine victim credibility and are the most important influence on prosecutorial decisions about whether to proceed with cases of sexual violence (Beichner and Spohn, 2005). The authors listed multiple victim characteristics that affect their credibility, such as age, race and gender (O'Donohue et al, 1998; George and Martinez, 2002; Davies and Rogers, 2009), moral character (Spears and Spohn, 1997; Spohn et al, 2001), voluntary victim intoxication (Kerstetter, 1990; Frohmann, 1991; Schuller and Stewart, 2000; Lonsway et al, 2001; Beichner and Spohn, 2012; Wentz and Keimig, 2019), inconsistency in statements (Alderden and Ullman, 2012), mental problems (Kerstetter, 1990), a previous sexual relationship with the suspect (Stanko, 1981–82; Spohn and Tellis, 2014), problems recalling details of the crime (Beichner and Spohn, 2012), delayed reporting (Rose and Randall, 1982; Kerstetter, 1990; Beichner and Spohn, 2012) and having previously engaged in sex work (Kerstetter, 1990; Kaiser et al, 2017). In their own research, Campbell et al interviewed police investigators about perceptions of victim credibility in sexual crime cases. They found that, when evidence is weak or unavailable, investigators resort to extralegal factors relating to victim credibility, which supports previous research showing the significance of a victim's moral character or their behaviour at the time of the assault for decisions about investigation and prosecution.

The verdict

On 21 November 1995, the jury in Rose West's trial returned guilty verdicts for the murders of Charmaine, Heather and Shirley Robinson. However, they deliberated for another evening on the remaining seven murder charges and, significantly, inquired whether the 'total absence of direct evidence' (Masters, 1997: 363), aside from the remains of the victims being found at Rose's home, was an obstacle to voting for a guilty verdict. They further inquired if they were permitted to reach a verdict based on a combination of similar fact evidence and the location of the remains. The answers were 'no' and 'yes', respectively. The next day, the jury returned guilty verdicts for all seven murder charges. The judge imposed the mandatory life sentence for murder and added: 'If attention is paid to what I think, you will never be released' (Masters, 1997: 363). 'What he thought' was presumably that Rose was guilty. Indeed, according to Masters's (1997: 353) observations, his summing up for the jury left no doubt about his view. Masters noted that the judge expressly warned jurors that, although they must not be influenced by his views, if they were to hear him say 'you might think that', then this was a signal that he was going to indicate what his view was. Masters noted that he used this phrase several times during the summing up, sometimes revealing a view pointing towards her guilt. The case was referred to the Lord Chief Justice, who decided that Rose should spend a minimum of 25 years in prison before being eligible for release on parole. However, two years later, and in response to public pressure, Jack Straw, then Home Secretary, imposed a whole life tariff for Rose, meaning that she will never be able to apply for parole (The Telegraph, 2018).

Conclusion

Although by no means the only explanation, using the research literature on credibility has enabled us to analyse its potential contribution to Rose West's conviction. We do not have the benefit of observing her courtroom demeanour ourselves because televised trials in the UK are not allowed. Thus, we must focus on the observations of those who watched and wrote about the trial. We have seen their descriptions of Rose's courtroom demeanour, and their comments on it, which show that her intrinsic and extrinsic credibility on the stand were weakened by her lack of competence, trustworthiness, goodwill and dynamism, and by her low social status, physical appearance and reputation. All of these were characteristics which aligned with lay conceptions of low credibility. Thus, in a case where the details of dates, times and locations of the killings could not be established, ruling out the possibility of presenting alibis, Rose could not dissuade the jury from thinking that 'she must have known' about the murders.

It seems clear, both from the strong objections lodged by the defence and the jury's question to the judge about it, that the introduction of similar fact evidence about Rose's history of sexual assaults was also a significant contributor to her conviction for seven of the murders. Without it, the prosecution would have had a difficult time alluding to Rose's sexual behaviour; with it, they were able to tell a story of a woman who had committed sexual assaults over the years, some in partnership with Fred, implying that she had also been involved in the murders. Against this powerful and sordid narrative, Rose offered denial but no alternative story with evidence to accompany it. If we turn to Bennett and Feldman's (1981) requisites for establishing guilt, Rose denied *presence* for every single one of the murders and none of the witnesses, including Rose's children, could say whether she was or was not directly involved in the murders. The prosecution therefore rested on a highly circumstantial case and so a story needed to be constructed to show that Rose possessed the *motivation* to commit the crimes. If, as we saw in Chapter 2, stories are important vehicles for constructing guilt and innocence, it is clear that the prosecution were successful in using the similar fact evidence to bolster their story and persuade the jury of its plausibility.

Another factor likely to have been important was the extensive publicity given to the case when the crimes were first discovered, when Fred committed suicide, and when Rose went on trial. Almost all the media reporting was misogynistic, unsympathetic to Rose, and much of it assumed that she was guilty. Wykes (1998) observed that many reports on the case emphasised Rose as the inadequate woman and paid little attention to Fred's sexual violence or indeed anything about the men who visited Rose for sex at her home. Winter (2004) further noted that a focus on Rose's sexuality revealed the prejudicial nature of exposing her violent, lesbian and bisexual sexuality. Wykes (1998) pointed out that there was no competing narrative that highlighted the problem of White masculinity and male violence as represented by Fred and the case was therefore embedded in masculine ideology. A powerful example of this misogyny was seen in Wilson's (2006) comments about Rose's 'betrayal of Fred', which made Wilson feel 'sad' and think that there was 'something evil' in her denying the love they shared. Wilson appeared to suggest that Fred committed a martyr-like act of self-sacrifice when he killed himself, 'He died in part to protect her and give her a plausible chance of acquittal' (Wilson, 2006: 501). The question, therefore, is whether this very negative publicity affected jurors' opinions about Rose's guilt. In Chapter 11, we will discuss the topics of pretrial publicity and prejudice, but they are also applicable here.

Furthermore, Rose was portrayed as egregiously deviant. Not only did she lack socially desirable qualities, but she was someone who defied every expectation of a woman. A woman who was emotionally, physically and sexually abusive to her children; a woman who was sexually deviant; a woman who was a sex worker; a woman who had a conviction and other accusations of indecent assault against her; a woman who stood accused of having been involved in the torture, rape and murder of women unknown to her; a woman accused of murdering eight-year-old Charmaine and, thus, a child killer; and finally a woman accused of murdering her own 16-year-old daughter. There was no possibility here, then, for any prognosis of 'mad' instead of 'bad' and, indeed, no scope for any reporting or analysis on her childhood circumstances and the nature of her relationship with her husband Fred. Storrs (2004) observed that after the trial, news stories did not draw any attention to the legal argument and debate about her conviction and instead great attention was given to the nature of her sexual depravity. As Wykes (1998: 238) suggested, at Winchester Crown Court femininity was put on trial and was 'tried by established icons of masculinity' and because of her gender Rose became a scapegoat (Storrs, 2004). In Chapter 7, we examine how 'social geometry' has been proposed as a determinant of case outcomes. It would predict that Rose, at the extreme end of the dimension of deviancy, would more likely than not have been convicted.

Recommended reading

Brian Masters's (1997) *She Must have Known* is a particularly useful book to read in terms of learning how the prosecution constructed a case against Rose West. Masters offers a detailed analysis of how similar fact evidence was applied as well as how *opportunity*, *capability* and *motive* (as we learned about in Chapter 1) were employed to prove that Rose was guilty of the murders of Charmaine, Heather and Shirley Robinson. Jo Winter's (2004) article offers a useful insight into the legal application of similar fact evidence and provides a critique of its use in Rose's trial.

Notes

[1] Wilson (2006: 502).

[2] A segment of Fred West's police interview where he blames Rose for the death of Heather can be listened to on YouTube: https://www.youtube.com/watch?v=MhNPpA08SQ4

[3] Source credibility may be defined as 'a term commonly used to imply a communicator's positive characteristics that affect the receiver's acceptance of a message' (Ohanian, 1990: 41).

[4] 'Brummie' is slang for someone from Birmingham.

[5] Extralegal factors are variables such as the defendant's race/ethnicity, gender, age, social class or social status which, according to the law, should not affect decisions about guilt or innocence (see Chapter 7).

[6] In Chapter 3 we reviewed research which shows that inconsistencies do not necessarily indicate that a witness is lying.

[7] In 1985, Cotton was convicted of rape and burglary in North Carolina and his conviction rested heavily on the eyewitness evidence of the victim, Jennifer Thompson-Cannino. His conviction was overturned ten years later when DNA testing proved that the assailant's semen did not belong to Cotton (Innocence Project, 2021). Jennifer Thompson-Cannino has since presented her story on a TED talk to educate the public about the problems with eye-witness testimony. Over the last fifty years, psychology scholars have persistently found problems with accurate eyewitness identification, and the prevailing opinion is that eyewitness testimony is unreliable (Wixted et al, 2018). The TED talk can be found here: https://www.youtube.com/watch?v=tbCvExeNsVk

5

Techniques of Neutralisation and the Conviction of the Oklahoma Bomber, Timothy McVeigh

I didn't go wrong.[1]

The crime, investigation and indictment

On the morning of 19 April 1995, 26-year-old Timothy McVeigh parked a Ryder rental truck, holding a homemade bomb, in the disabled zone in front of the Alfred P. Murrah Federal Building in Oklahoma City in the US. After parking the truck, McVeigh got out of the vehicle and walked away. At 9.02 am, the bomb exploded killing 168 people and injuring more than 500 others. Of those who died, 15 were children who attended the day-care centre on the second floor of the building, and another four children who were in or near the building also died. Other victims were employees of various federal government agencies and visitors to the offices. Meanwhile, McVeigh left the city and headed north in his yellow 1977 Mercury Marquis. State Trooper Charles Hanger stopped McVeigh's car on Interstate 35 because it did not have a licence plate. Hanger noticed that McVeigh was concealing a gun under his jacket and therefore arrested him for unlawfully carrying a concealed weapon and took him to the county jail in Perry, Oklahoma. Hanger ran McVeigh's social security number through a national crime database (Branson-Potts, 2015) but there were no outstanding warrants for his arrest. He was held in the jail for two days awaiting a court hearing for the firearms charge and failure to display a licence plate. No one at the jail suspected that he had any involvement in the Oklahoma City bombing. However, back in the city investigators discovered the Ryder truck's rear axle that had been flung two blocks from where the bomb had exploded. There was an identification number on the axle that enabled them to trace the vehicle to the Ryder agency that had rented it and then to the motel where McVeigh (registered under his real name) had stayed the night before the bombing. Staff at the motel also identified McVeigh from a composite sketch that was drawn from the description of staff at the rental agency. A check with the National Crime Information Center at FBI Headquarters meant that officers with the Bureau of Alcohol, Tobacco and Firearms (ATF) who were leading the investigation could see that Hanger had run McVeigh's details through the database on 19 April and they called the Noble County Sheriff's Office in Perry to ask if they knew anything about the wanted man. Fortunately for the ATF, McVeigh was still being held at the jail on the firearms and licence plate offences and he was immediately arrested for the bombing and transported back to Oklahoma City (Michel and Herbeck, 2001).

Investigators questioned McVeigh's father, Bill, who suggested that if his son was involved then it was likely that someone called Terry Nichols was an accomplice because Nichols, whose home McVeigh registered as his own, was a long-term associate and friend. When interviewed by the FBI, Nichols initially denied knowledge or involvement in the bombing and agreed that officers could search his truck and home. Incriminating evidence was found, and the subsequent indictment outlined the steps McVeigh and Nichols took to acquire and store bomb-making materials (Michel and Herbeck, 2001). It indicated that McVeigh and Nichols obtained explosive materials including ammonium nitrate, racing and diesel fuel, and a detonation cord. Furthermore, it was found that they had used storage units to conceal the explosives and other stolen property. Shortly before the bombing, Nichols robbed a firearms dealer, a previous associate of McVeigh's, to fund the crime. It was further outlined in the indictment that Nichols and McVeigh had purchased telephone calling cards under false names so that they could prevent calls being traced to them. Additionally, they had used various false names to conceal their identities and whereabouts in the build-up to the crime. Finally, the pair were indicted for constructing an explosive truck bomb which McVeigh had placed outside the Murrah Building where he detonated it (Transcript of Preliminary Hearing, 1995).

During the investigation stage, McVeigh's father also mentioned a person called Michael Fortier who was another of his son's friends. Fortier admitted to investigators that he had helped McVeigh and Nichols transport and traffic stolen firearms (from the robbery committed by Nichols). He later admitted that he was aware of McVeigh's intentions and failed to alert authorities about them. In exchange for a more lenient sentence, Fortier agreed to testify against McVeigh and Nichols. Additionally, Fortier's wife Lori also agreed to testify that she saw McVeigh demonstrating ways in which he might arrange his barrels of explosives in the van. In return, Lori received immunity from prosecution (Michel and Herbeck, 2001).

As you will see later in this chapter, McVeigh admitted his guilt to his lawyers, arguing that the bombing was necessary to teach the government a lesson. This makes his case an interesting one for us to study in relation to constructing guilt and innocence because McVeigh's rationalisations and claims that his actions were necessary can be understood by drawing on Sykes and Matza's (1957) influential concept of techniques of neutralisation. Although he pleaded not guilty and the case went to trial, he believed that everyone knew he was responsible and argued that if he could get his side of the story across the jurors would understand his reasons and some of them might sympathise with him. Ultimately, McVeigh's neutralisations and justifications were not accepted and this chapter will explore the many techniques available to neutralise deviant behaviour and, importantly, when and why they work, and when they do not.

McVeigh's desired defence strategy

McVeigh's desired defence strategy was based on his belief that his actions were justified because of the tyranny inflicted by the federal government. Thus, he wanted his defence team to construct a 'defence of necessity', which would mean he could admit the bombing but outline to the jury why the action was necessary. McVeigh believed that some of the jurors would understand and sympathise with his anger towards the government for what he saw as their violation of the right to keep and bear arms. Moreover, he was particularly angry about the government's actions in the events in Ruby Ridge, Idaho, in 1992 and Waco, Texas, in 1993. At Ruby Ridge, federal agents surrounded a remote cabin belonging to Randy Weaver, who was suspected of selling a sawn-off shotgun to a police informant. Weaver surrendered after an 11-day siege during which his wife, son and a US marshal were killed by gunfire, but the incident caused concerns about the overzealousness of the police. Then, in 1993, the ATF raided a religious compound near Waco, Texas. It belonged to a group known as the Branch Davidians led by David Koresh, who was suspected of stockpiling illegal weapons. The initial raid resulted in the deaths of six Branch Davidians and four government agents. This was followed by a 51-day siege which occupied the national headlines during which federal agents used everything from loud music to tear gas to force the Branch Davidians out. People from all parts of the US travelled to Waco to show their support for the Davidians, including McVeigh, who was interviewed by a local reporter. During a forced attempt to end the stand-off, fire broke out in the compound and 76 Branch Davidians (men, women and children) died (Michel and Herbeck, 2001).

Adding to the attraction he saw in this defence was the fact that McVeigh knew his trial would be under an enormous media spotlight, providing him with the opportunity to get his message across to the public (Michel and Herbeck, 2001). For a defence of necessity, he would need to be able to show that, although his actions were illegal, they were justified because there was no other way to avoid harm[2] (Justia, 2018). However, his lawyer, Stephen Jones, advised him that this defence would not succeed because they would not be able to prove that McVeigh was in 'imminent' danger from the federal government when he set off the bomb. Nevertheless, McVeigh argued that 'imminent' did not mean 'immediate' and drew on an analogy that 'If a comet is hurtling toward the earth, and it's out past the orbit of Pluto, it's not an immediate threat to Earth, but it is an imminent threat' (Michel and Herbeck, 2001: 285–6). In McVeigh's view, if the US government was able to get away with its actions at Ruby Ridge and Waco, there was an imminent threat to the lives of gun owners.

Discussions about McVeigh's criminal motivations and subsequent rationalisations for them make little sense unless we first explore key elements of his life history. The account of McVeigh's background introduced here has been drawn from Michel and Herbeck's (2001) book *American Terrorist*. As well as interviewing over 150 people who knew McVeigh throughout his life, including members of his family, they conducted 75 hours of interviews with McVeigh himself.

Born in 1968, McVeigh grew up in Lockport, New York. As a teenager he became increasingly and intensely interested in gun rights and in his mind the possibility that the federal government might start prohibiting law-abiding citizens from owning guns posed a very real threat. At the age of 20, McVeigh joined the US Army, where he met someone who shared his anger at the federal government over gun laws – his senior leader of the platoon, Terry Nichols. McVeigh also met another recruit with the same views, Michael Fortier. Additionally, during his time in the Army he read literature concerning a conspiracy between the United Nations and the United States to limit individual freedom and take over the world. This conspiracy theory was reflected in the novel *The Turner Diaries*, and McVeigh began to distribute the book to anyone who he thought might share his feelings. Published in 1978, *The Turner Diaries* was authored by a former American Nazi Party official, William L. Pierce. The story concerns a gun enthusiast who, in retaliation to the government's tightening of gun laws, plants a truck bomb next to the FBI headquarters in Washington, blowing up the building. The book illustrates how, gradually, individuals lost their rights to bear arms and, for McVeigh, this was a reflection of what was actually happening in the US. President George H.W. Bush had coined the term the 'New World Order' in 1990 and in the eyes of McVeigh and others who shared his beliefs, this 'Order' would involve the consolidation of governments into one central and global government. His concern was that the United Nations would establish a single world government and subsequently place severe limits on individual freedom. For McVeigh, gun owners would doubtlessly be at the top of the list for targets under the New World Order.

Having served in the Gulf War (1990–91), McVeigh returned home and left the Army feeling he could no longer work for a government that he was growing to despise strongly, a government that was seemingly fighting very hard to remove the US Constitution's Second Amendment guaranteeing the right to bear arms. After leaving the Army, his life began to drift. New York's economy was struggling, and he became deeply depressed. He found work as a security guard and part-time work in a store selling guns. His anger towards the government was vented through letters to a local newspaper where he argued about issues of crime, taxes and racism. McVeigh also began to feel that being a young White male was a disadvantage and viewed his failure to gain employment as the result of reverse discrimination. Feeling disillusioned with the lack of opportunity, McVeigh left his hometown in 1993 and travelled the US visiting gun shows, selling books and survival items and spending time with people who also felt strongly about the Second Amendment and the government's attempts to restrict the rights of gun owners. He often travelled back and forth between Fortier and his wife in Arizona and Nichols, who lived on his family farm in Michigan. As well as travelling to gun shows, McVeigh took it upon himself to investigate any rumours of evidence of the New World Order, sometimes driving hundreds of miles if necessary.

For McVeigh, Ruby Ridge and Waco reflected a wider pattern of the federal government breaking the law. Then, in 1994, new legislation was passed to ban assault weapons, reinforcing McVeigh's belief that the government was continuing to restrict people's right to carry firearms. McVeigh later explained to authors Michel and Herbeck that the threat he felt meant he worried at night that federal agents would first target someone like him in an effort to disarm American citizens. It was around this time, McVeigh explained, that he felt he needed to take action against the government. Gun legislation such as the Brady Handgun Violence Prevention Act (1993) (see ATF, 2019) required background checks on purchasers and the Federal Assault Weapons Ban (1994) (see ATF, 2020) saw the ban of semi-automatic weapons with large ammunition capacity. McVeigh viewed the increasing legislation as a move towards outlawing civilian ownership of firearms and even more concerning to him was a rumour that the ATF would demand floor plans of people's houses and make unannounced house checks on applicants for gun licences (Michel and Herbeck, 2001).

McVeigh began thinking about ways in which he could teach the government a lesson and reasoned that bombing a government building would be the strongest and most effective tactic for getting his message across. He considered various government buildings that he could attack but settled on the Murrah Building in Oklahoma City for several reasons.

First, it housed a cross-section of federal employees, namely the ATF, the Drug Enforcement Administration (DEA) and Secret Service. Producing a high body count, he reasoned, was also a tactic the American government employed in military conflicts because it delivered the loudest statement to the enemy. There were also other practical considerations such as the glass facing on the building which would shatter easily, the large car park that would serve to minimise collateral damage, and the open space around the building which would facilitate plenty of photo opportunities afterwards. During testimony for the prosecution, Fortier explained that McVeigh targeted Oklahoma City because he believed it was the ATF office there that had given the order for its agents to search the Branch Davidian compound in Waco (although this belief was later shown to be incorrect). McVeigh began purchasing fertiliser (ammonium nitrate) and cleaning solvent (nitromethane) to build a bomb that finally weighed 7,000 pounds and, with Nichols's help, stole several detonators. The bomb was assembled inside the van that he parked in front of the Murrah Building on the day of the attack (Michel and Herbeck, 2001).

The defence strategy in court, the verdict and the sentence

McVeigh's lawyer, Stephen Jones, would not accept his proposal to put up a defence of necessity because, as we have seen, he did not think it was a robust legal strategy. Ironically, he also argued that McVeigh's trial would become a forum for his political views, which seems to be what the latter wanted. Instead, Jones suggested that they should force the government to prove that it was McVeigh who bombed the building and unpick the State's evidence wherever they could. Jones went to great lengths to link the bombing to potential international associates. He hired a Harvard professor, an expert on Arab terrorists, to help with the defence case and argued that the FBI did not investigate in any real depth who else might have been involved in the bombing. He highlighted that the US Justice Department had indicated that McVeigh and Nichols were assisted by 'others unknown'. Thus, the defence case was that the government had the wrong man and that the bombing was the work of international terrorists.

Let's revisit Bennett and Feldman's (1981) requisites for assigning guilt that we discussed in Chapter 1. Remember it was argued that in order to establish guilt in a case involving circumstantial evidence, the prosecution must show *motive*, *opportunity* and *means/capability*. That is, the actor (in this case McVeigh) must be linked with the act (in this case a terrorist attack) via each of the requisites. In so doing, the jury would be able to conclude that McVeigh had the *motive* to commit the crime, that he had the *opportunity* to visit Oklahoma City and commit the act, and that he had the *means/*

capability, in other words that he was capable of making an explosive device and that he had the means of transport (a rented truck) in order to carry out the operation. However, the prosecution struggled somewhat to establish the requisite of *opportunity* because, despite an exhaustive criminal investigation, there were no eyewitnesses placing McVeigh at the scene of the crime and no evidence was presented showing that McVeigh and his alleged co-conspirator Nichols built the bomb. There were also no fingerprints on the rental agreement or the truck key which was found in an alley in the city, and no traces of fertiliser in the units that McVeigh and Nichols allegedly used to store their material for making the bomb (Romano and Kenworthy, 1997). However, the prosecution was able to establish other elements of *means/capability* by demonstrating that, under the name of Robert Kling, McVeigh had rented the truck two days before the bombing. Tom Kessinger, a mechanic at the rental shop offered a detailed description of two men who hired the Ryder truck. Investigators named them John Doe One and John Doe Two. From the composite drawing, McVeigh was identified as John Doe One, but John Doe Two was never conclusively identified. The prosecution also argued that phone records indicated that McVeigh had been shopping for bomb materials. Additionally, when stopped 75 minutes after the blast and 78 miles from the scene, anti-government propaganda was found in his car, while his pockets, jeans and earplugs had traces of PETN, a compound used in detonator cords (Romano and Kenworthy, 1997). Furthermore, the prosecution sought to establish guilt by demonstrating McVeigh's *motive* which included his anger at the federal government's raids on Ruby Ridge and Waco, letters to his sister Jennifer indicating his loathing for the federal government, and the damaging testimony of Fortier and his wife (Michel and Herbeck, 2001).

Jones told the jury that the defence would prove McVeigh's innocence (Gumbel and Charles, 2013). Their case rested on poking holes in the prosecution's case. During the opening statement Jones challenged the requisite of *motivation* by arguing that his client was far from alone in his political views and that having such deep-seated beliefs did not equate to taking action. In so doing, Jones was able to make reference to, and indeed emphasise, McVeigh's belief that the federal government 'executed seventy-six people at Waco, including thirty women and twenty-five children' (Jones, 1997: opening statement) as well as mentioning Ruby Ridge and his upset at the threat to the Second Amendment. *Capability* was challenged by arguing that McVeigh could not carry out the bombing alone. To this end, Jones suggested that it could not be proved that McVeigh was John Doe One and, furthermore, no one could be certain that John Doe Two did not exist (Gumbel and Charles, 2013). Jones further highlighted the contamination of evidence at the scene and the laboratory and the deficient skills of the professionals who were 'more law enforcement oriented than scientific oriented' (Jones, 1997: opening statement). Jones *redefined* the Fortiers' testimonies, arguing that they persistently insisted their friend was innocent of the charges and that the reason for their change of heart was because of the threat of criminal charges against them unless they testified for the prosecution (Jones, 1997: opening statement).

It is worth noting that before the trial began, Jones's colleague leaked information to the *Dallas Morning News* which revealed that McVeigh admitted his guilt and said that he bombed the building at a time when he knew he would achieve a higher 'body count'. Other media outlets such as NBC News, ABC News, *Newsweek* and *Playboy* also reported on leaked documents relating to McVeigh's discussions with his defence team. Jones requested that the trial be delayed, but Judge Richard Matsch refused, suggesting he did not consider the news stories were as widely circulated or accepted as the defence team thought. However, because of concerns about pretrial publicity and the fairness and impartiality of the jury, McVeigh's trial was moved from Oklahoma to Denver, Colorado (Thomas, 1996). In 1997, he was found guilty and convicted of conspiracy to use a weapon of mass destruction, use of a weapon of mass destruction, destruction by explosive of a federal building and eight counts of premeditated murder of federal law and enforcement officers (Romano and Kenworthy, 1997). The jury unanimously recommended that McVeigh receive the death penalty.[3] In 2000, McVeigh asked a federal judge to stop all appeals regarding his convictions and requested a date be set for his execution. On 11 June 2001, McVeigh was executed by lethal injection at the US Penitentiary at Terre Haute, Indiana (Linder, nd). In a separate federal trial, McVeigh's associate Terry Nichols was found guilty of conspiracy and eight counts of involuntary manslaughter and sentenced to life in prison. In a later Oklahoma state trial, Nichols was charged with and convicted of 160 counts of first-degree murder, one count of first-degree manslaughter for the death of an unborn child, and one count of aiding in the placement of a bomb near a public building. Nichols was sentenced to 160 consecutive life sentences without the possibility of parole (Linder, nd). Michael Fortier received a 12-year prison sentence and a $200,000 fine (Michel and Herbeck, 2001).

McVeigh said that he never doubted the outcome of his trial, that he would be found guilty and receive the death sentence. He viewed the trial as a charade since he considered that everyone knew he was guilty (Michel and Herbeck, 2001). Instead, he said he hoped that the news coverage during his trial would draw the public's attention to events like Ruby Ridge and Waco and help them understand them the way that he did: 'as a watershed moment in the emergence of a new American tyranny' and he hoped he communicated the message during the trial proceedings that his 'actions were righteous' (Michel and Herbeck, 2001: 308). Thus, McVeigh did not directly oppose his conviction and execution but sought to establish his lack of guilt in the sociopolitical rather than legal domain. This is where Sykes and Matza's concept of techniques of neutralisation is relevant because it may be applied to understand how McVeigh rationalised and justified his crime and attempted to neutralise his guilt.

Techniques of neutralisation

Sykes and Matza's (1957) article 'Techniques of neutralization: a theory of delinquency' was a response to the dominant theories of the time that centred on Cohen's (1955) subcultural theory of crime, which posited that delinquent boys rejected middle-class standards and replaced them with their own set of values, which tended to be delinquent ones. Sykes and Matza challenged this hypothesis, arguing that delinquents do not entirely reject the dominant social order and values. For example, if a delinquent truly believed that their own norms and values were valid then they would feel no guilt or shame for their behaviour once they were caught. Instead, Sykes and Matza suggested that delinquents do in fact experience guilt and shame, that they admire law-abiding others, and to some extent engage in law-abiding activities within the community, for example through churches and schools. In short, their argument is premised on the proposition that delinquents know right from wrong and are influenced by both conventional and delinquent subcultures (Maruna and Copes, 2005). To avoid feelings of guilt and shame, the delinquent must employ ways of rationalising their behaviour and neutralise the subsequent feelings that might arise from it. Central to Sykes and Matza's argument is that delinquents employ excuses and justifications to rationalise their behaviour. By using talk that neutralises guilt, linguistic devices enable the individual to engage in deviant behaviour while maintaining a 'sense of morality' (Maruna and Copes, 2005: 230).

In their influential article, 'Accounts', Scott and Lyman (1968: 46) built on Sykes and Matza's work noting: 'An account is a linguistic device employed whenever an action is subjected to valuative inquiry'. Thus, by rationalising and neutralising their behaviour, the delinquent is able to lessen the impact of social controls and to this end 'the delinquent both has his cake and eats it too, for he remains committed to the dominant normative system and yet so qualifies its imperatives that violations are "acceptable" if not "right"' (Sykes and Matza, 1957: 667). For Maruna and Copes, the accounts people give for their actions is a way of understanding how they attach meaning to events. To do so provides insight into the 'psychology of the individual – his or her personality, identity, or self – as much as it does about the events and structural conditions experienced' (Maruna and Copes, 2005: 222; see also, McAdams, 1985, 1993; Bruner, 2002).

Sykes and Matza's (1957) article, which originally focused on the behaviour of young delinquents, remains 'one of the most frequently cited and influential explanations of criminal behavior' (Maruna and Copes, 2005: 222). Maruna and Copes's (2005) article offers an exhaustive review of research on techniques of neutralisation and highlights how the theory has been used to account for a variety of social misdemeanours and crimes such as rape (Bohner et al, 1998), murder (Levi, 1981), genocide (Alvarez, 1997; Stewart and Byrne, 2000), white-collar crime (Benson, 1985; Jesilow et al, 1993; Shover and Bryant, 1993; Simon and Eitzen, 1993), deer poaching (Eliason and Dodder, 1999), being a hitman (Levi, 1981), hate crimes against the Amish (Byers et al, 1999; Byers and Crider, 2002), assaulting prostitutes (Miller and Schwartz, 1995), stealing office supplies (Hollinger, 1991), and snitching on peers (Pershing, 2003). Interestingly, Maruna and Copes noted that scholars have also utilised the theory to help explain less serious behaviours such as entering pre-teen daughters into beauty pageants (Heltsley and Calhoun, 2003). Since their review, other studies have examined techniques of neutralisation in relation to wildlife crime in rural England and Wales (Enticott, 2011), deviant consumer behaviour such as verbal abuse and deceitful and fraudulent actions (Harris and Daunt, 2011), alcohol consumption (Piacentini et al, 2012), animal rights activism (Liddick, 2013), cannabis-using divers (Martin et al, 2019), and child sexual abuse and the Roman Catholic Church (Weir, 2020). Hazani (1991: 135) pointed out that, in fact, neutralisation theory has 'universal applicability' because it can be used to understand any situation where there are discrepancies or inconsistences between a person's actions and beliefs.

Sykes and Matza identified five major types of techniques of neutralisation. The *Denial of Responsibility* occurs when the offender argues that their actions were caused by forces outside of their control. For example, the person may blame their mistreatment at the hands of parents, or the company they keep in a disorderly neighbourhood. Sykes and Matza (1957: 667) suggested that by seeing themself as 'more acted upon than acting', the delinquent begins to follow a path that deviates from the 'dominant normative system' without attacking the norms themselves. In this regard, a psychiatrist who assessed McVeigh prior to his trial noted that his childhood was disrupted by his parents' divorce and his mother's subsequent move to Florida. His mother took McVeigh's sisters but left him to live with his father. McVeigh described how his parents' arguments were so intense that he thought they might kill one another. The psychiatrist suggested that as a result, McVeigh created a fantasy world where he played the part of the superhero and 'As an adult, McVeigh came to see the US government as the ultimate monster – especially after the Waco incident' (Michel and Herbeck, 2001: 289). He also confided in a friend that he blamed his mother for breaking up the family and expressed anger towards her. Despite this and the psychiatrist's observations, McVeigh maintained that his childhood was no different from that of any other person who grew up with divorced parents. In fact,

Exercise 1:

Let's think about Hazani's (1991) suggestion that neutralisation theory can help us to understand inconsistencies between a person's behaviour and their beliefs. Can you think back to a recent situation where your behaviour was not aligned with your beliefs or values? For example, you might strongly value and believe in health foods that are low in sugar but perhaps the other day you found yourself at the fridge staring at the chocolate truffles. The next thing, you find yourself eating them! What might you have told yourself to neutralise the behaviour? Examples might include:

'I have had a hard day, I deserve a treat';

'I have been so good with my diet for so long';

'One won't do any harm'.

Sound familiar? If you find yourself using any of these types of justifications then you are already unknowingly familiar with Sykes and Matza's 'techniques of neutralization'! As Hazani pointed out, the concept can be applied universally. Think about it for a moment – neutralising these behaviours serves to protect you (Maruna and Copes, 2005) since if you took responsibility for every single one of your faults or failings, you might end up feeling quite depressed! Maruna and Copes (2005: 227) expressed this point well: 'there is nothing pathological about neutralising negative behaviours. ... Taking full responsibility for every personal failing does not make a person "normal." It makes them extraordinary'.

according to Michel and Herbeck (2001: 21), he 'would angrily deny' that his parents' divorce had any influence on his crime. Thus, McVeigh did not deny responsibility for his actions.

The *Denial of Injury* arises when the offender makes a distinction between acts they consider wrong and acts that are illegal but not immoral. Sykes and Matza (1957: 667) used the example of an offender vandalising a property but then telling themself afterwards that the owner of the property 'can well afford it'. Similarly, they suggested, the stealing of a car might be justified as 'borrowing' and so no real injury or harm to the owner has taken place. Importantly, Sykes and Matza (1957: 668) emphasised that the offender's behaviour is seen as an 'extension' of common practices such as truancy and 'pranks' rather than viewing themself in complete opposition to the law. McVeigh had considered blowing up a federal building in the middle of the night where there would likely be only a few employees working. However, for him, to destroy an almost empty building at night would have had no impact on the government since 'They've got bottomless pockets of cash to build a new one' (Michel and Herbeck, 2001: 224). Rather, he conceded, he needed a 'body count' to successfully convey his message (Michel and Herbeck, 2001). Thus, he sought to maximise rather than deny the injury.

Denial of the Victim is made when the offender positions himself as the avenger and the victim as the villain. Sykes and Matza used the example of someone taking revenge on an unfair teacher, or a Robin Hood character who seeks justice outside of the law. Additionally, denial of a victim might take place because of the apparent absence of one. For example, think about white-collar crimes for a moment. If an employee decides to steal items from an office or fraudulently claims expenses, he or she may not think that anyone has been victimised. For McVeigh, *Denial of the Victim* was an important justification. As mentioned previously, for the government to take notice of his message, McVeigh thought that the bombing required a high body count and the Murrah Building contained more than 500 workers during the day. McVeigh consistently argued that he took no pleasure in killing but that it was justified in the name of underscoring a message to the American government. The Murrah Building housed employees of the ATF and the DEA, and the Secret Service, whom he vehemently despised. Other government employees from Social Security, the Department of Housing and Urban Development, and the Department of Agriculture were in the building and McVeigh could also see them as legitimate targets. According to Michel and Herbeck (2001), McVeigh acknowledged that many of the people he was about to kill had nothing to do with the agencies involved in the incidents at Waco and Ruby Ridge and so to justify his actions, he recalled the image he had used since childhood, which was the destruction of the Death Star in the 1977 movie *Star Wars*:

> McVeigh saw himself as a counterpart to Luke Skywalker, the heroic Jedi knight whose successful attack on the Death Star closes the film. As a kid, McVeigh had noticed that the Star Wars movies showed people sitting at consoles – Space-Age clerical workers – inside the Death Star. Those people weren't storm troopers. They weren't killing anyone. But they were vital to the operations of the Evil Empire, McVeigh deduced, and when Luke blew up the Death Star those people became inevitable casualties. When the Death Star exploded, the movie audiences cheered. The bad guys were beaten: that was all that really mattered. As an adult, McVeigh found himself able to dismiss the killings of secretaries, receptionists, and other personnel in the Murrah Building with equally cold-blooded calculation. They were all part of the Evil Empire. (Michel and Herbeck, 2001: 224–5)

Fortier's testimony for the prosecution reflected this rationale when he said he asked McVeigh about who would become victims of the bombing:

> He explained to me that he considered all those people to be as if they were the storm troopers in the movie *Star Wars*. They may be individually innocent, but because they are part of the – the Evil Empire, they were guilty by association. (Michel and Herbeck, 2001: 333)

To underscore this view, McVeigh regularly wore a T-shirt depicting the Liberty Tree with droplets of blood falling from it. Thomas Jefferson's words were written over the top: 'THE TREE OF LIBERTY MUST BE REFERESHED FROM TIME TO TIME WITH THE BLOOD OF PATRIOTS AND TYRANTS' (Michel and Herbeck, 2001: 154). In McVeigh's own words, he declared that he:

> didn't define the rules of engagement in this conflict. The rules, if not written down, are defined by the aggressor. It was brutal, no holds barred. Women and kids were killed at Waco and Ruby Ridge. You put back in [the government's] faces exactly what they're giving out. (Michel and Herbeck, 2001: 225)

However, *Denial of the Victim* became much more difficult for McVeigh when he learned that 19 of those fatally wounded were children (15 from the day-care centre). He always denied knowledge of there being a day-care centre in the Murrah Building and expressed regret that children were killed. Yet according to Michel and Herbeck (2001: 324–5), trial observers noted McVeigh sharing jokes and smiling with his lawyers. This provoked questions about why he did not appear to show any respect for the victims and their families and McVeigh responded:

> The victims are looking for some show of remorse. I understand and empathize with the victims' losses, but at the same time, I'm a realist. Death and loss are an integral part of life everywhere. We have to accept it and move on. To these people in Oklahoma who lost a loved one, I'm sorry, but it happens every day. You're not the first mother to lose a kid, or the first grandparent to lose a grandson or granddaughter. It happens every day, somewhere in the world. I'm not going to go into that courtroom, curl into a fetal ball, and cry just because the victims want me to do that. (Michel and Herbeck, 2001: 324–5)

McVeigh described a strong and positive relationship with his younger sister Jennifer and her hostile response to the FBI demonstrated her reciprocal feelings (Michel and Herbeck, 2001). During the investigation, it emerged that she had sent her brother several bullets in the mail. According to Michel and Herbeck she was forced to testify against McVeigh or face criminal prosecution for sending the ammunition. McVeigh later told Michel and Herbeck that he sympathised with his sister when she testified, but not enough to cause regret for the bombing:

> In any kind of military action, you try to keep collateral damage to a minimum. But a certain amount of collateral damage is inevitable. (Michel and Herbeck, 2001: 331)

The *Condemnation of the Condemners* means that the offender refocuses the attention from themself to the motivations and behaviours of those who disapprove of their behaviour. Sykes and Matza (1957: 668) suggested that the condemners such as the police may be viewed as 'corrupt, stupid and brutal' and 'by attacking others, the wrongfulness of [the offender's] own behavior is more easily repressed or lost to view'. Additionally, those who criticise offenders can be characterised as 'hypocrites, deviants in disguise, or impelled by personal spite' (Sykes and Matza, 1957: 668) and therefore they 'have no right to pass judgment on others' (Maruna and Copes, 2005: 233). The act is considered irrelevant because others have committed far worse acts, 'and these others are not caught, not punished, not condemned, unnoticed, or even praised' (Scott and Lyman, 1968: 51). McVeigh wrote an essay in 1998 for *Media Bypass* magazine, an alternative media outlet, in which, to emphasise his condemners' hypocrisy, he compared his crime to American military actions. He argued that for the government, the bombing of buildings containing children is legitimate and acceptable if it is part of a military operation, yet they condemned McVeigh for bombing a building in which he did not know that children were present:

> Hypocrisy when it comes to death of children? In Oklahoma City, it was family convenience that explained the presence of a day-care center placed between street level and the law-enforcement agencies which occupied the upper floors of the building. Yet when discussion shifts to Iraq, any day-care center in a government building instantly becomes 'a shield'. Think about that.
>
> (Actually, there is a difference here. The administration has admitted to knowledge of the presence of children in or near Iraqi government buildings, yet they still proceed with their plans to bomb – saying that they cannot be held responsible if children die. There is no such proof, however, that knowledge of the presence of children existed in relation to the Oklahoma City bombing.) When considering morality and '*mens rea*' (criminal intent) in light of these facts, I ask: Who are the true barbarians? (Michel and Herbeck, 2001: 368)

After watching the documentary *Waco, the Big Lie*, McVeigh was further convinced that the government's intention was to kill the Branch Davidians and he subsequently took it upon himself to spread the message about Waco. At gun shows he distributed leaflets with titles such as 'US Government Initiates Open Warfare Against American People' and 'United States Government or Nazi Germany?' As a way of promoting his message, McVeigh greeted telephone callers with messages like 'Give me liberty or give me death' (Michel and Herbeck, 2001: 140). Other forms of advocacy included distributing leaflets with various quotes on subjects ranging from gun control to taxes. He also wore a T-shirt with a picture of Waco and the words 'FBI – FEDERAL BUREAU OF INCINERATION', along with an ATF baseball cap that was punctured with two bullet holes and he began selling the caps himself. He further distributed cards with the name and address of the FBI agent, Lon Horiuchi, who shot and killed Randy Weaver's wife, Vicki Weaver, at Ruby Ridge. He also sold flares and flare launchers that could be used like rockets to shoot at ATF helicopters. While the bombing reflected what had been described in the novel *The Turner Diaries*, there was a new book, which McVeigh read following his conviction, that he said was even more important. Rather than destroying a government building, the new novel told a story of assassins who murder government agents one by one:

> 'If people say *The Turner Diaries* was my Bible,' McVeigh said recently, '*Unintended Consequences* would be my New Testament, I think *Unintended Consequences* is a better book. It might have changed my whole plan of operation if I'd read that one first.' (Michel and Herbeck, 2001: 304)

The *Appeal to Higher Loyalties* occurs when the offender feels they are in a dilemma that can only be resolved by breaking the law. Thus, the act was permissible 'or even right since it served the interests of another to whom he owes an unbreakable allegiance or affection' (Scott and Lyman, 1968: 51). The dominant norms are not rejected as such; rather, there are other norms that are seen as more important such as having a higher loyalty to another group or cause to which they belong. The technique may be employed by an individual seeking 'higher' goals such as profit or justice for their peer group. This justification is particularly relevant to McVeigh's motivations. His loyalty to another cause – gun owners' rights and the threat the FBI posed to gun owners' lives – was evident when he first joined the Army. Other soldiers at Fort Riley observed his collection of several books on firearms and gun laws. McVeigh argued to his defence team that his crime was one of 'necessity' because the US government posed an imminent threat to the lives of gun owners following the incidents at Waco and Ruby Ridge, incidents, he argued, that were not isolated. Fortier and Nichols told McVeigh that they thought the FBI was guilty of manslaughter having started the fire at Waco, although for McVeigh it was murder. Infuriated, McVeigh visited the ruins of the Branch Davidian Compound in Waco and according to Michel and Herbeck (2001: 139) his desire for information about events there became 'all-consuming'. For McVeigh, even if David Koresh was guilty of child abuse, as alleged by the federal government, he and his followers should not have suffered because of it.

When techniques of neutralisation work and when they do not

Kaptein and van Helvoort (2019) developed a model that aimed to help better understand how neutralisations work. Reviewing previous research (see, for example, Scott and Lyman, 1968; Schlenker, 1980; Schönbach, 1990; Benoit and Hanczor, 1994; Bandura et al, 1996; Barriga and Gibbs, 1996; Robinson and Kraatz, 1998; Fritsche, 2002; Ashforth and Anand, 2003; Gellerman, 2003; Geva, 2006; Goffman, 2009; Murphy and Dacin, 2011; Banerjee et al, 2012; and Shigihara, 2013), they argued that none of these studies was based on a systematic inventory of identified techniques for all types of deviant behaviour and that the model has been extended and developed arbitrarily and inconsistently. They suggested that the limited yet broad and overlapping techniques identified by researchers are one reason for the inconsistent research findings on neutralisation. To this end, Kaptein and van Helvoort conducted an exhaustive multidisciplinary search of the literature to find as many examples of neutralisations as possible. The neutralisations included those behaviours that were deemed 'immoral, unethical, nonconforming, delinquent, and criminal' (2019: 1263). The authors found 1,251 different neutralisations which they classified into four categories: *Distorting the facts*, *Negating the norm*, *Blaming the circumstances* and *Hiding behind oneself.* These four categories are broadly based on the types of neutralisations identified in the literature (and within those four categories are 12 techniques and a total of 60 sub-techniques). Because the neutralisations are clustered, the relationship between the techniques and sub-techniques may be better understood. For example, individuals may use sub-techniques in a particular sequence, that is, where one technique fails, another can be drawn on, thus facilitating better understanding on how and when neutralisations may be accepted or rejected.

The result is a model presented in a wheel that is divided into the four categories and within that the 12 techniques and 60 sub-techniques. The wheel presents the first category and its corresponding techniques and sub-techniques beginning at the top (in the 12 o'clock position) and each subsequent technique and sub-technique follows in a clockwise direction.

The further on in the wheel the neutralisations are, the less room there is for people (whose neutralisation is not accepted) to select another (sub-)technique before having to admit their guilt. Thus, the earlier on their neutralisation appears in the wheel, the more room they have to utilise another before having to acknowledge their guilt. Additionally, by using a particular (sub-)technique, the person cannot rely on earlier sub-techniques to justify or rationalise their deviant behaviour in a logical way. Kaptein and van Helvoort (2019) noted, however, that the sequence in which the (sub-)techniques are presented does not indicate that the subsequent (sub-)techniques become more invalid or that every person begins with the first technique or indeed that they move around the wheel in a linear fashion.

Based on Kaptein and van Helvoort's (2019) model, McVeigh can be seen to have employed the following sub-techniques of neutralisation: *Reducing the norm to the immorality of the accusers, The appeal to higher goals, The appeal to rights, The limitation to one option* and *The limitation of others being responsible*. Table 5.1 depicts the sub-techniques' corresponding techniques and categories.

Kaptein and van Helvoort's (2019) *Reducing the norm to the immorality of the accusers* corresponds closely with Sykes and Matza's (1957) *Condemnation of the condemners*. The neutralisation does not aim to dismiss one's accountability towards others but only towards particular people, and in McVeigh's case this was the federal government. Also under the same category is *The appeal to higher goals*. Like Sykes and Matza's *Appeal to higher loyalties*, the deviant behaviour is based on achieving a goal that the person perceives as more important than the norm being breached such that the action is ultimately 'for the greater good' (Martin et al, 2014: 303). McVeigh's higher loyalties to gun owners' rights evidently did not demonstrate appeal to the public or elicit their acceptance because of the unusually cruel nature of the crime. Thus, the nature and characteristics of the audience may also determine whether

Table 5.1: The categories and their associated techniques and sub-techniques of neutralisation that McVeigh attempted to utilise as per Kaptein and van Helvoort's model

Category	Technique	Sub-technique
Negating the norm	4th Technique *Reducing norms to facts*	Reducing the norm to the immorality of the accusers
	5th Technique *Appealing to another norm*	The appeal to higher goals The appeal to rights
Blaming the circumstances	7th Technique *Blaming the limited options*	The limitation to one option
	8th Technique *Blaming the limited role*	The limitation to others being responsible

or not neutralisations are accepted. For example, there have been cases of animal rights activists breaking into farms to expose the poor treatment of animals raised for consumption. Their neutralisation of the law against breaking and entering by claiming loyalty to animal welfare will likely be accepted by an audience which is also against animal cruelty but will be less accepted by those who are indifferent. However, acceptance could also depend on the nature of the crime. For example, breaking and entering to rescue harmed animals is unlikely to be viewed the same way as if the actions extend to physical harm of the farmers themselves.

The appeal to rights is utilised when the person hides behind moral and legal rights, also known as the defence of necessity (Coleman, 2005). We know that this was, indeed, McVeigh's desired legal defence and that his lawyer countered that it would not be accepted on the grounds that he was not in 'imminent' danger from the government. The technique labelled *The limitation to one option* is also recognised as the defence of necessity because, as the neutralisation suggests, the person claims that they have no other option under such circumstances but to engage in the deviant act (Minor, 1981). McVeigh's lawyer clearly found such a defence implausible because there was no imminent threat to life and there were alternative acts that McVeigh could have chosen to demonstrate his point. However, there are occasions when the defence of necessity may be successfully applied. In England and Wales, there are three requirements in order to apply for the defence of necessity: the act is needed to avoid inevitable and irreparable evil; no more should be done than is reasonably necessary for the purpose to be achieved; and the evil inflicted must not be disproportionate to the evil avoided. Medical cases appear to yield most success in using this type of neutralisation and defence. For example, there was a high-profile case in 2001 (Re A (conjoined twins) [2001] 2WLR 480) when the defence of necessity was allowed for the offence of murder in relation to a life-saving operation to separate conjoined twins. Joined at the pelvis, one of the twins was completely dependent on the other for survival and if left conjoined both babies would die. If the twins were separated, however, the stronger twin would survive and the weaker one would die. The parents refused consent for the operation and the doctors applied to the court for a declaration that it would be lawful and in the best interests of the children to operate. The High Court granted the declaration on the grounds that the operation was akin to withdrawal of support. The procedure was carried out and the weaker twin did die but the stronger one, now a teenager, went on to live a healthy life (Malvern, 2014). However, the defence of duress is now more commonly used than the defence of necessity and is available when a defendant was forced (either by a person or circumstances) to commit a crime. It can be used for all types of crimes except murder, attempted murder and treason. Elliott and Quinn (2016) provide clear outlines of the legal definitions and a variety of examples of cases when the defence of necessity and defence of duress have been used.

The limitation to others being responsible is a technique in the model that expands on Sykes and Matza's *Denial of Responsibility*. When discussing Sykes and Matza's (1957) model, we noted that McVeigh did not attempt to deny his responsibility. However, under Kaptein and van Helvoort's (2019) model there is scope to recognise McVeigh's acknowledgement of his responsibility but at the same time his attempt at reducing it by arguing that his behaviour was the result of the behaviour of others (Fulkerson and Bruns, 2014). In other words, although McVeigh never denied his responsibility for the bombing, he made it clear that it would not have happened if it were not for the tyranny that the government persistently inflicted on civilians, and the incidents at Waco and Ruby Ridge were examples of that tyranny. According to Kaptein and van Helvoort (2019), partially attributing responsibility to others should be a less risky strategy than holding the other person or entity *entirely* responsible. However, notwithstanding the blame that McVeigh apportioned to the federal government, the seriousness of his crime negated serious consideration of such a neutralisation.

We will see in Chapter 9 that defendants may use the defence of diminished capacity if they were mentally unwell and were unable to understand the consequences of their act at the time of the crime. Moreover, there may be times when the cause of diminished responsibility is attributed to other people or circumstances, wholly or partially neutralising a person's guilt, which may be accepted by courts and the public. This type of strategy proved controversial in the Californian 'Twinkie defense' used in 1979 by defendant Dan White. White was convicted of voluntary manslaughter (the less serious charge for homicide) after his lawyer successfully argued that White's diet of junk food created a chemical imbalance, affecting his ability to judge properly (Cornell Law School, Legal Information Institute, nd). The defence of diminished responsibility may also be successful in cases involving domestic violence. For example, if a woman who kills her violent partner as a result of cumulative abuse cites the concept of the 'battered woman syndrome' to support her claim of diminished responsibility, this then becomes relevant in the jury's consideration that she was acting under provocation.

We have seen that Sykes and Matza's theory (1957) and Kaptein and van Helvoort's (2019) model can be applied to understand how McVeigh validated his actions to the extent that, even up until his execution, he considered them justified. However, clearly his techniques of neutralisation were not accepted by the jury, the wider audience, and probably even those who shared his political views. Thus, the acceptance of neutralisation techniques seems to depend – at least partly – on the nature of the action itself. Indeed, a photograph of a rescue worker carrying a deceased baby from the Murrah Building was widely circulated, no doubt underscoring the heinous and cruel nature of McVeigh's crime. Convicted Unabomber Theodore Kaczynski argued that McVeigh's 'bombing was a bad action because it was unnecessarily inhumane' and that a more effective protest would have been to target a:

> small number of people who were personally responsible for the policies or actions to which the protesters objected. Such a protest would have earned far more sympathy than the Oklahoma City bombing did, because it is safe to assume that many anti-government people who might have accepted violence that was more limited and carefully directed were repelled by the large loss of innocent life at Oklahoma City. (Michel and Herbeck, 2001: 400–1)

Exercise 2:

You have so far learned that the defence of duress is now more commonly used than the defence of necessity in England and Wales. For it to succeed, the defence must show that although the defendant had the *mens rea* to commit the crime, they acted out of compulsion and were therefore not exercising freedom of choice. For example, the defendant reasonably believed that unless they committed the said offence, threats of death or serious injury to themself, or someone they were responsible for, would be carried through. A clear explanation of the defence of duress and elements that must be established for it to succeed can be found in Ahluwalia and Rafferty's (2017) briefing note for the Criminal Bar Association for England and Wales. They wrote specifically about the defence of duress available to female defendants who are victims/survivors of domestic abuse. Drawing on a factual case study from Ahluwalia and Rafferty's briefing note, consider for a moment your views on the guilt or innocence of the defendant.

A woman (YS) is charged with driving while disqualified, driving with excess alcohol, driving without insurance and dangerous driving. The permanently illuminated brake lights and swerving of the car caught a police officer's attention who then activated the siren, trying to stop the woman's vehicle. The woman did not stop and the police officer chased the car for five minutes.

The woman driving explained that her abusive partner had dragged her partially dressed from her home. She claimed that her partner forced her to drive and threatened to kill her if she did not continue to drive, that he screamed continuously at her, punched her in the ribs and tried to grab the steering wheel.

The findings of fact were presented at the Magistrates' Court:

> There is no doubt that [YS] has been involved in an abusive relationship with R who has a history of violent offences in the domestic setting. We believe that [YS] drove dangerously to escape the Police at the behest of R, although, as the

driver of the car, she could have halted the vehicle. We are prepared to believe that the reason she drove at speed was because [YS] believed if she did not R might kill or seriously injure her. (Ahluwalia and Rafferty, 2017: 7)

Would you find YS guilty of all, or any, of the following:

driving while disqualified;
driving with excess alcohol;
driving without insurance;
dangerous driving?

1. What are your reasons and justifications for your judgement?
2. Do you think the court found her guilty or not guilty?

The defence of duress in this case failed because the Magistrates' Court concluded: 'We do not find that a reasonable person with the defendant's beliefs, history of domestic violence, and of her age, in her situation, would have done what she did. She admits to having consumed alcohol before driving' (Ahluwalia and Rafferty, 2017: 7). Furthermore, the conviction was upheld on appeal to the High Court, noting: 'Even taking that background [of domestic abuse] they found that a reasonable person having experienced violence and threats which, on occasion, had not always been carried out would not have acted as the Appellant did' (Ahluwalia and Rafferty, 2017: 7). The Criminal Bar Association for England and Wales has criticised the defence of duress for failing to reflect cases of domestic abuse whereby the victim cannot always predict when they are under the threat of immediate or almost immediate physical harm, 'thus ignoring the true and complete mechanisms of compulsion' (Ahluwalia and Rafferty, 2017: 4). What do you think?

Conclusion

It is emphasised throughout this book that each chapter draws on one perspective to help explain why the defendant in the case was acquitted or convicted. Of course, apart from his failure before the court and public opinion to neutralise his guilt, there are other factors that possibly contributed to McVeigh's conviction. Arguably, the prosecution's evidence was strong enough to prove McVeigh's guilt beyond a reasonable doubt and he did not publicly deny the crime. Defending a client with the knowledge of his culpability clearly provoked his lawyer's colleague into leaking information to the press that confirmed McVeigh's guilt. Additionally, Jones's two and a half hour opening statement sought to delve into very fine detail about the case they were going to present to challenge the prosecution's case. The *ABA Journal* noted his performance was 'rambling and disjointed' (Gumbel and Charles, 2013: 318), implying that it made little impression on the jury. Indeed, the art of language and persuasion in the courtroom and its influence on jury decision-making is the focus for the next chapter.

However, there is evidence that techniques of neutralisation will be accepted by the legal system in some cases. For example, the defence of duress in the UK allows for some mitigation in cases where the individual acted because they were under threat of some kind. Notwithstanding this, you observed in Exercise 2 that meeting the criteria for the defence of duress can be challenging and complex and that justifications are not readily accepted and are perhaps treated suspiciously. This certainly appears to be present in the culture of offender rehabilitation programmes too; justifications are treated as a symptom of denial and are deemed risky to the offender's ability or willingness to desist from crime. However, the concept of neutralisation provides a useful insight into the cognitive and decision-making mechanisms of the individual. In the future, we will hopefully see the more comprehensive model of Kaptein and van Helvoort (2019) being utilised by scholars to better understand more consistently how neutralisations work (or not).

Recommended reading

As you have seen in this chapter, Maruna and Copes's (2005) article is an exhaustive review of the research utilising Sykes and Matza's (1957) 'Techniques of neutralization' and offers a thorough critique of the strengths and weaknesses of the theory. It is also worth reading Kaptein and van Helvoort's (2019) 'A model of neutralization techniques' because of its comprehensive overview of the concept that has been used by researchers in order to develop a contemporary model for scholars to draw on.

Notes

[1]   This was McVeigh's reply to an inmate on death row who asked him where he went wrong (Michel and Herbeck, 2001: 376).

[2]   There are some important requisites in order to successfully apply the necessity defence in the US. For example, the defendant must show that at the time of the crime, they believed there was a clear and specific threat that required immediate action; they must also show that they had no realistic alternative to committing the crime; the harm caused by their crime must not have exceeded the harm avoided; and the defendant did not contribute to, or cause, the threat (Justia, 2018).

[3]   McVeigh was subject to a federal trial, hence the charges of eight counts of premeditated murder of federal law and enforcement officers. In 1998, McVeigh was preparing to face a state trial on multiple charges of murdering civilians; however, Oklahoma decided against bringing him to trial for those murders on the condition that the federal government carry out his execution (Michel and Herbeck, 2001).

6

Language Style and Persuasion in the Criminal Trial of O.J. Simpson

If it doesn't fit, you must acquit.[1]

The murders of Nicole Brown Simpson and Ronald Goldman

On the evening of 12 June 1994, Nicole Brown Simpson (35), her two young children and other family members dined at the Los Angeles (LA) restaurant Mezzaluna, in California. Ronald Goldman (25) was a waiter at Mezzaluna and an acquaintance of Nicole. Ronald (hereafter Ron) left Mezzaluna at around 9.50 pm and, following a brief stop at his apartment to change his clothes, he walked to Nicole's condominium at 875 South Bundy Drive, LA, to return a pair of glasses that belonged to Nicole's mother, who had left them at the restaurant. Just before midnight, Nicole's agitated and blood-stained dog was found by a man walking around the neighbourhood. The dog led the man to Nicole's condominium where he could see two bodies (later identified by the police as Nicole and Ron) lying on the walkway to the house. They had both been stabbed multiple times (Cotterill, 2003). At approximately 11.50 pm on the evening of the murders, Nicole's ex-husband, Orenthal James (O.J.) Simpson, was picked up by a chauffeur from his house in another part of LA: he was leaving to attend a Hertz conference in Chicago (Buckleton, 2005). The following morning, when informed by the police of the murders, Simpson returned to Los Angeles where he was questioned for almost four hours. He was subsequently released without charge. Simpson maintained his innocence throughout the interview and claimed to have no knowledge of the murders (Cotterill, 2003).

However, the day after Nicole's funeral, on 17 June 1994, a warrant for Simpson's arrest for the murders was issued. He failed to surrender and instead left his home with his friend A.C. Cowlings and got into a 60-mile slow-speed car chase, with Cowlings driving his Ford Bronco around the Southern California freeways. Simpson was reported to be suicidal in the back of the vehicle, apparently with a gun to his head. The Bronco was followed by several police officers and helicopters. Because Simpson was a celebrity icon with a Hall of Fame football career behind him, the Bronco was also followed by several news crews, and fans of Simpson even cheered him on during the chase. Finally, Cowlings drove Simpson back to his home where he surrendered and was arrested. On the same evening, Simpson was formally charged with two counts of first-degree murder, a capital offence under California law (Cotterill, 2003). Following a six-day preliminary hearing, on 8 July 1994, Judge Kennedy-Powell ruled that there was 'ample evidence' for Simpson to be put on trial for the first-degree murder of both Nicole and Ron (Cotterill, 2003).

Simpson's trial began on 28 January 1995. Presiding Judge Lance Ito allowed the trial to be televised and it quickly became a media spectacle (Furno-Lamude, 1999), attracting such intense interest that it was thought to be the most reported trial in history (Schuetz, 1999a). The cost to Los Angeles County and Simpson himself was noteworthy: $9 million and $10 million, respectively. Twelve jurors and 12 alternates were sequestered for 266 days, during which the prosecution presented evidence for 99 days and the defence for 34 (Simpson Trial Statistics 1997, cited in Schuetz, 1999a). On 2 October 1995, after less than four hours' jury deliberation, Simpson was acquitted of both murders (Schuetz, 1999a), a decision that shocked many, mainly White, followers of the trial. However, Simpson was subsequently called to a civil trial when the victims' families charged him with the wrongful deaths of Nicole and Ron. On 4 February 1997, he was found liable for wilfully and wrongfully causing their deaths: $12.5 million were awarded to Nicole's children and $12.5 million to Ron's father, Fred Goldman, and $8.5 million in compensatory damages (Schuetz, 1999a). The money has never been paid by Simpson (Goldman and Goldman, 2007).

The criminal trial

The criminal trial of O.J. Simpson was widely described at the time as 'the trial of the century' and it is easy to see why. Schuetz (1999a) suggested that, from Simpson's arrest on 17 June 1994 up until the verdict on 2 October 1995, this trial received more media coverage than any other trial in history. More recently, the notion of the 'celebrity suspect' is no longer uncommon (Chamberlain et al, 2006). There have been a number of highly publicised cases involving celebrities who have been accused or convicted of serious crimes, perhaps most famously the British celebrity Jimmy Savile (although he did not go to trial because criminal accusations against him only emerged following his death); and American actor Bill Cosby who was convicted of sexual offending in 2018. Another very famous case was that of Michael Jackson, who is the focus of our case study in Chapter 7. In 2005, Jackson was acquitted of charges made against him for child molestation. However, in 1994 the idea of a famous celebrity accused of a double homicide was unheard of and, arguably, perhaps still is. Notwithstanding this, it is worth noting here the 2009 conviction of the famous US music producer Phil Spector for the murder of actress Lana Clarkson (Li, 2009).

Simpson's acquittal at trial led to the publication of dozens of books about the case in light of the controversy caused by the verdict. Doubts about the rightness of Simpson's acquittal were evident and some reservations were even raised among his defence team. Robert Kardashian, who was one of his lawyers and a good friend, gave a television interview to Barbara Walters in which he openly admitted that he had doubts about Simpson's innocence. He acknowledged, 'I'm so conflicted because of that blood evidence. It's very difficult for me' (Kardashian, 1996). Kardashian further claimed that the lead attorney at the time, Robert Shapiro, told him that he thought the murders occurred because Simpson went to Nicole's condominium to 'pop' her tyres and got caught. Kardashian claimed that he overheard Shapiro encouraging Simpson to enter a plea bargain (Kardashian, 1996). Doubts about Simpson's innocence extended much more widely and books were published in an attempt to explain why, in the face of what looked like convincing physical evidence for conviction, Simpson was acquitted. Notably, in 2008 Bugliosi, a famous prosecutor who wrote *Outrage: The Five Reasons Why O.J. Simpson Got Away with Murder*, placed much blame for the acquittal on the prosecution's performance. Additionally, Bosco's (1996) title *A Problem of Evidence: How the Prosecution Freed O.J. Simpson* echoed the same perception regarding the prosecution's performance. Dershowitz, who was part of the 'dream team' of defence attorneys in the Simpson trial, also highlighted problems with the prosecution in his 1996 book *Reasonable Doubts: The Criminal Justice System and the O.J. Simpson Case*. Simpson himself wrote the highly controversial book that contains a hypothetical confession, titled *If I Did It* (Simpson, 2006). On the cover the letter 'f' in the word 'If' in the title is so small that it is barely visible, making it seem to read as 'I did it'. On the opposite side of the debate, other books have sought to question Simpson's guilt, most notably Dear's (2014) book *OJ Is Innocent and I Can Prove It*, which presents controversial evidence implicating Simpson's son Jason in the murders. Perhaps the best-known account of the murders and criminal trial, is the Netflix series *The People vs O.J. Simpson: An American Crime Story*, based on the *New York Times* bestseller *The Run of His Life: The People v. O.J. Simpson*, written by Toobin (1996), a legal analyst who argued that Simpson was guilty of the murders.

Cotterill (2003) listed several possible reasons for Simpson's acquittal. First, one of the aspects of this case that made it so famous was the accusation that the defence played the 'race card'. The lead defence attorney, Johnnie Cochran, introduced race as a key factor in the case when it came to light that one of the detectives working on the investigation was shown by the defence to have used highly emotive and strongly racist language in the past. This enabled the defence to claim that officers of the Los Angeles Police Department (LAPD) framed Simpson for racist motives by planting evidence at the crime scene and elsewhere. It has also been widely commented that the jury was predominantly composed of African American citizens and Toobin (1996) argued that this was the basis for race to influence the jury's decision-making. Second, Cotterill suggested that the jury may have found it impossible to believe that a famous sporting celebrity was capable of double homicide. Third, Cotterill speculated that the acquittal may be simply understood by the reasonable doubts raised by the defence. In a similar vein, Bugliosi (1996) proposed that there were five key reasons for Simpson's acquittal including the location where the case was tried (downtown Los Angeles) and the influence of pretrial publicity. However, for Bugliosi the main explanations for Simpson's acquittal involved the introduction of the 'race card' by the defence, the incompetence of the prosecution and the quality of the closing statements made by each side.

All of these factors could be important in explaining Simpson's acquittal, and each could be assessed in relation to the relevant theoretical perspectives on the workings of the criminal justice process. However, in this chapter we focus on an additional factor which was arguably important: the quality of the rhetoric (the persuasive dimension of discourse) and oratory (the style of delivery) used by the lawyers on both sides to try and persuade the jury of Simpson's guilt or innocence. Although discursive tactics are a constant feature of courtroom performance, in this chapter we examine parts of the closing statements to the jury made by the prosecution and defence, for it is in the closing statements that they brought together their arguments and attempted to prevail over the opposing side. We do not think that differences in the quality of the rhetoric and oratory can completely account for Simpson's acquittal, but his trial offers a good opportunity to explore this dimension of constructing guilt or innocence.

What are closing statements in a criminal trial?

Once the presentation of evidence for and against the defendant has been completed, the prosecution and defence prepare to make their closing statements. In both the US and the UK, the prosecution delivers their closing statement first, followed by the defence, and then the prosecution is afforded the opportunity for rebuttal (Schuetz, 1999c). Closing statements are structured and organised in such a way that the favourable evidence is emphasised and presented 'in its best possible light: a theory of what happened supported by evidence and common sense' (Tanford, 1983: 133). Schuetz and Snedaker (1988) observed that the closing statement typically deals with opponents' allegations, offers suggestions about how to reconcile conflicting evidence, gives advice on how the jury should apply the law to the case and, finally, highlights the reasons why jurors should deliver a favourable verdict. However, there are rules to be obeyed: the closing statements must not introduce any new evidence, and attempting to elicit sympathy or emotion from the jury is – at least formally – prohibited (Schuetz and Snedaker, 1988). Persons (2005: 55), a practising lawyer in the US, held that the closing statement is 'your best opportunity to persuade them [the jury] to find for your client and show them how to do it'. For Persons, to be persuasive a closing statement must possess certain features. *Structure* is the first, because the structural framework in which the arguments are presented enables jurors to follow a logical sequence and hang thoughts on to it. (Colloquially, Persons described it as 'tell 'em what you're going to tell 'em; tell 'em; then tell 'em what you told 'em'; Persons (2005: 56).) *Theme:* for Persons, this is a critical ingredient because it answers the question of what the case is about. *Purpose:* everything the lawyer says during closing statements should have a purpose and speaking should not be used for self-promotion or to 'sound off' to the audience. *Focus:* this requires the lawyer to remain focused on the target and to guide the jury methodically to reach this point. *Phrase:* a memorable phrase keeps the jury engaged and increases conviction in the message. *Pulse:* the closing statement needs beat and changing rhythm to keep the audience engaged. *Delivery:* the lawyer's 'belief in his/her case and his/her cause becomes contagious to the jury' (Persons, 2005: 56) because the manner in which the speech is delivered should be fascinating. While most of these features would be important for closing statements made in any courtroom, we note that Persons was here describing the discursive culture of many US criminal courts. Such things as a memorable phrase or a beat and changing rhythm might be viewed very critically in a British courtroom.

Schuetz (1999c) noted that there is disagreement among practitioners and scholars about the influence a closing statement might have on the outcome of a trial. However, she also observed that there is general agreement that the way in which the closing statements are constructed is relevant to their persuasive capacity. Academic analyses of the closing statements in the Simpson case have certainly been conducted, most notably Schuetz's (1999c) narrative analysis of both the criminal and civil trials and Cotterill's (2003) analysis of the metaphors used. This chapter draws on these analyses although its key focus is the rhetorical and oratorical features of language used by the prosecution and defence lawyers.

In the Simpson trial, the prosecution told the story of a 'rage' killing, rooted in jealousy and a long history of domestic abuse. The defence claimed that Simpson's prosecution was part of a conspiracy to frame a Black man (Schuetz, 1999b). A great deal of attention has been paid to the prosecutors, Marcia Clark and Christopher Darden, with Bugliosi (1996) describing their performance as incompetent and their closing statements as poorly constructed and ill-prepared. Similarly, Dershowitz publicly told Darden on television that he 'screwed up' and that the prosecution's performance would be used in law schools as an example of incompetence:

> The first trial [criminal trial] is a classic of how not to try a case; it's going to be taught in law schools all over the country for generations: how not to try a murder case. Christopher Darden and his colleagues are going to be remembered as the lawyers who readily messed up a case that possibly could have been won had it been done in a more refined way. (Dershowitz nd)

Interestingly, one juror, Tracy Kennedy, described Johnnie Cochran's performance for the defence as 'magnificent' (quoted in Lilley, 1999: 36) in comparison to that of the prosecution.

The forensic technique and rhetorical structure in closing statements

Amsterdam and Hertz (1992) analysed the closing statements delivered by the prosecution and defence counsel in a homicide trial in New York in 1991. They found that the closing statements conformed to a well-worn and favoured approach among lawyers. That is, they adopted what is known as a forensic technique and a rhetorical structure. A forensic technique is based on a textbook model of what a closing statement to a jury should contain in relation to content and style (see Mauet, 2017). The rhetorical structure refers to the first segment of the closing statement and is likened to Aristotle's formal model for rhetorical presentation whereby a proem (which means a preamble to a speech) enhances the worthiness (and perhaps likeability) of the speaker and, in turn, serves to secure the cooperation of the jurors. Aristotle himself said that 'good character always commands more attention' (Amsterdam and Hertz, 1992: 60): think back to Chapter 4 on credibility!

An analysis of the closing statements in the Simpson trial parallels Amsterdam and Hertz's observations in that both the prosecution and defence adopted a forensic technique and a rhetorical structure during their closing statements. The text-book model of the forensic technique, in the trial observed by Amsterdam and Hertz, first included praise offered to the jury for their approach in undertaking their responsibilities (as well as a reminder of the obligation that rested on them to determine guilt or innocence); they identified the issues that were and were not in dispute; each stated the facts, law and logic that supported their case; they dissected the evidence, highlighting favourable evidence and explaining away detrimental evidence; and, finally, the jury was urged to deliver a verdict in accordance with justice. Below the surface of the forensic technique and rhetorical structure, Amsterdam and Hertz also identified more complex techniques: a narrative structure in which the prosecution and defence dealt with an identical set of events and yet they told entirely different stories. You will recall this from Chapter 1, which drew on the work of Bennett and Feldman (1981) to analyse the conflicting stories about Casey Anthony told by the prosecution and the defence. Similarly, the prosecution and defence in the Simpson case each adopted their own narrative structure. The prosecution identified Simpson and Nicole as their central characters and told a tale about a fractious marriage and divorce marred by continuous discord and domestic violence. Their story underpinned the alleged motivation for Simpson to murder Nicole. For the defence, their central characters included Simpson, who was portrayed as a victim of the racist attitudes and behaviour of their other central character, Detective Mark Fuhrman, and indeed of the more general racism that they claimed was commonplace in the LAPD at that time. Thus, in the prosecution's closing statements, Marcia Clark summarised the evidence and Christopher Darden presented the story of domestic abuse that led to the murders. In the defence's closing statements, Johnnie Cochran presented the story of his client having been framed because of his race, while Barry Scheck dealt with the DNA evidence. Clark and Darden shared the rebuttal (Schuetz 1999c).

The elements of forensic technique and rhetorical structure can be observed in both Clark's and Cochran's closing statements. Towards the beginning of the closing address, both Clark and Cochran drew on the forensic technique by emphasising the obligation resting on the jurors' shoulders:

> Now, you as jurors sit as judges of the evidence. You are called the trier of fact. And as such your job is to be neutral and to be impartial as you examine the testimony presented. And in this regard you are guided, just like any Judge, by the law. And the jury instructions that were read to you on Friday is the law that you will apply to the evidence to determine the answers to the question that is posed here: who murdered Ronald Goldman and Nicole Brown? (Clark, 1995: prosecution closing statement)

However, Cochran began the defence's closing statement by placing stronger emphasis on the jury delivering a verdict in accordance with justice:

The final test of your service as jurors will not lie in the fact that you've stayed here more than a year, but will lie in the quality of the verdict that you render and whether or not that verdict speaks justice as we move towards justice. (Cochran, 1995a: defence closing statement)

Perhaps the key difference to be observed here is Clark's emphasis on her reminder to the jury of their responsibility to base their verdict on evidence and common sense. In contrast, Cochran referred specifically to the trial itself while offering the metaphor of a 'journey towards justice' that simultaneously served to infer what the verdict 'ought to be'. Importantly, Cochran's choice of words for the forensic technique reflected the defence's central theme throughout the trial: that their client was the victim of a frame-up because of his race.

The rhetorical structure helps to reinforce and establish rapport between the lawyer and jurors (Amsterdam and Hertz, 1992). Amsterdam and Hertz noted that the lawyers first remind the jurors of when they last spoke, which was during *voir dire* (a pretrial procedure in which jury members are selected from a pool of citizens). They suggested that this standard technique serves to remind the jury of the good relationship established between the jurors and the lawyer and that their selection as jury members reflected their demonstrated ability to be good jurors. If we take a look at the way Clark and Cochran opened their closing statements, we can easily observe the classic rhetorical model that Amsterdam and Hertz referred to:

Finally. I feel like it has been forever since I talked to you. It kind of has. It is very weird being in the courtroom sitting next to you every day not getting a chance to talk to you. It is very unnatural. I have to tell you as long as I've been doing this, as many years as I've been doing this, at this moment in the trial I always feel the same. I feel like I want to sit down with you say, 'And what do you want to talk about?' (Clark, 1995: prosecution closing statement)

Similarly, Cochran adhered to this rhetorical model at the start of his closing statement:

We met approximately one year and one day ago on September 26th, 1994. I guess we've been together longer than some relationships, as it were. But we've had a unique relationship in this matter in that you've been judges of the facts. (Cochran, 1995a: defence closing statement)

119

Clark and Cochran's preamble reflected what Amsterdam and Hertz (1992) noted: the prelude enables lawyers to appeal to the values shared between themselves and their audience:

> I want to thank you from the bottom of my heart. You have been through so much. You have made a tremendous sacrifice. You haven't seen your children enough; you haven't seen your family enough; you haven't seen your loved ones enough, and all of this in the name of justice and the service of justice. Your dedication and your selflessness are truly beyond the pale.[2] (Clark, 1995: prosecution closing statement)

Cochran appealed to the commonly shared value of taking a murder trial seriously:

> At the outset, let me join with the others in thanking you for the service that you've rendered. You are truly a marvellous jury, the longest serving jury in Los Angeles County, perhaps the most patient and healthy jury we've ever seen. I hope that your health and your good health continues. ... We have been advocates on both sides. The judge has been the judge of the law. We all understand our various roles in this endeavour that I'm going to call a journey toward justice. ... Now, you'll recall during a process called voir dire examination, each of you were thoroughly questioned by the lawyers. You probably thought, 'Gee, I wish they'd leave me alone'. But you understood, I'm sure, that this is very serious business. (Cochran, 1995a: defence closing statement)

The use of the forensic technique and rhetorical structure by both the prosecution and defence in the Simpson trial highlights the common elements of lawyers' closing statements as identified by Amsterdam and Hertz (1992). Nevertheless, the trial of O.J. Simpson was also unique because of its high-profile nature and media attention. Additionally, the opposing counsels told entirely different stories, with their associated plots and themes. However, lawyers on both sides made use of well-established discursive techniques in attempting to persuade the jury. Yet as Amsterdam and Hertz point out, there are more complex techniques going on beneath the surface of the forensic technique and rhetorical structure. Indeed, they go on to analyse the trial they observed in relation to its 'dialogic structure' which, put simply, refers to assigning meaning to events to help the jury interpret the evidence in the way intended by the lawyer. However, the focus of our analysis is on the linguistic style adopted by the prosecution and defence in the closing statements. This is because the closing statements of the prosecution and defence can be compared and contrasted for their powerless and powerful speech styles respectively.

The oratorical features of language style

In a widely cited early study, O'Barr (1982) explored the influence of language on legal decision-making. He argued that we can form strong impressions of someone simply based on the way they communicate. Thus, the way in which someone communicates can have a bearing on whether we accept their message or not. Qualities of good sense, good moral character and good judgement can help to persuade an audience in a particular direction (see, also, Rieke and Stutman, 1995). Having conducted a linguistic analysis of how court participants speak, O'Barr and his colleagues identified different types of speech patterns: 'powerful' versus 'powerless' speech style, narrative versus fragmented testimony, hypercorrection, and simultaneous speech (see O'Barr, 1982). We have seen that the prosecution attorneys in the Simpson trial were widely criticised for their performances during the closing statements and it is arguably the instances of powerless speech throughout their delivery that offer a more detailed insight into why their arguments were so poorly received. According to O'Barr, people who communicate with a powerless speech style appear nervous or hesitant and therefore their ability to persuade and their perceived integrity is compromised. In contrast, a person employing a powerful speech style will present statements as though they are facts and speak in short and concise sentences. Consequently, the speaker will more likely be persuasive because they are perceived as competent, credible and reliable (O'Barr, 1982).

The concepts of powerless and powerful speech were originally proposed by Lakoff (1975) in her study of women's use of language. Lakoff argued that women were more likely to adopt a powerless speech style and men a powerful one. O'Barr (1982) found no differences in speech style between genders but attributed a powerless speech style to those occupying a lower social status. O'Barr (1982: 67) identified a number of components to powerless language used in the courtroom:

- *Intensifiers:* this is a form of speech that places emphasis on the assertion being made, for example, 'very', 'definitely', 'very definitely', 'surely' and 'such a'.
- *Hesitation forms:* this form of speech is made up of meaningless utterances such as 'uh', 'you know', 'um' and 'well'.
- *Hedges:* refers to words that serve to minimise the assertion such as 'sort of', 'a little', 'kind of', 'I think' and 'I guess'.
- *Tag questions:* these are questions that give the impression of decreasing the speaker's certainty of an issue such as 'don't you think?'.

O'Barr's work has been built on extensively since it was published, most notably by Hosman and Siltanen. A study of theirs in 1994 found that perceptions of a speaker's self-control and control over others are influenced by their speech style. A later study by them in 2006 further supported this: hedges were associated with lower perceived speaker competence, control of self and control of others. In 2011, these authors found that tag questions negatively affect speaker credibility and perceptions of message quality, supporting the findings of Blankenship and Holtgraves (2005). Other contemporary research studies support the notion that powerful and powerless speech styles are respectively associated with positive and negative perceptions (see Parton et al, 2002; Areni and Sparks, 2005; Hosman and Siltanen, 2006; Blankenship and Craig, 2007; Zuraidah, 2009; Jules and McQuiston, 2013; and Gadzhiyeva and Sager, 2017). However, it is important to note that other studies have found powerful and powerless speech to operate in different ways in the courtroom. Innes (2007) found that powerless speech, for example, did not necessarily operate in a powerless way in the courtroom. This was supported by Hildebrand-Edgar and Ehrlich (2017) who examined a rape trial and found that the complainant's powerful speech style appeared to undermine her credibility because her assertiveness was inconsistent with her identity as a rape victim. Thus, the authors posited that certain speech styles are favoured according to the contexts in which they are used. Like Innes (2007), the current analysis of oratorical features and language style in the closing statements for the Simpson case shows that powerless speech is not only used by people who on other criteria (for example, low social status) are relatively powerless: we will see that it was also a significant element of the prosecution's discourse.

Exercise 1:

Watch 10–15 minutes of the following segment of Marcia Clark's closing statement. What are your thoughts on her style? Her clarity? How assured, organised and convincing did she look? Was she beginning to tell a good story?

https://www.youtube.com/watch?v=irpFV4SQjkM

The prosecution's powerless speech style

Perhaps the most common example of the powerless speech style in Marcia Clark's closing statement was her tendency to *hedge* (minimising the assertion). In fact, we can observe many instances when Clark referred to witness testimony and reduced the certainty of the evidence by the use of *hedges* such as 'I think'. For example, she discussed the testimony of Stewart Tanner, a witness who testified that he was due to meet his colleague, the victim, Ron, on the evening of the murders:

and I think [hedge] Stewart Tanner testified that he was … they had plans to meet at the Baja Cantina. (Clark, 1995: prosecution closing statement)

Mark Storfer, witness for the prosecution, was a neighbour of Nicole and testified to hearing her dog barking when he was putting his son to bed:

> Mark Storfer testified as well. Let me back up [hesitation]. I'm sorry [hedge]. … And at one point I think [hedge] he pointed out where he was able to see, and he indicated that the dog bark seemed to come from the location of Nicole's condo. (Clark, 1995: prosecution closing statement)

You might agree with Schuetz (1999c: 109–10) in her observations that Clark's delivery of the closing statement 'lacked structure and precision' and 'suffered from digressions or examples not relevant to the case'. Indeed, it is easy to find examples of Clark's lack of precision and coherency:

> If someone else was involved, that certainly does not mean that the defendant didn't do it; it just means that he got somebody else to help him. That doesn't necessarily mean he didn't do it, though. I'm not saying that he did. (Clark, 1995: prosecution closing statement)

> In this section I'm going to talk to you – I'm not going to start this way, but ultimately I'm going to talk to you about the law of homicide. (Clark, 1995: prosecution closing statement)

General hesitation from Clark during her closing statement served to highlight the inarticulate and sometimes confusing nature of her delivery:

> Let me tell you briefly what I forgot to tell you in the very beginning. (Clark, 1995: prosecution closing statement)

> If you remember, Mr. Deedrick testified about the microscopic comparisons of hair and fibre in this case, and when he did so – well, first, let me point something out. (Clark, 1995: prosecution closing statement)

For his part, Darden identified Simpson's motive for the murders by drawing on the evidence of domestic violence between Simpson and his ex-wife Nicole. He used this to support Clark's claim that the motive demonstrated malice aforethought, but his argument was undermined by hesitation:

Miss Clark talked to you about premeditation and malice aforethought and whether or not the killing was willful and deliberate and all of that [hesitation]. (Darden, 1995a: prosecution closing statement)

Exercise 2:

It might be argued that repetition in a sentence could serve to emphasise an important point. This clip shows 20 minutes of Darden delivering his closing statement. Does Darden's style of repetition help to achieve emphasis on the point being made? What are your thoughts on his style? His clarity? How assured, organised and convincing did he look? Was he beginning to tell a good story?

https://youtu.be/JEGBj5r6iW8

Powerless and powerful speech styles and the physical evidence

A key element in the defence's case was their accusation that Simpson's blood was planted at the crime scene. Thus, rebutting this attack from them was imperative for the prosecution. It might be argued that at a time when DNA evidence was in its relative infancy, explaining it to jurors in the simplest of terms was necessary. However, we can discern here that the quality of Clark's argument against the defence's allegations was compromised by her use of the double negative, which you may have noticed from watching the YouTube clip in Exercise 1:

If what they are saying is true with this aerosol effect, flying DNA all over the place, then Mr. Simpson's blood type ought to be showing up in other cases somewhere. You know [hesitation], somewhere out or down in another department in a rape case Mr. Simpson's type should be showing up because it is everywhere. Or even let's confine it to this case. Talk about that. That, how come if the argument is that his blood is flying all over the place, DNA is flying all over the place, why didn't we find his blood type showing up where obviously it shouldn't be? [double negative]. (Clark, 1995: prosecution closing statement)

Gary Sims, witness for the prosecution, was a scientist with the California Department of Justice DNA laboratory and testified to finding blood spatter on Simpson's socks:

Gary Sims testified, and when he did, he told you about the fine spatter that he found above – on a sock that he found above the Nicole Brown stain on sock A. Little dots. I think [hedge] he said there were like ten of them above the Nicole Brown stain. (Clark, 1995: prosecution closing statement)

I think [hedge] there were two smaller stains of Nicole Brown that were only good enough for PCR testing and there was one large stain that was good enough for RFLP testing. (Clark, 1995: prosecution closing statement)

Douglas Deedrick, witness for the prosecution, was an FBI Special Agent and testified that Ron Goldman's shirt was cut with a knife. Dr Lakshmanan Sathyavagiswaran, witness for the prosecution, was the Los Angeles County Chief Medical Examiner:

I think [hedge] we had Doug Deedrick testify that he examined the damage in Ron Goldman's shirt and he determined that – and a shirt of course is less elastic and less messy, if you will, than flesh, and he was able to see the damage in the shirt and see that it was the knife – that the cuts in the shirt were made with a single-edged very sharp knife, which tends [hedge] to support and corroborate what Dr. Lakshmanan said. (Clark, 1995: prosecution closing statement)

Dr. Lakshmanan told you, there were – there was – she was rapidly, I think [hedge] that is what he said, rapidly incapacitated. (Clark, 1995: prosecution closing statement)

Dr Henry Lee, witness for the defence, was a forensic expert:

First of all, obviously that blood drop, and I think [hedge] Henry Lee even testified to this, was dripped on the sole and Ron Goldman was already down when it was dripped on the sole. (Clark, 1995: prosecution closing statement)

Barry Scheck delivered the second part of the closing statements for the defence, specifically dealing with the physical evidence. In contrast to Clark's powerless speech style, Scheck adopted a powerful one in the form of short, concise statements that were presented as fact. In the following extract, only one example of a powerless speech style can be observed, in the form of an *intensifier* (placing emphasis on the assertion being made):

The integrity of this system is at stake. You cannot convict when the core of the prosecution's case is built on perjurious testimony of police officers, unreliable forensic evidence and manufactured evidence. It is a cancer at the heart of this case and that's what this evidence shows. When you go through it patiently, when you go through it carefully, when you go through it scientifically, logically, that's what the evidence shows, and you cannot convict on that evidence. There are many, many [intensifier] reasonable doubts buried right in the heart of the scientific evidence in this case, and we have demonstrated that. And we don't have to prove them, but the evidence shows it. So in the words of Dr. Lee, something is wrong. Something is terribly wrong with the evidence in this case. You cannot trust it, it lacks integrity, it cannot be a basis for a verdict of beyond a reasonable doubt. (Scheck, 1995: defence closing statement)

In contrast to Scheck's powerful use of speech in relation to the physical evidence, Christopher Darden's rebuttal to this is plagued by unconcise, lengthy sentences and repetitions. We see an example here of hesitation whereby meaningless words are added to the sentence, coupled with a hedge, serving to minimise the assertion that Darden is trying to make:

And the defence would have you believe that this is a complex series of facts and evidence and law and science and all of that [hesitation]. Not really. Not really [hedge]. (Darden, 1995a: prosecution closing statement)

Powerless and powerful speech styles and the integrity of witnesses

The integrity of some of the key witnesses for the prosecution had previously been significantly compromised under attack from the defence. We have already mentioned the consequences of this for prosecution witness Detective Mark Fuhrman. Additionally, forensic scientist Dennis Fung was heavily criticised for his mistakes in the collection of physical evidence at the crime scene. Significantly, Clark concurred with this view and not only acknowledged the witnesses' eroded credibility but also recognised that Fung was 'not the model of efficiency', thereby weakening the validity of his testimony:

Dennis Fung, whom you can see is not the model of efficiency, forgot to collect it [blood from the rear gate], and from this we get a theory that they seem to imply that the blood was planted. (Clark, 1995: prosecution closing statement)

The emphasis on Fuhrman's lack of integrity was particularly strong:

Let me come back to Mark Fuhrman for a minute. Just so it is clear. Did he lie when he testified here in this courtroom saying that he did not use racial epithets in the last ten years? Yes. Is he a racist? Yes. Is he the worst LAPD has to offer? Yes. Do we wish that this person was never hired by LAPD? Yes. Should LAPD have ever hired him? No. Should such a person be a police officer? No. In fact, do we wish there were no such person on the planet? Yes. But the fact that Mark Fuhrman is a racist and lied about it on the witness stand does not mean that we haven't proven the defendant guilty [double negative] beyond a reasonable doubt. (Clark, 1995: prosecution closing statement)

Similarly, Christopher Darden further criticised Fuhrman in his closing statement:

And I'm not even going to call him Detective Fuhrman if I can help it because he doesn't deserve that title. (Darden, 1995a: prosecution closing statement)

This is a recurring theme because, later, Darden again impressed upon the jury the damaged credibility of Fuhrman as a witness despite presenting his testimony as useful:

But in 1985, Detective Fuhrman was not a detective. I just called him Detective, geez. (Darden, 1995a: prosecution closing statement)

These sentiments were at odds with the prosecution's plea to put Fuhrman's racism 'into perspective'. Furthermore, Darden then gave an unclear instruction to the jury to 'decide' what Fuhrman's behaviour meant to them. The vague outcome to that instruction was compounded when Darden indicated that he did not know how the jury should assess Fuhrman:

You have to consider everything Fuhrman said on the witness stand because that's evidence in this case. And I want you to consider it. I want you to consider all the evidence. So don't think I'm saying, hey, just overlook it, just overlook what he said, just overlook the fact that he lied about having used that slur in the past 10 years. But I am asking you to put it in the proper perspective. You decide what it's worth. You decide what it means. It if helps you in assessing his credibility – and it should, or his lack of credibility, I don't know – then you use it. (Darden, 1995a: prosecution closing statement)

Shortly after giving this instruction on assessing Fuhrman's credibility, Darden repeated it, although he was no clearer:

This evidence, just like all the other evidence in the case: attach whatever value you think is appropriate. I would say use it to assess his credibility, and other use you want to put to it. (Darden, 1995a: prosecution closing statement)

While acknowledging Fuhrman's damaged credibility, the prosecution highlighted Simpson's celebrity status – a notion incongruent with what he was on trial for. Thus, while not necessarily delivering the following segments of the closing statement using a powerless speech style, the quality of the argument was weakened because of their positive references to the defendant. For example, Clark referred to the chauffeur Allan Park who testified that on the evening of the murders he collected Simpson to take him to the airport and that Simpson was not at home at the agreed time for his pick-up:

> Now, he looked at his watch many times that night and the reason he did is very obvious. He is a driver. It is important that he be on time. It is important to him, it is not just me, somebody like that, or somebody that – ordinary average folk. He [Simpson] is important. He has to do well. (Clark, 1995: prosecution closing statement)

Darden also referred to Simpson's stardom and talent, perhaps unhelpfully serving to highlight a difficult paradox for the jury:

> He is a murderer. He was also one hell of a great football player, but he is still a murderer. (Darden, 1995b: prosecution closing statement)

Towards the end of his closing statement, Darden referred again to the defence strategy of playing the so-called 'race card', but in doing this, he undermined the prosecution's case against Simpson:

> It really is all smoke. And you know [hesitation], you are going to have to be careful when you deal with that defence evidence. Some of it was pretty good, though. I mean [hedge], that stuff they did to Fuhrman [laughs] was textbook stuff from a legal perspective. (Darden, 1995b: prosecution closing statement)

In contrast to the prosecution's lapses into powerless speech, during the closing statements for the defence Cochran highlighted the prosecution's views about Fuhrman while skilfully employing a powerful speech style of highly emotive and condemnatory words that, notably, were presented as facts:

> both prosecutors have now agreed that we have convinced them, beyond a reasonable doubt by the way, that he is a lying perjuring

genocidal racist and he has testified falsely in this case on a number of scores. (Cochran, 1995b: defence closing statement)

Exercise 3:

Watch the first 10–15 minutes of Johnnie Cochran's closing statement for the defence. What are your thoughts on his style? His clarity? How assured, organised and convincing did he look? Was he beginning to tell a good story?

https://youtu.be/apelbRFm5dE

Powerless and powerful speech style and the use of metaphors

In 2003, Cotterill, a language and communication lecturer, published *Language and Power in Court: A Linguistic Analysis of the O.J. Simpson Trial*. In that study, she analysed the frequency and use of metaphors employed by the lawyers on both sides during the closing statements. Metaphors refer to a figure of speech whereby a phrase is used to describe something that, although it cannot literally be applied, serves as a representation of it and is easily understood by the audience (Cotterill, 2003). Metaphors can also refer to feelings and emotions (Kövecses, 2000). For example, Darden described Simpson as the 'ticking time bomb', a metaphor that portrayed a man who was increasingly abusive and violent towards his wife – violence that would eventually culminate in her murder. Cotterill (2003: 201) argued that metaphors hold a 'coercive rhetorical aspect' that can provide a powerful framework for persuading in courtroom argumentation. From the practitioner perspective, Bugliosi (1996) advocated the use of metaphors in closing statements and suggested that drawing on examples, metaphors and humour could hold the jury's attention for days if necessary.

In her analysis, Cotterill (2003) found that the defence employed metaphors almost twice as frequently as the prosecution. However, this only applied to Cochran's delivery because Cotterill found that Barry Scheck kept his delivery almost completely free of metaphor. Cochran made metaphorical references to 'sport' and 'war' by using words such as 'winning' and 'losing', 'victory' and 'defeat', 'sides' and 'battles' (Cotterill, 2003: 203). The use of such metaphors may have served to reinforce Simpson's status as 'a national sporting hero' (Cotterill, 2003: 203). Perhaps because it would undermine their representation of him as a double murderer, the prosecution did not utilise the same metaphors (Cotterill, 2003).

Clark employed the metaphor of the 'jigsaw puzzle' to illuminate and reinforce the evidence. Cotterill's analysis demonstrated that, as Clark summarised each piece of evidence in her closing statement, she added a piece to the computerised jigsaw puzzle which she displayed to the jury. Once the puzzle was complete, it revealed the infamous police 'mugshot' photograph of O.J. Simpson following his arrest. (A simple Google search and click on 'images' will enable you to see the photograph for yourself!) Cotterill observed that, from that point on, this metaphor was no longer used in the prosecution's closing statements. Defence attorney Cochran skilfully dealt with Clark's 'jigsaw puzzle' metaphor by undermining the credibility of a jigsaw puzzle as no more than a trivial game:

> and so that little example, a jigsaw puzzle, was clever, but really it trivialises a man's fight for his freedom, who has always said that he was innocent from day one. (Cochran, defence closing statement, cited in Cotterill, 2003: 213)

Following Clark's closing statement, Darden made use of the 'time bomb' metaphor. Toobin (1996: 419) pointed out that Darden explained each of the domestic violence incidents in chronological order and then 'punctuated them with the phrase "And the fuse is burning"' (see, also, Cotterill, 2003: 206). Cotterill noted that Darden's metaphor demonstrated his skill in 'hiding' and 'highlighting' (Lakoff and Johnson, 1980), whereby the jury's attention was drawn to focus on one particular aspect of events, thus taking the focus off other elements that did not reflect the metaphor (Lakoff and Johnson, 1980). Cotterill further noted that when Cochran picked up the metaphor in his closing statement he sought to 'highlight' aspects of the 'burning fuse' metaphor that the prosecution had attempted to 'hide'. To reinforce the metaphor of the 'burning fuse', Darden played the 911 (emergency) call made by Nicole to the police a year prior to her murder, and displayed photographs of her injuries to the jury (Cotterill, 2003). She suggested that Darden's use of this metaphor was skilled and powerful, illustrating to the jury that Simpson was an 'unpredictable, dangerous and out of control wife-beater' (Cotterill, 2003: 207). However, his powerless language style remained problematic for the delivery of the metaphor. The following excerpt initially appears to highlight effectively the build-up to the murder, thereby serving to underline Simpson's motivation for the murders. Metaphors are used such as 'a step further', 'set him off', and 'out of control', all of which could have worked in Darden's favour because they are consistent with the metaphor of the 'burning fuse'. However, hesitations and repetitions were evident and, confusingly, Darden revealed at the end of his metaphorical turn that he was not referring to the night of the murders:

> The fuse is burning, folks, and it is getting shorter and it is getting shorter and it is just getting shorter. But this morning, you know

[hesitation], I want to take things a step further, if I may, if you will allow me to [hedge]. Let's just cut right to the chase. Imagine the defendant in his Bronco. He is full of anger [metaphor] and he is full of rage and it is night-time and he is driving that Bronco and he is full of jealousy and the fuse continues to burn and the focus of his anger is Nicole. For some reason in his mind she has done something that he can't ignore, something that has set him off. He is jealous, he is raging, he is out of control. And he is in that Bronco and he is driving as fast as he can towards Nicole's house and it's about ten o'clock. He is out of control, folks, he is completely out of control. He is at Nicole's house. It is night-time. But we are not even talking about June 12th. We are not talking June 12th, 1994. We are talking about October 25th, 1993. (Darden, 1995b: prosecution closing statement)

Cochran sought to neutralise the seriousness of domestic violence in the Simpson marriage, describing an incident in 1985 as 'unfortunate' and underscoring that there was only 'one' incident in 1989. There were no intensifiers, hesitations, hedges, or tag questions:

We talked about his analogy about a fuse. And I referred to him as Dr. Darden with regard to what he had to say, and I thought I would just summarise briefly this morning the response to what he had to say and what he tried to weave together. As I said, he talked about an incident in 1985, an unfortunate incident between two people who were married. There was no arrest, there was no physical violence. The one incident in '89, the one he is not proud of, the one he wrote those letters about, the one he apologised for and said he was sorry, and there is no physical violence after that. (Cochran, 1995b: defence closing statement)

Cochran appeared to use a metaphor when he suggested that Darden tried to 'weave together' an analogy about a burning fuse. This implied that Darden's arguments for motive had unravelled. Cochran developed the argument further in seemingly justifying Simpson's distress because of Nicole's behaviour:

In the 1993 call, the 911 call, you listen to that entire tape when they cut it off and you will remember that it is unfortunate when anyone has an argument, but you listen carefully to what Mr. Simpson is arguing about, what he is talking about and what the discussion is about. Mrs. Simpson mentions the children and he says, 'You weren't worried about the children when you were doing so and so on the couch'. He is pretty graphic, but any man or woman would be upset over what he is talking about on that tape. There was no physical violence. (Cochran, 1995b: defence closing statement)

The prosecution claimed that on the day of the murders, despite being in a relationship with Paula Barbieri, Simpson still held out hope for his relationship with Nicole. They referred to a four-minute telephone call Simpson made to Nicole on the same afternoon, followed by an immediate telephone call to Paula; but his call to Paula went unanswered and he did not know her whereabouts. Clark described Simpson being seen at his daughter's recital on the afternoon of the murders in a 'very unusual mood, glowering, spaced out … simmering' (Clark, 1995: prosecution closing statement). The prosecution argued that Simpson felt abandoned by both Nicole and Paula while also conceding that they did not know the nature of the telephone conversation between Simpson and Nicole. Darden told this story in the context of the 'burning fuse' metaphor to help facilitate an understanding of what ultimately 'triggered' Simpson that day:

> This is a very, very tense relationship and things are about to explode because he has that conversation with her; he has that conversation with her; he can't find Paula. And by the time he gets to that recital that afternoon around five o'clock he is fit to be tied. He is angry. (Darden, 1995b: prosecution closing statement)

Cotterill (2003: 207) noted that the defence could have chosen to ignore the prosecution's metaphor of Simpson as a 'ticking time bomb' and formulate a different one. However, Cochran chose to deal with the 'burning fuse', referring to it as a 'specious theory' and 'speculation' and highlighting the absence of evidence for a 'trigger'. For example, Clark claimed that Simpson was providing himself with an alibi by visiting Nicole's good friend Kato Kaelin (who lived in Simpson's annexe) to ask him for some five dollar bills to tip the skycap at the airport. In turn, Clark argued, this enabled Simpson to inform Kaelin that he was about to drive to McDonald's, providing further evidence, if later required, that another person knew of Simpson's whereabouts during the murder. Because Kaelin invited himself along on Simpson's trip to McDonald's, Clark argued that this disrupted Simpson's plan to murder his ex-wife. In contrast to the powerless speech that can be observed in both Clark and Darden's closing statements, powerful speech was evident when Cochran challenged Darden's metaphor of the 'burning fuse' by rejecting Clark's theory that Simpson was trying to provide himself with an alibi. Short sentences presented as fact were evident, although some hedges, unusual for Cochran's speech style, were also present:

I suppose [hedge] that if you're in this jealous rage, if the fuse is running short, it's interesting, isn't it, to stop, go get a hamburger at McDonald's? Does that make any sense to any of you? Does it make sense to you to drive to McDonald's? There's no evidence that he tried to tell Kato Kaelin not to come. The evidence is that these two men got in the Bentley and went to McDonald's. The evidence is that while O.J. Simpson is in this murderous rage, he's worried about money to tip the skycaps at the airport because he has 100 dollar bills. So he gets 20 dollars from Kato Kaelin. What's unusual about that? Kato Kaelin is living there for free. So I suppose [hedge] he could give them 20 dollars. Then Kato Kaelin wants to get something to eat. And Miss Clark said they could have gone to a restaurant. Well, you can do anything I suppose [hedge]. But the facts are, they went to McDonald's to get a hamburger. O.J. Simpson ate the hamburger. Presumably [hedge] he was hungry. (Cochran, 1995a: defence closing statement)

Cochran commented on Darden's lack of oratorical energy during the closing statement:

You notice how at the end he kind of petered out of steam there, and I'm sure he got tired and he petered out because this fuse he kept talking about kept going out. It never blew up, never exploded. There was no triggering mechanism. There is nothing to lead to that. (Cochran, 1995a: defence closing statement)

He also highlighted that there were no domestic violence incidents from 1989 up until the murders:

Those are facts. He kept going back and forth to '85, '89, '93, but there is no physical violence. (Cochran, 1995a: defence closing statement)

As we have already seen, for the prosecution the portrayal of Simpson as the 'ticking time bomb', because of his history of domestic violence towards Nicole, was imperative to demonstrating motive. It was therefore equally important that, when describing the motive of domestic violence, there was no confusion about what was being described. However, Darden's persuasiveness was perhaps undermined by his lack of certainty and confidence in the message he was delivering:

So hey, Fuhrman testified. Fuhrman described for you a 1985 domestic violence, domestic abuse incident or incident of violence or incident of abuse or disturbing – what do you call it – disturbing the peace incident, whatever you want to call it. (Darden, 1995a: prosecution closing statement)

Probably without realising it, Darden diluted the power of the 'burning fuse' metaphor by his use of a tag question in relation to the number of times the police had been called to a domestic violence incident between Simpson and Nicole:

You know [hesitation], it was – it was a slow burn. We talked about the – the 1989 incident and the fact that the police had been there eight times before. Both the defendant here and Nicole Brown both – both admitted that, so I guess it is true, right? [tag question]. (Darden, 1995b: prosecution closing statement)

Darden continued to emphasise the metaphor of the 'burning fuse', but his apparent uncertainty about Simpson's behaviour undermined its power:

Let me tell you something, the fuse is burning. The fuse is burning, folks. The fuse is burning. And at some point, the fuse is going to run out and it is going to play out. It is going to get so short and so close to the bomb that at some point, the bomb is going to explode. ... And I don't know [hedge]. This is the evidence in the case. You're going to have to decide what that means. You can interpret what he says. You don't have to just take it literally. You decide what that means. It could mean a couple of things. (Darden, 1995a: prosecution closing statement)

In order to weaken even more the 'burning fuse' metaphor in the jurors' minds, Cochran played a video clip of Simpson who was filmed at his daughter's recital at 6 pm in the evening on the day of the murders. Simpson can be seen laughing and smiling, allowing Cochran to contradict the prosecution's claim that he was in a 'murderous rage'. A photograph was also shown to the jury of Simpson and his daughter at the recital. While talking to the jury about the photograph, Cochran's tone of voice became increasingly animated and passionate as he pointed out the apparent incongruity between the photograph and the prosecution's claims:

And even after that video, like any proud papa, you know what O.J. Simpson did? Took a picture, a photograph with his daughter. Let's look at this photograph for a minute, if you want to see how he looks while he is in this murderous rage, while this fuse is going on that Darden talks about. Where is the fuse now, Mr. Darden? Where is the fuse? Look at that look on his face like any proud papa! He is proud of that little girl and who wouldn't be proud of her? And this is post the dance recital. She has the flowers apparently he went out and bought for her. He is standing there with her. The photograph is taken. There is no way – we have no way of knowing that would be important. We have no way of knowing that Chris Darden someday would stand before you and try to make you believe that that man was in a murderous rage at that time and that we would bring forward that same picture so you would see it with your own eyes, so you would see that. (Cochran, 1995a: defence closing statement)

The metaphor is further undermined by Darden's vagueness about the nature of Simpson and Nicole's relationship in the build-up to the murders:

despite everything that had happened, that happened up until this point, 1994, she moves in January to Bundy and in the spring she begins dating the defendant again. And Kato Kaelin told you from the witness stand that they had some kind of commitment, either to each other or she to him, I'm not sure of all the details [hedge], but you heard the testimony, and if my memory fails me [hedge], then, you know [hesitation], rely on the testimony in case I'm incorrect. But they had some kind of agreement or commitment that she would date only him or wouldn't date anybody else before he left to go to New York for football season. (Darden, 1995b: prosecution closing statement)

Cochran accused the prosecution of having a 'vivid imagination' with which Darden cloaked himself in an armour of expertise on relationships. In powerful speech with the use of short statements, Cochran negated these arguments and emphasised the jury's 'journey towards justice' as well as employing a second metaphor when he referred to 'tying it together' (implying that he was going to do better than the prosecution's attempt to 'weave' the evidence into a plausible claim):

Dr. Darden for the love and forlorn. He speculates on and on. This isn't imagination. This is real life. This isn't anything for *Murder She Wrote*. If they tried to sell this story to *Murder She Wrote* they would send it back and say it is unbelievable. You are going to see it as we tie it together. It is nice to have vivid imaginations, but here in this courtroom we are searching for truth as we tie it together. It is nice to have vivid imaginations, but there in this courtroom we are searching for truth on this journey for justice. (Cochran, 1995a: defence closing statement)

Finally, Darden suggested to the jury that he was glad that he did not have to decide on Simpson's guilt or innocence, thus reinforcing his own uncertainty:

> And whatever you do, the decision is yours, and I'm glad that it is not mine. (Darden, 1995b: prosecution closing statement)

By examining the speech style of both the defence and prosecution, it has been possible to observe the potential contribution and effect of powerful and powerless speech style on the jury's perceptions and interpretations. Undermining the physical evidence and the integrity of witnesses was a key strategy for the defence and one that required an equally skilful strategy by the prosecution to deal with it effectively. However, with persistent powerless language (and acknowledgement of Simpson's celebrity status) the prosecution arguably failed to deal successfully with the more compelling tactics employed by the defence. Although both sides utilised metaphors in their arguments, the prosecution's attempts were, again, seemingly undermined by their powerless speech style.

Conclusion

This chapter has drawn on the discipline of linguistics to help us analyse the closing statements in the criminal trial and attempt to explore more deeply its possible contribution to Simpson's acquittal. Specifically, the research on the effects of powerless and powerful speech has enabled us to compare and contrast the style and quality of the competing closing statements in a famous trial that continues to cause much controversy and debate. The recordings of the closing statements that are now available on YouTube further offer us a unique opportunity to observe precisely how the lawyers' language styles may have been perceived by the jury. Importantly, Geiger (2004) argued that there could be other factors that also support the persuasive effect of an argument in a criminal trial. For instance, the lawyers' tone of voice, body language, theatrical performance, visual aids and emotional appeals to the jury may all be present and discernible in their delivery. Certainly, Cochran's style of argumentation was passionate (Schuetz, 1999c), particularly in contrast to Darden's.

There is no doubt that the criminal trial of O.J. Simpson affords academics and commentators the opportunity to analyse various aspects of the trial that draw on a range of theoretical perspectives and academic disciplines. We noted at the start of this chapter that this analysis is only one perspective that may help to explain Simpson's acquittal. Indeed, you may have recognised other perspectives in this chapter that have already been covered in the book so far, namely, *the requisites for establishing guilt* (Chapter 1); *storytelling in the courtroom* (Chapter 2), and *credibility* (Chapter 4). Additionally, there are other perspectives relevant to the trial of O.J. Simpson which are discussed in later chapters, for example, *social status* (Chapter 7) and the *role of the media* (Chapter 11). A full explanation for Simpson's acquittal would also need these perspectives to be applied and evaluated to the case.

Recommended reading

Schuetz and Lilley's (1999) *The O.J. Simpson Trials: Rhetoric, Media, and the Law* offers a comprehensive academic analysis of both the criminal and civil trials. Similarly, Janet Cotterill's (2003) *Language and Power in Court: A Linguistic Analysis of the O.J. Simpson Trial* is particularly useful for learning more about the trial from a linguistic perspective.

Notes

[1]   Cochran, defence closing statement in the Simpson trial, cited in Cotterill (2003: 111).

[2]   This was an unfortunate use of the phrase 'beyond the pale', which designates unacceptable behaviour. Perhaps Clark meant to say 'above and beyond', which is a laudatory phrase.

7

Social Geometry and the Acquittal of Michael Jackson

The man has a wonderful kind heart.[1]

Background

On 1 March 2005, Michael Jackson went on trial for the sexual molestation of a child and related charges including conspiracy involving child abduction, false imprisonment and extortion (McDonell-Parry, 2019). The alleged victim was a friend of Jackson's, Gavin Arvizo, who at the time of the alleged offences was 13 years old (Wardrup, 2009). The trial lasted 73 days, involved 90 witnesses for the State of California, 50 for the defence, and nearly 700 items of evidence. At the end, on 13 June 2005, Jackson was acquitted of all charges (Dimond, 2005).

Jackson was born in 1958; his musical career began when he was five years old. Under the management of his father, Jackson and four of his brothers formed a musical group called the 'Jackson 5'. Jackson became the lead vocalist and the band was signed to a Motown record label after they were talent-spotted in 1969. The Jackson 5 experienced enormous success and, as well as being part of the group, Jackson launched his solo career when he was 13. In 1982, he released his sixth solo album, *Thriller*, which remains among the best-selling albums in history (Biography.com Editors, 2020). According to the website 'Celebrity Net Worth' Jackson was worth $500 million (£380 million) at the time of his death in 2009. At the height of his career, between 1985 and 1995, he sold 750 million albums and earned between $50 million and $100 million per year.

Jackson's accuser, Gavin Arvizo, has been described as a 'poor Latino boy' who lived with his mother and two siblings in a studio flat in east Los Angeles (Dimond, 2005: 219). When he met Jackson for the first time, Gavin was suffering from stage-four kidney cancer. It was his wish to meet his idol, and he and Jackson developed a relationship through several telephone calls in

2000. Gavin appeared to have a difficult background, marked by his parents' acrimonious divorce, his sister's allegations of sexual abuse against their father and the loss of his father's parental rights after pleading guilty to child cruelty. In 1998, the family were caught shoplifting at JCPenney and Tower Records stores. A confrontation and physical altercation ensued between the family and security guards. Gavin and his mother, Janet Arvizo, were injured and won a settlement of $152,000. Additionally, at the time of Jackson's trial, Janet Arvizo was under investigation for welfare fraud (Dimond, 2005).

Concerns about Jackson's relationship with Gavin Arvizo and other male children were sparked following the 2003 documentary *Living with Michael Jackson* for which the singer agreed that British documentary filmmaker Martin Bashir could follow him for eight months (Shaw and Bashir, 2003). According to Dimond (2005), the singer was hoping that he could reinvent himself after his career had virtually stalled. The documentary included a short interview clip with Gavin resting his head on Jackson's shoulder and the pair holding hands. Jackson claimed in the interview that he saw nothing wrong in sleeping with young children in his bed. The clip portrayed a close relationship between the two although, in actual fact, they did not know each other very well. Following the development of their friendship through telephone calls, Gavin and his family visited Jackson's Neverland Ranch several times although Jackson was not always present. For example, during his chemotherapy sessions, Gavin had been permitted to go home and, in the summer of 2000, he visited the ranch with his siblings and parents. In 2001, Gavin and Jackson did not see each other at all and then, in late 2002, Jackson asked Gavin to join him at the ranch and to take part in the interview (Dimond, 2005). Concern had grown among viewers of the documentary about the singer's parenting skills when he famously dangled his baby son from a hotel in Berlin with a towel over the infant's face to disguise his identity (Dimond, 2005). Rather than giving Jackson the positive reinvention he was hoping for, the documentary raised serious questions about his relationship with young boys. Because of the interview that featured him, a school official who knew Gavin Arvizo called the welfare authorities, while activist attorney Gloria Allred also made a formal complaint urging an investigation into whether Jackson's three children were in danger (Dimond, 2005).

Gavin Arvizo subsequently reported that Jackson had sexually molested him between 20 February and 13 March 2003. Then, on 18 November 2003, more than 70 investigators from the Sheriff's Department and District Attorney's Office in Santa Barbara County, California, carried out a search, looking for evidence at Jackson's Neverland Ranch (Madigan and Newman, 2003). The day after the raid on the ranch, Santa Barbara District Attorney Tom Sneddon announced in a news conference that 46-year-old Jackson was being charged with multiple counts of child molestation as well as giving an 'intoxicating agent' to a minor for the purpose of committing child molestation (Dimond, 2005: 208).

Witnesses for the prosecution included fingerprint experts who testified that the fingerprints of both Jackson and Gavin were identified on pornographic magazines in the singer's bedroom. The fingerprints of Gavin's younger brother, Star, were also found on another pornographic magazine (Dimond, 2005). During the trial, Gavin and his younger brother testified that on the evening of their first visit to Neverland they stayed in the master bedroom with Jackson and a friend of his, Frank Cascio. The brothers said that Jackson and Cascio showed them pornographic images on a laptop (Dimond, 2005).

Following their initial brief friendship, the Arvizo family had little contact with Jackson until September 2002, when, according to Gavin, the family unexpectedly heard from Jackson. Gavin and his two siblings were invited to Neverland for a day of fun and an overnight stay without their parents. The Arvizo siblings testified that they did not know that part of the documentary *Living with Michael Jackson* (Shaw and Bashir, 2003), was being filmed during their stay. Gavin testified that, when being interviewed by Martin Bashir, Jackson wanted him to say certain things such as having helped him to recover from cancer. He further explained that the sexual abuse occurred after the making of the documentary. He could not be sure how many times Jackson had sexually abused him, although under direct examination he recounted two incidents of sexual abuse between February and March 2003 which followed drinking alcohol in the arcade at Neverland. Gavin and his brother claimed that Jackson told them the alcohol was 'Jesus Juice' (Dimond, 2005).

Exercise 1:

So now you know that Jackson was acquitted of child molestation charges. Given what you have learned about Jackson's and Gavin Arvizo's backgrounds and lifestyles, how likely do you think a conviction of Jackson would be and why?

It might be helpful to think back to Chapter 6, which examined the acquittal of O.J. Simpson. Folklore would suggest that the rich get acquitted but why do you think this is so?

The old Broadway saying 'You can't convict a million dollars' (Furneaux, 2006: 407) is underpinned by the popular thinking that rich defendants can 'buy' their acquittal. Michael Jackson and O.J. Simpson are among other wealthy celebrities whose famous acquittals were fraught with dispute. In

1995, Calvin Cordozar Broadus Jr, the rap singer better known as Snoop Dogg, and his bodyguard were acquitted of the murder of a member of a rival gang. Allegedly, Snoop Dogg was driving the car while his bodyguard fired the gun. Johnnie Cochran, the lead defence lawyer in the O.J. Simpson trial defended both men (Helmore, 1995). In 2005, the American actor Robert Blake was acquitted of murdering his wife and while thanking his defence team and declaring he had no money left, he quoted Johnnie Cochran saying, 'You're innocent until proven broke' (Sweetingham, 2005). However, like Simpson, he was later found liable for her death in a civil court (Associated Press, 2005). The well-known R&B singer R. Kelly was found guilty in 2021 of sex trafficking and racketeering (Spencer et al, 2021). However, in 2008, he had been famously acquitted of child pornography charges (Tarm, 2019).

The undisputed fact that these defendants were famous and wealthy does not tell us anything about the workings of the criminal justice system that helps us to understand the acquittals in any depth. Justice is supposed to be blind, in that the evidence presented in court is the only influence in making a decision about guilt or innocence. However, famous acquittals like Jackson's suggest that the weighing up of evidence presented in a criminal case may be only one aspect of the decision-making process. How jurors arrive at judgements of guilt is sometimes explained by extralegal factors that have nothing to do with the evidence presented in the case. In one of the largest studies on juror decision-making, Kalven and Zeisel (1966) found that when evidence is weak or ill-defined jurors become 'liberated' from the constraints on making decisions based solely on the evidence. Instead, they argued, jurors employ extralegal factors to help them reach a verdict. Extralegal factors are legally impermissible variables such as the defendant's characteristics, for example, their race/ethnicity, gender, age, social class, social status, and having a criminal and/or deviant record. In Chapter 4 we noted the effects that a regional accent can have on perceptions of guilt (see Dixon et al, 2002) as well as the significance of victim characteristics and credibility in the processing of sexual assault reports (see LaFree, 1981; Spears and Spohn, 1997; Beichner and Spohn, 2012). Pretrial publicity is another extralegal variable. These factors impact on the key processes involved in constructing guilt and innocence.

Devine and Caughlin's (2014) meta-analysis of extralegal variables that included both juror and defendant characteristics indicated weak to modest support for the Liberation Hypothesis. On the other hand, sociologist Donald Black (1976) theorised that extralegal factors explain most, if not all, criminal case outcomes. A key extralegal factor is social position and Black's theory would propose that the relative positions of Jackson, the defendant, and Gavin Arvizo, the alleged victim, determined the case outcome. For example, because of Jackson's social position, he was able to hire a prestigious defence team and when such a team is strong, the prosecution struggles (think back to Chapter 6 and the prosecution's struggles in the Simpson trial!). In this chapter, we use Black's theory to highlight some of the ways in which extralegal factors worked in the trial of Michael Jackson.

Black's theory on the behaviour of law

Donald Black theorised about the influence of extralegal factors on criminal case outcomes in an influential book, which he titled *The Behavior of Law*, published in 1976. Central to his thinking is the idea that law can be quantified and therefore thought of in terms of 'more' law or 'less' law. Thus, in relation to criminal law: 'an arrest is more law than no arrest ... detention before trial is more law than release ... conviction is more than acquittal ... [and] the longer a prison term, ... the more law' (1976: 3). It is the variation in amount that he termed the 'behaviour' of law, and he proposed that this behaviour can be explained and predicted by the relative social positions of those involved in any legal procedure, be it a police stop-and-search, a decision to prosecute, or a jury trial. Apart from criminal justice personnel, most stages of the criminal justice process also involve suspects/offenders and victims, and some include witnesses. Each of these participants has a location in social space and they are connected by the legal procedure, just as they can be connected with others through decisions about hiring and firing, dating apps, political elections and so on.

Black proposed that social space is five-dimensional, such that individual locations are fixed in several ways simultaneously. The first dimension is *stratification*, which describes the 'vertical aspect of social life' (1976: 1) and maps inequalities in access to resources, including money. This dimension accords with popular conceptions of socio-economic status and the distinctions sometimes made between 'upper', 'middle' and 'lower' classes. The second dimension is *morphology*, which charts the 'horizontal' aspect of social life in terms of integration and intimacy (1976: 1). It is reflected in common distinctions that people make between family, friends, acquaintances and strangers, or between in-groups and out-groups. The third dimension is *culture*, which refers to the 'symbolic aspect of social life' (1976: 1), a concept which is not easy to define but which Black argued can be seen in religion, folklore, science, technology, morals, art and music. We might think of these different domains as generators of meaning. At the individual level, Black refers to differences in 'cultural status', for example between people with different levels of education, and also to differences in 'conventionality', for example between people with different levels of alignment with dominant moral codes. The fourth dimension of social space is *organisation*, which refers to 'the capacity for collective action' (1976: 1). It is typically observed in groups or institutions and can vary greatly in the degree of formality, from highly informal groups such as friends or family, to highly formal institutions such as a university or government department. An individual's level of organisation depends on the number of organisations to which they belong and the level of formality of those organisations. The fifth and final dimension identified by Black is *social control*, defined as 'the definition of deviant behavior and the response to it' (1976: 2). At the individual level, Black paid particular attention to differences in respectability, which varies between 'upright' or 'honest' citizens and 'deviant' or 'immoral' characters. This five-dimensional model of social space means that there are many different unique locations within it. For example, one individual could be wealthy (stratification), solitary (morphology), not well educated (culture), highly organised (organisation) and respectable (social control); another could be poor (stratification), belong to a large family (morphology), be an accomplished musician (culture), a community organiser (organisation), and a preacher (social control); and so on.[2]

Black, however, did not dwell on the complex matrix of social positions, but on the way in which each dimension predicted the behaviour (amount) of law between any two individuals based on their relative positions along it. Thus, in relation to stratification, he predicted that there will be more law when the two individuals are of high status than if they are of low status, and to support this he cited studies on the sociology of law that show that, for example, rich people are more likely than poor people to use law to solve their disputes. Additionally, different positions on the stratification scale have a significant influence on the behaviour of law: rich people are more likely to invoke the law against poor people than vice versa. As he put it: 'downward law is greater than upward law' (1976: 21). Let us visualise this for a case of common assault. Black's theory predicts that victims of higher social status will be more likely to report the crime (and set the criminal justice process in motion) than victims of lower social status. If the victim and offender are of different social statuses, more law will be invoked when the offender is of lower social status than the victim and less law when the offender is of higher social status than the victim.[3] The same types of prediction are also developed for the other dimensions of social space: law is more likely to be invoked by people who are integrated, cultured, organised and respectable, and its maximum expression appears when directed at individuals who are at the other end of the scale. In contrast, isolated, uneducated, unorganised and unrespectable individuals are least likely to use the law and less likely to be successful if they do so; they are also more likely to be the object of serious legal action (including convictions and harsher sentences).

One of the most radical aspects of Black's theory is its focus on the social positions of those involved in criminal events and their aftermath, to the apparent exclusion of anything else. As he put it in an interview: 'the shape of social space – geometry – determines everything' (2002: 119). From this, we are given to understand that whether or not, and to what extent, the law is activated depends entirely on the statuses of the people who come into contact with each other. However, status is not *action*, yet the law *behaves*, so a connection between the two needs to be made if an explanation of the latter is to be complete. For example, in a study of decisions to seek or impose the death penalty in Texas, Phillips found that a convicted defendant was approximately six times more likely to receive the death penalty if the victim was of high social status, that is, 'integrated, sophisticated, conventional, and respectable' compared to a victim who was 'marginal, unsophisticated, unconventional, and disrespectable' (Phillips, 2009: 809).[4] While this finding aligns with Black's theory, Phillips noted that it cannot tell us why the victim's social status influences death penalty decision-making. In discussing possible explanations, he focused on the impact of social status on the development of the case. For example, the supporters of higher status victims may mobilise through personal efforts and the media to pressure for the death penalty; the families of higher status victims may be more organised and capable of more collective action; prosecutors and jurors may be more sympathetic to higher status victims; or the death of a higher status victim might be seen as more tragic. These possibilities reveal that the behaviour of law is not only seen in key decisions, such as whether to impose the death penalty, but equally in the processes leading up to those decisions where the influence of social status can also be examined.

There have been numerous tests of Black's theory, but almost all of them have – like Phillips – compared social status variables with specific outcomes such as arrest, conviction or sentence, and much of the behaviour of law remains as a 'black box'. For example, in one of the first tests of the theory, Gottfredson and Hindelang (1979) used victim survey data to see what predicts reporting a crime incident to the police (more law) or not reporting it (less law). They found that almost none of Black's predictions were supported by the evidence: wealthy victims (stratification) were not more likely to report the incident, nor were those who were employed (morphology) or better educated (culture). Furthermore, the best predictor of reporting was the seriousness of the crime, something that they felt was not accounted for in the theory.[5] However, the survey data did not capture details about the reporting process (mode of contact, frequency of contact regarding the case, response by the police, further outcomes and so forth), so a simple yes/no answer on reporting is quite a superficial measure of the behaviour of law.[6]

More insightful have been studies which involve detailed consideration of case handling. For example, Cooney (1994) argued that evidence, which is considered to be the foundation for many legal decisions, is socially produced and that status is a key determinant in this process. He drew on the concept of 'partisanship' proposed by Black (1993) in his subsequent writing on the behaviour of law. Partisanship involves taking sides (in this case, with either the victim or the offender) and Black theorised that partisans are more likely to gravitate towards the party with higher status and those with whom they are socially closer. This has consequences for both the amount and credibility of evidence: higher status parties are more likely to 'attract' greater amounts of evidence, and that evidence is given greater credibility. For example, the police usually collect much more information about cases involving high-status victims than those involving low-status victims; defence lawyers collect less evidence when representing low-income clients but much more for high-status defendants (see, also, Emmelman, 1994); higher-status parties can attract more witnesses for their case and having more witnesses increases the chances of success; higher-status witnesses are also perceived to be more credible (see Chapter 4). All of these processes inhere in the construction of evidence, which in turn affects decisions about guilt and innocence. As Cooney (1994) pointed out, these and other propositions need to be examined through the lens of social geometry, which interrelates victims, offenders and criminal justice personnel. This is exactly the kind of approach that can be used in exploring specific cases, such as the one discussed in this chapter.

Celebrities on trial

In the same year that Cooney published his study, events were unfolding which would lead to the trial of O.J. Simpson in 1995 (see Chapter 6). If that case was a late candidate for the 'trial of the [20th] century', it was partly a contender for the title because the defendant was a celebrity. And although celebrities had occasionally gone to trial before, it is arguably the Simpson case that focused attention on the role of celebrity status in the conduct and outcome of criminal investigations and trials. If Black and Cooney had published their main ideas in the current century rather than the previous one they would probably have given some attention to celebrity status not only because, by definition, it puts cases in the public eye but also because a celebrity is someone who is high in cultural status (Black's third dimension of social space).[7] A focus on celebrities such as O.J. Simpson and Michael Jackson therefore allows further exploration of the link between social location and the behaviour of law.

Research to date has focused on celebrities as defendants, rather than victims, perhaps because high-profile acquittals such as that of O.J. Simpson have led to the perception that celebrity defendants are relatively advantaged in criminal cases, something which is also predicted by Black's theory. However, what motivates these studies is a concern with unequal treatment before the law rather than an interest in its social geometry. While their findings help to understand the behaviour of law, they are not produced with the intention of testing the theory.

There are some relatively obvious benefits available to celebrity defendants in criminal cases (Chamberlain et al, 2006). First, they can secure the expensive services of prominent defence lawyers, partly because they have the income to do so, and partly because the high profile nature of the case provides publicity for the lawyers. Second, in the US at least, juries in high-profile cases may be 'sequestered' for the duration of the trial; that is, confined to a hotel and cut off from news media sources that might prejudice their opinion about the case. (As we saw in Chapter 6, this measure was taken in the trial of O.J. Simpson.) Third, their lawyers have good access to news media and can put the case for their client's innocence to the public, at the same time criticising and putting pressure on the prosecution and the victim, who – of course – also have access to the media. Given that publicising details about a celebrity (as inevitably happens in criminal cases) can have a negative effect on judgments (Sanbonmatsu et al, 2012), media strategies can become particularly important. There are also some less obvious benefits; for example, physical attractiveness (possessed or manufactured by many celebrities) may diminish perceptions of guilt (Knight et al, 2001).

Several studies have used mock jurors to test whether celebrity defendants are less likely to be convicted. Skolnick and Shaw (1997) conducted a study using a defendant on trial for murder. One defendant held a high celebrity status, that is, a successful, award-winning author and the other defendant held a low celebrity status, that is, an unemployed writer. The study found that celebrity status did not influence verdicts although it did influence evaluative judgements (likeability, trustworthiness, competence) about the defendant. Thus, participants viewed the defendant with a high celebrity status as less responsible for the crime than the defendant with a low celebrity status. Participants were also more likely to view the defendant positively if they were of the same race. Knight et al (2001) examined the role of race and celebrity status in decisions about rape cases. Participants – all White students – read a fictitious news story about an allegation of rape made against a person whose characteristics were randomly varied (Black or White; famous or non-famous) and were asked to make a judgement about the defendant's guilt or innocence. The study found that White celebrities were judged more favourably than White non-celebrities, but Black celebrities were judged more negatively than Black non-celebrities. Using fictional characters in mock trial summaries, Chamberlain et al (2006) found no effect of celebrity status on judgements of guilt, although their measure of celebrity (celebrity, semi-celebrity, non-celebrity) may have affected the results. In another study with mock jurors, Wong et al (2010) presented a murder trial of a movie star, a televangelist celebrity, and an office worker. Interestingly, the movie star was slightly more likely to be convicted than the other two defendants, although participants who scored high on the

Celebrity Attitude Scale ('celebrity worshippers') were less likely to convict the movie star than those with a low score. The mixed findings from these studies indicate some support for the impact of celebrity status on decisions about guilt and innocence, although it should be noted that all used fictional rather than real cases, and each used differently designed scenarios. More importantly, from the perspective of Black's theory, they did not explore the social geometry of the cases by systematically manipulating the status of offenders, victims and mock jurors.

Dimension 1: Stratification/socio-economics

As mentioned earlier in this chapter, the dimension of stratification describes the 'vertical aspect of social life' (Black, 1976: 1) and a person's positioning on the vertical scale determines their access to resources, including money. According to Ridgeway and Walker (1995), social status may be defined by a person's social recognition and prestige. Schooler (2013) suggested that a person's social status relates to their position in a hierarchical social system. Within that system, the actors occupy roles that determine their expected pattern of interrelationships with others. Statuses are ranked according to the individual's prestige, the unequal distribution of resources and unequal opportunity, and power over others. Schooler described social status as being measured along a linear continuum, such as years of education or income. According to Black (1976), the distance on the vertical scale between defendant and accuser is important in determining how much law will be applied to the defendant.

Jackson's high-powered attorneys were estimated to have charged around $5 million to defend him (Davis, 2005). Principal among them was Thomas Mesereau Jr. A high-profile lawyer, Mesereau had been involved in other celebrity cases and, since the Jackson trial, has successfully defended other well-known and famous people of serious charges (Mesereau Law Group, 2020). It may not surprise you that Johnnie Cochran, O.J. Simpson's defence lawyer, mentored Mesereau and, according to Dimond (2005: 271), a journalist who observed Jackson's trial, those who have seen his courtroom skills describe him as 'mesmerising'. Along with Mesereau as lead defence attorney were three other lawyers including his long-term associate, Susan Yu. In contrast, because the prosecution is state-funded, resources for the prosecution team are usually much more restricted. Lead prosecutor Tom Sneddon had previously sought charges against Jackson in the 1993 case and he was now assisted by senior district attorneys Ron Zonen and Gordon Auchincloss (Dimond, 2005).

With access to valuable resources and relationships, Jackson's social capital was high. As Portes (1998: 6) defined it, social capital is 'the ability of actors to secure benefits by virtue of membership in social networks or other social structures'. Jackson's durable network of similar friends and acquaintances offered him the benefit of drawing on their support during his trial, including becoming witnesses for the defence. In sum, high-status litigants (that is, the defendant or alleged victim), are likely to generate more investigative effort for their case and more cooperation and support from witnesses, while the quality and credibility of the evidence is stronger. Therefore, they are more likely to receive a favourable outcome. High-status individuals are more likely to have relationships with, or know, others of high status. This is beneficial should any of them become involved in a legal dispute and require support because when witnesses are of a high status their evidence is deemed more credible (Stanko, 1981–82; O'Barr, 1982; Wolf and Bugaj, 1990). Additionally, high-status litigants can also attract high-status witnesses even if there is relational distance between them and, in fact, an unrelated witness is of greater value than one who is a close relative of either litigants (Pospisil, 1971). Because of their 'strong gravitational attraction', high-status litigants are able to more easily attract relationally distant partisans. For example, as well as eliciting the support of celebrity witnesses, Jackson was able to mobilise very reputable attorneys and expert witnesses. The chances of a low-status litigant prevailing against a high-status opponent is low because their version of events will seem less convincing (Cooney, 1994: 850). These advantages are less available, if at all, to low-status litigants like Gavin Arvizo.

Witnesses for the defence included famous comedians Jay Leno and Chris Tucker as well as the famous actor Macaulay Culkin and the differences in the social status of the witnesses for both sides were persistently evident. Starting with the Arvizo family, Jackson's defence team sought to portray them as 'con-artists, actors and liars', words that were repeatedly used during the trial. Mesereau emphasised this theme during his opening statement for the defence:

> First of all, ladies and gentleman, I am going to prove to you in this case that there is a pattern by Janet and her children of ensnaring people for money. ...
>
> We will prove to you, the mother, with her children as tools, was trying to find a celebrity to create their life and give them advantages they didn't have. And they were looking far and wide for that celebrity. And unfortunately for Michael Jackson, he fell for it. That's where it all begins. (Mesereau, 2005a: defence opening statement)

As well as highlighting Jackson's naivety to the ploys of the Arvizos, the defence persistently emphasised his 'genius' and socio-economic status:

... the creative genius, generating hundreds of millions of dollars in his lifetime. (Mesereau, 2005e: defence closing statement)

The theme of manipulation continued during the questioning of witnesses and dominated almost the entirety of Mesereau's summary of the evidence in the closing statement: 'the list of people she hustled is endless' (Mesereau, 2005d: defence closing statement). He supplied the jury with an inventory of Janet Arvizo's and her children's 'hustling' activities to get money from celebrity comedians; hustling for free dance lessons for her children; and hustling a newspaper editor to include her bank account details in an article to help cover chemotherapy costs for Gavin. It was argued that the Arvizos were a family of hustlers and that the family manipulated others into giving them money:

> When she took her children to The Laugh Factory, placed them on stage, had them do skits and plays about their poverty, how poor they were, about the part of town they came from. (Mesereau, 2005d: defence closing statement)

Mesereau told the jury about the family's 1998 lawsuit against JCPenney and Tower Records, from which Janet and Gavin won a settlement of $152,000. However, Mesereau highlighted the inconsistences in her account of the altercation with security guards at the store (Dimond, 2005) and referred to it as a 'fraudulent lawsuit'. Additionally, he emphasised that Janet applied for emergency welfare ten days after the settlement and, again, denoted her actions as 'welfare fraud' for which she was under investigation during Jackson's trial (Dimond, 2005). Think back to Chapter 4 for a moment: these allegations undermined her trustworthiness (intrinsic credibility) and perhaps compounded her already questionable reputation (extrinsic credibility) (Rieke and Stutman, 1995).

The family's greed and lack of credibility was evoked through phrases such as 'these people' and 'these kinds of witnesses'. In parallel, Jackson was portrayed as a victim whose benevolent, vulnerable and naive character attracted people who wanted to 'steal money' from him:

> There's only one thing they need. A conviction, by you. You cannot let these people prevail. ... She [Janet Arvizo] wanted to be part of Michael Jackson's world. She wanted to benefit from the financial, the celebrity, the public relations advantages she had with Michael Jackson. ...
>
> And you have that power in your hands to make them rich, and they'll never have to work a day in their life. You have the power. (Mesereau, 2005d: defence closing statement)

The portrayal of Jackson as a victim of economically disadvantaged people was a theme that extended beyond the Arvizo family. This enabled the defence to skilfully undermine some key witnesses for the prosecution as well as comparing them to the defendant. Past attempts by the prosecution witnesses to make money in unlawful ways or by selling stories about Jackson were revealed:

> They don't want to work. They want to be millionaires at Mr. Jackson's expense. Ladies and gentlemen, when he settled those two cases in the early '90s, he became a real target for people who don't want to work. And he still is. (Mesereau, 2005d: defence closing statement)

Again, Jackson's high socio-economic status and the witnesses' low status were displayed for the jury. For example, a former maid at Neverland, Blanca Francia, testified that she saw Jackson in bed with his ten-year-old friend Wade Robson and also saw them in the shower together. Francia further claimed that eight-year-old Macaulay Culkin slept in Jackson's bed during his visits. The defence undermined this damaging testimony by drawing the jury's attention to the $20,000 she was paid for an interview with the magazine *Hard Copy*, thereby eroding Francia's credibility. Mesereau also juxtaposed the defendant's generous character with Francia's apparent irresponsibility when he questioned her about Jackson increasing her pay cheque because of her unpaid bills. Additionally, Mesereau pointed to Francia's status as an illegal alien as well as her inability to arrive at work on time and her reprimands for issues on her time card. To compound the damage to her credibility, Francia admitted that she was caught looking inside her co-worker's bag to look at her pay cheque (Dimond, 2005).

Another witness for the prosecution was Ralph Chacon, who had been a security guard on the Neverland Ranch between 1991 and 1994. He testified that he saw Jackson perform a sexual act on 13-year-old Jordie Chandler. Mesereau highlighted Chacon's unsuccessful lawsuit against Jackson for wrongful termination. He was one of five employees who sued Jackson, claiming that their employment had become intolerable after being harassed by other employees, allegedly to instil fear about speaking out against their employer who was shortly to stand trial (Dimond, 2005). Mesereau also mentioned a counter-lawsuit launched by Jackson against Chacon which resulted in a judgment for $25,000 against him for stealing goods from Jackson.

Another witness for the prosecution was Adrian McManus, a former maid at Neverland. She told the jury that she witnessed inappropriate touching between Jackson and Macaulay Culkin, Brett Barnes, and Jordie Chandler. To overcome this damaging testimony, Mesereau brought into doubt McManus's credibility by questioning her about the mishandling of $30,000 from a child's account, for which she was found guilty. In his closing statement, he described the act in powerful and persuasive language by arguing that McManus 'stole from a child's account'. He further argued that McManus knew that Blanca Francia and Jordan Chandler had received money from Jackson in previous settlements and therefore wanted money too.

Wade Robson (whose family became friends with Jackson in the early 1990s) was a witness for the defence and denied Blanca Francia's claim that she had seen him with Jackson in the shower. He denied that Jackson had ever sexually molested him. Robson explained during his testimony that, between the ages of 7 and 14, he had slept with Jackson in his bed at various locations. Brett Barnes, another witness for the defence, stayed with Jackson at Neverland several times, sometimes with his family and sometimes alone, and he testified that he shared a bed with Jackson until he was 19 years old. He denied that Jackson had ever sexually molested him. Macaulay Culkin also testified that he had known Jackson during his childhood and slept in the same bed with him, but no sexual abuse had taken place. We can see that the socio-economic status of these defence witnesses was higher than that of the Arvizos and other witnesses for the prosecution, something which Mesereau emphasised to the jury:

> Macaulay Culkin is 24 years old. He is very wealthy and very successful. He's on top of the world. He's in his 20s. You're immortal in your 20s. He didn't have to come here and testify for his friend. He did it because he wanted to do the right thing. The same with Wade Robson. He's a successful choreographer now. They came here to stand up for their friend in a time of need and tell the truth. (Mesereau, 2005d: defence closing statement)

By contrast, Mesereau dwelt on the low status of the prosecution witnesses:

> McManus is found with materials from Neverland stored in her house. She steals from a children's trust. She steals from Mr. Jackson. She has judgments against her. They want you to believe her over these alleged victims [Robson and Culkin] who come in and say, 'He didn't do anything to us'.
>
> Put your faith and trust in Ralph Chacon, who said he wanted to be a millionaire in his deposition in that case. ... Put your faith and trust in Adrian McManus. Put your faith and trust in all the trips to the tabloids they made through that agent they hired, who they claim their lawyer was responsible for. Don't believe these three young men who say, 'We were never touched'. (Mesereau, 2005d: defence closing statement)

Dimension 2: Morphology/radial status

Morphology refers to the extent to which a person is integrated into social life. On this dimension, Jackson and the Arvizos were remarkably dissimilar in their level of integration into social life. Jackson was at the centre of US society, in the music and television industries. In contrast, the Arvizo family were of Latino descent, living in a disadvantaged area of Los Angeles in a studio apartment and therefore arguably towards the margins of US society. Jackson's integration into society could be observed in his benevolence and charity with children in need, a point underscored in the defence's opening statement:

> And you'll see an invitation to play and be childlike. And as I think you already know, children come there [to Neverland] all the time. Most of them inner city children from poverty, drugs, violence, problems. They go there for recreation. It is an invitation for them. And he wanted a place where children, particularly these kinds of children from the inner city with problems, could come and have fun and be free and spontaneous, innocent, have a wonderful time. (Mesereau, 2005a: defence opening statement)

Witnesses for the prosecution appeared acutely aware of their marginal status compared to the defendant. During the trial, Phillip LeMarque, a live-in chef at Neverland, explained that he did not report what he witnessed at the time 'Because nobody would have ever believed us. … Michael was on the top of everything then' (Dimond, 2005: 263). As Dimond noted, during the early 1990s, Jackson's career was flourishing and he was planning for the Dangerous Tour. Additionally, Dimond pointed out that Macaulay Culkin was an international movie star himself (and therefore, like the defendant, was at the centre of US society): 'Who would have believed a foreign-born cook over big names like that?' (Dimond, 2005: 264). Indeed, Mesereau posed the question to the jury:

> You're going to trust him [LeMarque] over Macaulay Culkin? (Mesereau, 2005d: defence closing statement)

Dimension 3: Cultural status

Jackson's cultural status, as an accomplished musician and mainstream cultural icon, was superior to that of the Arvizo family. One way in which these differences manifested during the trial was the witnesses' ability or inability to articulate themselves well while giving testimony to the jury.

For example, according to Dimond (2005: 236), Janet Arvizo's testimony was 'rambling and convoluted' and courtroom observers thought that she cost the prosecution the case. Dimond further described her 'tortured' testimony coupled with 'exaggerated gestures' which indicated an uneducated woman with possible emotional and mental health problems. Janet Arvizo was questioned about the charge against Jackson of abduction and false imprisonment.[8] Mesereau pointed out that, while claiming she was imprisoned, she also left and returned to Neverland, and, on one occasion, left to have a leg wax. Asked how many times she escaped the 'dungeon Neverland', Arvizo said:

'I'm asking you. I'm asking you. Please.' (Mesereau, 2005c: cross-examination of Janet Arvizo)

Arvizo's inarticulateness was perhaps symbolic of her lack of cultural status:

'If you could simplify the questions, that would be easier for me.'
'I don't understand what you're saying.'
'Well, you lost me now.' (Mesereau, 2005c: cross-examination of Janet Arvizo)

Further undermining her credibility as a prosecution witness, Arvizo was questioned about the allegations of child abuse that her son Gavin made against her when he was in kindergarten. In 'powerless' language (think Chapter 6), Arvizo explained:

'I feel ... If I'm correct.'
'I think it was.' (Mesereau, 2005c: cross-examination of Janet Arvizo)

Macaulay Culkin testified for the defence. Dimond (2005: 288) noted that one of the jurors appeared 'starstruck' as Culkin, a celebrity himself, entered the courtroom. Although there are examples of 'powerless' speech in Culkin's testimony, when it came to direct questions about whether or not Jackson had molested him, his answers offered certainty and clarity:

Zonen:	Did Mr. Jackson ever molest you?
Culkin:	Never.
Zonen:	Did Mr. Jackson ever improperly touch you?
Culkin:	Absolutely not.
Zonen:	What do you think of these allegations?
Culkin:	I think they're absolutely ridiculous. (Zonen, 2005a: cross-examination of Macaulay Culkin)

Jackson's intelligence and talent made it easy to emphasise and compare his cultural status to that of the Arvizos who were described several times through the closing statement as 'con-artists, actors and liars':

> He has a reputation for being a very childlike person, very naive, very idealistic, a musical genius. ... A person who, from an early age, was such a genius at what he did that he attracted millions of dollars before he even knew what it meant. (Mesereau, 2005d: defence closing statement)

Because of Jackson's superior cultural status, Mesereau was able to enhance the theme that this made the very hard-working genius vulnerable to falling victim to those of a low cultural status:

> He's known to have developed Neverland as a Disney-like environment to bring inner city children so they can have some fun. He's known to have developed his own lifestyle in a very idealistic and naive kind of way. And he is an unbelievable target because he's attracted millions and millions and millions of dollars through the years because of his genius and his talent and through his hard work. (Mesereau, 2005d: defence closing statement)

> Michael Jackson had to work hard from the age of five to develop his musical talents and his musical genius, and he did so. He went to school, he came home, he did his homework. And a success that you know about has come about through a combination of genius, and very, very hard work. (Mesereau, 2005a: defence opening statement)

In stark contrast, unfavourable descriptions of the Arvizo's inferior cultural status featured heavily in the defence's closing statement:

> This is a family where children have been taught to con, and children have been taught to lie, and children have been taught to very brashly and brazenly, and with no embarrassment or any type of restraint, call one celebrity after another. (Mesereau, 2005d: defence closing statement)

Details about the uncultured behaviour of the Arvizo children were also accentuated:

> And you know that everywhere the Arvizo children went, they would rummage through drawers, rummage through the house. They did it at the dentist's office. ... This is the way they behave. (Mesereau, 2005e: defence closing statement)

Interestingly, even prosecutor Ron Zonen alluded to the idea that there is room to 'bend' the rules of perceived acceptable behaviour for a person with such an elevated cultural (and social) status:

> In your entire lifetime you never will hear of another middle-aged man doing that with a child. You would be outraged if you were to find out that there was somebody who lived in your neighborhood who was taking young boys into his bedroom amidst a sea of pornography and alcohol. You'd be on the phone with the police in a second. And yet in this case, we're expected to say that that is normal. It is loving, it is kind, it is nurturing, and it is nonsexual. (Zonen, 2005b: prosecution closing statement)

Dimension 4: Organisation

Jackson was the centre and pinnacle of a strong organisational network, including several of his employees, advisers, famous family members and friends and, of course, a powerful legal team. Furthermore, he had plenty of supporters from his fans as can be observed when he stood on the top of a car to greet some of them following the first day of his trial. Black and Baumgartner's (1983) theory of partisanship can help us to further understand Jackson's acquittal. Partisanship is the strong support of a party, cause or person. Phillips (2009) suggested that families are the most important group of people that a person belongs to and that some families are cohesive and persistently act as a group and support one another. It can be observed from Jackson's trial that his family behaved as a unit: his mother, father and siblings attending the trial every day. They were also a famous family with power and wealth. Let's compare Jackson's family to that of the alleged victim. As we have seen, Gavin Arvizo's family was fractured and littered with examples of problems and dysfunction. The success of the Jackson family, on the other hand, appears to overshadow the historical physical and emotional abuse the children experienced from their father, Joe Jackson (see the documentary *Living with Michael Jackson*; Shaw and Bashir, 2003).

In 2010, Black suggested that he did not originally properly appreciate the relevance of third parties, for example, judges, juries, lawyers and witnesses. According to his theory of partisanship (which predicts whose side someone will take in a conflict), the location of those third parties is important and 'may have a major impact on what happens at each stage of the legal process' (Abramowitz and Black, 2010: 44). For example, Cooney (1994) applied Black's theory of partisan behaviour to show how attracting supporting evidence in a criminal case is distributed differently according to the social geometry of the defendant and alleged victim.

Dimension 5: Social control/normative status

Jackson had been subject to civil and criminal proceedings (social control) ten years prior to the 2003 allegations, which was potentially very damaging to his reputation and perceived guilt in the Arvizo case. In 1993, a lawsuit had been filed against Jackson for sexual battery. The father of 12-year-old Jordan Chandler filed the suit after his son disclosed to a psychiatrist that he had been sexually abused by Jackson. Jordan Chandler met Jackson when the pop star's car broke down in Los Angeles and the owner of the rental agency asked him to call his stepson, Jordan, who was a fan of the singer. A telephone relationship between the pair developed and Jackson offered gifts and trips abroad to the family. A criminal investigation was opened against Jackson, but on 25 January 1994 an out-of-court civil settlement between Jackson and the Chandlers was negotiated for $25 million. By September of that year, the criminal investigation was closed (Dimond, 2005). Chandler's mother, June, testified for the prosecution in the Arvizo case and, to neutralise potential damage from this testimony, Mesereau employed the same strategy observed in the cross-examination of Janet Arvizo:

Mesereau:	… you and Evan [Jordan's father] hired attorneys and tried to negotiate a financial settlement before you ever talked to any police officer, right?
Chandler:	No.
Mesereau:	You were negotiating for money before you ever reported anything to any police officer in Los Angeles, correct?
Chandler:	Not correct. (Mesereau, 2005b: cross-examination of June Chandler)

During the closing statement, Mesereau drove home the theme of Jackson's accusers being money grifters. Beginning with an attack on Janet Arvizo's character, he repeatedly used the words 'fraudulent', 'perjuring' and 'disguised' when describing her activities for monetary profit:

> When she fraudulently sought food stamps, when she fraudulently sought disability, when she fraudulently sought every state benefit she could get her hands on by perjuring herself and perjuring herself and perjuring herself through constant welfare applications, where she disguised settlements, disguised bank accounts, disguised benefits. (Mesereau, 2005d: defence closing statement)

Mesereau described Janet Arvizo's deviant actions as part of a wider pattern of behaviour:

I'm going to show you where they have repeatedly committed perjury in this trial. But that's nothing new. Eventually JCPenney settled in a fraudulent lawsuit for $152,000. Ten days after she gets the money, she doesn't just seek welfare under penalty of perjury, she seeks emergency welfare assistance using violence [by her husband] in the home as a reason. (Mesereau, 2005d: defence closing statement)

Other unsavoury and damaging claims made by Janet Arvizo were highlighted:

You note in the middle of Janet's spousal abuse case with her ex-husband David, suddenly the claim that David had molested Davellin [their daughter] surfaced. The slow evolution of a claim of molestation. (Mesereau, 2005d: defence closing statement)

Mesereau demonstrated how this pattern of behaviour was borrowed by Gavin:

You know that Gavin Arvizo, at a very young age, made a false claim of abuse against his mother in the 1990s to the Department of Children and Family Services. He then withdrew the claim. He was very young. He was very street smart. He'd been schooled by his parents, David and Janet. (Mesereau, 2005d: defence closing statement)

Mesereau highlighted the constant tangles the Arvizo family found themselves in with the law. For example, following his parents' divorce, Gavin's father lost parental rights after pleading guilty to child cruelty. Furthermore, the defence undermined Gavin's credibility by emphasising his repeated poor behaviour and disciplinary issues at school (Dimond, 2005). Indeed, several of Jackson's employees testified that the Arvizo brothers were ill-behaved, littering, cursing and throwing things at other people from the top of the Ferris wheel at Neverland. One employee told the jury that Gavin demanded alcohol and that his younger brother demanded, 'Get me the f***ing Cheetos'. They also claimed that the younger brother had brought along an adult magazine and both had created a 'filthy mess' (Dimond, 2005: 294–5). Jackson's younger cousin also recounted incidences of bad behaviour by the brothers, suggesting that they were drinking alcohol and watching pornography (Dimond, 2005).

Because of the family's persistent entanglement with the law, Mesereau could effectively bring into question their credibility as witnesses and construct the whole case as a fraud:

You can't count the number of lies under oath by all of the Arvizo witnesses. You can't count them. They lie directly. They lie to your face. They lie under oath. They exaggerate. They give run-around answers to try to avoid the question. How many does it take to let you know this case is a fraud? (Mesereau, 2005e: defence closing statement)

Having dealt with explaining away any potential room to perceive Jackson as deviant, Mesereau went further by constructing Jackson's conventionality (and therefore non-deviance) as a heterosexual man:

Now, ladies and gentlemen, the prosecution has tried to focus your attention on what they now call pornography at Neverland. And they found for the last ten years' worth of *Hustler*, *Playboy*, *Penthouse*, things of that sort. All legal. All heterosexual. (Mesereau, 2005d: defence closing statement)

Exercise 2:

We can now see how Jackson and the Arvizos were simultaneously located on each of the dimensions of social space identified by Black.

1. Do you think that some dimensions are more relevant than others in helping to explain Jackson's acquittal? If so, which one(s) and why?
2. Are there characteristics of the Jackson case which you think might contradict Black's theory?
3. Which other perspectives reviewed in the book so far might also explain Jackson's acquittal?

Conclusion

Although due process in a court trial is usually followed, if we put aside legal factors that contributed to Jackson's acquittal such as the credibility of the witnesses for the defence, extralegal factors may have heavily influenced the outcome of this case. As we noted in Chapter 4, jurors may be 'liberated' from making decisions based only on the evidence when the evidence itself is unclear. Because of the nature of child abuse, there is probably a lack of physical evidence. Prosecutor Tom Sneddon himself said that murder cases are easier to win than child abuse trials because crimes involving murder are more likely to produce clearer and stronger evidence (Dimond, 2005). Furthermore, Rieke and Stutman (1995) suggested that jurors generally do not believe children as witnesses. They proposed that jurors consider children as incapable of remembering as much information as adults and are vulnerable to manipulation, resulting in false accounts of child abuse. Thus, the very nature of the charges against Jackson may help explain why extralegal factors influenced the decision on conviction or acquittal. In this case, the social geometry of the defendant and the alleged victim placed them far apart on each dimension, and importantly, the positioning of Jackson was favourable to his case. Not only did the alleged victim occupy a disadvantageous social position, the latter also offered a theory of motive for the allegations; that is, the accuser was set to win financial compensation should a conviction be secured. No doubt, as you read through this chapter, you may have noticed yourself applying Black's theory to other cases you have either read about in this book or in other notable trials. For example, O.J. Simpson's social and cultural status was superior to those he was accused of murdering: Nicole Brown Simpson and Ronald Goldman. Could this also help to explain Simpson's acquittal?

You may now be aware of the documentary *Leaving Neverland* in which Wade Robson reversed his position, claiming that Jackson did in fact sexually abuse him from the age of 7 to 14. He said that it was not a case of 'repressed memory. I never forgot one moment of what Michael did to me. But I was psychologically and emotionally completely unable and unwilling to understand that it was sexual abuse' (Robson, 2013). Following Robson's disclosure, James Safechuck alleged that as a child he too suffered long-term sexual abuse by Jackson. Safechuck and Jackson appeared in a Pepsi advert together when Safechuck was eight years old and from then on Jackson became close friends with the family (*Leaving Neverland: Michael Jackson and Me*, 2019). O'Grady and Matthews-Creech (nd) who discuss support and advocacy for victims of child sexual abuse outlined several reasons why victims do not always disclose. As well as self-blame, shame and fear, protection and admiration for the perpetrator may also be compelling reasons for victims not wishing to disclose information about what happened.

The trial of an individual with Jackson's social status is unique and therefore cannot be compared to any other case. Additionally, the trial took place in 2005 and since then there has been an increase in celebrities and high social status individuals accused of crimes and subsequently standing trial for them. Thus, it is no longer such an unusual phenomenon that celebrities do not necessarily hold social influence and referent power (Chamberlain et al, 2006). Academic research about child sexual abuse has consistently increased over the years, bettering our knowledge and understanding about its nature and impact on victims. Indeed, increased understanding about why victims may not disclose until later in life, if at all, helps to explain why Wade Robson and James Safechuck eventually made disclosures. However, Mesereau has since argued that their claims reflect greed and a desire to gain money from Jackson's estate (Mesereau, 2013), once again drawing attention to Jackson's social status.

Exercise 3:

We will close this chapter with one final question to you: how might the outcome of the trial differed if Robson and Safechuck had been the accusers and why?

Recommended reading

We would recommend reading Chapters 1 and 2 of Black's (1976) *Behavior of Law* because the theory is explained in a clear and accessible way.

Notes

[1] Mesereau, 2005d: defence closing statement.

[2] While many scholars have focused on other status variables such as gender (for example, Morash, 2006) or race (for example, Bowling and Phillips, 2002), and their impact on the behaviour of law, Black argued that these are not dimensions of social space but map onto them through stratification, morphology and so on. Although he acknowledged that they could be used as indicators of social status if other data were not available (Black, 1993), Geiger-Oneto and Phillips (2003: 23) found that in the US the correlation between race and social status is 'strong, but far from perfect' while the correlation between sex and social status is 'more tenuous'.

[3] Black's predictions about the impact of victims' and offenders' statuses on the behaviour of law also extend to criminal justice personnel, who themselves have a social location, determined largely by their position in the corresponding criminal justice agency. Thus, the behaviour of law is also predicted by the relative social locations of criminal justice personnel, victims and offenders. In one striking illustration of 'downward law', he used the example of homeless people who 'lack social status of every kind' and are 'a social magnet' not only for arrest and prosecution but also for being 'kicked, clubbed or otherwise degraded' (2002: 124): 'If a homeless man protests that kicking him is against the law, for example, the police officer involved might well reply, "I *am* the law." And sociologically he would be right. Perhaps he would even kick the homeless man again to emphasise his point' (2002: 125; original emphasis).

[4] However, another extralegal variable (race) and some of the case characteristics, such as the gender of the victim and the participation of more than one offender, were also significant predictors of the death penalty. The results therefore suggest that Black's theory can only provide a partial explanation of criminal case outcomes and that other variables are also relevant. In fact, Phillips emphasised that his study was *not* a test of Black's theory, because the data only included measures of victim status but not of offender status and therefore the directionality of the relationship between victims and offenders – a vital part of the theory – could not be established.

[5] Black (1979) responded that the seriousness of a crime is itself an example of the behaviour of law, because law both defines and responds to deviant behaviour.

6   Subsequent tests of the theory using a similar 'black box' approach report varying levels of empirical support for it, from little (for example, Myers, 1980; Doyle and Luckenbill, 1991; Avakame et al, 1999; Litwin, 2004; Golladay, 2017) to partial (for example, Borg and Parker, 2001; Copes et al, 2001; Geiger-Oneto and Phillips, 2003; Holtfreter, 2008; Clay-Warner and McMahon-Howard, 2009; Kuo et al, 2012) to robust (for example, Kruttschnitt, 1980; Dawson, 2003; Wong, 2010).

7   Additionally, by virtue of their acquired wealth many celebrities are high on the stratification scale.

8   The Arvizo family claimed that they were held at Neverland ranch against their will following the airing of the documentary *Living with Michael Jackson* (Shaw and Bashir, 2003).

8

The Role of Vulnerability in the Alleged False Confession and Subsequent Conviction of Brendan Dassey

They got to my head.[1]

Wiegert:	Show me again. Grab, take this pen like it's the knife, OK. Tell me how you stabbed her and how hard you stabbed her. Right here. [Mark Wiegert demonstrates.] I mean, how hard did you do it? [Brendan demonstrates.] That's it? I don't think so. You do that you're not even gonna pierce the skin. Be honest here. How hard did you stab her? Show me. [Brendan demonstrates.] OK. Now if you do that, you know what happens? Blood spurts out, right? So where did the blood go on you? Where did you have blood on ya?
Brendan:	My pants and my hands.
Wiegert:	How did you get that blood off your hands?
Brendan:	Washed it off.
Wiegert:	You know how I can tell when you're lying to me, Brendan? Your voice changes. I've been doing this job a long time along with Tom, OK? You can't fool us, OK? You can't continue to lie and expect us to believe this. Do you think you're that smart that you can fool us, Brendan? Do you want to talk with us and tell us the truth?
Brendan:	Yeah.
Wiegert:	OK, then tell us the truth. Where did that knife go?
Brendan:	It was in the jeep.
Fassbender:	OK. We'll give you that. It was in the jeep. What Steven say he did aft..., he did with it after that?

162

Brendan:	He didn't tell me nothin' about it.
Fassbender:	What, what happened to her underwear?
Wiegert:	That we know you know.
Brendan:	No I don't.
Wiegert:	You do.
Brendan:	I didn't see um. (Interrogation of Brendan Dassey, 2006c)

The segment above is part of Brendan Dassey's interrogation and confession to participating in the sexual assault and murder of Teresa Halbach with his uncle, Steven Avery. He was interviewed by Investigator Mark Wiegert and Special Agent Tom Fassbender.

Exercise 1:

1. Are there moments in the interview where the police are pressuring Dassey? If so, why would that be?
2. If the police say that they knew Dassey was lying, why did they not mention the evidence they had which contradicted his statements?
3. What evidence can you see in this transcript which might support the claim that Dassey's confession was false?
4. Confession evidence is often referred to as 'The Queen of Proofs' (Peters, 1997). Why do you think this is?
5. How powerful do you think Dassey's confession is without any scientific evidence linking him to the murder?
6. How easy or difficult do you find it to believe that someone might confess to a crime that they didn't do? Think about the reasons for your answer.

The murder of Teresa Halbach

On 3 November 2005, the mother of 25-year-old Teresa Halbach called the local sheriff's office (in Calumet County, Wisconsin, US) to report that her daughter was missing. She was last seen on 31 October taking photographs of a car for the *Auto Trader* magazine at a business called Avery's Auto Salvage in nearby Manitowoc County. Halbach was taking the photographs for Steven Avery, who, along with other members of the family, lived in one of the cabins on the Auto Salvage lot. On 5 November, Halbach's vehicle, a Toyota RAV4, was discovered on the lot, and a few days later police found the key to it in Avery's bedroom. On the same day, bones and teeth were found in a burn pit adjacent to Avery's cabin. On 15 November, Avery was charged with the murder of Halbach (Griesbach, 2014). In the days following the discovery of Halbach's vehicle, the police interviewed other members of Avery's family including his 16-year-old nephew, Brendan Dassey. Dassey, who had learning disabilities, was interrogated multiple times, on 6 November 2005, and 27 February, 1 March and 13 May 2006, each time without a lawyer present (Gallini, 2019). During the 1 March interrogation, he confessed to participating in the murder of Halbach with his uncle, Steven Avery. When Dassey's mother was permitted to see him after the interrogation, he immediately threw doubt on his confession telling her 'They [the police] got to my head' (Interrogation of Brendan Dassey, 2006b). Nevertheless, on 3 March 2006, he was arrested and charged with being party to a first-degree homicide, sexual assault and mutilation of a corpse, and in the final interrogation on 13 May continued to provide details of his participation (Interrogation of Brendan Dassey, 2006c). At his trial in April 2007 he formally retracted his confession, but was found guilty of all three crimes and was sentenced to life in prison with eligibility for parole in 2048. In a separate trial, Avery was convicted of intentional homicide and sentenced to life in prison with no possibility of parole (Griesbach, 2014).

The cases of Avery and Dassey became internationally famous following the ten-episode Netflix documentary *Making a Murderer* released in 2015, with a follow-up series in 2018. The documentaries chronicled the arrests, charges, trials, convictions and appeals of both Avery and Dassey. Following Avery's arrest for the murder of Halbach, the producers of *Making a Murderer* became interested in documenting the case because of Avery's extraordinary background. He had previously been wrongfully convicted for the sexual assault, false imprisonment, and attempted murder of a local woman named Penny Bernstein in 1985 after she misidentified him as the assailant. After serving 18 years of a 32-year sentence, he was exonerated by DNA evidence and, with support from the Innocence Project, was released from prison in 2003 (Demos and Ricciardi, 2015). He filed a $36 million lawsuit against Manitowoc County for hostility, obstruction of justice and punitive damages (Rodriguez et al, 2018). Separately, the 'Avery Bill' was passed by the state legislature, which included provisions regarding the retention and testing of DNA, the requirement that interviews of juveniles and adults be electronically recorded, and policies concerning the procedure of eyewitness identification (2005 Wisconsin Act 60). Ironically, it was during this time that Avery was arrested and charged for the murder of Halbach (Rodriguez et al, 2018).

The first series of *Making a Murderer* chronicled the contentious evidence against both Avery and Dassey; and in the second series, Avery's post-conviction lawyer, Kathleen Zellner (whose previous successes included the exonerations of 17 men), unpicked the prosecution's case, casting serious doubt over the legitimacy of the police investigation. Zellner proposed that the blood and DNA evidence and the victim's bones had been planted by the police to frame Avery. (In Wisconsin, to raise reasonable doubt, the defence are permitted to 'point the finger' at someone else (Zellner, 2018).) In the second series of *Making a Murderer*, this is precisely what Zellner did; she theorised that Halbach was murdered by Dassey's older brother, Bobby (for a review, see Appellant Brief, 14 October 2019). Avery's latest request for a new trial was denied by the Wisconsin Court of Appeal (Robinson, 2021). In a Twitter post, Zellner outlined the next steps that include a habeas corpus petition, meaning the court would need to determine whether Avery's imprisonment is lawful. Zellner further indicated that she would be submitting a new petition with the circuit court (Zellner, 2021). Interestingly, a new court filing submitted by Zellner outlines new eyewitness evidence from a delivery driver who claims he saw Bobby Dassey pushing a Toyota RAV4 with an unidentified man on 5 November 2005. The eyewitness explained that he did originally report what he saw but was told by the Manitowoc County Sheriff's Office that they already knew who murdered Halbach (Freedman, 2021).

The work of Dassey's post-conviction lawyers was also documented in the second Netflix series (Nirider and Drizin, 2018). Laura Nirider and Steve Drizin, specialists in juvenile false confessions, argued that Dassey's confession to the murder of Halbach was unreliable. An appeal reached the Wisconsin Supreme Court, where a review of his case was denied in 2013. Nirider and Drizin then took his case to the Federal District Court in 2015, petitioning to overturn his conviction and secure his release from prison (via habeas corpus). In 2016, federal judge William Duffin granted Dassey habeas corpus relief, overturning his conviction and declaring in his 91-page ruling that Dassey's confession was involuntary. The judge's ruling was founded on the argument that the interrogating officers had made false promises to Dassey and repeated several times, 'We already know what you did'. He also took into consideration Dassey's age, his intellectual disabilities and the absence of legal assistance during the interrogations. Referring to the rarity of winning in a federal court, Judge Duffin wrote:

> While the circumstances for relief may be rare, even extraordinary, it is the concern of this court that this case represents the sort of extreme malfunction in the State criminal justice system that federal habeas corpus relief exists to correct. (Cited by Nirider and Drizin, 2018)

Wisconsin prosecutors were given three options: to release Dassey, retry him or appeal Judge Duffin's decision. They chose the last. In 2017, the Federal Seventh Circuit Court of Appeals affirmed Judge Duffin's decision to overturn Dassey's conviction but they also ordered that Dassey remain in prison while the Wisconsin Department of Justice lodged a second appeal against Judge

Duffin's ruling. The Department of Justice requested a rehearing by the full Seventh Circuit, known as an 'en banc' review, and as a result, Dassey's conviction was reinstated on the grounds that his confession was not coerced. Dassey's final hope rested with the US Supreme Court but they refused to hear the appeal (Nirider and Drizin, 2018). Having exhausted his appeals, Nirider and Drizin's only option was to petition for executive clemency with Wisconsin Governor Tony Evers. (Clemency, or a pardon, is the forgiveness from the governor for a criminal conviction and is not the vacation of a conviction (Dall'Osto et al, 2019).) If Dassey were to be granted clemency then his freedom would be restored and he would be released from prison. However, on 20 December 2019, the Wisconsin Pardon Advisory Board denied Dassey's request for clemency, stating that the petition did not meet the eligibility criteria (Hagerty, 2019). Nirider and Drizin also requested that Governor Evers consider commuting Dassey's sentence if clemency was not an option. However, the Advisory Board stated that they do not consider commutations. In response, Nirider and Drizin (2019) argued:

> Governor Evers is not bound by these rules. He does have the power to issue commutations under the Wisconsin Constitution and should do so when, as here, courts fail to deliver justice. Our partners around the country stand ready to work with the Governor to develop an appropriate process for the review of commutation petitions.

Unless the Wisconsin Pardon Advisory Board engages in a review of commutations, it is almost certain that Dassey will remain in prison, at least until becoming eligible for parole in 2048.

False confessions

A confession is defined as:

> A detailed written or oral statement in which a person admits to having committed some transgression, often acknowledging guilt for a crime. (Kassin and Gudjonsson, 2004: 35)

Relatedly, a false confession is defined as:

> An admission to a criminal act – usually accompanied by a narrative of how and why the crime occurred – that the confessor did not commit. (Kassin et al, 2010: 5)

Falsely confessing to a crime is against a person's self-interest to such a degree that it seems unlikely to happen. Indeed, confession evidence is so powerful that it is considered to trump other evidence such as DNA (Kassin, 2012). Thus, the United States Supreme Court has stated that '[a] confession is like no other evidence' (Waxman, 2020); and as Perske (1994: 377) commented, 'Confessions for heinous crimes continue to be seen in many legal circles as the "queen of the case"'. It is not possible to determine exactly the prevalence of false confessions (Kassin et al, 2018); however, the Innocence Project (2019) in the US estimated that false confessions contribute to around 30 per cent of wrongful convictions in that country.

Most of the research on false confessions has been undertaken in the US and in 1985 Kassin and Wrightsman sought to distinguish three different types of false confessions: *voluntary*, *coerced-compliant* and *coerced-internalised*. A *voluntary* false confession is made freely and without pressure or coercion. Such confessions may be offered to protect someone else; to gain fame in a high-profile case; because mental illness means that an individual cannot distinguish reality from fantasy; or because there is a need for self-punishment to alleviate feelings of guilt (Kassin and Gudjonsson, 2004). High-profile examples include the 200 volunteered confessions to the kidnapping of US aviator Charles Lindbergh's 20-month-old son in 1932. Still in the US, and more recently, in 2006, John Mark Karr voluntarily and falsely confessed to the murder of JonBenét Ramsey in 1996 (Millstein, 2016).

A *compliant false confession* is a type of admission elicited from a person who wants to escape a stressful situation. The confessor knows that they are innocent; however, under intense pressure, they may believe that by confessing to the crime they will not be punished, or they perceive from their interrogators that they will somehow be rewarded. For example, being allowed to sleep, eat or go home may serve as strong incentives for people to comply and falsely confess (Gudjonsson, 2003). High-profile examples include the 1975 British case of Stefan Kiszko. Kiszko, who had developmental problems and repeatedly asked for his mother during the police interrogations, falsely confessed to the sexual assault and murder of 11-year-old Lesley Molseed after an interviewing detective told him 'As soon as we get this wrapped up we can all go home for Christmas'. Kiszko later explained that he subsequently believed that if he confessed, he would be allowed to go home (O'Connell, 2017: 103). A high-profile example from the US was the 1989 Central Park Jogger case when five teenagers confessed to a sexual assault that they did not commit (Burns, 2011). This is also the type of false confession allegedly made by Dassey.

An *internalised false confession* occurs when the suspect comes to distrust their own memory so much that they believe that they may have committed the crime because they have been told that there is strong and indisputable evidence against them. Additionally, the person may even begin to experience false memories. Kassin et al (2010) used the case of 14-year-old Michael Crowe in California to illustrate how an internalised false confession may occur. Crowe was interrogated for the murder of his younger sister, Stephanie. Presented with (false) overpowering evidence against him, he came to believe he was responsible saying: 'I'm not sure how I did it. All I know is I did it'. Perhaps most concerning is that the interrogators convinced Crowe that he had two sides to him: 'Good Michael' and 'Bad Michael'. You can watch the YouTube clip showing part of his interrogation which evidences the emotional distress and confusion that he was experiencing as a result of his internalised false confession.[2] Another suspect was caught and convicted for the crime (although subsequently acquitted at a retrial), and thus, the charges against Crowe were dropped (Kassin et al, 2010).

Leo (2009) suggested that there is no single cause for a false confession. Rather, compliant and internalised false confessions are elicited with the interrogators' persuasion and psychological coercion. Additionally, certain conditions, known as situational factors, are likely to increase the likelihood of a suspect falsely confessing (including voluntarily), as are dispositional factors such as suspects with certain characteristics and personality traits. Note that at the time of his interrogation, Dassey was a 16-year-old special education student with an IQ of 74 and speech-language functioning in the bottom percentile (Nirider et al, 2019). This means that Dassey possessed two of the key risk factors associated with falsely confessing to a crime during interrogation: adolescence and intellectual disability.

Those at risk of making a false confession

Adolescents

Dispositional risk factors include the suspect's age (that is, being an adolescent), those with cognitive and intellectual disabilities, and elements of personality and psychopathology.[3] Kassin et al (2010) argued that research demonstrates the cognitive and psychosocial immaturity of children and adolescents compared to adults and that being young is associated with suggestibility, immature decision-making and increased obedience (see, also, Kassin, 2002). Also, Paus (2009) argued that the prefrontal cortex, which is the part of the brain associated with planning and decision-making is still developing into early adulthood. Therefore, children and adolescents are more prone to risk-taking behaviours, impulsiveness and a lack of understanding of long-term consequences. Kassin et al (2010) noted that juveniles are at an increased risk of making a false confession and that several studies provide strong evidence of this (see Drizin and Colgan, 2004; Redlich et al, 2004; Owen-Kostelnik et al, 2006; Redlich, 2007). Indeed, studies indicate the over-representation of juveniles in proven false confessions. For example, one study analysed the reasons for exoneration and 44 per cent of juveniles and 69 per cent of individuals with mental impairment were exonerated because they had falsely confessed (Gross et al, 2005). Drizin and Leo (2004) found that 35 per cent of individuals who falsely confessed were under the age of 18 and within that sample 55 per cent were aged 15 or younger.

Grisso et al (2003) designed a hypothetical mock-interrogation situation and asked adolescents and young adults whether they would confess to the police, remain silent or deny the offence. Participants aged between 11 and 15 were significantly more likely to report that they would confess to the crime than participants aged 16 and over. In their survey of more than 10,000 students aged between 16 and 24 in Iceland, Gudjonsson et al (2006) found that, of those having experience of an interrogation, 7 per cent said they had falsely confessed. In a later study by Gudjonsson et al (2009), involving more than 23,000 adolescents with an average age of 15 from seven different countries, 11.5 per cent reported having been interrogated, and of those 14 per cent said that they had falsely confessed.

Adolescents are less likely than adults to properly understand what in the US are called their Miranda rights (Redlich and Goodman, 2003), which establish the suspect's right to remain silent and to be accompanied by an attorney during police interrogation (Trocchio, 2015). Similarly, in the UK, there is the Right to Silence, and also to be assisted by a lawyer. Grisso (1981) studied the Comprehension of Miranda Rights tests and found that adolescents struggle to comprehend their rights. Other research supports this finding; for example, Goldstein et al (2003) found that age, IQ and special education were predictors of difficulty in comprehending Miranda rights. Additionally, they concluded that an understanding and appreciation of Miranda rights among young delinquents has not improved since the 1970s. This finding is also supported by Viljoen et al's (2007) study, which found that lack of understanding and appreciation of Miranda rights were particularly high among defendants aged between 11 and 15. Similarly, Viljoen et al (2005) found that suspects aged 15 years or under were significantly more likely to waive their right to counsel and to confess, compared to those aged 16 and 17. These findings suggest that such comprehension is a developmental, age-related skill. Importantly, the authors argued that simply citing the Miranda rights to a young/mentally impaired suspect is not enough to ensure their legal rights and protections.

Waxman (2020) argued that, unlike adults, adolescents are unable to appreciate the long-term consequences of their actions and are therefore more likely to offer a confession believing it will end the interrogation and that they will be allowed to go home. Thus, having confessed to his participation in the sexual assault and murder of Halbach, Dassey inquired how long the interrogation would last because he had a project due at school. He later asked his interrogators (Investigator Mark Wiegert and Special Agent Tom Fassbender) if he would be back in classes before the end of the day. When Fassbender asked Dassey what he thought would happen, he replied 'I don't know' and when it was explained that he would be arrested and not be going home that night, Dassey asked, 'Is it only for one day or …?' Still confused about the consequences of his confession, he asked his mother:

Dassey: Where am I going?
Barb Janda: Where do you think you're going?
Dassey: I don't know? (Interrogation of Brendan Dassey, 2006b)

Intellectual disability

Suspects with cognitive and intellectual disabilities are also over-represented in the statistics on false confessions (see Gudjonsson and Mackeith, 1994; Gudjonsson, 2003). According to the *Diagnostic and Statistical Manual of Mental Disorders*, fifth edition (*DSM-5*; APA, 2013), intellectual disability is a 'disorder with onset during the developmental period that includes both intellectual and adaptive functioning deficits in conceptual, social and practical domains'. According to the *DSM-5*, people with intellectual disability will experience challenges in 'reasoning, problem solving, planning, abstract thinking, judgment, academic learning, and learning from experience' (APA, 2013: 33). In the UK, it is similarly defined as having an IQ of less than 70 and significant impairment for understanding new or complex information, and impaired social functioning that begins in childhood (Department of Health, 2001).

Additionally, a person with intellectual disability is more likely to respond to coercion and pressure (Ellis and Luckasson, 1985). They are also more suggestible to leading questions and, in turn, the likelihood of investigators presenting false evidence to the suspect increases (Gudjonsson, 1984; Perlman et al, 1994). People with intellectual disability struggle socially and at school. Bybee and Zigler (1992) suggested that people with intellectual disability exhibit 'outerdirected' behaviour which means relying on others to provide social and language cues because they are not able to rely on their own problem-solving abilities. Importantly, Bybee and Zigler noted that although people without intellectual disability may also rely on 'outerdirected' behaviour, they are able to identify more readily when another person's cues are misleading or inaccurate.

Importantly, Anderson and Hewitt (2002) found that suspects with intellectual disability cannot learn and remember the necessary knowledge and skills to perform competently under questioning. Other studies have found that this group of individuals tend to confess during police interrogations (see Atchison and Keyes, 1996). Still other studies have also found that individuals with intellectual disability significantly lack understanding and appreciation of their Miranda rights (see Fulero and Everington, 1995; Everington and Fulero, 1999; Cloud et al, 2002; O'Connell et al, 2005). Leo (2009) suggested that suspects with limited intellectual intelligence will also lack social intelligence. This, Leo argued, means that these suspects will not fully comprehend complex situations including police interrogations. Importantly, Leo (2009: 336) observed that 'the police detective who appears to be friendly is really their adversary'. Note that, having waived his Miranda rights, Dassey's interrogators referred to him as 'buddy' or 'bud' several times.

Clare and Gudjonsson (1995) conducted a study that involved asking people with and without intellectual disabilities to watch a video clip of a suspect making a true and false confession during an interrogation. They found that 38 per cent of participants with intellectual disabilities, compared to 5 per cent of participants without, believed that the suspect would be allowed to go home while awaiting trial. Thus, Dassey's youth coupled with his intellectual disability may have further compounded his lack of comprehension about the consequences of his confession.

In his petition for clemency, Dassey's lawyers argued that as well as being a juvenile, he had 'a range of intellectual disabilities clustered around his inability to speak and process language – precisely the skills to navigate an interrogation' (Nirider et al, 2019: 6). The lawyers further argued that tests undertaken at his school showed that Dassey had a 'well below' to 'below average' cognitive ability. Additionally, the lawyers noted in the petition that, six months prior to his interrogation, Dassey had gone through a speech-language evaluation which indicated that he had the language abilities of a 5- to 11-year-old.

On a related matter, Shaw and Budd (1982) found that people with intellectual disability have a strong desire to please people, especially those in authority.

> The bias toward providing a 'socially desirable' response is so strong that many persons with mental retardation will literally tell the questioner whatever they perceive that he or she wants to hear. (Fulero and Everington, 2004: 169)

Another characteristic of this group is their tendency to agree with the questioner; that is, when asked a 'yes' or 'no' question, they are much more likely to answer 'yes' even if it implies something that obviously cannot be true (Sigelman et al, 1982). This behaviour is known as acquiescence and generally refers to behavioural compliance (Finlay and Lyons, 2002). For example, Sigelman et al (1981) found that 73 per cent of people with intellectual disability answered 'yes' to the question 'Does it usually snow in the summer here?' when they live in Texas. And the more difficult a question, the more likely this group is to answer 'yes'. Finlay and Lyons (2002) suggested that earlier research (see Cronbach, 1942, 1950) on acquiescence found that when asked a 'true' or 'false' question, students tend to reply 'true' when in doubt.[4]

It is therefore significant to note that during the interrogations on 27 February and 13 March, Dassey was asked a total of 26 'yes' or 'no' questions and he offered a 'yes' reply on 20 occasions. For example:

Wiegert:	He said that he [Steven] cut himself, while he was stabbing her [Teresa]? Yes or no?
Dassey:	Yes.
Wiegert:	Tell, just try to go through in your mind exactly what he told you about him cutting himself. Put it in your own words.
Dassey:	... He ... he said ...
Wiegert:	OK. Is everything you're telling me today, Brendan, the truth? Yes or no?
Dassey:	Yes.

When asked to affirm who killed Halbach, Dassey replied 'Steve'.

Wiegert:	And Steven did it by how again, tell me that again.
Dassey:	That he stabbed her.
Fassbender:	OK. He had told you that? Yes or no?
Dassey:	Yes. (Interrogation of Brendan Dassey, 2006a)

The Gudjonsson Suggestibility Scale (Gudjonsson, 1984) measures how people respond to leading questions and to disapproval during an interrogation. Studies using this scale in the UK demonstrate that individuals with intellectual disability are more likely to exhibit suggestibility than those without intellectual disability. This group of individuals is also more likely to change the answers when presented with mild disapproval (see also O'Connell et al, 2005). So it is not surprising that, in the petition for clemency, Dassey's lawyers argued that 'At trial, psychological testing indicated that his disabilities rendered him more compliant and suggestible than 95% of the population' (Nirider et al, 2019: 7).

How a compliant or internalised false confession occurs

The misclassification error

Leo (2009) suggested that law enforcement officers make a sequence of errors during the interrogation and it is this psychological process that leads to a suspect falsely confessing. These are: the misclassification error, the coercion error and the contamination error. These errors are observed in the most widely used interrogation strategy in the US, the Reid Technique, which according to Pérez-Sales (2017: 199) is 'the most well-known coercive interrogation paradigm'. The technique involves a three-stage process: first, investigators should undertake a factual analysis of the offence before they interrogate the suspect; second, a non-accusatory interview should take place to provide investigators with the opportunity to undertake a Behavioural Analysis Interview (BAI). This involves the investigators making observations of behavioural cues of deception in order to determine whether the suspect is guilty or not. If the investigators believe that the suspect has not told the truth, then the third stage, the accusatory interrogation, is initiated.

Exercise 2:

During Dassey's interrogation on 1 March 2006, he confessed to the sexual assault and murder of Halbach. One of the interrogators talking to Dassey was Investigator Mark Wiegert. Conduct a Google search of 'Brendan Dassey interrogation' and you will find several still images of the interrogation.

1. What do you observe about the body language of Dassey and of Wiegert?
2. Does Dassey's body language indicate anything about his honesty or dishonesty? Think about the reasons for your answer.

Officers trained in the Reid Technique observe non-verbal behaviours of suspects in order to identify deception. Inbau et al (2001), who promote the technique, claimed that deceptive suspects sit in a slouched position and that they will not directly face the interrogator. Accordingly, deceptive suspects will convey 'protective gestures' such as covering their eyes or mouth. Other deceptive indicators include foot bouncing, decreased eye-contact with the interrogator, greater response latency (time taken for the suspect to answer the question), and speaking more slowly and with an increased pitch of the voice. Inbau and his colleagues have also claimed that investigators are able to detect deception via verbal and non-verbal cues and behavioural attitudes with a success rate of 85 per cent (Gudjonsson, 2018), although Leo (2008) suggests that trainees are told that the rate of accuracy is actually 100 per cent. We can see evidence of behavioural analysis during one of Dassey's interrogations when Investigator Wiegert explained to him:

> You know how I can tell when you're lying to me, Brendan? Your voice changes. I've been doing this job a long time along with Tom, OK? You can't fool us, OK? You can't continue to lie and expect us to believe this. (Interrogation of Brendan Dassey, 2006c)

This first error, the *misclassification error*, is rooted in the investigators' false confidence that they are able to accurately discern between truth-tellers and deceivers; thus, a mistake is made when an innocent suspect is deemed guilty.

Inbau et al (2013: 187) defend the Reid Technique arguing:

> It must be remembered that none of the steps is apt to make an innocent person confess and that all the steps are legally as well as morally justified.

However, Leo (2009) argued that detectives are falsely taught that they are able to accurately discern truth-tellers and deceivers. What do you recall about the research on detecting deception in Chapter 4? Does it support the claims of Inbau et al? Note that the petition for clemency quoted Dassey's Individualized Education Program (IEP)[5] which stated 'Brendan will occasionally ask questions when he is unsure; however, eye contact and participation during discussions with adults and peers is limited' (Nirider et al, 2019: 7).

Leo (2009: 334) contended that the misclassification error is necessary for false confessions to occur and to this end 'it is both the first and the most consequential error that police make'. Once the misclassification error has been made and the investigators have determined that the suspect's guilt 'seems definite or reasonably certain' (Inbau et al, 2013: 187), then the guilt-presumptive nine-step process of the Reid Technique can begin. The suspect is confronted, deceived, manipulated and presented with suggestions and themes, which are all tactics designed to break down resistance (Gudjonsson, 2018). This is known as the *coercion error*. With the coercion error, innocent suspects are at risk of falsely confessing. Coercive methods are characterised by maximisation and minimisation tactics, both of which can be observed during the interrogations of Dassey. Investigators may 'maximise' the evidence or possible punishment to the suspect; that is, they may imply that there is *more* evidence than there actually is or that punishment will be *more* severe if suspects are not forthcoming with information. Conversely, investigators may 'minimise' the suspect's culpability or possible punishment, that is, they may imply that the suspect is *less* culpable than their co-defendant or because they were provoked. Additionally, they may imply that the severity of the punishment will be *less* if they provide the investigators with information that will facilitate the investigation.

The coercion error: maximisation tactics

In the US, it is legal for investigators to deceive suspects and tell them that they have evidence against them when they do not and, in fact, this is endorsed in the Reid Technique (Kassin et al, 2010). Because of the investigators' apparent certainty of the suspect's guilt, the nine-step process of interrogation begins with a strong presumption of guilt and the strategies employed aim to send a message to the suspect that their denials are futile (Kassin et al, 2010).

Maximisation tactics may include presentations of false evidence such as telling the suspect that a witness positively identified them as the assailant or that the police have found their fingerprints or blood at the crime scene. In relation to adolescents specifically, Kassin et al (2010) reviewed some experiments with this population and their responses to mock crimes and interrogations. For example, Redlich and Goodman (2003) found that in studies using the Kassin and Kiechel (1996) computer crash paradigm, adolescents were more likely to confess than young adults, particularly when presented with false evidence against them. In another study, Candel et al (2005) did not present the children with false evidence and yet more than a third of the sample confessed to pressing the shift key[6] and, interestingly, 89 per cent of the confessors internalised their confession (meaning they believed that they were guilty). This kind of deception has been shown to leave suspects vulnerable to manipulation, leading to their perceptions of various phenomena becoming significantly altered.

In Dassey's case, during his second interrogation he explained that he and Avery put some branches, a cabinet, tyres and a vehicle seat on the fire. When Dassey's interrogators asked him who put the vehicle seat on the fire, he said that both he and Avery did. In response, Fassbender said:

> I gotta believe you did see something in the fire. You wanna know why I believe that? Because Teresa's bones were intermingled in that seat. And the only way her bones were intermingled in that seat is if she was put on that seat or if the seat was put on top of her. (Interrogation of Brendan Dassey, 2006a)

This was a presentation of false evidence; Halbach's bones were not found intermingled in the vehicle seat (Nirider et al, 2019). Additionally, Fassbender and Wiegert persistently told Dassey that they knew 'what happened', serving as prompts to overcome his denial.

During Dassey's interrogation on 1 March 2006, in which he confessed to the sexual assault and murder of Halbach, his interrogators told Brendan 'we know [what happened]' 26 times. For example:

Wiegert: You know. Honesty is the only thing that will set you free. Right? And **we know**, like Tom said, **we know**, we reviewed those tapes. **We know** there's some things you left out and **we know** there's some things that maybe weren't quite correct that you told us. OK. We've done, we've been investigating this a long time. **We pretty**

much know everything, that's why we're talking to you again today.

Wiegert: Brendan, **I already know. You know we know.** OK. Come on, buddy. Let's get this out, OK?

Wiegert: **We know** what happened, it's OK.

Wiegert: Brendan, be honest. You were there when she died and **we know** that. Don't start lying now. **We know** you were there. What happened?

Wiegert: **We know** you shot her too. (Interrogation of Brendan Dassey, 2006b)

During the interrogation on 27 February 2006:

Wiegert: That burn pit, Brendan, was no bigger than this table. OK? You know how big it was. I find it quite difficult to believe that if there was a body in that, Brendan, that you wouldn't have seen something like a hand, or a foot, a head, hair, something. OK? **We know** you saw something. And maybe you've tried to block it out but it's really important that you remember. Think back.

Wiegert: Was there blood on those clothes? Be honest, Brendan. **We know. We already know you know.** Help us out. Think of yourself here. Help that family. (Interrogation of Brendan Dassey, 2006a)

On 13 May 2006, the same tactic was utilised at different points during the interrogation:

Wiegert: Come on, Brendan. What's he telling her at this time? **We know** there's some talking going on, OK. **We, we know** that.

Fassbender: **We know** you were involved in this. There's no question about that.

Wiegert: **We know** you lied to us in the past, right? (Interrogation of Brendan Dassey, 2006c)

During this final interrogation of Dassey, as we saw at the beginning of this chapter, Fassbender asked him what happened to the victim's underwear and he was immediately followed by Weigert:

Wiegert: That **we know you know.**

Dassey: No I don't.

Wiegert: You do. (Interrogation of Brendan Dassey, 2006c)

The coercion error: minimisation tactics

Kassin et al (2010) argued that minimisation increases the risk of innocent suspects falsely confessing. Minimisation tactics include investigators implying that the suspect is less culpable than their co-accused or minimising the legal consequences of a confession. The Reid Technique advises developing a 'theme' which involves placing 'the moral blame for [the] actions on some other person or some outside set of circumstances'. According to Reid and his colleagues, such a technique is founded on a fairly common tendency to minimise actions by blaming someone or something else. Interrogators are advised to present as sympathetic and understanding while emphasising their desire to work with the suspect to resolve the issue (John E. Reid and Associates Inc., nd). Evidence of theme development according to the Reid Technique (and therefore of this kind of minimisation tactic) can be observed during Dassey's interrogations. Thus, Fassbender and Wiegert frequently reassured Dassey that it was not his fault, and that Avery, his uncle, was to blame instead. For example:

Wiegert:	Did you help him put that body in the fire? If you did, it's OK. (Interrogation of Brendan Dassey, 2006a)
Wiegert:	Let's be honest here, Brendan. If you helped him, it's OK, because he was telling you to do it. You didn't do it on your own. (Interrogation of Brendan Dassey, 2006b)
Fassbender:	He used you for this. (Interrogation of Brendan Dassey, 2006b)

In their attempt to elicit a confession to the sexual assault of Halbach, Wiegert and Fassbender minimised Dassey's involvement by continuing with the theme that Steven 'made him do it':

Wiegert:	OK. What happened next? Remember, we already know, but we need to hear it from you. It's OK. It's not your fault. What happens next?
Fassbender:	Does he [Steven] ask you?
Wiegert:	He does, doesn't he?
Fassbender:	We know.
Wiegert:	He asks you doesn't he? What does he ask you?
Dassey:	That if I wanted a girlfriend. (Interrogation of Brendan Dassey, 2006b)

The same theme can also be observed at other points during the interrogation:

Fassbender:	What does Steven make you do?

Wiegert immediately followed with the comment:

Wiegert: It's not your fault, he makes you do it. (Interrogation of
                Brendan Dassey, 2006b)

During the same interrogation, both Fassbender and Wiegert appeared to
warn Dassey that Avery was and would likely continue implicating Dassey
in the crime:

Fassbender: It's going to be a lot easier on you down the road, ah,
                if this goes to trial and stuff like that. We need to know
                that, because it's probably going to come out. Think of
                Steven for a second. Steven is already starting to say some
                things and eventually he is gonna potentially lay some
                crap on you and try and make it look like you are the bad
                person here. Um, and we don't want that. (Interrogation
                of Brendan Dassey, 2006b)

The investigators also utilised the other minimisation tactic of understating
the legal consequences of a confession. For example, Wiegert reassured
Dassey that because he was being the 'good guy', he would be the one to
get a 'better deal':

Wiegert: Because you're being the good guy here. You're the
                one that's saying 'You know what? Maybe I made some
                mistakes but here's what I did.' The other guy involved
                in this doesn't want to help himself. All he wants to do is
                blame everybody else. OK? And by you talking with us,
                it's, it's helping you. OK? Because the honest person is
                the one who's gonna get a better deal out of everything.
                You know how that works. (Interrogation of Brendan
                Dassey, 2006b)

The minimisation through implied leniency is designed to have the effect
of making it seem that confessing is a means of escape (Kassin et al, 2010).
Kassin et al suggested that when hearing speech people tend to 'read between
the lines', that is, rather than recalling precisely what was said, they state
what was implied instead. For example, when people hear the sentence 'The
flimsy shelf weakened under the weight of books', people often mistakenly
recall that the shelf in fact collapsed (see Harris and Monaco, 1978; Hilton,
1995; Chan and McDermott, 2006; Kassin et al, 2010). Thus, suspects may
perceive leniency when minimising comments are made (for example, 'it's
not your fault') or suggestions that they were pressured into committing

the crime. Research supports this theory (see Kassin and McNall, 1991; Russano et al, 2005; Klaver et al, 2008). For example, Ofshe and Leo (1997) analysed 125 recorded transcripts of interrogations and found that police often employ minimisation techniques that imply leniency, while harsher sentencing was implied should a confession not be offered.

Another example of minimising the legal consequences of a confession can be observed in the interrogation of Kiszko, mentioned earlier, where it was implied that if he provided information then everyone could go home for Christmas. Such beliefs of leniency are also relevant in the interrogations of the suspects in the Central Park Jogger case where the defendants claimed that promises of going home were made to them (Kassin et al, 2010). Leniency was also a tactic employed by Fassbender and Wiegert up until Dassey confessed to the murder of Halbach. As we have seen, during his second interrogation, Dassey was questioned about what he saw burning in the fire pit next to Avery's residence on the night Halbach went missing. Fassbender asserted that Dassey must have seen Halbach's body on the fire pit because her bones were intermingled with a car seat that Dassey acknowledged helping Avery put on the fire. At the start of the interrogation, Fassbender implied that he and Wiegert were actually protecting him from being charged as their colleagues would have seemingly preferred:

Fassbender: … how old are you 16, 17? You're a kid, you know and we got, we've got people back at the sheriff's department, District Attorney's office, and they're looking at this now saying there's no way that Brendan Dassey was out there and didn't see something. They're talking about trying to link Brendan Dassey with this event. They're not saying that Brendan did it, they're saying that Brendan had something to do with it or the cover up of it, which would mean Brendan Dassey could potentially be facing charges for that. And Mark and I are both going well, ah he's a kid, he had nothing to do with this, and whether Steve got him out there to help build a fire and he inadvertently saw some things that's what it would be. It wouldn't be that Brendan act-actually helped him dispose of this body. (Interrogation of Brendan Dassey, 2006a)

This assertion is later repeated:

Fassbender: We've gotten a lot of information and you know some people don't care, some people back there say 'No, we'll just charge him'. We said 'No, let us talk to him, give him the opportunity to come forward with the information that he has, and get it off of his chest'.

Examples of implied leniency can also be observed in other parts of the interrogation:

Fassbender:	I promise I will not let you high and dry, I'll stand behind you.
Fassbender:	Mark and I both can go back to the district attorney and say, ah, ... Dassey ... came forward and finally told us. Can imagine how this was weighing on him? They'll understand that.
Wiegert:	We'll go to bat for ya, but you have to be honest with us.
Wiegert:	We're not gonna run back and tell your grandma and grandpa what you told us or anything like that.
Fassbender:	Mark and I, yeah we're cops, we're investigators and stuff like that, but I'm not right now. I'm a father that has a kid your age too. I wanna be here for you. There's nothing I'd like more than to come over and give you a hug 'cause I know you're hurtin'. (Interrogation of Brendan Dassey, 2006a)

Leniency was implied in different parts of the third interrogation during which Dassey confessed to the crime:

Wiegert:	We know you were back there. Let's get it all out today and this will all be over with.
Fassbender:	Your cooperation and help with us is gonna work in your favor.
Fassbender:	I'm thinking you're all right. OK, you don't have to worry about things.
Fassbender:	We're in your corner.
Wiegert:	Honesty here, Brendan, is the thing that's gonna help you. OK? No matter what you did, we can work through that. OK? We can't make any promises but we'll stand behind you no matter what you did. OK?
Fassbender:	We, we feel that, that maybe, I think Mark and I both feel that maybe there's a, some more that you could tell us, um, that you may have held back for whatever reasons and I wanna assure you that Mark and I both are in your corner, we're on your side, and you did tell us yourself that one of the reasons you hadn't come

forward yet was because you're afraid, you're scared, and, and one of the reasons you were scared was that you would be implicated in this, or people would say that you helped or did this. (Interrogation of Brendan Dassey, 2006b)

Towards the end of the interrogation, Fassbender explained that Dassey would need to write down everything he had said:

Fassbender: So just make sure it's the truth and you have nothing to worry about, OK?

With these minimisation tactics being used during his second and third interrogations, it is noteworthy that during the fourth and final interrogation, Dassey had already confessed to the crime and the minimisation strategies were absent. The tone of Fassbender and Wiegert was markedly different from the previous interrogations and their frustration with Dassey's many inconsistencies was apparent:

Fassbender: If the truth doesn't match up with the facts, you know I'm ready to tell Mark we're leaving.
Wiegert: And I'm not gonna sit here, Brendan, and allow you to lie to me any more ... I've got enough evidence without you. ... Do you wanna help yourself? Then why are you lying? Look at me, Brendan. Brendan? Brendan? Brendan?
Wiegert: Do you think you're that smart that you can fool us, Brendan? Do you want to talk with us and tell us the truth? (Interrogation of Brendan Dassey, 2006c)

The contamination error

Drizin (2018) explained that in order to secure a conviction, interrogators need the suspect to talk about details of the crime that are only known to the perpetrator. Because an innocent suspect is unable to do this, the contamination error is made. This is when the investigators feed the suspect facts about the crime. Drizin concluded that investigators offered Dassey three key facts that were unknown to the public at the time of his interrogation. First, they told Dassey that Halbach was shot in the head; second, they said that a burn barrel in the Avery salvage yard contained the victim's personal items; and third, Dassey was told that someone opened the hood [bonnet] of the car and did something to the engine. The process of providing these facts to Dassey and then eliciting them from him meant that he appeared to 'guess' the answers to the investigators' questions when it became clear that his responses were not what they were hoping to hear. During the interrogation on 1 March in which Dassey confessed, he spoke about Avery stabbing the victim. However, knowing from the forensic evidence that Halbach was shot in the head, Fassbender and Wiegert made several attempts to elicit this information from Dassey:

Wiegert:	What else did he do to her? We know something else was done. Tell us, and what else did you do? Come on. Something with the head. Brendan?
Dassey:	Huh?
Fassbender:	What he made you do, Brendan, we know he made you do somethin' else.
Wiegert:	What was it? [pause] What was it?
Fassbender:	We have the evidence, Brendan, we just need you ta, ta be honest with us.
Dassey:	That he cut off her hair. (Interrogation of Brendan Dassey, 2006b)

Following a dialogue about the reasons for cutting off the victim's hair, the interrogators continued to prompt Dassey to confess that he and/or Avery shot Halbach in the head:

Wiegert:	OK, what else?
Fassbender:	What else was done to her head?
Dassey:	That he punched her.

The answer was not what the interrogators hoped to hear so they continued with their prompts:

Wiegert:	What else? [pause] What else?
Fassbender:	He made you do somethin' to her, didn't he? So he-he would feel better about not bein' the only person, right?
Fassbender:	What did he make you do to her?
Wiegert:	What did he make you do, Brendan? It's OK, what did he make you do?
Dassey:	Cut her.

To overcome his persistent denials about the shooting, more prompts were offered:

Wiegert:	Come on Brendan, what else?
Wiegert:	We know, we just need you to tell us.
Dassey:	That's all I can remember.

The contamination error occurred when one of the officers, seemingly frustrated, fed the facts directly to Dassey:

Wiegert:	All right, I'm just gonna come out and ask you. Who shot her in the head?
Dassey:	He did.
Wiegert:	Then why didn't you tell us that?
Dassey:	'Cause I couldn't think of it. (Interrogation of Brendan Dassey, 2006b)

Dassey's response that he 'couldn't think of it' indicates that he was guessing the answers to the interrogators' questions. In the final interrogation, by the same officers, and after Dassey was charged for the crime, Dassey's inconsistency about the details of the crime was evident throughout. Notably, Dassey said that neither he nor Avery cut off Halbach's hair. When Fassbender challenged Dassey on this inconsistency, Dassey replied:

I don't know, I was just guessing. (Interrogation of Brendan Dassey, 2006c)

Part of the forensic evidence included a DNA trace from Avery on the hood latch of Halbach's RAV4. Thus, it was helpful for the investigators if Dassey could provide evidence of witnessing Avery lifting the hood of the car following the murder:

Fassbender:	Go ba... I wanna back just a bit, you're down at the car, and you're hiding the car, right? Do you recall him taking the plates off?
Dassey:	Yeah.
Fassbender:	OK, what else did he do, he did something else, you need to tell us what he did, after that car is parked there. It's extremely important [pause]. Before you guys leave that car.
Dassey:	That he left the gun in the car.
Fassbender:	That's not what I'm thinking about. He did something to that car. He took the plates and he, I believe he did something else in that car.
Dassey:	I don't know.

| Fassbender: | OK. Did he, did he, did he go and look at the engine, did he raise the hood at all or anything like that? To do something to that car? |
| Dassey: | Yeah. (Interrogation of Brendan Dassey, 2006b) |

Kassin et al (2010) noted that false confessions tend to occur after lengthy interrogations when a suspect is isolated from people familiar to them. When in a state of stress, people seek emotional support from others (Schacter, 1959; Rofé, 1984; Uchino et al, 1996; Kassin et al, 2010) and because of this deprivation, the suspect's primary concern will be to remove him or herself from the situation. Because of lengthy interrogations, false confessions have occurred when suspects have been deprived of sleep. Sleep deprivation can impair a person's ability to making decisions and increase their vulnerability to manipulative influence. In one experiment on sleep deprivation, Frenda et al (2016) found that participants who had been awake for 24 hours were 4.5 times more likely to make a false confession than participants who had eight hours' sleep. For a review of other research on the effects of sleep deprivation, see Harrison and Horne (2000); and Kassin et al (2010) offered a review of the research from outside of experimental settings on how sleep deprivation affects medical students, motorists and pilots. Moreover, Kassin et al noted that, according to Amnesty International, many victims of torture reported having been deprived of sleep for more than 24 hours.

Scherr et al (2020) described a cumulative disadvantage that suspects experience, stretching from interrogation to conviction and beyond. For example, the disadvantage begins when a suspect naively enters a police interrogation with interrogators who have already presumed their guilt. This presumption of guilt, coupled with the use of the Reid Technique, can lead to a false confession, which considerably increases the disadvantage for the suspect. Scherr et al argued that a false confession is so powerful that it has the ability to corrupt later evidence-gathering. For example, once the 'confession' is released it can sway eyewitnesses to change their identifications and alibi witnesses to retract their evidence, and cause bias among forensic scientists in the way that they interpret evidence. At this point, Scherr et al suggested, the case is so compelling against the defendant that a wrongful conviction is virtually certain. Let us think back to Dassey's appeal for a moment. How compelling might you have found the argument his lawyers made that he falsely confessed and was therefore not guilty of the crime? According to Scherr et al, appeal efforts are severely hampered because of the evidence that has been built up against the individual. Indeed, they argue that the criminal justice system is not layered with safety nets whereby prosecutors correct the mistakes of police officers; where judges recognise overzealous prosecutors; and where an appeals court carefully critiques the conviction. Instead, Scherr et al (2020: 4) argued that rather than innocence mattering more over time, errors are compounded throughout each stage of the criminal justice system. In fact, 'actual innocence matters less over time, not more'.

The experts agree ...

According to Kassin et al (2018), there has been increasing use of psychologists and social scientists to serve as expert witnesses in trials that contain disputed confession evidence. However, their use in the US is inconsistent among courts and depends on whether judges consider such testimony reliable or valid or, alternatively, it may be considered the job of the jury to decide on the confession evidence. In an online survey with 87 experts from different countries on the psychology of confessions, Kassin et al (2018) set out to discover the experts' opinions and agreement on deception detection, police interrogations, and confessions.

Kassin et al (2018) suggested that two findings are particularly noteworthy. Experts agreed that innocent people are at an increased risk of falsely confessing when interrogators offer explicit promises of leniency, when they make threats of harm or punishment, and when 'enhanced' interrogation (that is, torture) is conducted. Additionally, the experts agreed that presenting suspects with false evidence, as is legal in the US, is equally dangerous. In relation to minimisation tactics such as offering the suspect a moral justification for the crime, for example, 'your uncle made you do it' as in the case of Dassey, experts mostly agreed that this is likely to cause the suspect to infer leniency if they confess. Kassin et al argued that these tactics are fundamental to the Reid Technique and yet it is heavily critiqued among the scientific experts. Experts strongly agreed that the risk of false confessions is increased for adolescents, those who are particularly compliant and suggestible, those with intellectual disabilities and those with diagnosed psychological disorders. Nearly all respondents indicated that their primary role as expert witnesses was to educate the jury to facilitate their competence in evaluating confession evidence. Kassin et al concluded that the results of the survey should inform courts and, indeed, expert witnesses about what is accepted evidence in instances of suspected false confessions. In turn, Kassin et al argued, this helps experts when constructing their argument in court to show that a confession has been coerced.

The jury's still out

Mindthoff et al (2018) conducted a survey with 825 potential jurors about their perceptions of confession behaviours, the waiving of Miranda rights, interrogation methods, risk factors, and the admissibility of confession evidence in court and how much weight they would give to it. The results are interesting because it seems that perceptions about confessions are changing. That is, although confession evidence continues to be perceived as a strong indicator of guilt, 60 per cent of participants accepted the idea that suspects might falsely confess. Mindthoff et al compared this to Henkel et al's (2008) study, in which 49 per cent of participants accepted the possibility and occurrence of false confessions. Woestehoff and Meissner (2016) suggested that increased knowledge and understanding about false confessions may be explained by the popularity of high-profile cases that highlight the problems with coercive confessions. For example, how many of you have seen *Making a Murderer*, *Amanda Knox*, and *Now They See Us* (about the Central Park Five) on Netflix?

Another interesting finding was that these potential jurors generally indicated that they do not think suspects understand their Miranda rights and, indeed, that innocent suspects are more likely to waive their rights than guilty suspects. Additionally, participants held the perception that police are likely to use manipulative tactics so that suspects waive their rights. However, Mindthoff et al suggested that it remains unclear what, if any, influence such knowledge would have on jurors in a trial. Participants accurately indicated the extent to which investigators use threats and false evidence ploys, which reflect findings of police self-reports (see Kassin et al, 2007). Potential jurors in the study also recognised the use of promises of leniency, which Mindthoff et al suggested is a new and encouraging finding since this was not recognised in Leo and Liu's (2009) study sample. Mindthoff et al's sample recognised the risk of a suspect falsely confessing when coercive tactics are used. However, Mindthoff et al argued that this does not necessarily mean that potential jurors can apply this new knowledge in a real-life trial. They refer to Woody et al's (2014) study which found no difference between coercive and non-coercive interrogation methods and verdict outcome. Participants in Mindthoff et al's study did not recognise adolescence as a dispositional risk factor although they did indicate that this population of suspects should have the right to a parent or guardian being present during interrogation. Notwithstanding this, the findings also revealed that almost one third of participants indicated their belief that interrogation tactics used on adults are also appropriate for use on adolescents of 17 years and younger. Mindthoff et al's sample indicated that they would place more weight on DNA and forensic evidence than on confession evidence, which is contrary to the claim among the academic community that confessions are perceived as the 'queen of proofs' or that they trump DNA evidence. Participants also generally indicated that confessions elicited via coercive methods should not be admissible in court; however, as Mindthoff et al warned, this does not necessarily mean that they would disregard such evidence should it be presented in court. In conclusion, the authors recommended that the notification of Miranda rights to suspects should be recorded for the purposes of evaluation in court. Additionally, they suggested that further research should examine how potential jurors might apply their knowledge. Because of contemporary knowledge and understanding about coercive tactics, Mindthoff et al argued that increased acquittals might be observed and so it is in the interest of prosecutors to cease the use of interrogation methods and instead employ evidence-based interviews such as information-gathering approaches.

The PEACE model

Deception tactics are illegal in Britain and, according to Gudjonsson (2018), nowhere in the world has evidence about the nature of false confessions impacted on legal and policy change as much as it has in the UK. He provided an overview of six signal crimes (Innes, 2014) that influenced these changes: the 'Confait' case; the 'Guildford Four'; the 'Birmingham Six', the 'Tottenham Three'; the case of Judith Ward; and the 'Cardiff Three'. In 1978, the Royal Commission on Criminal Procedure was set up to examine law and procedure in relation to the investigation and prosecution of criminal offences in England and Wales. It was recommended that the powers of the police be balanced with protecting the rights of the public (Munday, 1981). Subsequently, the Police and Criminal Evidence Act (PACE) was introduced in 1984 and implemented in 1986 (Gudjonsson, 2018). The Act comprises a number of Codes of Practice, of which Code C concerns the detention of suspects. For example, suspects must be provided with a full briefing of their legal rights (Kassin et al, 2010) and have access to a solicitor and to free legal advice (Card and English, 2017). Suspects must be provided with a warm, clean and well-ventilated cell with access to a toilet (Davies, 2015). Additionally, suspects must be given frequent breaks and eight hours' rest within a 24-hour period (Kassin et al, 2010). All adolescents and those with mental health disorders or with intellectual disability should be interviewed in the company of an 'appropriate adult' (Card and English, 2017). The Act stipulates that confession statements that are disputed cannot be used in evidence unless the prosecution can prove beyond reasonable doubt that the confession was not obtained by coercion. To this end, suspects must be interviewed, not interrogated (Gudjonsson, 2018). Gudjonsson argued that following the implementation of PACE, coercive interviews were still being conducted and were influenced by the Reid Technique (Gudjonsson, 2018). Then the PEACE model was introduced in 1993 and has been used by British police since then as an information-gathering approach (Kassin, 2017). First, investigators are encouraged to Prepare and Plan, that is, examine the evidence and plan the interview; then Engage and Explain, that is, build a rapport with the suspect; Account, that is, conduct a cognitive interview to enable the suspect to speak freely; Closure, that is, addressing discrepancies in the suspect's account; and Evaluation, that is, comparing the suspect's narrative to the evidence, resolving inconsistences and drawing conclusions. Following the rolling out of a national training programme in 1993, the PEACE model has been used in the UK ever since (Gudjonsson, 2018).

Meissner et al (2014) conducted a review of the research comparing accusatorial and information-gathering interrogation techniques. The research indicated that, unlike interrogation techniques, information-gathering methods garnered more true confessions without also increasing false confessions. For example, Williamson (2006) found that since the use of the PEACE model there has been a decrease in false confessions in the UK. Thus, the evidence indicates that information-gathering methods are more effective and, as Kassin (2017: 8) suggested, they 'can be used to solve crimes without unnecessary risk to suspects who turn out to be innocent'. However, there is another kind of problem that exists, both in the US and the UK. This is plea bargaining, which to some extent is a variant of the minimisation tactic. McConville et al (1994) conducted the largest study of legal professional practice ever undertaken in the UK. The study was a critical examination of defence lawyers in Britain from initial contact with clients through to the routine preparation and representation of defences in court. Specifically, the researchers examined how the assumption of guilt can critically undermine defendants' rights. Indeed, they found that most defendants pleaded guilty, even those who were in fact innocent. The defendants were routinely informed that in exchange for pleading guilty they would receive a reduction in charges or a lesser sentence. Lawyers admitted that they had no desire to go to trial and defendants were fearful of the process and did not possess the legal understanding of their rights. Although this study is relatively old now, plea bargaining remains a key part of American and British justice and in future is worthy of further exploration in relation to the nature, extent and consequences of this practice.

Conclusion

This chapter has shown that there is an abundance of literature and research on false confessions. In the US, the growth in DNA evidence has facilitated the exoneration of the wrongfully convicted, and in turn this has provided some indication of the nature and prevalence of false confessions. Popular documentaries highlighting the issue mean that public knowledge and understanding of how and why a suspect comes to falsely confess to a crime is increasing. The research highlighted in this chapter has provided us with an understanding of the different types of false confessions as well as how the Reid Technique in the US facilitates the pathway of errors that lead to a suspect confessing to a crime they did not commit. Suspects in the UK are better protected. Since the introduction of PACE 1984 and the PEACE model, evidence-gathering techniques are used and research suggests that such techniques are more effective in garnering true confessions and reducing the risk of a suspect falsely confessing.

Years later, Dassey continues to be at the centre of debate among lawyers, politicians and the media. His lawyers have persistently argued that his adolescence and intellectual disability rendered him deeply vulnerable to his interrogators who, they suggest, made the classic misclassification, coercion and contamination errors which led to his false confession. Having exhausted all of his appeals, Dassey's journey through the criminal justice process may be an example of what Scherr et al (2020) referred to as 'cumulative disadvantage'. Because of the documentary *Making a Murderer* and the subsequent vast public support for Dassey's release and exoneration, it might have been assumed that his potential innocence of the crime became increasingly significant throughout the process of his appeals. However, Scherr et al (2020: 356) argued that rather than mattering more, errors are compounded during each stage, 'with each successive stage tainted by its predecessor'. To this end, it looks increasingly likely that Dassey will serve the remainder of his prison sentence, at least until he is eligible for parole in 2048.

Recommended reading

Gudjonsson's (2018) book *The Psychology of False Confessions: Forty Years of Science and Practice* draws on two murder cases in the author's native Iceland. In so doing, the book provides a comprehensive account of the latest research on false confessions. Additionally, there is a chapter devoted to discussing some key British cases that led to new developments in legislation and policy.

Notes

[1] Brendan Dassey speaking to his mother after being interrogated by the police (Interrogation of Brendan Dassey, 1 March 2006).

[2] See https://www.youtube.com/watch?v=z0tdOWZK4AA

[3] Personality and psychopathology relate to conditions contained within the DSM-IV Axis I and II diagnostic framework (Kassin et al, 2010). There is research evidence to suggest that individuals with antisocial personality traits, personality disorder, psychological disorders, substance abuse, traumatic life events or ADHD are vulnerable to making false confessions. Because these factors are not relevant to Dassey's case, we will not discuss them here. For an overview of the research see Kassin et al (2010).

[4] For a review of the literature supporting and countering acquiescence among those with intellectual disabilities, see Finlay and Lyons (2002).

[5] In the US, an IEP allows students with delayed skills or disabilities to receive special education services at school (Bachrach, 2016).

[6] Participants are told that they are taking part in a computer-based reaction time task. They are warned not to press the shift key because this would cause the computer to crash. After a minute, the computer crashes and the participants are accused of having pressed the forbidden key. The participants are then asked to sign a statement admitting that they pressed the key.

9

The Defence of Diminished Responsibility and the Trial of Peter Sutcliffe

[U]nless I can convince people in here I am mad and maybe
then [I'll serve] ten years in the loony bin.[1]

Background

On 5 May 1981, 34-year-old Peter William Sutcliffe went on trial at the
Old Bailey, charged with the murders of 13 women: Wilma McCann,
Emily Jackson, Irene Richardson, Patricia Atkinson, Jayne MacDonald, Jean
Jordan, Yvonne Pearson, Helen Rytka, Vera Millward, Josephine Whitaker,
Barbara Leach, Marguerite Walls and Jacqueline Hill. He was also charged
with the seven attempted murders of Anna Rogulskyj, Olive Smelt, Marcella
Claxton, Maureen Long, Marilyn Moore, Upadhya Bandara and Theresa
Sykes (Smith, 2013). Sutcliffe attacked and murdered his victims (some of
whom were sex workers and whose ages ranged between 16 and 47) late at
night in West Yorkshire and Manchester between 1975 and 1981 (Bilton,
2012). His modus operandi typically involved hitting the unsuspecting
woman on the back of the head with a ball pein hammer. He also stabbed
his victims with a sharpened screwdriver and mutilated their bodies. The
expensive and lengthy police investigation attracted enormous media
attention because it took West Yorkshire detectives more than five years to
capture Sutcliffe. The police were heavily criticised, not least because Sutcliffe
had been interviewed nine times during their investigation. The reasons for
their failure to apprehend Sutcliffe more quickly have been the subject of
most true crime books and documentaries covering the case. First, senior
investigators were misled in their belief that the man they were looking

for was solely motivated by a 'hatred of prostitutes' (Yallop, 1981: 65); and second, a hoaxer from north-east England wrote letters and sent tapes to detectives falsely confessing to the murders. This had the effect of seriously derailing the investigation because every suspect was eliminated if they did not have a Geordie accent (Bilton, 2012). Eventually, on 2 January 1981, Sutcliffe was approached by police in Sheffield while sitting in his car with a prostitute. The car had false number plates and Sutcliffe was taken in for questioning. Two days later, he confessed to being the so-called 'Yorkshire Ripper' (Bilton, 2012).

However, the history of the police investigation is not the focus of this chapter. Rather, we are interested in exploring the defence of diminished responsibility raised at Sutcliffe's trial. That is, the defence argued that he was suffering from paranoid schizophrenia at the time of his offences and therefore he should be found guilty of the lesser charge of manslaughter rather than murder. After several weeks of interviews, Sutcliffe claimed to the police that he heard voices from God instructing him to kill prostitutes and he was diagnosed with paranoid schizophrenia by three consultant forensic psychiatrists. What is particularly interesting about this case is that the prosecution initially accepted Sutcliffe's plea of guilty to manslaughter. Prosecutors were satisfied that the outcome would be the same as if he were found guilty of murder, except that he would spend the rest of his life in a psychiatric hospital rather than prison. Additionally, it meant that the families of the victims would be spared the ordeal of a trial with details of the injuries the victims had sustained (Bilton, 2012). However, the judge, Mr Justice Boreham, observed that there was an issue which could not be ignored: during his initial interview and confession Sutcliffe had failed to mention to the police what he later called his 'mission' from God. The judge, who disfavoured plea bargains (Bilton, 2012), told the prosecution that there was no factual evidence behind Sutcliffe's plea of diminished responsibility:

> The matter that troubles me is not the medical opinions because there is a consensus. It seems to me that all these opinions – and I say this without criticism – all these opinions are based simply on what this defendant has told the doctors, nothing more. Moreover, what he has told the doctors conflicts substantially with what he told the police on the morning of arrest. I use the word 'conflict' advisedly. In statements to the police he expressed a desire to kill all women. If that is right – and here I need your help – is that not a matter which ought to be tested? Where lies the evidence which gives these doctors the factual basis for these pleas? It is a matter for the defendant to establish. It is a matter for a jury. We have in a sense conducted a trial which has satisfied us. It seems to me it would be more appropriate if this case were dealt with by a jury. (Mr Justice Boreham, cited in Bilton, 2012: 506)

As a result, a trial before a jury went ahead and the prosecution, who had readily accepted the plea of diminished responsibility, were now required to argue against Sutcliffe's defence. The question for the jury to decide was whether they believed the psychiatric diagnoses or whether they believed that Sutcliffe was feigning paranoid schizophrenia (Bilton, 2012). Thus, in this chapter we will explore how the defence sought to establish the partial defence of diminished responsibility and the questions the prosecution raised around the credibility and plausibility of the defence's arguments. First, however, we will review some of the legal definitions of the plea of insanity and diminished responsibility and review the research exploring the factors that affect the success or failure of an insanity defence.

The defence of insanity

The discipline of psychiatry advanced considerably during the 20th century and provides a framework for understanding the relationship between mental illness and crime. According to Tsimploulis et al (2018), Anglo–American law and every modern jurisdiction demands that for a defendant to be deemed criminally responsible, they need to have *voluntarily* committed a prohibited act (known as *actus reus*) and additionally, the person must have known and intended to do wrong (known as *mens rea*) (see also Morse, 1999; Hart, 2008; Torry and Billick, 2010). Because both elements must be proven beyond a reasonable doubt (Torry and Billick, 2010; Tsimploulis et al, 2018), the mental condition of the defendant must also be considered (Hart, 2008; Tsimploulis et al, 2018). If a psychiatrist assesses a defendant as suffering from a relevant mental condition at the time of the crime, then the defence of insanity may be raised. However, it is important to note that insanity is a legal term, not a psychiatric one (Tsimploulis et al, 2018).

The main psychiatric defences available to defendants in England and Wales include unfitness to plead and to stand trial (as outlined in the Criminal Procedure (Insanity and Unfitness to Plead) Act 1991),[2] automatism,[3] insanity, and diminished responsibility (the defence that concerns us here). The criminal law has long sought to treat defendants with some kinds of mental illness differently. Thus, in the 13th century suspected defendants underwent the 'Wild Beast Test' meaning a defendant could not be convicted for a crime if they understood their actions no better than 'an infant, brute, or wild beast' (Allnutt et al, 2007: 292). Then, in 1581, an English legal treatise first recorded the insanity plea and pronounced that ' "a madman, a natural fool or a lunatic in the time of his lunacy" cannot be held accountable for his crime' (Tsimploulis et al, 2018: 370). Legislation was further refined following the trial of Daniel M'Naghten who, in 1843, intended to murder Prime Minister Sir Robert Peel but misidentified him and instead shot and killed his personal secretary, Edward Drummond. M'Naghten believed that the government was involved in a conspiracy against him and he was later acquitted by a jury on the grounds of diminished responsibility (Allnutt et al, 2007). Subsequently, the British House of Lords stipulated new rules that set out the criteria for the defence of insanity and the M'Naghten rules were established in the Trial of Lunatics Act 1883 as follows:

> to establish a defence on the ground of insanity, it must be clearly proved that, at the time of committing the act, the party accused was labouring under such a defect of reason, from disease of the mind, as not to know the nature and quality of the act he was doing; or, if he did know it, that he did not know what he was doing was wrong. (Tsimploulis et al, 2018: 371)

In 20 US states, the M'Naghten rule still applies.

The American Law Institute (ALI) Model Penal Code rule adopted a wider conception of insanity by drawing on both the Durham Rule[4] and the Irresistible Impulse Test.[5] Under the Model Penal Code, a Not Guilty by Reason of Insanity (NGRI) verdict can be considered when 'at the time of the crime as a result of mental illness or defect the defendant lacks substantial capacity either to appreciate the criminality of his conduct or to confirm his conduct to the requirements of law' (Tsimploulis et al, 2018: 371). The interpretation of insanity is shared in most US states[6] and most European countries[7] (Tsimploulis et al, 2018). When a defendant pleads insanity, there is no dispute that he or she is responsible for the *actus reus* (the guilty act); however, the defence lies in the claim that the defendant did not possess the *mens rea* (the willingness to commit the act). If successful, the defendant receives a 'special verdict' and is found not guilty by reason of insanity (White, 1985).

Over time, the insanity defence became less appealing to defendants in the UK, because of its restrictive rules of interpretation. Furthermore, during the 1950s significant legal developments led to it being used much less frequently. Thus, from the 1840s onwards the death penalty had been restricted to offences of murder and the introduction of the Homicide Act 1957 limited its use to just five types of murder conviction.[8] The death penalty was then completely abolished in the 1965 Murder (Abolition of the Death Penalty) Act and it was replaced with a mandatory life sentence. Interestingly, according to White (1985), for some defendants, indefinite detention in prison was preferable to indefinite detention in a special hospital (which could still be imposed if the defendant is found not guilty by reason of insanity). Importantly, the Homicide Act 1957 introduced diminished responsibility, a partial defence for murder that, if successful, enables the jury to convict the defendant on the lesser charge of manslaughter. Thus, the insanity defence has rarely been used in the UK.[9] Similarly, the insanity defence is seldom used in the US (Nusbaum, 2002) and there, as with diminished responsibility in the UK, the defence of diminished capacity can be raised and, if successful, the defendant is convicted of a lesser offence (Testa and Friedman, 2012).

Diminished responsibility

Diminished responsibility in England and Wales is one of the special defences which exists only for murder cases. Introduced in the Homicide Act 1957, it was later modified in the Coroners and Justice Act 2009. Diminished responsibility under the Homicide Act 1957 is a partial defence to murder and is different to a complete defence, such as self-defence. If successfully argued, murder could be reduced to manslaughter (CPS, 2019), and in turn, this enables judges to exercise discretion when considering the length of sentence (Mackay and Mitchell, 2003). The 1957 legislation stated that a person displayed diminished responsibility if, at the time of the crime, the accused was suffering from an 'abnormality of mind (whether arising from a condition of arrested or retarded development of mind or any inherent causes or induced by disease or injury)', and the abnormality must have 'substantially impaired his mental responsibility for the killing' (Kennefick, 2011: 756). An abnormality of the mind covers several different conditions including psychopathy, volitional insanity, alcoholism (Tennant, 2001) and mercy-killing (Griew, 1988). It is for the defence to prove, on the balance of probabilities (CPS, 2019), that the defendant is not liable to be convicted of murder but instead is liable for manslaughter. Thus, the aim of the defence is not to absolve the defendant from complete liability (Kennefick, 2011).

The 1957 legislation received much criticism, specifically on the issues of clarity, fairness and effectiveness. Kennefick (2011: 755–6) noted that there was a lack of clarity around the term 'abnormality of mind', 'which has been deemed obscure and inadequate in a medical diagnostic sense'. Additionally, 'substantial impairment of mental responsibility' has been viewed as an unclear concept. In response to the criticisms on clarity, the Coroners and Justice Act 2009 introduced a revised partial defence referring to a 'recognised medical condition', replacing the original wording. This aimed to outline much more clearly 'what aspects of a defendant's functioning must be affected in order for the partial defence to succeed' (Kennefick, 2011: 756). The new element of a 'recognised medical condition' sought to address the criticism of the original legislation regarding its lack of psychiatric terms and the subsequent interpretations that varied from court to court. The change was commended by the Royal College of Psychiatrists for ensuring that the defence of diminished responsibility is 'grounded in valid medical diagnosis' (cited in Kennefick, 2011: 757). Notwithstanding this, Kennefick argued that the new wording narrows the defence because it excludes disorders that may not yet be accepted medical conditions. Under the original legislation, a person suffering from depression and a heightened state of emotion because of a loved one's suffering, who subsequently commits a mercy killing, may be able to use the defence of diminished responsibility. However, under the new legislation such a defence is narrowly restricted (Kennefick, 2011).

The defence of diminished responsibility has sometimes been applied successfully and, under the original legislation, some recognised medical conditions were established in case law: for example, psychopathy (*R v Byrne* 1960); chronic depression (*R v Gittens* 1984); premenstrual syndrome and postnatal depression (*R v Reynolds* 1988); battered women's syndrome (*R v Ahluwalia* 1992); personality disorder (*R v Martin* 2002); Asperger's (*R v Reynolds* 2004); and epilepsy (*R v Campbell* 1987).

Factors that affect the success or failure of an insanity defence

Research, predominantly conducted in the US, has focused on examining the factors that contribute to the success or failure of an insanity defence. While the insanity defence is not to be confused with the defence of diminished capacity in the US or diminished responsibility in the UK, some of the findings are relevant to understanding the likely success of the latter defences and thus we review them briefly here.

Motive

Pickel (1998) noted that a belief which might inform jurors' judgements of insanity is the presence of a 'crazy' or unreasonable motive even though the ALI standard does not require jurors to look for an unreasonable motive and, similarly, UK legislation does not make this requirement for jurors either. Interestingly, Stone (1993: 175) suggested that in homicide cases 'we look for motives, and when there is no apparent motive we look to psychiatry'. According to Pickel (1998: 576), a crazy motive is one 'that cannot logically explain why a mentally healthy person would commit murder'. Pickel's study supported the hypothesis that jurors are more likely to judge a defendant insane if there is a 'crazy' or unreasonable motive, something also found in previous studies (see McGlynn and Dreilinger, 1981; Finkel and Handel, 1989; Helm et al, 2016). While not cited by Sutcliffe's defence, Pickel's (1998) notion of a 'crazy' or unreasonable motive appeared to underpin their case because their client claimed that he heard voices from God telling him to rid the streets of prostitutes. His motive was situated by three psychiatrists in the context of their diagnosis of Sutcliffe as suffering from paranoid schizophrenia.

Psychiatric and criminal history

Conner (2006) examined newspaper articles in the US covering all court trials for 102 homicide cases over the period of a year (2000–01), in which a plea of not guilty by reason of insanity was made. From the information contained in the articles, it was found that the defendant's chances of a successful insanity plea depended on having a diagnosed and documented psychiatric condition as well as prescribed medication prior to the crime, and previous institutionalisation for mental illness. Gulayets (2016) pointed to other studies that support the view that defendants are more likely to avoid a criminal conviction when there is a diagnosis of a major mental illness (Packer, 1987; Janofsky et al, 1989; Cirincione et al, 1995; Warren et al, 2004) and a history of having been previously institutionalised (Packer, 1987; Cirincione et al, 1995; Warren et al, 2004; cf Janofsky et al, 1989).

Conner's (2006) study suggested that defendants are more likely to succeed in their insanity plea if they have no previous convictions. This is because having a criminal history appears to indicate that the defendant should have understood the wrongfulness of their actions. Other studies support this finding (Packer, 1987; Cirincione et al, 1995; Ohayon et al, 1998; Warren et al, 2004; Appelbaum et al, 2015). According to Gulayets (2016), the influence of psychiatric opinion has received little attention. However, Gulayets referred to studies in the US that have found psychiatric opinion to be highly correlated with verdicts of 'not guilty by reason of insanity' (Steadman et al, 1983; Howard and Clark, 1985; Janofsky et al, 1989). Two Canadian studies further support these findings (Ohayon et al, 1998; Gulayets, 2016).

Nature of the crime

We saw in Chapters 4 and 7 that jurors are sometimes affected by extralegal variables that influence their judgement of guilt or innocence. Similarly, previous research indicates that jurors may rely upon their personal beliefs about insanity rather than following the legal instructions provided by the judge (Roberts et al, 1987; Finkel and Handel, 1989; Roberts and Golding, 1991; Pickel, 1998; Skeem and Golding, 2001).[10] Pickel (1998: 572) suggested that one such schema might be the 'bizarreness' of the crime even though case law in some states in the US stipulates that a defendant's sanity should not be judged on the bizarreness of the crime alone. State v Neutzel suggested that a bizarre crime is either 'oddly committed or unusual' or 'especially vicious or heinous' (cited in Pickel, 1998: 572). Indeed, Roberts et al (1987) found that mock jurors were more likely to judge a defendant guilty but mentally ill when they considered the crime to be bizarre. Additionally, Pickel's study of mock jurors found that they were more likely to judge the defendant NGRI when the crime was of an unusual nature. However, Pickel noted that the effect of unusualness in her study was not identical to the effect of bizarreness in Robert et al's study. For example, bizarreness was judged as guilty but mentally ill rather than increasing the likelihood of a verdict of NGRI. Roberts et al made the defendant's actions both odd and vicious whereas Pickel made the actions just 'odd'. Pickel theorised that when acts are described as vicious, jurors may see them as more reprehensible and therefore more deserving of punishment than they otherwise would be. However, the influence of heinousness is mirrored in a more recent study by Appelbaum et al (2015).

Evidence of planning

Pickel (1998) found that crimes that appeared to be well planned and organised tended to negate the insanity plea and the finding supports previous mock juror research by Roberts and Golding (1991). Similarly, Conner (2006) found that evidence of planning, such as taking a weapon to the crime scene, was associated with decreasing the chances of a successful plea of insanity. She suggested that this may be because impulsive murders appear more irrational and pointless and give rise to the belief that the defendant was incapable of controlling their actions.

Victims

Conner (2006) found that the success of the NGRI plea is less likely when there were multiple victims and if the victims were children. She suggested that a jury's rejection of the insanity plea could be a reflection of their desire for vengeance. Additionally, multiple victims may be perceived as a risk of further crimes should the defendant be acquitted or receive a lesser sentence. The study indicated the significance of the victim's age: when victims were children under the age of 13 there was a reduced chance of the defendant being found NGRI. Conner posited that the murder of children may be perceived as particularly heinous to jurors.

Neurobiological evidence

Since Sutcliffe's trial, scientific work to support other psychiatric evidence has advanced significantly. In the US in particular, there has been an increase in the use of neurobiological research as mitigating evidence for criminal responsibility (McSwiggan et al, 2017), particularly for violent crimes (see Gurley and Marcus, 2008; Mowle et al, 2016; Remmel et al, 2019). Neuroimaging is used to indicate reduced amygdala activity which is associated with psychopathy and callous/unemotional traits (DeLisi et al,

2009). Genetic evidence is also being increasingly presented; for example, the enzyme monoamine oxidase (MAOA-L) has been associated with an increase of aggressive and antisocial behaviour (McSwiggan et al, 2017). However, Tabb et al (2019) suggested that the success of genetic evidence in mitigating legal responsibility for a crime has been inconsistent. Having reviewed cases where evidence of the MAOA-L genotype was included in criminal cases, McSwiggan et al suggested that genotype evidence may not be successful in its persuasiveness because its impact on the defendant is difficult to prove.

Berryessa et al (2020) compared the influence of neurobiological evidence to psychological evidence on judgments of insanity and found no significant effect for either, reflecting previous mock-juror studies (Appelbaum and Scurich, 2014; Appelbaum et al, 2015; LaDuke et al, 2018; Remmel et al, 2019). However, they pointed out that other studies have found a strong effect of neuroscience-based evidence on judgments of psychopathic defendants (see Gurley and Marcus, 2008; Rendell et al, 2010; Schweitzer and Saks, 2011; Greene and Cahill, 2012). The authors hypothesised that different vignettes describing different violent crimes might explain the mixed results. The fact that they used vignettes which lacked viciousness could have appeared to mock jurors as an indicator of the defendant's ability to know right from wrong as well as the ability to control their behaviour. Weiss et al (2020) examined mitigation arguments at appellate courts (courts of appeal) when genetic evidence was presented. Their study found that expert witnesses lacked scientific detail in what they said and that their testimony elicited few positive results in achieving habeas corpus hearings[11] or new trials. The authors concluded that the inclusion of hereditary or genetic influences alone in a defence argument is insufficient to reduce culpability and it is more persuasive when coupled with other mitigating factors related to the defendant's life experiences.

The defence strategy to establish the partial defence of diminished responsibility

Usually, the burden of proof lies with the prosecution to persuade the jury that the defendant is guilty beyond a reasonable doubt. However, in a trial where the defendant is pleading diminished responsibility, the burden of proof rests on the defence. It is for them to persuade the jury that the defendant should be found guilty of the lesser charge of manslaughter rather than murder because of their mental condition at the time of the offence(s). Thus, there is no dispute about the *actus reus*. We saw in Chapter 1 that, to prove their case, the prosecution must demonstrate what Bennett and Feldman (1981) termed the *presence*, *action* and (criminal) *state of mind* of the defendant. In response, the defence seek to raise doubt by *challenging* and/or *redefining* the *evidence* and/or *reconstructing* the story entirely. However, what we will see this time is the roles reversed, with the defence focusing specifically on *state of mind* (remember there is no dispute in this case about Sutcliffe's *presence* and *action* at the scenes of his crimes). In turn, the prosecution *challenged* the defence's evidence on Sutcliffe's *state of mind*. Specifically, the prosecution sought to raise doubts about his diagnosis of paranoid schizophrenia and to demonstrate that, rather than hearing the voice of God to instruct him to murder prostitutes, the *motive* for his crimes was in fact sexual.

The defence: direct examination of Peter Sutcliffe

Although the defence had three diagnoses of paranoid schizophrenia in their favour, they needed to overcome the problem that the diagnoses arose simply from what Sutcliffe had told the psychiatrists. Additionally, despite claiming that his symptoms of paranoid schizophrenia began when he was a young adult, he had never disclosed his mental condition to friends, family or a doctor. It was important, then, that the defence strategy focus on Sutcliffe himself, explaining the symptoms of his mental condition, when and how his symptoms first emerged, and how it eventually led him to commit multiple murders. The central theme for the defence was that Sutcliffe heard voices from God instructing him to rid the streets of prostitutes. As well as being fundamental to his plea of diminished responsibility, it also helped to establish an unreasonable motive (Pickel, 1998), which, according to the research outlined previously, should have augmented the credibility of his plea.

During his testimony at the trial, Sutcliffe described his first experience of hearing God's voice when he was 19 or 20 and working in a cemetery. He said that this had a 'terrific impact' on him, and he felt that he had 'just experienced something fantastic' (direct examination of Sutcliffe 12 May 1981, cited in Davies and Rusbridger, 1981a). He then outlined the chronology of events that led him to hearing voices from God that began instructing him to murder following a negative encounter with a prostitute in 1969. He explained that his motive for seeing a prostitute was an act of revenge towards Sonia, his soon-to-be wife, after her affair with another man. He told the jury that the prostitute charged him £5 and because he only had a £10 note, they drove to a local garage to get it changed. According to Sutcliffe, the men at the garage escorted the woman away and he had to leave, minus his £10.[12] Sutcliffe claimed that his hatred for prostitutes was sparked by this incident (Bilton, 2012) and when, some three weeks after the incident, he saw the prostitute in a pub he confronted her about it. She treated what had happened as a joke, reinforcing his attitude towards prostitutes:

> She just thought this was a huge joke and, as luck would have it, she knew everybody in the place and went round telling them all about

the incident. Before I knew what was happening most of the people around me were laughing. (Direct examination of Sutcliffe 12 May 1981, cited in Davies and Rusbridger, 1981a)[13]

Sutcliffe testified that he carried out his first attack on a prostitute between one and four weeks following the incident at the pub. He was in a car with his friend, Trevor Birdsall, when he got out, and, disappeared from view, attacked a woman (who he said he believed was a prostitute) over the head with a sock containing a stone. The victim did not press charges and so no conviction appeared on his record. He claimed at the trial that he saw it as a sign that he was not meant to be 'caught or punished for the attempt' (direct examination of Sutcliffe 12 May 1981, cited in Davies and Rusbridger, 1981a).

A very pressing issue for the defence was that there was some evidence of a sexual motive to his crime therefore raising doubt about Sutcliffe's claim that his motive was to rid the streets of prostitutes. To this end, when asked by the defence, he denied that he enjoyed or took any pleasure from hitting the victims over the head or stabbing them (Bilton, 2012).

Some weeks after Sutcliffe's first attack, he was arrested in the garden of a house in the red-light area of Manningham in Bradford for being in possession of a hammer and was fined for going equipped for theft (Davies and Rusbridger, 1981a). Following this, he said he experienced a long period of disinterest in prostitutes and did not attempt another attack until six years later in 1975 (Bilton, 2012). He put this down to the fact that he was living in London, seeing Sonia, and had taken a job where he had to work at night and thus there was no opportunity for killing. He claimed that the voice would reassure him whenever he complained about the mission and asked 'why it should be me that did it, because I found it so difficult' (direct examination of Sutcliffe 12 May 1981, cited in Davies and Rusbridger, 1981a). However, after he was made redundant in 1975, he could no longer deny the voices, and this provoked his attack on Anna Rogulskyj in Keighley, hitting her with a ball pein hammer. Sutcliffe claimed he believed her to be a prostitute although she was not. Rogulskyj survived the attack because Sutcliffe was disturbed by someone passing nearby (Bilton, 2012).

Next, Sutcliffe testified about his subsequent attack on Olive Smelt, whom he believed was a prostitute (she was not). Once again, he was sitting in the car with his friend Trevor Birdsall when he saw the victim in the street. He told Birdsall that it was the prostitute they had seen in the public house where they had just been drinking. Sutcliffe got out of the car, followed the victim, and hit her. Smelt survived the attack because Sutcliffe was again disturbed by a passing car (Bilton, 2012). He testified that he hoped his feelings about his mission would subside, but they did not:

I found it very difficult. I just couldn't restrain myself. I couldn't do anything to stop myself, because it was God who was controlling me. (Direct examination of Sutcliffe 12 May 1981, cited in Davies and Rusbridger, 1981a)

Sutcliffe further emphasised his motive and the great discomfort he experienced while hearing voices:

Before doing it, I had to go through a terrible stage each time. I was in absolute turmoil, I was doing everything I could do to fight it off, and asked why it should be me, until I eventually reached the stage where it was as if I was primed to do it. (Direct examination of Sutcliffe, cited in Jones, 2019: 48)

The defence barrister, James Chadwin, QC, continued his line of questioning to further underscore the lack of a motive other than 'the mission' and asked Sutcliffe about whether he ever looked forward to killing someone with pleasure, to which he replied, 'No, certainly not' (direct examination of Sutcliffe, cited in Jones, 2019: 48). Sutcliffe offered an example to demonstrate just how much he did not want to commit the murders and how hard he tried to resist the voices when driving to the red-light area in Leeds one evening:

I got halfway there, and I was still in turmoil. I do not think I was quite in that state where I could possibly do it. I was arguing all the time. I was not always getting answers, quite a lot I did not understand. ... I finally stopped the car. I turned it round. I was shouting in the car. I set off back, changing the gears, jamming the gearbox. I put the car in the garage, and went to bed. I felt a great sense of achievement. (Direct examination of Sutcliffe 12 May 1981, cited in Davies and Rusbridger, 1981a)

Sutcliffe testified that God had instructed him ahead of time to commit every attack and murder except that of Yvonne Pearson because, as a prostitute, she was the one who approached Sutcliffe and did so by chance. She knocked on his car window asking him for business, and he said he saw this chance encounter as evidence that his mission was arranged by God:

I ask her where she sprung from. She said, 'It's just good timing' or 'You can put it down to fate.' Unfortunately for her, I thought this was my direct signal. ... After I killed her, I apologised to her. I said I was sorry, and she could get up, and that she would be alright, and she would be able to get up. (Direct examination of Sutcliffe 12 May 1981, cited in Davies and Rusbridger, 1981a)

Adding credence to the prosecution's case was that not all of Sutcliffe's victims were prostitutes and this therefore was another important issue for the defence to address and allow Sutcliffe to explain himself. He told the jury how he felt when he learned from a newspaper that one of his victims, Jayne MacDonald, was not a prostitute:

> I was really shattered mentally. I just couldn't accept it. I felt terrible, full of remorse.

He said that it took him several weeks before he finally felt reassured by the voice of God (direct examination of Sutcliffe 12 May 1981, cited in Davies and Rusbridger, 1981a).

Another of Sutcliffe's victims, Josephine Whitaker, was also not a prostitute. Sutcliffe admitted that he had doubts about her being a prostitute because she was talking about having just visited her grandma. However, the voice of God reassured him:

> This is a likely tale. She is really trying to play tricks on you. You are not going to fall for all this are you? (Direct examination of Sutcliffe 12 May 1981, cited in Davies and Rusbridger, 1981a)

Continuing to draw on and enhance the defence that he was suffering from paranoid schizophrenia, Sutcliffe said that when he heard about the hoax letters and tape that were sent to the police, he saw it as God intervening and creating a diversion so that he could carry on with his mission. He also described the several 'near misses' because, having been interviewed several times following some of the murders, the police did not catch him:

> Everything was in God's hands. The way I escaped, the way I went away satisfied. (Direct examination of Sutcliffe 12 May 1981, cited in Davies and Rusbridger, 1981a)

Arguably the most damning evidence to undermine his plea of diminished responsibility was that a prison officer overheard Sutcliffe telling his wife that if he could convince people he was insane then he would receive a lesser sentence (Bilton, 2012). The officer testified that he had heard Sutcliffe telling his wife:

> I wouldn't feel any animosity towards you if you started a life on your own. I am going to do a long time in prison, thirty years or more,

unless I can convince people in here I am mad and maybe then ten years in the loony bin. (Prison hospital warden John Leach, cited in Yallop, 1981: 350–1)

On the stand, Sutcliffe defended his comments, explaining that he was simply trying to reassure his very distraught wife.

Direct examination of Dr Hugo Milne

Following Sutcliffe's testimony, the consultant forensic psychiatrist Dr Milne testified for the defence, claiming that there was no evidence that Sutcliffe was simulating (feigning) paranoid schizophrenia and that he had maintained a conscious awareness of this possibility throughout the interviews (Bilton, 2012). He insisted that he was 'very much on my guard' (Clark and Tate, 2015: 32) about being fooled. Because one of the key issues for the defence was that the psychiatrists made their diagnosis based on what Sutcliffe had told them rather than any other evidence, Chadwin asked Milne if Sutcliffe presented with symptoms. Milne explained:

> The way he might behave as if he was suspicious of other people's behaviour. The way he may misinterpret people's behaviour and the way he may react to what he believes. (Direct examination of Milne, cited in Clark and Tate, 2015: 33)

Judge Boreham interrupted and repeated his initial concerns when the prosecution had originally accepted Sutcliffe's plea of diminished responsibility:

> It sounds as if you are saying that you are very much dependent upon what you are told, and rather as we in the courts, you have to test its accuracy. (Direct examination of Milne, cited in Clark and Tate, 2015: 34)

Milne listed 19 symptoms of paranoid schizophrenia and suggested that the primary schizophrenic experience was 'the most crucial symptom in the diagnosis of schizophrenia' (direct examination of Milne, cited in *The Washington Post*, 1981), which was when he first heard the voice while working in the cemetery. Milne described Sutcliffe as having: a belief that he had special powers and a sense of grandeur (Clark and Tate, 2015); over-controlled behaviour; illogical thinking; lack of insight into the reasons for his behaviour; feelings that his mind was being controlled; and distortions in thought and perception (Hollway, 1981). He concluded that there was more than enough evidence to diagnose Sutcliffe with paranoid schizophrenia (direct examination of Milne, cited in Davies and Rusbridger, 1981c).

Milne described the signs and symptoms of Sutcliffe's illness which included 'suspicion and uncontrollable impulse', and such a degree of preoccupation with prostitutes that he became deluded:

> I am referring to his phrases that have come out in court here about prostitutes being the scum of the earth and being responsible for all sorts of problems to the extent that he could not see beyond that idea. (Direct examination of Milne, cited in Clark and Tate, 2015: 34)

Milne identified Sutcliffe's 'over-controlled' behaviour and referred to his ability to remain very calm when making his admission to the police. Whereas most people would be anxious, he 'behaved with an abnormal degree of calmness, detachment and quiet' (direct examination of Milne, cited in Davies and Rusbridger, 1981c).

Finally, another key issue for the defence to address was that there was no dispute that Sutcliffe was always in possession of weapons, suggesting that there was clear planning and forethought in his actions. As we have observed from the research outlined earlier in this chapter, evidence of premeditation is very often associated with a negation of the plea of insanity. To this end, Milne testified that, although Sutcliffe had a sharpened screwdriver in his possession with the intent of stabbing his victims, such premeditation was not inconsistent with someone suffering from paranoid schizophrenia (direct examination of Milne, cited in Davies and Rusbridger, 1981c).

Exercise 1:

Having read some key excerpts of the testimony for the defence, consider the following questions:

1. In light of the research presented earlier in the chapter, how strong do you think the evidence is that Sutcliffe was suffering from paranoid schizophrenia at the time of his offences?
2. How credible do you think Dr Milne's testimony is and do you think his diagnosis of Sutcliffe was correct? What reasons can you give for your answer?

The prosecution strategy: challenging the state of mind (motive)

The prosecution's case was premised on Sutcliffe feigning insanity, most notably because the diagnoses were made based on what he told the psychiatrists and also because he failed to mention 'the mission' when first interviewed by the police. In his opening statement, Sir Michael Havers, QC suggested that the reason for the trial was simple:

> There is a marked significant difference between the version which Sutcliffe gave to the police and the version he gave to the doctors. You will have to consider whether the doctors might, in fact, have been deceived by this man; whether he sought to pull the wool over their eyes; or whether the doctors are just plain wrong. You will have to decide whether as a clever, callous murderer he has deliberately set out to provide a cock and bull story to avoid conviction of murder. (Havers, prosecution opening statement, cited in Clark and Tate, 2015: 10)

Later on, Harry Ognall, QC, also for the prosecution, emphasised that the defence had no case unless there was a clear absence of sexual motive:

> I expect he has never wanted to be seen as a sexual killer, because, if he puts himself forward as a sexual killer, the Divine mission goes out of the window. (Cross-examination of Milne, cited in Bilton, 2012: 519)

The prosecution: cross-examination of Peter Sutcliffe

Drawing attention to the fact that Sutcliffe had never disclosed his mental condition to anyone, Havers put to him during cross-examination that it was not until two months after his arrest and during the eighth interview with a consultant forensic psychiatrist that Sutcliffe claimed to be hearing the voice of God telling him he had a mission to kill prostitutes (Burn, 2019). Havers further questioned Sutcliffe about his relationship with his wife, Sonia, whom he said he trusted, and confirmed his relationship to his 'devoted' mother:

Havers:	That [his mental condition] was the most stunning thing in your life and you did not tell Sonia?
Sutcliffe:	No.
Havers:	You didn't tell your devoted mother?
Sutcliffe:	No.
Havers:	You didn't tell anyone until years and years had gone by and then you told them on the eighth interview in Armley Jail? (Cross-examination of Sutcliffe, cited in Burn, 2019: 311–12)

Following on from his testimony during direct examination, Sutcliffe confirmed that it was after the incident of being short-changed by a prostitute and later taunted by her that he came to develop a hatred for prostitutes. Challenging the defence's account, congruent with the type of unreasonable motive cited by Pickel (1998), Havers suggested:

> So God very conveniently jumped on the bandwagon after that and says: 'You have a divine mission, young Peter, to stalk the red-light districts and avenge me by killing prostitutes?' (Cross-examination of Sutcliffe, cited in Davies and Rusbridger, 1981b)

Turning to the details of the murders, Sutcliffe confirmed that, as well as receiving instructions to carry out the crimes, God also offered specific instruction to him in the process of the attacks. For example, he claimed that God had instructed him to force horsehair (from a nearby abandoned sofa) down the throat of Yvonne Pearson to quieten her and that God further instructed him to hide behind a garden wall after attacking Theresa Sykes. Havers's further probing on this issue caused Sutcliffe's testimony to become inconsistent and, in turn, weakened what would have been his unreasonable motive (Pickel, 1998) for the crimes:

Havers:	When Yvonne Pearson was lying there gurgling and moaning and there was someone in a car nearby, with your high average intelligence you must have known you were in danger of being caught. You don't need God to tell you to ram [the horsehair stuffing from the sofa] down her throat?
Sutcliffe:	No.
Havers:	Did God tell you?
Sutcliffe:	No. (Cross-examination of Sutcliffe, cited in Bilton, 2012: 513)

As noted earlier, if the prosecution could replace the unreasonable motive (Pickel, 1998) of a mission from God with a sexual motive, then Sutcliffe's plea of insanity would not be plausible and this is precisely what the prosecution sought to do. Sutcliffe's defence for removing some of the victims' clothes was to help him stab them to death quickly. He claimed it was also to 'show them for what they were [scum of the earth]'. He further denied gaining sexual gratification when stabbing some of his victims in the breasts and vagina. However, as well as omitting information about the voices from God in his police interview and confession, he also acknowledged that if the victim was not a prostitute it did not matter. When referring to the murder of Josephine Whitaker, he said: 'The mood was in me and no woman was safe ... I realised she wasn't a prostitute but at that time I wasn't bothered. I just wanted to kill a woman' (police statement from Sutcliffe, 2

January 1981, cited in Bilton, 2012: 744). He also admitted that he raped one of his victims, Helen Rytka, while she was dying. When Havers questioned him about this, Sutcliffe replied:

> I didn't have sex. I entered her, but there was no action. It was to persuade her that everything would be all right. I had no choice, it was important to keep her quiet. (Cross-examination of Sutcliffe, cited in Bilton, 2012: 514)

Havers pointed out that, to persuade the doctors of his mental illness, Sutcliffe could not admit that some of the women he attacked were not prostitutes:

Havers: Is that why you had to maintain through thick and thin in the face of the clearest evidence that these six women were prostitutes?

Sutcliffe: No, I knew when I did it that each one was.

Havers: Your story would have gone straight down the drain if you had to say to the doctors that six of them were not prostitutes?

Sutcliffe: It is not a story, sir.

Havers: But the mission requires them to be prostitutes.

Sutcliffe: It didn't require them to be, they were. (Cross-examination of Sutcliffe, cited in Burn, 2019: 313–14)

Havers referred Sutcliffe to the statement he made to the police about one of his victims, Josephine Whitaker, which was 'I realised she was not a prostitute':

> Had you got to the stage where your lust for killing meant that everybody that you saw, if in a quiet spot, could meet their death at your hands? (Cross-examination of Sutcliffe, cited in Davies and Rusbridger, 1981b)

Sutcliffe's answer was 'no', but also that God was giving him detailed instructions in the build-up to Whitaker's murder (Davies and Rusbridger, 1981b).

Remember that Conner (2006) found that evidence of rational thinking or forethought decreases the likelihood that jurors will perceive the defendant to be insane. The possession of a weapon at the crime scene will support the view that the defendant had forethought about his intentions. Indeed, the central argument for the prosecution was that the evidence showed that Sutcliffe's crimes were calculated and premeditated. Even during the unplanned murder of Yvonne Pearson, he admitted to having weapons in his possession (Bilton, 2012). During cross-examination, Havers noted Sutcliffe's ability to resist God's instructions sometimes by pointing out how he carefully chose where to carry out the attacks, demonstrating quick thinking to avoid being caught, while able to act in a way to fool his victims into believing they were safe with him. As well as demonstrating forethought and planning, Havers argued that these facts indicated Sutcliffe's ability to control himself. When Sutcliffe denied this, Havers asked him:

Havers:	Are you saying that if the urge came over you in the middle of Piccadilly Circus, you would have done it there?
Sutcliffe:	Yes. That's exactly what I said in my police statement. (Cross-examination of Sutcliffe, cited in Davies and Rusbridger, 1981b)

Havers continued to challenge this by asking Sutcliffe if he had ever murdered anyone inside his car. As well as suggesting that there would be no room, Sutcliffe commented:

Sutcliffe:	They would probably make a lot of noise and there would be evidence all over the car.
Havers:	That's it. Well done. Stop there. There would be blood all over your car. It would make your detection more likely. A messy job to get rid of it. That's what I am getting at: your capacity for control. Do you see? (Cross-examination of Sutcliffe, cited in Davies and Rusbridger, 1981b)

Cross-examinations of psychiatrists Dr Hugo Milne, Dr Terence Kay and Dr Malcolm MacCulloch

Ognall cross-examined Dr Milne and began by asking him what he thought of Sutcliffe's suggestion about convincing people he was mad so that he could do just 'ten years in the loony bin':

Milne:	I think it is a very straightforward decision to make. Is this man pretending to be mad, and has duped me and my colleagues, or am I, from my clinical examination right in saying that he is a paranoid schizophrenic? ... either he is a competent actor, or I am an inefficient psychiatrist ... paranoid schizophrenics are extraordinarily cunning, extremely involved in premeditation and determined not to be found. (Cross-examination of Milne, cited in Bilton, 2012: 517)

Ognall redefined Milne's assertion:

A very great proportion of normal criminals are also cunning, clever and anxious not to be found. That isn't the hallmark of a schizophrenic. It is the hallmark of a normal criminal. I suggest that this pattern is a badge of a premeditated killer. (Cross-examination of Milne, cited in Bilton, 2012: 517)

Ognall addressed the fact that Sutcliffe's wife had been diagnosed with schizophrenia early on in their relationship and Milne conceded that he could have learned 'ideas of reference' (Yallop, 1981: 357). He further emphasised Sutcliffe's deception to the police and the doctors, in turn forcing Milne to acknowledge that he could not be certain that Sutcliffe had not lied to him:

Perhaps I have been duped. It is for the jury to decide. (Cross-examination of Milne, cited in Yallop, 1981: 357)

Consultant forensic psychiatrist Dr Kay testified that he felt sure of his diagnosis, although he conceded:

The prison officers, who are with him twenty-four hours a day, told me that we [the three doctors] were being fooled. (Cross-examination of Kay, cited in Yallop, 1981: 358)

Havers asked Kay if he was aware of a US experiment in which eight 'perfectly normal' people successfully simulated the symptoms of schizophrenia, for example hearing voices. Kay acknowledged that he knew of the experiment and the diagnoses psychiatrists made of all the participants, admitting them to various hospitals:

Havers:	I understand they fooled doctors at seventeen mental institutions, but the patients considered them fakes.
Kay:	That is correct. (Cross-examination of Kay, cited in Yallop, 1981: 359)

MacCulloch conceded that he had not made additional inquiries to help validate his diagnosis nor had he read the police interview transcripts:

Yes, Mr Ognall, I would agree that in reaching my diagnosis I made no enquiries of Sutcliffe's family, friends, workmates or general practitioner. (Cross-examination of MacCulloch, cited in Yallop, 1981: 358)

He also conceded:

I will admit that I could not determine whether Sutcliffe was a liar. (Cross-examination of MacCulloch, cited in Yallop, 1981: 358)

The judge asked:

Mr Justice Boreham:	If what he has told you is not true, then what of your diagnosis?
MacCulloch:	It falls. (Cross-examination of MacCulloch, cited in Yallop, 1981: 358)

In seeking to establish a sexual motive for the crimes, during his cross-examination of Milne Ognall held up the screwdriver with which Sutcliffe stabbed Josephine Whitaker in the vagina. He suggested that it was done for sexual gratification:

Ognall:	What else could the attack with the screwdriver be but sexual?
Milne:	It may have been sexual.
Ognall:	What else could it have been? I will have an answer.
Milne:	I do not think it could have been anything else other than sexual.
Ognall:	Did Peter Sutcliffe tell you that there was no sexual elements in the attacks?
Milne:	Yes.
Ognall:	Well, that doesn't seem to be right, does it?
Milne:	No. (Cross-examination of Milne, cited in Bilton, 2012: 519)

Ognall further highlighted the sexual intercourse Sutcliffe admitted to having with Helen Rytka as she was dying after being hit with a hammer and referred to the police statement where Sutcliffe complained:

Ognall:	'She just lay there limp and didn't put much into it.' Normal?
Milne:	Not normal, no. (Cross-examination of Milne, cited in Clark and Tate, 2015: 39)

Milne rationalised Sutcliffe's sexual behaviour as an attempt to 'avoid detection, quieten her and get away'. Ognall pointed to the implausibility of this:

Ognall:	Why did he have to have intercourse with her to keep her quiet? I don't suppose he could have just put his hand over her mouth?
Milne:	As he himself said, this was what the girl expected.

The judge intervened and asked Milne whether, given the attack the victim had just sustained, it was really likely that this was what she expected. Milne conceded that he did not know.

Ognall: Look Dr Milne, he is having intercourse with a woman who has been cruelly attacked and is near death. I ask you again – no underlying sexual component?

Milne: A sexual component, yes. (Cross-examination of Milne, cited in Clark and Tate, 2015: 39)

Ognall continued to emphasise Sutcliffe's sexual motivation, for example the fingernail scratches on the vagina of murder victim Marguerite Walls:

Ognall: I put it to you that the injuries to these women betray quite clear sexual components in the attacks. Do you agree?

Milne: Yes. (Cross-examination of Milne, cited in Clark and Tate, 2015: 39)

Ognall: This isn't a missionary from God, it is a man who gets a sexual pleasure out of killing these women. (Cross-examination of Milne, cited in Rumbelow: 2013: 353)

Underscoring the fundamental importance of the psychiatric diagnosis to the defence's case, Ognall commented:

> If there's a sexual component in the attacks, how is that to be reconciled with the Divine Mission simply to put their lives to an end? If the central point of the Divine Mission doesn't bear close analysis in the eyes of the jury, where then lies your diagnosis of paranoid schizophrenia?

Milne: Very simple. Nowhere. (Cross-examination of Milne, cited in Davies, 1981)

When cross-examining MacCulloch, Ognall asked him to confirm when he first learned of the nature of the prosecution's case. The psychiatrist admitted that he only knew of the Crown's case the day before the trial began:

Ognall: You say that with remarkable calm and apparent indifference. How were you going to, if called upon, justify your diagnosis on oath, without knowing

MacCulloch:	the nature of the Crown's case? How on earth do you diagnose a man's psychiatric condition without knowing the nature and quality of that which he is alleged by outside evidence to have done? By examining the mental state and taking history. (Cross-examination of MacCulloch, cited in Yallop, 1981: 358)

The judge again intervened, drawing attention to the incongruence between Sutcliffe's words (he was hearing voices from God) and his actions (the sexual assault of his victims):

Mr Justice Boreham:	Are there not truly occasions when that homely old phrase applies, that a man's actions speak louder than his words?
MacCulloch:	Yes, I am sure there are occasions. (Cross-examination of MacCulloch, cited in Yallop, 1981: 358)

Interestingly, Havers reverted from the technical and legal terminology of diminished responsibility to the more non-technical language of 'bad rather than mad':

Havers:	Would you accept that if Sutcliffe was a cold-blooded killer who had an enormous desire to kill prostitutes or just to kill women, he would be 'bad rather than mad'.
Kay:	Yes, I would accept that. (Cross-examination of Kay, cited in Yallop, 1981: 359)

Perhaps Havers considered that the lay language of 'bad rather than mad' was a more persuasive tool to encourage the jury's view that Sutcliffe's motive was to kill any woman available for sexual pleasure, and therefore the plea of diminished responsibility simply could not stand.

The verdict, aftermath and beyond

Three weeks after the trial began, by a verdict of ten to two, Sutcliffe was found guilty of murder and sent to prison for life (Smith, 2013). A year into his prison sentence at HMP Parkhurst, two prison service psychiatrists recommended that Sutcliffe be moved to a mental hospital to receive treatment. Sutcliffe was presenting with continued hallucinations. The Home Secretary, William Whitelaw, denied the request and denied a second application from Sutcliffe's family following a violent attack he suffered from a fellow inmate. Then, in

---

Exercise 2:

Having read some key excerpts of the prosecution's cross-examination, consider the following questions:

1. What questions did the prosecution raise around the credibility of the defence's plea of diminished responsibility?
2. How plausible did you find the testimony of the psychiatrists? What reasons can you give for your answer?

1984, a new Home Secretary, Leon Brittan, accepted the request after being informed that Sutcliffe's mental condition had greatly deteriorated. Sutcliffe was refusing to take any medication at prison and the Home Office said he could not be forced to, 'the implication being that if he was sent to Broadmoor [secure psychiatric hospital], this would change' (Bilton, 2012: 571). This was an interesting turn of events because it suggests that perhaps the psychiatrists who diagnosed Sutcliffe with paranoid schizophrenia were correct in their original assessments of him. However, according to Bilton, some employees of the prison service believed Sutcliffe's transfer happened because the service could not guarantee his safety from other inmates. Bilton also pointed out that, despite the implication that Broadmoor could impose mandatory medication on Sutcliffe, he refused to take any during his first ten years at the psychiatric facility. Eventually, he began taking Depixol, a drug prescribed for schizophrenia. Several people who knew Sutcliffe claimed that he had manipulated authorities so that he could be detained in Broadmoor where he received more benefits than he would have in prison. One such person was his primary nurse, Frank Mone, whose story appeared in a newspaper article in 1995, claiming that Sutcliffe pretended to be schizophrenic:

> He killed because he enjoyed it. ... He is an evil man, it's as simple as that. Peter did not show any signs of schizophrenia. His original diagnosis when he came to Broadmoor talked about the voice in his head which led him to commit murders, but he told me there was no voice. He was on no medication, did not suffer hallucinations and did not show any of the classic signs of schizophrenia. ... He just enjoys the perks at Broadmoor. This voice would appear again if he was being reassessed and then mysteriously disappear. (Mone, quoted in Bilton, 2012: 574–5)

There was another very interesting development in the case relating to evidence of a sexual motive that was not brought into evidence at the trial.

It was revealed in the first edition of Bilton's book in 2003. A retired West Yorkshire detective told the author that, following Sutcliffe's confession, he was stripped and searched and the police found that instead of wearing underwear, he wore a V-neck sweater upside down, 'with his legs placed inside the long sleeves ... allowing the V-neck at the front to expose his genitals' (Bilton, 2012: 493). Additionally, knee pads had been sewn into the garment. Bilton reasoned that the knee pads allowed him to comfortably kneel over his victims while he masturbated and stabbed them. Arguably, the garment suggests both sexual motivation and clear evidence of planning, both of which would be wholly incongruent with the nature of his plea of diminished responsibility. It is something of a mystery that the evidence was not brought to trial, although Bilton speculated that the junior detectives were placed in a difficult position, having strip-searched Sutcliffe *after* the interview and confession.

During the 1980s and 1990s, Sutcliffe confessed to two other assaults in which the victims survived. In 1975, Tracey Browne was 14 when she was attacked by Sutcliffe with a hammer in the 'small, leafy town' (Smith, 2013: 168) of Silsden, Bradford. He had struck up a conversation with Browne as she walked home from a party. Despite the very accurate sketch composite that Browne helped produce, Sutcliffe was not caught for the attack. Had Sutcliffe been caught for his attack on Browne, there would have been very little room to argue that he thought she was a prostitute given the victim's age and location. However, at the time, the investigators were convinced that the person responsible for the other attacks and murders was motivated by a 'dreaded hatred of prostitutes' (Jim Hobson, Acting Assistant Chief Constable of West Yorkshire, cited in Smith, 2013: 189). Indeed, it is widely documented that the hunt for a man with a Geordie accent, who police were convinced hated prostitutes, derailed the investigation so that Sutcliffe was able to murder women for five more years (Smith, 2013). As Smith observed, investigators envisaged a 'reincarnation of Jack the Ripper' and in searching for a mythical figure 'you are not likely to come up with a lorry driver from Bradford' (Smith, 2013: 164). A former West Yorkshire detective who interviewed Sutcliffe after his arrest also believed that Sutcliffe was guilty of other attacks and murders including an attack on a taxi driver, John Tomey, and the murder of a 60-year-old man, Fred Craven, in 1966[14] (Bilton, 2012).

Despite a campaign to Home Secretary David Blunkett in 2003, psychiatrists at Broadmoor continued to defend Sutcliffe's place there. Finally, in 2016 and after 32 years at Broadmoor, a tribunal ruled that Sutcliffe's treatment for schizophrenia was successful, that he no longer required treatment and ordered him to be returned to prison (*The Guardian*, 2016), where he spent the rest of his life in HMP Frankland near Durham. On 13 November 2020, Sutcliffe died of COVID-19 at the University Hospital of North Durham, aged 74 (Topping, 2020).

Conclusion

This chapter illuminates the challenges and complexities of raising the defence of diminished responsibility. It is notable that the verdict in Sutcliffe's case was ten to two in favour of conviction for murder rather than manslaughter. Sutcliffe's case supports previous research indicating that jurors prefer evidence that aligns and sits in context with their personal beliefs and intuition about mental illness and crime. It is likely that the jury's verdict is reflected in the doubts raised by the prosecution, that is, doubts about the validity of his psychiatric diagnosis and therefore doubts about his motive: doubts that were only heightened further by evidence to the contrary. Of course, Sutcliffe's failure to get the defence of diminished responsibility accepted by the court is by no means the only explanation for his conviction for murder. The large number of victims attracted enormous media attention to the case and the pressure of punitive public opinion may have been felt, even if not acknowledged, in the courtroom. Anything other than a conviction for murder might have been perceived as Sutcliffe 'getting away with it'. Furthermore, as we saw in Chapter 7, the social geometry of defendants and victims may influence the outcome of a criminal trial. Perhaps then, if Sutcliffe had been of a higher social status, his defence of diminished responsibility might have been successful. Finally, we saw in Chapter 3 that inconsistency in testimony can damage a defence and, significantly, Sutcliffe was inconsistent in his testimony about the victims who were not sex workers. Perhaps this inconsistency decreased the credibility of his claim to be acting on instructions from God.

Recommended reading

Most of the true crime literature covering the case of Peter Sutcliffe focuses mainly on the pitfalls of the investigation. However, some authors also cover the evidence given at trial in at least one of the chapters. Those books are Yallop (1981), Bilton (2012), Rumbelow (2013), Clark and Tate (2015), and Jones (2020). Kennefick's (2011) article 'Introducing a new diminished responsibility defence for England and Wales' offers a comprehensive and critical overview of the original Homicide Act 1957 and the subsequent Coroners and Justice Act 2009.

Notes

[1]   Prison Officer John Leach testified that he overheard Sutcliffe saying this to his wife while he was in prison awaiting trial (Yallop, 1981: 351).

[2]   A jury can assess the appellant's fitness to plead based on a set of criteria such as whether the appellant has the capacity to understand the charges against them, is able to follow the course of the proceedings and whether they can effectively participate in the trial.

For an overview of the history and contemporary issues related to fitness to plead, see Brown (2019). If deemed not fit to plead, a trial of facts will occur and the court may dispose a Hospital Order, Supervision Order or an Absolute Discharge (Brown, 2019).

[3] Automatism refers to an involuntary behaviour over which an individual has no control (Fenwick, 1990). The appellant is not liable for their behaviour because of an unconscious or involuntary action, for example a crime committed while the person was diabetic and suffering with hypoglycaemia (low blood sugar caused by too much insulin in the bloodstream) (see Broome v Perkins). Non-insane automatism is a complete defence and if successful the defendant is fully acquitted with no requirement for hospital treatment (DeFreitas and Hucker, 2015).

[4] Used only in New Hampshire, the Durham Rule considers that a Not Guilty by Reason of Insanity (NGRI) verdict can be given when the crime is the result of a mental illness. Simply suffering from a mental illness per se could be sufficient to warrant an NGRI verdict. That is, the definition does not rely on evidence to show how the mental illness affected the cognitive and emotional consequences for judgment (Tsimploulis et al, 2018).

[5] Used in Alabama, this definition focuses on volitional control: 'as a result of mental illness the defendant was unable to control his impulses leading to the criminal act' (Tsimploulis et al, 2018: 371).

[6] Except Montana, Idaho, Utah and Kansas, where NGRI was replaced with 'guilty but insane' (Tsimploulis et al, 2018: 371).

[7] Countries such as the US, UK, Canada, Australia and New Zealand adopt a binary system indicating the presence or absence of criminal responsibility whereas other countries such as the Netherlands, Belgium and Germany adopt a system that allows for varying degrees of criminal responsibility (Grossi and Green, 2017; Tsimploulis et al, 2018). See Grossi and Green (2017) and Tsimploulis et al (2018) for a description of how other countries apply the insanity defence.

[8] One of the types of crimes to remain a capital case was committing a murder during the course of a theft. However, this was strongly criticised because murder during the course of a rape remained a non-capital offence (Knowles, 2015). Other crimes that remained capital offences included murder by shooting (for example, the Hanratty case reviewed in Chapter 2) or causing an explosion; murder while resisting arrest or effecting or assisting an escape from custody; murder of a police officer or of a person assisting a police officer; and murder of a prison officer or of a person assisting a prison officer (see Knowles, 2015, for an interesting overview of the history and abolition of the death penalty in the UK).

[9] In 2014, the insanity defence was successfully used in the UK. A 16-year-old defendant who murdered his mother was deemed to have been suffering from severe psychotic mental illness and the jury found him not guilty by reason of insanity. A Hospital Order was imposed (Bajwa, 2014).

[10] See, also, Chapter 10 in this book where we briefly discuss 'common sense' views on insanity.

[11] The determination of whether a person's detention or imprisonment is lawful.

[12] The value of £10 in 1969 is the equivalent value of about £142 today (Inflation Tool, 2021).

[13] A full transcript of Sutcliffe's trial is not available; however, several of the true crime books written about the case include various excerpts that, when taken together, provide sufficient detail.

[14] For a full description, see Chapter 19 in Bilton's 2012 book *Wicked Beyond Belief: The Hunt for the Yorkshire Ripper*.

10

Common Sense and the 'Reasonable Person' in the Trial of Oscar Pistorius

I am not persuaded that a reasonable person with the accused's disabilities in the same circumstances would have fired four shots into that small toilet cubicle.[1]

The shooting of Reeva Steenkamp

At 3.19 am on 14 February 2013, in Pretoria, South Africa, a distraught Oscar Pistorius phoned one of his neighbours, Johan Stander, to ask for help: 'Johan, please, please come to my house. I shot Reeva. I thought she was an intruder. Please, please, please come quick' (Carlin, 2014: 8). In that first brief and urgent request, five minutes after the shots were fired, Pistorius gave an account that determined the way that the criminal case against him would develop. He had shot Reeva (he did not say that someone else had shot her); and although he was not quite accurate in saying he thought that 'she' was an intruder, he thought that he was shooting at an intruder (he did not say, for example, that he was angry with Reeva). He would say the same to others who he called that morning, to the neighbours, security guards, emergency services and police who went to his house, to the magistrate who committed him for trial, and to the judge who presided over it. In terms of the requisites for establishing guilt (see Chapter 1), Pistorius admitted that he was at the scene of the incident and had fired the shots, but he denied criminal intent, claiming that he had fired in self-defence and that Reeva's death was a tragic mistake. As we will see, in evaluating Pistorius's account of events two questions were the focus of attention. First, was the shooting of Reeva a mistake, as Pistorius claimed, or had he really intended to kill her? And second, even if he thought that he was shooting at an intruder, was his action lawful and did it conform to what would be reasonably expected for self-defence in a situation such as this? In this chapter we will explore the role of 'common sense' in influencing answers to the first question and ideas about 'reasonableness' in deciding answers to the second.

The victim of the shooting was Reeva Steenkamp. She was a 29-year-old model and minor TV celebrity in South Africa, having been raised in Port Elizabeth and later moving to Johannesburg. She met 26-year-old Pistorius at a motor-racing track on 4 November 2012 and they began dating immediately (Carlin, 2014). Pistorius was one of South Africa's foremost sports celebrities at the time. He had been born with a congenital defect to his lower legs and feet, which were amputated when he was 11 months old, leaving what he and others called his 'stumps'. From that early age he used prosthetic limbs. Showing great enthusiasm for sports, in 2004, at the age of 18, he took up running using specially designed prosthetic 'blades'. He had great competitive success, both in South Africa and internationally, notably at the Beijing Paralympics (2008) and the London Olympic and Paralympic Games (2012). The 'Blade Runner', as he was nicknamed, also attracted lucrative sponsorship deals for advertising from companies such as Nike and BT (a British telecommunications company), and by 2013 he was estimated to be earning $2 million a year from them (Forbes Africa, 2013). In 2008, he had purchased a four-bedroom house in the wealthy gated community[2] of Silver Woods Estate, Pretoria. It was here that the shooting took place.

The trial of Oscar Pistorius

By February 2013, Pistorius and Reeva had been dating for three months. They had not moved in together, but Reeva quite often spent the night at his house, as she did on the night of 13–14 February. In his testimony during the subsequent trial, Pistorius's narrative of the circumstances which led to the shooting was as follows. He and Reeva had retired to his bedroom quite early on the night of 13 February, around 9 pm. (His was a large bedroom, with a balcony on one side, and a passageway with closets which connected to an en suite bathroom. There was no door between the bedroom and the bathroom, but the toilet inside the bathroom was behind a door). It was a very warm and humid night and the air conditioning was not working; so, to cool the bedroom down, Pistorius put two electric fans on the balcony. He fell asleep between 9 pm and 10 pm, while Reeva was still awake, watching TV and texting on her phone. He woke up 'in the early hours of February 14th' (Pistorius Testimony, 2014: 113),[3] presumably at or just before 3 am. Reeva was still awake and Pistorius noticed that the fans were still running, so he got out of bed, brought them into the bedroom and closed the door and curtains to the balcony. The bedroom was now dark, except for a small

LED light from the TV cabinet. As Pistorius was about to cover the light with some jeans, he heard the bathroom window slide and thought that it was being opened. Although his bedroom was on the first floor of his house, he thought that there was a burglar coming up a ladder from the outside and getting into the bathroom. Pistorius (who was a gun enthusiast) kept a pistol by his bed and he pulled this out, thinking that he needed to 'put myself between the person that had gained access to my house and Reeva' (Pistorius Testimony, 2014: 115). He whispered to Reeva to get down and phone the police and then made his way, cautiously and on his stumps, to the bathroom. Just before he got there, he heard a door slam and thought that this could only have been the door to the toilet, further confirming his fear that someone was in the bathroom. On looking into the bathroom, which was not well lit, he could see that the window was indeed open. Thinking that the intruder had gone into the toilet, he 'started screaming again for Reeva to phone the police' (Pistorius Testimony, 2014: 119). He was not sure whether someone was going to 'come out of the toilet to attack me ... [or] come up the ladder ... and start shooting'. He stayed where he was and 'kept screaming', 'and then I heard a noise from inside the toilet what I perceived to be somebody coming out of the toilet. Before I knew it, I had fired four shots at the door' (Pistorius Testimony, 2014: 119).

Still shouting for Reeva, he went back to the bedroom, only to find that she was not in bed, or on the floor beside it, or hiding behind the curtains to the balcony. At this point, he realised that she might be in the bathroom, so he went back and tried to open the toilet door, but it was locked. He was now panicking; and he went back to the bedroom, opened the balcony doors to shout for help, put on his prosthetic legs, returned to the toilet and tried – but failed – to kick the door open. He took a cricket bat from his bedroom, hit the door three times and knocked out one of the top panels. Leaning through the door, he picked up the key from the floor and opened it. Reeva was on the floor inside, seriously injured and hardly breathing. Not long after this, Pistorius called his neighbour, Mr Stander, and then the emergency services and the estate's security office. By the time Mr Stander and his daughter reached the house, Pistorius had carried Reeva part way downstairs and they helped him carry her to the ground floor (Pistorius Testimony, 2014: 119–26).

Exercise 1:

Now that you have read Pistorius's account of what happened, how plausible do you think it is? Do you think that it makes sense? List any doubts that you have.

Forensic examination would later show that three of the four shots fired through the toilet door had hit Reeva and she sustained wounds to her right thigh, left upper arm and head. Because Pistorius had Talon (expanding) bullets in his pistol, each wound was very serious, but the wound to the head was 'immediately incapacitating' and meant that she could not have breathed for very long after that. At 3.50 am, the paramedics who had arrived pronounced that she was dead. Five minutes later, the police arrived (High Court, Gauteng Division, 2014a).

Was the shooting a mistake?

The police questioned Pistorius about what had happened, while they also searched his house. Perhaps suspecting that his story was not convincing, they arrested Pistorius and took him into custody. He was sent to hospital for a check-up and returned to spend the night in the police jail. The following day, 15 February, he was taken to the Pretoria Magistrates' Court where he was told that prosecutors were planning to charge him with premeditated murder. This charge was formally announced by prosecutor Gerrie Nel at a bail hearing which began on 19 February, and was based on evidence gathered by the police, mainly from Pistorius's neighbours who reported hearing loud voices, bangs and gunshots at his home. Nel alleged that a quarrel between Pistorius and Reeva had ended with the shooting. To counter this, Pistorius's defence team, led by Barry Roux, read a prepared statement from the defendant which would be repeated and amplified in his testimony at trial. Magistrate Desmond Nair granted Pistorius bail while the case progressed, requiring a surety of one million rand (equivalent to £73,000) (Carlin, 2014).

Interestingly, in his comments on the case Magistrate Nair posed some 'sharp questions' about Pistorius's account of events: 'why he had fired into the bathroom door without asking who was there, why he had not seen that Ms. Steenkamp was not in the bed beside him when he arose to check out a strange noise, and why he had not fled rather than confront an intruder' (Polgreen and Cowell, 2013). These were similar to questions circulating in the media and public opinion, where many commentators thought that Reeva would have said something to Pistorius while he was in the bedroom if she had also been there (see, for example, HLN After Dark, 2013). In other words, his version of what happened just did not make sense to them. His claim that he acted in self-defence against someone he thought was an intruder therefore seemed of doubtful plausibility; his account did not square with 'common sense'.

Common sense and world knowledge

The law does not direct judges and jurors to use their common sense when deciding a case, but they do it anyway. For example, feminist scholars have shown that commonly held beliefs about victims' behaviour in alleged rape incidents conform to what they call 'rape myths': 'attitudes and beliefs that are generally false but are widely and persistently held, and that serve to deny and justify male sexual aggression against women' (Lonsway and Fitzgerald, 1994: 134). Typical examples are that sex is consensual if the victim does not resist ('I think it's instinct, if you've got a hand free you'd grab for his eyes or his face or anything'; Ellison and Munro, 2009: 371); and that men have uncontrollable sexual urges ('a woman can stop right up to the last second ... a man cannot, he's just got to keep going, he's like a train, he's just got to keep going'; Ellison and Munro, 2010: 793). Crucially, these kinds of beliefs have been shown to influence judgements about guilt. Thus, Leverick (2020) reported that in 28 studies all but three found that mock jurors who held rape myths were less likely to convict a suspect of rape.

A similar situation holds in relation to suspects who claim an insanity defence. Perlin (1990: 24) observed that 'where defendants do not conform to "popular images of 'craziness,'" the notion of a handicapping mental disability is flatly and unthinkingly rejected'. Skeem and Golding (2001) reported that studies with mock jurors repeatedly show that, in deciding whether or not to support an insanity defence, they do not use the legal definition of insanity that has been given to them by the court but rely on their own views of what insanity looks like. Studying people who had been called for jury service, Skeem and Golding (2001: 586) found that their definitions of insanity could be reduced to one of three different 'prototypes' (or models): 'moral insanity' (manipulative, violent, unpredictable individuals), 'severe chronic disability' (individuals with serious mental illness), and individuals with an 'impaired mental state at the time of the offence'. They also found that jurors who held this latter conception of insanity were more likely than other jurors to accept an insanity defence. We saw in Chapter 9 that a 'crazy' or unreasonable motive in a crime influences jurors' judgements as to whether the defendant was insane at the time of the offence (Pickel, 1998).

Skeem and Golding's work provided good evidence that 'common sense' may not be as common as sometimes thought, because people differ in their beliefs and perceptions about insanity. And what could be said for 'common sense' about insanity could also be applied to 'common sense' about other phenomena that are relevant to matters of crime and justice: different types of crime, offenders and victims, witness credibility, and so on. As Perlin (1990: 26) put it:

> the content and style of expression of common sense varies markedly from one place to another. The truth claims to which [ordinary common sense] gives rise are complex and conflicting, and stem from diverse situational factors, such as geography, culture, class, education, familial background, religion, and current events.

Thus, to speak of 'common sense' may be to impose one individual's views and beliefs as against those of others, or to try to abstract a commonly held view and belief from a variety of individual postures. It is probably for this reason that Pennington and Hastie (1986) used the term 'world knowledge' to describe the views and beliefs derived from real-world experience that people apply to what they judge. World knowledge does not have to be common sense; its importance lies in providing a referential framework with which to evaluate what is said in a trial. As we saw in Chapter 2, Pennington and Hastie argued that evidence is usually presented through the development of a story, which is judged by its consistency, completeness and plausibility. In their words, 'A story is plausible to the extent that it corresponds to the decision maker's knowledge about what typically happens in the world and does not contradict that knowledge' (1991: 528). Against Pistorius's seemingly implausible story that he had not realised that Reeva was in the bathroom, the prosecution developed an alternative story which posited a quarrel between them, with Reeva fleeing to the bathroom and shutting herself in the toilet, only to be followed by Pistorius who angrily shot at her through the door.

Choosing between the stories

The trial was set to start more than a year after Reeva's death, on 3 March 2014 in the High Court of North Gauteng, Pretoria. On 15 August 2013, the Director of Public Prosecutions for North Gauteng filed four indictments against Pistorius.[4] The first was for the murder of Reeva Steenkamp, while the other three were for firearms offences. Two of the latter were for discharging a firearm in a public place (once through the open sunroof of a car in 2010, once in a restaurant in January 2013), and the third was for illegal possession of ammunition found when the police searched his house in February 2013. None of the firearms indictments were related to the murder and could have been processed in a separate hearing, but it was thought that the prosecution wished to include them in his trial for murder in order to demonstrate Pistorius's prior reckless behaviour with guns (Carlin, 2014). The four charges were put to Pistorius by prosecutor Nel at the beginning of the trial and to each he replied 'not guilty' (Carlin, 2014: 155).

Nel called 21 witnesses for the prosecution, whose testimony lasted for 15 days. His objective was to establish that Pistorius and Reeva had been in a heated argument just before she died. The first five lived at varying distances from Pistorius's house and testified to hearing what they thought was a woman screaming, followed by gunshots. Cross-examination by Roux attempted to variously demonstrate that: if there was an argument, they could not have heard what was being said; they might have confused the gunshots and the sounds of the cricket bat that Pistorius used to break open the toilet door; and they mistook Pistorius's high-pitched screams for help for those of a woman in distress. Nel also presented evidence from WhatsApp messages sent between Pistorius and Reeva, placing much weight on one in which she wrote 'I'm scared of u sometimes and how u snap at me and of how u will react to me', which appeared to show a conflicted and potentially aggressive relationship between them. For his part, Roux asked that the next line of the same message also be read out to the court – 'You make me happy 90% of the time and I think we are amazing together' – arguing that no such tension existed. For the defence, Roux called three neighbours of Pistorius who, in sum, testified that they had been awoken by a loud bang and then heard Pistorius calling for help. They were followed by an acoustics specialist who testified that at longer distances the screams of a man or a woman could be indistinguishable. Roux then called Pistorius to the stand and, in direct examination, he gave the account of events that we have already summarised.

We will halt our narrative of the trial at this point, before Pistorius was cross-examined by Nel, because at the end of the trial one of the tasks of the court was to decide between these two stories. If the prosecution's version was considered to be more credible, Pistorius would be convicted for the premeditated murder of Reeva and face a sentence of life imprisonment (with eligibility for parole after 25 years), or a minimum sentence of 15 years in prison if premeditation had not been demonstrated (Terblanche and Mackenzie, 2008: 408). On the other hand, if the court accepted Pistorius's claim that he had not intended to kill Reeva it would need to decide how to categorise this 'mistake'.

Juries were abolished in South Africa in 1969, and decisions on conviction or acquittal are in the hands of a judge, accompanied in serious cases such as murder by two assessors with experience in criminal justice. The judge and assessors form a 'jury of three' which decides on the conviction or acquittal of the defendant by a unanimous or majority vote, while sentencing is a matter reserved for the judge (van Zyl Smit and Isakow, 1985). The judge assigned to Pistorius's trial was Thokozile Masipa, who by then had been on the bench for 16 years, having been only the second Black woman to be appointed as a High Court judge in South Africa. The assessors, both lawyers, were Janette Henzen-Du Toit and Themba Mazibuko. It fell to this jury of three to decide on Pistorius's 'mistake'. Its verdict was prepared in written form – a 73-page document – and read out to the court by Judge Masipa beginning on 11 September 2014.

Through a careful analysis of phone records from Pistorius and his neighbours, an evaluation of the evidence relating to the shouts and shots, and the WhatsApp messages between Pistorius and Reeva, Judge Masipa concluded that there had been no quarrel between them in the early morning of 14 February. Interestingly, she noted that:

There are ... a number of aspects in the case which do not make sense, such as:

- Why the accused did not ascertain from the deceased when he heard the window open, whether she too had heard anything.
- Why he did not ascertain whether the deceased had heard him since he did not get a response from the deceased before making his way to the bathroom.
- Why the deceased was in the toilet and only a few metres away from the accused, did not communicate with the accused, or phone the police as requested by the accused. This the deceased could have done, irrespective of whether she was in the bedroom or in the toilet, as she had her cell phone with her. It makes no sense to say she did not hear him scream 'get out'. It was the accused's version that he screamed at the top of his voice, when ordering the intruders to get out. Another question is:
- Why the accused fired not one, one shot but four shots, before he ran back to the bedroom to try to find the deceased. (High Court, Gauteng Division, 2014a: 42)

While these queries echoed those made by Magistrate Nair and by commentators in the media, in the court's view 'These questions shall unfortunately remain a matter of conjecture' (High Court, Gauteng Division, 2014a: 42); they were not sufficient to undermine Pistorius's claim that he had made a mistake. Moreover, Judge Masipa added that Pistorius's distraught reactions after the shooting were consistent with the shock at discovering the consequences of his mistake and could not have been faked.

The question that the court then considered was how to judge Pistorius's behaviour in light of the mistake. Here, it followed the perspective on criminal intent which, according to legal scholar Phelps (2016), is now increasingly prevalent in South Africa. This perspective holds that if X intends to kill Y but in fact kills Z by mistake, X cannot be found guilty of the *murder* of Z because they had no intent to kill Z. Instead, X would be guilty of the *culpable homicide* of Z because they failed to take precautions to safeguard Z. Transferred to the Pistorius case, this would mean that if he intended to kill an intruder but in fact killed Reeva, he could be guilty of culpable homicide, an offence that carries a discretionary rather than minimum sentence. In this regard, Judge Masipa asked:

How could the accused reasonably have foreseen that the shots he fired would kill the deceased? Clearly he did not subjectively foresee this as a possibility that he would kill the person behind the door, let alone the deceased, as he thought she was in the bedroom at the time. (High Court, Gauteng Division, 2014a: 50)

And she concluded that, because of this, Pistorius could not be convicted of murder. Nevertheless, a conviction for culpable homicide did not automatically follow because the court also had to consider Pistorius's claim that he had fired in self-defence.

Was the shooting lawful?

In South Africa, self-defence is known as a 'private defence' and, if successfully demonstrated, will lead to an acquittal. There is an additional concept of 'putative private defence' where a person thinks or fears that they are about to be attacked and takes action to protect themself (Phelps, 2016; Snyman, 2004). Because no one had yet emerged from behind the toilet door in Pistorius's bathroom, and he reported only that he heard a noise in the toilet, an attack had not begun and his plea of not guilty was therefore a case of putative private defence – he had made a mistake in thinking that someone was about to attack him. While both a private defence and a putative private defence require the defendant to demonstrate the type of harm they would have suffered from the attack, its imminency and the proportionality of the response to it, the putative private defence also requires an assessment of what the defendant perceived:

> [With a] putative private defence, the focus shifts to the perpetrator as an individual, and the question then is whether that person, in the light of his or her personal aptitudes, gifts, shortcomings and knowledge, could fairly be blamed by the legal order for the unlawful act. (Snyman, 2004: 192)

The claim of putative private defence by Pistorius meant that the trial focused a lot of attention on his state of mind and behaviour in front of the toilet door. As we will see, closely entwined with an assessment of his actions were considerations about what a 'reasonable person' would do in the same circumstances.

Self-defence and the 'reasonable person'

Whereas common sense is not a standard of evaluation explicitly recognised by the law, the concept of a 'reasonable person' is central to cases where self-defence is claimed (Moran, 2010). As Lee (2003: 127; emphasis added) expressed it:

> Under traditional self-defense doctrine ... a defendant is justified in using *a reasonable amount of force* against another person if *she honestly and reasonably believes* that (1) she is in imminent or immediate danger

of unlawful bodily harm from her aggressor, and (2) the use of such force is necessary to avoid the danger.

Thus, to decide if the force used is reasonable, the court has to determine what a 'reasonable person' would have done in the same circumstances.

However, just as there may be questions about whose 'common sense' is being invoked when it is used to support a judgement about a case, there are also questions about who the 'reasonable person' is – or should be. Forell (2010) noted that for a very long time both the law and legal practitioners in the US referred to the 'reasonable man', reflecting a patriarchal conception in which women were to be judged by male standards. It was only in the 1970s and 1980s that the genderless term 'reasonable person' began to appear, although Forell noted that some members of the judiciary continue to refer to the 'reasonable man'. However, even with the increased recognition that the hypothetical figure of reference should be the 'reasonable person', legal scholars have continued to raise questions and concerns regarding the characteristics of that person. Two schools of thought and practice have emerged, advocating either an 'objective' or 'subjective' definition of the reasonable person.

The objectively defined reasonable person would be an 'average person who is statistically similar to most other people' (Miller, 2010: 264). The problem here is that the 'average person' may be an unavoidable abstraction: how can we decide their characteristics and, more significantly, who decides them? Rothstein (1999: 118) held that 'The hypothetical reasonable person is not the average person or the average juror, but the personification of a community ideal of reasonable behavior. This is an objective and largely unitary standard'. However, Miller (2010) argued that even this 'objective' standard is not gender-neutral because the community ideal of reasonable behaviour reflects male, rather than female, beliefs and values. It could, for example, include some of the rape myths mentioned previously, and feminist scholars have pointed to the ways in which women are judged by male standards, either as victims of rape (Burgin and Flynn, 2021) or killers of their partners (Keegan, 2013). Moving beyond the gender framework, Lee (2003: 4) argued that 'social norms, particularly those regarding gender, race, and sexual orientation, can influence legal decision makers'. For example, as she critically expressed it, 'It is "reasonable" to kill a Black man in self-defense if pervasive race norms stereotype Blacks as dangerous criminals' (2003: 5).

The subjective approach to visualising the reasonable person calls for attention to some of the personal characteristics of defendants, such as their gender or race. Thus, if the defendant is a Black man, jurors should be instructed to put themselves 'in the defendant's shoes' (Lee, 2003: 224) in order to decide whether he acted reasonably. The same would apply to a case involving a White female defendant: would her actions have been those of a 'typical' White woman under the circumstances? While this is an important principle, supported by many critical scholars (Lee, 2003), the subjectivist approach confronts two interrelated problems. The first is, which of the defendant's characteristics should be taken into account and why? It is a matter of logic that the more characteristics are included, the smaller the number of subjects in the reference group and, as Lee (2003: 207) put it, 'Total subjectivism – taking into account all of the defendant's characteristics, including ways of thinking – would eliminate a "reasonable person"'. The second is the difficulty that jurors may face in trying to imagine a 'reasonable person' whose social and cultural characteristics differ greatly from their own. For example, how easily could a young White middle-income female juror 'put herself in the shoes' of an older, minority, low-income male? For these reasons, most proposals for a subjective definition of the reasonable person usually focus on a single characteristic, such as gender, race or sexual orientation.

As a hybrid approach, blending objective and subjective models of the reasonable person, Lee proposed that jurors should engage in 'switching' exercises. For example, Miller (2010: 250) argued that 'voluntary manslaughter continues to accommodate men who kill their wives in the heat of passion, but not women who kill their husbands for the same reason' (who are more likely to be convicted of murder). In line with Lee's proposal, if the defendant is a man who 'in the heat of passion' has killed his female partner because of her infidelity, to decide whether this was a 'reasonable' response to provocation jurors should switch the genders of the defendant and victim: if a woman had killed a man in the same circumstances, would this also be seen as a 'reasonable' response to provocation? If jurors find that their opinions change according to the respective genders of the aggressor and victim, this would indicate that they are applying different standards of reasonableness and that they need to re-examine their attitudes and beliefs. In relation to race, Lee proposed that switching could be used where the racial characteristics of the defendant and victim differ. Keeping all the circumstances of the crime the same, jurors should ask themselves whether their decision in a case with a White defendant and Black victim would be the same as when the defendant is Black and the victim is White.

Was Pistorius's behaviour reasonable?

As is well known, defendants are not required to testify at their trial. Whether or not to take the stand is their choice, for it falls to the prosecution to prove guilt, not to the defence to prove innocence. Although Pistorius had previously given his version of events through a statement read at his bail hearing in 2013, and a further statement read by his legal team at the start of the trial giving the explanation for his plea of not guilty, we have seen that he also chose to take the stand. Apparently, his decision was motivated by his desire to persuade the court through his own words that he thought he was shooting at an intruder (Carlin, 2014: 195). Roux took him through some of his background and then the events of 13–14 February which we have summarised previously, and as Pistorius narrated the latter, he broke down more than once, crying and retching (something he had done frequently during earlier parts of the trial).

Nel's cross-examination of Pistorius lasted for five days and was often confrontational in tone. Numerous times, he accused Pistorius of lying, of 'tailoring [making things up] as we go', of making mistakes in his testimony, and of not taking responsibility for what he had done (Pistorius Testimony, 2014; see also, Carlin, 2014: 191). His questioning was detailed, and his method was to switch back and forth between topics, particularly in the search for inconsistencies in Pistorius's testimony by comparing it with things that he had recently said on the stand, or in his bail application or explanation of plea.[5] Apart from the objective of portraying Pistorius as an unreliable and untruthful witness and trying to get him to admit to a quarrel with Reeva, Nel also identified crucial differences in the way in which he described the shooting. In his answer to Nel's very first questions, Pistorius said 'I made a mistake' (Pistorius Testimony, 2014: 142). Later, he referred to the shooting as 'an accident':

Nel: Mr Pistorius … you referred in your plea explanation to this incident, or this occurrence as 'an accident'. Is that correct?

Pistorius: That is correct, My Lady.[6]

Nel: What was the accident?

Pistorius: The accident was that I discharged my firearm in the belief that an intruder was coming out to attack me, My Lady.

Nel: So the discharge was not accidental? Or was the discharge accidental?

Pistorius: The discharge was accidental, My Lady. I believed that somebody was coming out. I believed the noise that I heard inside the toilet was somebody coming out to attack me, or to take my life.

Nel: No. Do you know what an 'accidental discharge' is?

Pistorius: My understanding is that I did not intend to discharge my firearm.

Nel: I am going to be rude, Mr Pistorius, but I have warned you before. … The fact is, did you shoot at the intruders with the intention to shoot them?

Pistorius: My Lady, I shot because I was at that point with that …
                 that split moment I believed somebody was coming out
                 to attack me, that is what made me fire my … out of fear.
                 I did not have time to think. I discharged my firearm.
                 (Pistorius Testimony, 2014: 199–201)

And still later, Nel challenged Pistorius to clarify his testimony about
the shooting:

Nel: Is it your defence that you fired at the attacker?
Pistorius: No, My Lady.
Nel: Or wait, I will put it differently. Did you fire at the
                 perceived attacker?
Pistorius: I fired at the door, My Lady.
Nel: No, no. Listen to my question, Mr Pistorius! I am not going
                 to let this one go. Now the way I understand the case is
                 that you acted in putative self-defence and I know it is a
                 big word, but I will try and assist you with that. That you
                 perceived an attack, that you fired at the attacker to kill him,
                 or to ward off the attack. That is not true. Am I right?
Pistorius: I did not fire to kill anyone, My Lady.
Nel: Or to ward off an attack.
Pistorius: My Lady, I did not have time to think, I heard this noise
                 and I thought it was somebody coming out of to attack
                 me, so I fired my firearm.
Nel: Your defence has now changed, sir, from putative self-
                 defence to involuntary action. Is that what you are
                 telling me?
Pistorius: I do not understand the law, Madam, what I can reply
                 and tell the court is what I am asked and I can reply as
                 to what I thought.
Nel: But I would not say I understand the law, I would not
                 say that, but that is what I hear. That your defence is
                 not one of putative self-defence anymore. You can forget
                 that. … It is now I have … I do not know why I fired.
Pistorius: No, I am not saying I do not know why. I have given
                 a reason to why I fired, My Lady. I thought somebody
                 was coming out to attack me.
Nel: But you did not fire at that person.
Pistorius: I fired in the direction of where I thought the attack was
                 coming from, My Lady.
Nel: No. You see, Mr Pistorius, you are now. … You now
                 have to give a lot of answers and you know why, Mr

Pistorius? It is because you know exactly you fired at
Reeva. These other versions of yours cannot work.
(Pistorius Testimony, 2014: 498–500)

Through his cross-examination, Nel exposed vagaries in Pistorius's
narrative of what happened. He focused particularly on what he saw as
his incompatible descriptions of his behaviour: on the one hand, Pistorius
claimed that he shot because he *believed* that an intruder was about to attack
him, but on the other Pistorius claimed that *he did not have time to think* and
had simply fired at the door, in the direction of an expected attack. Nel
argued that Pistorius had changed his version from putative self-defence to
involuntary action.

To bolster this argument, in cross-examination Nel might also have referred
to Pistorius's evidence in chief to Roux, in which he had said 'Before I knew
it, I had fired four shots at the door' (Pistorius Testimony, 2014: 119), because
to say 'Before I knew it' was to signal unthinking and perhaps involuntary
action. Nevertheless, this and other phrases and descriptions from Pistorius
were included by Nel in his closing statement to the court as evidence of
Pistorius's 'contradictory versions' of how and why the shots came to be
fired (State's Heads of Arguments, 2014: 53). Nel's objective was not only
to portray Pistorius as 'an appalling witness' (State's Heads of Arguments,
2014: 23), but also to support the prosecution's claim that Reeva's murder
was premeditated. Nevertheless, recognising that the court might see things
differently, he also argued that the evidence in the case would support a
conviction for murder, either because of a clear intent to kill 'the intruder'
or because he must have foreseen that the person in the toilet might die,
but nevertheless decided to shoot.[7] And he went so far as to argue that,
even if the court accepted Pistorius's version of the events, he should still
be found guilty of culpable homicide: 'A reasonable man, armed with a
firearm, facing a closed door would not have fired four shots through the
door if "provoked" only by a sound' (State's Heads of Arguments, 2014: 106).
He was thus seeking by all arguments possible to rebut Pistorius's claim of
putative private defence.[8]

In closing for the defence, Roux went even further than Nel by listing all
of the different ways in which Pistorius had described his shooting behaviour
(Defence's Heads of Arguments, 2014: 189–91). However, he did not dwell
on the 'contradictions' alleged by Nel but argued that all of Pistorius's
statements were consistent with what he, Roux, now put to the court:

[I]t is respectfully submitted that the version of the Accused as to the
circumstances which prevailed both prior to and during the discharge of
his firearm came about as a result of him having in a fearful and vulnerable

state discharged his firearm in reflex during the episode of an exaggerated startle response.[9] (Defence's Heads of Arguments, 2014: 191–2)

In other words, Roux argued for involuntary action on the part of Pistorius rather than putative private defence. He added to this that Pistorius had no intent to kill Reeva, because he did not think that she was in the toilet, and therefore he could not be convicted of murder. He also argued that Pistorius could not be convicted of culpable homicide because his behaviour was not negligent. Here, Roux appealed to the well-established legal principle that negligence can only be determined by comparing a defendant's behaviour with that of a 'reasonable person' in the same circumstances: would the reasonable person have done what the defendant did? Additionally, he pointed to precedents arguing that the 'reasonable person' should not be defined as simply anyone but must take into account significant characteristics of the accused, and in this case Pistorius's disability was the significant characteristic. He cited a previous ruling from the South African courts that established criteria for subjective definitions of reasonableness: 'One must test negligence by the touchstone of the reasonable person of the same background and educational level, culture, sex and race of the accused. The further individual peculiarities of the accused alone must be disregarded'. He then added: 'There can be no doubt that disability does not form part of 'individual peculiarities' and therefore it must be taken into account in the concept of the reasonable person. ... To deny disability in determining reasonableness, would mean that disability is unreasonable' (Defence's Heads of Arguments, 2014: 238). Thus, the question was not whether *anyone* faced with the circumstances which Pistorius described would have acted as he did, but whether *anyone with a similar disability* would have done so. Thus, Roux concluded, 'We respectfully submit that the Accused, in the peculiar circumstances and having regard to his disability and the effects of such disability, did not act negligently' (Defence's Heads of Arguments, 2014: 242). In other words, he should not be found guilty of culpable homicide because of his 'reflex' action in firing the gun.

In considering Pistorius's claim to putative private defence, Judge Masipa described Pistorius as 'a very poor witness' (High Court, Gauteng Division, 2014a: 39) and, in alignment with the prosecution's argument, noted that his varied versions of events represented 'a number of defences or apparent defences' (High Court, Gauteng Division, 2014a: 30). She disagreed with the defence's claim that the shooting was simply a reflex action and, citing Pistorius's statements that he did not intend to shoot anyone, argued that, if this was so, he could not claim that he had acted in putative private defence. She then focused on his act of firing the shots through the toilet door and whether this was a reasonable action or constituted negligence.

In her judgment, Judge Masipa chose to frame disability as a form of 'vulnerability' which was not 'unique [that is, an individual peculiarity] as millions of people in this country can easily fit into that category' (High Court, Gauteng Division, 2014a: 53). Although disability and vulnerability had not been cited in previous rulings as relevant referents for reasonableness, Masipa nevertheless considered them in this case. She pointed out that, on hearing the sound in the bathroom, Pistorius could have immediately called security or the police, or he could have run to the balcony to shout for help.[10] Indeed, in her view, 'The accused had reasonable time to reflect, to think and to conduct himself reasonably' (High Court, Gauteng Division, 2014a: 55). From there, she proceeded to consider his action in front of the toilet door:

> On the facts of this case I am not persuaded that a reasonable person with the accused's disabilities in the same circumstances would have fired four shots into that small toilet cubicle. Having regard to the size of the toilet and the calibre of the ammunition used in the firearm, a reasonable person with the accused's disability and in his position would have foreseen that if he fired shots at the door, *the person inside the toilet might be struck and might die as a result*. ... *I am of the view that the accused acted too hastily and used excessive force*. In the circumstances it is clear that his conduct was negligent. (High Court, Gauteng Division, 2014a: 55–6; emphasis added)

Given this negligent behaviour, Pistorius was convicted of culpable homicide and on 21 October 2014 sentenced to five years in prison.[11]

Many people thought that Pistorius should have been convicted of murder (DJILP, 2014), as did the prosecution, which was given leave by Judge Masipa to appeal the verdict in December 2014 (Smith, 2014). The case was heard in the Supreme Court of Appeal in November 2015, where the Director of Public Prosecutions argued that Pistorius's conviction for culpable homicide should be set aside and replaced with a conviction for murder (*dolus eventualis*). The panel of five judges delivered its ruling on 3 December, read by Judge Eric Leach. The Court of Appeal disagreed with Judge Masipa's view that Pistorius's behaviour had been merely negligent:

> As a matter of common sense, at the time the fatal shots were fired, the possibility of the death of the person behind the door was clearly an obvious result. And in firing not one, but four shots, such a result became even more likely. But that is exactly what the accused did. ... In these circumstances I have no doubt that in firing the fatal shots the accused must have foreseen, and therefore did foresee, that *whoever was behind the toilet door might die, but reconciled himself to that event occurring and gambled with that person's life*. This constituted dolus eventualis on

his part, and *the identity of his victim is irrelevant to his guilt.* (Supreme Court of Appeal, 2015: 27–8; emphasis added)

It is significant that the appeal court took a different position to the trial court on the identity of the victim. Whereas Judge Masipa had ruled out the possibility of murder because Pistorius did not intend to kill Reeva, the appeal court took the view that Pistorius's intent was the sole consideration and that the identity of the victim was not relevant.[12] By reasoning in this way, the appeal court broadened the possible verdicts beyond culpable homicide to include murder.

Indeed, it argued that it was 'a matter of common sense' that a case of shooting like this represented *dolus eventualis* and therefore murder. The conviction for culpable homicide was set aside and replaced by a conviction for murder.[13]

Comparing the arguments from the High Court and the Court of Appeal, we can see that they coincided in attributing to Pistorius the knowledge that whoever was behind the door might die as a result of the shots he fired, but they diverged in relation to his motivation. For the trial court, he had 'acted too hastily and used excessive force'; in other words, he had not taken steps to avoid the death of the victim and his behaviour was unreasonable. For the Court of Appeal, he had 'reconciled himself' to the possibility of death and pressed ahead regardless; his behaviour was not just unreasonable, it was criminal. The fact that Pistorius did not give a consistent and clear account of how the shooting happened may have allowed these differing judgments about his behaviour, but it is also important to observe the ways in which common sense and conceptions of reasonableness fed into each. The High Court, which seemingly saw a lack of common sense in Pistorius's failure to raise the alarm *before* moving towards the bathroom, did not think that a reasonable person with his condition would have fired the shots at the toilet door. The Court of Appeal argued that common sense supported a conclusion that firing 'not one, but four' shots through the toilet door indicated that the accused knew that death could result, leading to the inference that Pistorius saw this as an acceptable outcome.

From this, we see how different notions of common sense and what is reasonable could lead to different judgments in the Pistorius case, although their content is not entirely clear because neither the High Court nor the Court of Appeal fully explicated their reasoning. Perhaps one way to excavate those notions would be to use Lee's (2003) proposal on 'switching' to see if different verdicts might arise, and why. For example, if the events had transpired in exactly the same sequence, but with Pistorius in the toilet and Reeva in the bedroom, how might she have been judged if she had shot him? Equally significant, what if the person in the toilet had been an intruder, as Pistorius claimed to have thought? How would his actions have been judged? Carlin (2014: 3) observed that 'the faceless intruder of his imagination had to have had a black face, because the fact was that for white people crime mostly did have a black face' (see also, Langa et al, 2020). Thus, if Pistorius's victim had been a Black male, how would he have been judged?[14]

Exercise 2:

In deciding the first sentence for Pistorius for the conviction of culpable homicide, the court referred to several previous cases which were fairly similar, including the following:

> In the matter of the State v Siyabonga Mdunge (RC777/12 Regional Court Pietermaritzburg), the accused and the deceased were sleeping at their home when at about 00:30 the accused was awoken by a noise as if a window was opening. He thought a burglar was trying to get into the house. Fearful for his life he grabbed his firearm from his bedside pedestal drawer and made his way to the entrance of the room. He could hear the noise coming from the bathroom. Slowly he made his way to the bathroom door to investigate. As he reached the bathroom door it suddenly opened. Startled and afraid for his life, he discharged his firearm thinking that the person who opened the door was a burglar. That person, however, was not an intruder, but his wife. He rushed her to hospital, but it was too late.
>
> The accused in Mdunge was arrested for murder, but entered a plea and sentence agreement with the National Prosecuting Authority (NPA) in terms of section 105A of the Criminal Procedure Act. In terms of the agreement, the National Prosecuting Authority accepted a plea of guilty to culpable homicide. (High Court, Gauteng Division, 2014b: 23–4)

Analyse the similarities and differences between the Mdunge case and the Pistorius case. Do you think that a charge of murder was appropriate in the Mdunge case? Do you think that his conviction for culpable homicide was appropriate?

Conclusion

Our objective in this chapter has been to examine how 'common-sense' reasoning and beliefs about the 'reasonable person' featured in judgements about Pistorius's behaviour and led to different verdicts: that proposed by the defence (acquittal because his disability led him to act in putative private defence, or involuntarily), by the High Court (guilty of culpable homicide), and by the Court of Appeal (guilty of murder with *dolus eventualis*). Different notions of common sense or beliefs about what a reasonable person would do led to different evaluations of the case, and if the courts or the public had engaged in a 'switching' exercise further variants (and possible verdicts) would likely have appeared.

Common sense appears to contribute to many judgments about criminal cases. Research by Pennington and Hastie (1986, 1991) and others (Willmott et al, 2018) has shown that 'world knowledge' is used to assess the plausibility of stories told in trials, although identifying and probing such knowledge may be difficult (Wagenaar, 1995). Additionally, Friedland (1989) highlighted the use of common sense in evaluations of witness credibility. We saw in Chapter 3 that a lack of 'common sense' was used by both the prosecution and the judge to question the plausibility of Crippen's account about his wife's disappearance. In Chapter 4, we saw that common sense fuelled a powerful indictment of Rosemary West's claim of innocence because many people felt that 'she must have known' about the murders (Masters, 1997). Similarly, given the debates about Sutcliffe's insanity (see Chapter 9), if we apply Skeem and Golding's (2001) research (reviewed earlier), it is possible that the jurors in Sutcliffe's trial were less likely to accept a defence of insanity because the evidence did not fit their beliefs about what insanity looks like. And where the law directs attention to the 'reasonable person', common sense may be an important point of reference. Its role in judgements about guilt or innocence therefore looks to be very significant and difficult to diminish.

Of course, as in the other chapters in this book, we do not claim that the verdicts on Pistorius were driven entirely by the use of common sense, world knowledge or beliefs about reasonableness. We have already mentioned another factor that undoubtedly contributed to the outcomes, which was his failure to give a clear and consistent account of his actions and mental state at the time of the shootings (see Chapter 3 on the role of inconsistencies in testimony). This led to the High Court's rejection of his claim of self-defence and allowed both that court and the Court of Appeal to construct slightly different versions of what happened. Additionally, if we apply 'social geometry' (see Chapter 7) to this case, rather in the mode of 'switching', we would predict that, if the victim had been of lower social standing (for example, an intruder), Pistorius would have been less likely to have been arrested, prosecuted and convicted of either culpable homicide or murder. However, given that Reeva belonged to a very similar social and cultural world to Pistorius, his celebrity status did not appear to favour him in many ways.

Recommended reading

John Carlin's book (*Chase Your Shadow: The Trials of Oscar Pistorius*, 2014) offers a good account of the trial and also includes a lot of material about Pistorius, Reeva Steenkamp and the media interest in the case which we have not included in this chapter. Cynthia Lee's book on *Murder and the Reasonable Man: Passion and Fear in the Criminal Courtroom* (2003) gives a detailed, readable and thought-provoking analysis of the debates and dilemmas surrounding the definition of the 'reasonable person'.

Notes

[1] High Court, Gauteng Division (2014a: 55).

[2] Gated communities are walled off from surrounding neighbourhoods, with a single point of access and often a security kiosk that is staffed permanently or part-time. Among other things, they are designed to protect the residents from burglary, theft and violent crime. They are particularly common in countries, such as South Africa, with high crime rates. For South Africans who followed the Pistorius case, his residence in a gated community and the associated cluster of meanings relating to race, inequality and fear of crime were unremarkable, and unremarked. However, this was the context which informed Pistorius's portrayal of his actions (Langa et al, 2020).

[3] The information and quotes from Pistorius's testimony, here and in what follows, are taken from a transcript from the trial which is available online. There is no author indicated on the transcript, but we verified its accuracy by comparing it with recordings of the testimony which were available on YouTube, for example *Sky News*, 2014.

[4] The document was published online at https://www.news24.com/news24/Archives/City-Press/Full-document-Oscar-Pistorius-indictment-20150429-2. Appended to the indictments was a list of 107 witnesses who the prosecution might call, including Frank Chiziweni. Chiziweni was Pistorius's housekeeper and had a room on the ground floor of the property. At the trial, Johan Stander's daughter testified that when she arrived at Pistorius's house Chiziweni was standing at the foot of the stairs, along with a security guard. When the police questioned Chiziweni about the events of 13–14 February, he said that he had been asleep while the shooting took place and did not hear anything. Although many believed that this could not have been possible (Gutman and Thom, 2014), Chiziweni was not called to testify for the prosecution, or for the defence, and Pistorius mentioned him only once (and not by name) during his testimony, in connection with the location of a magazine rack in the toilet.

[5] As we saw in Chapter 3, the identification and exploitation of inconsistencies in a witness's testimony is often a key focus of cross-examinations.

[6] In South African courts, the convention is that witnesses answer questions as if speaking to the judge.

[7] This latter form of intent, in which the perpetrator knows that someone could be killed and nevertheless proceeds, is known in South African law as *dolus eventualis*. In such cases, from the perspective of the offender, the victim's death would be an acceptable outcome. Murder with *dolus eventualis* is not the same as culpable homicide, where the perpetrator knows that their action might cause death and takes no steps to avoid it. In culpable homicide, the offender does not see the victim's death as an acceptable outcome; they have killed through negligence rather than intent.

[8] In Chapter 1, we identified how the formulation of several alternative charges can weaken the prosecution's case, because they are unable to tell a single story about the crime. Here, we see a similar example of arguing for alternative charges that could be used to convict the defendant.

[9] A startle response is a reflexive and defensive response – such as closing the eyes, hunching the shoulders, bending the trunk and the knee – to a sudden event, such as a loud noise

or flash of light (Corsini, 2002). In Pistorius's case, Roux argued that there were three 'startle events': the opening of the bathroom window, the slamming of the toilet door and a noise from inside the toilet (thought to have been the movement of a magazine rack).

10   We could interpret this as common-sense thinking which informed her judgment about the reasonableness of Pistorius's actions.

11   Pistorius was acquitted of two of the firearms offences (shooting through an open car roof; illegal possession of ammunition) and convicted for the remaining one (discharging a firearm in the restaurant), and sentenced to a suspended sentence of three years, which was to run concurrently with the sentence for culpable homicide.

12   Phelps (2016) claimed that this perspective, which did not take account of mistaken identity, had been replaced by the perspective adopted by Judge Masipa which links intent with the identity of the victim. However, we can see its continued presence in this argument made by the Supreme Court of Appeal.

13   Having set aside Pistorius's conviction for culpable homicide and replaced it with a verdict of murder, the Court of Appeal referred the case back to the High Court for resentencing. In July 2016, Judge Masipa increased Pistorius's sentence to six years in prison, well below the presumptive minimum of 15 years for murder. This led to a further appeal by the prosecution (National Prosecution Authority, 2016), arguing that the sentence was 'shockingly lenient'. In November 2017, the Supreme Court of Appeal increased Pistorius's sentence to 15 years, deducting 19 months for time already served and leaving 13 years and five months still to be served (Supreme Court of Appeal, 2017).

14   Langa et al (2020: 511) also commented that a local journalist had wondered 'whether it would have been an issue if Pistorius had in actual fact killed a black man who was in his home'. The 'issue' here might have been the amount of publicity that a case involving a Black victim would have received, presumably much less than for the killing of Reeva. However, it might also have been whether killing someone behind a closed door was reasonable. If the victim were a Black male, how much police and prosecutorial attention would have been given to whether or not he represented the imminent threat which is integral to the concept of self-defence, or would the violent Black male of the popular imagination have been seen as always representing an imminent threat?

11

Amanda Knox's Trial in
the Media

> I exist only through the lens of Meredith's murder in some
> people's minds. They forget that I'm a human being with my
> own life and my own experiences.[1]

The American student accused of murdering Meredith Kercher covered
her ears to block out the sound of her housemate's dying screams, say
Italian police.

In an extraordinary statement to detectives Amanda Knox claims she
sat in the kitchen of their house and listened to the British student
being killed.

The 20-year-old said she knew Miss Kercher was in her bedroom with
musician Patrick Diya Lumumba – but did nothing to help.

The student wasn't clear if she heard 'thuds' but 'I could imagine what
was going on', she told police in Perugia after 'crumbling' under days
of questioning.

'I can't remember how long they were together in the bedroom but
the only thing I can say is that at a certain point I remember hearing
Meredith's screams and I covered my ears.

'Then I don't remember anything else. There is such a lot going on
in my head.'

The bizarre extracts from a rambling 'confession' by Knox
emerged yesterday.

The girl, her Italian boyfriend Raffaele Sollecito, 23, and Congolese
father of one Lumumba, were arrested in a series of dawn raids
on Tuesday.

The trio are accused of murdering Miss Kercher, 21, as she fought off a violent sexual attack. She was found lying semi-naked in her bedroom six days ago with her throat cut. (Hale and Pisa, 2007)

Exercise 1:

1. Having read the newspaper article, how much of it is familiar to you?
2. Can you find parts of it where the article assumes that you have knowledge of the case?
3. What information did you think was missing from the article?
4. Do you think the article is assuming someone was guilty?
5. Do you think Amanda Knox was guilty? Or do you think it is too quick to judge? Why do you think you made that decision?

The crime, convictions and acquittals

On 2 November 2007, 21-year-old British exchange student Meredith Kercher was found sexually assaulted and murdered in her bedroom in Perugia, Italy. The alarm was raised by one of her flatmates, 20-year-old American exchange student, Amanda Knox. Knox reported that she had spent the night at the residence of her boyfriend, Raffaele Sollecito, and had returned to her flat on the morning of 2 November to shower and change her clothes. Apart from Kercher, there were two other flatmates, Italian students, who were away for the weekend. Knox noticed droplets of blood in the bathroom; Kercher's bedroom door was closed and locked, and she did not respond to knocks and shouts. Knox returned to Sollecito's flat, told him about her concern, and he called the police. When the police arrived, they forced open the door and discovered Kercher's body. Despite having raised the alarm, Knox and Sollecito quickly fell under suspicion because the authorities thought that their behaviour was odd. As they waited outside the small house in which the flat was located, the couple were observed embracing and kissing and the lead prosecutor later said it was not what would be expected of someone supposedly grieving for her murdered friend (Knox, 2015).

Five days after the murder, the police interrogated Knox for several hours during the middle of the night. She was not offered a lawyer and the interrogation was not recorded. After repeated questioning, she said that she had been in the flat when Kercher was killed and she implicated Patrick Lumumba, the owner of a local bar where Knox worked part-time, in the murder. Based on her statement, Lumumba was arrested; however, he was released following confirmation of his alibi, that he was in his bar at the time of the murder. Knox was deemed to have falsely implicated Lumumba, thereby arousing further suspicion about her involvement in the murder of Kercher (Knox, 2015).

Knox retracted her statement the following day, claiming that the police bullied her, asked her to 'imagine' what had happened, offered her Lumumba's name (leading to his implication) and hit the back of her head calling her a 'stupid liar'. Nevertheless, the prosecution continued to gather evidence against both her and Sollecito. Forensic investigation found Knox's DNA on the handle of a knife discovered in the kitchen at Sollecito's flat and Kercher's DNA was on the blade of the same knife (Simon, 2015). Additionally, Kercher's blood was found in the bathroom mixed with Knox's DNA (Wise, 2009) and there was evidence implicating Sollecito because of a bloody shoeprint in the bathroom believed to be his. Forensic analysis also found Sollecito's DNA on Kercher's bra clasp. It was further alleged that Knox and Sollecito had staged a break-in and attempted to clean up the crime scene (Wise, 2009).

DNA found at the crime scene also led to the arrest of a 20-year-old male, Rudy Guede. He was an Ivory Coast immigrant with a history of minor theft who was an acquaintance of the male students who lived in the flat below Kercher and Knox and they had once met him briefly (Burleigh, 2012). Guede fled to Germany the day after the murder and, in a recorded Skype conversation with a friend, he claimed that he was using the toilet when Kercher was murdered and caught a glimpse of the perpetrator when he subsequently went to Kercher's room to try to help her. He also wrote, 'Knox has nothing to do with it' (Burleigh, 2012: 209). He was arrested in Germany and sent back to Italy.

In Italy, prosecutors oversee the police investigation and subsequently take the evidence to court. The lead prosecutor for this case, Giuliano Mignini, theorised that Kercher, Guede, Knox and Sollecito could have been on drugs, such as cocaine, and that a sex game they were involved in spiralled out of control. Also, some of the symbolic aspects of the evidence were not lost on him. A bloody shoeprint was found leading away from Kercher's bedroom and historical Masonic rites require initiates to remove one shoe. Blood was found in the apartment below Kercher's, later determined to come from the black cat that lived there. And the murder occurred during Hallowtide, when Catholic religious ceremonies remember the dead. Could Kercher's death have been some sort of satanic, sacrificial rite (Burleigh, 2012)?

Guede was tried first, convicted of murder and sexual assault and sentenced to 30 years in prison, subsequently reduced to 24 years. Knox and Sollecito were tried together in 2009 in a Perugian criminal court headed by Judge Giancarlo Massei. At the start of the trial, both entered pleas of not guilty. Apart from the DNA evidence, during the trial the prosecution presented a video showing a simulation of how Knox might have wielded the knife while Sollecito held Kercher down. Guede also testified for the prosecution saying that Knox was present at the crime scene (YouTube Documentary, 2016). Other evidence against Knox included eyewitness testimony in which one witness claimed to have seen Knox with her co-accused defendants on the night of the murder (Nadeau, 2010). Another witness, Marco Quintavalle, reported that he saw Knox in his shop early in the morning on 2 November, contradicting her claim that she had been at Sollecito's flat (Injustice Anywhere, nd).

On 6 December 2010, Knox and Sollecito were found guilty of murdering Kercher and received 26-year and 25-year custodial sentences, respectively.[2] However, on 3 October 2011, both Knox and Sollecito were acquitted by the Perugian Court of Appeals headed by Judge Claudio Pratillo Hellmann. During the appeal, the defence was granted an independent review of the DNA evidence and it was declared that the forensic science presented in the prosecution's case at the trial was unreliable (Court of Assizes of Appeal of Perugia, 2012). In relation to Knox's confession to the police, Judge Hellmann referred to the 'obsessive length' of the interrogation of a young girl not yet fluent in Italian and without a lawyer present to assist her (Court of Assizes of Appeal of Perugia, 2012: 21). He also criticised the trial and referred to 'the dubious reliability of witness Quintavalle'; and 'the substantive groundlessness ... not to mention the ambiguity of this evidence' (90). Knox and Sollecito were released from prison, and Knox returned to the US. However, Francesco Maresca, the lawyer representing the Kercher family said, 'We are asking and confirming our initial request, which is upholding the original verdict' (Maresca, 2011).

In 2013, Italy's Court of Cassation (Supreme Court) reviewed the case and quashed the findings of the appeal and on 30 January 2014 the Florentine Court of Appeals overturned Knox and Sollecito's acquittal and they were once again found guilty of the murder of Kercher (Gill, 2016). The outcome of this new appeal confirmed Knox's conviction and increased her sentence to 28 and a half years in prison. Although she had now left Italy, it was argued that a request should be made for her extradition from the US. Meanwhile, Sollecito's sentence was confirmed as 25 years of imprisonment. In disagreement with this third verdict, lawyer Ted Simon, representing Knox, said 'There is no meaningful difference, there is no new evidence' (YouTube Documentary, 2016).

Finally, in an appeal to the Court of Cassation, on 27 March 2015 Knox and Sollecito were once again acquitted. In the official explanation, the Court said that there were no definitive biological traces of Knox and Sollecito in the room where Kercher was murdered, nor on the victim's body. The Court also identified and criticised errors in the investigation, including the improper handling of DNA evidence. Guede's involvement in the murder was acknowledged and the Court was quoted as having stated that the media attention and the nationalities of those involved led to 'a spasmodic search for one or more guilty parties to offer up to international public opinion' which 'certainly did not aid the search for the truth' (Ognibene and Binnie, 2015). The Court also stated that re-examining the case was pointless because of the inability to draw reliable conclusions from scarce evidence. However, the Court upheld the separate conviction and sentence of Knox for falsely implicating Lumumba in the murder (Ognibene and Binnie, 2015).

The Court of Cassation's mention of 'international public opinion' was unavoidable in this case because it attracted huge attention on a par with that given to some of the other cases reviewed in this book, such as those involving O.J. Simpson or Oscar Pistorius. The victim was British, one defendant was American and the others were Italian, thereby engaging public attention in each country. From the start of the investigation, the Perugian police and prosecution shared a lot of their information and hypotheses with reporters, and the trial was televised; thus, there was ample opportunity to disseminate the theory that this had been a sex game (with an unwilling victim) gone wrong. If the defendants had all been male, the crime might have been catalogued as one more unfortunate case of rape and murder and have received relatively little attention in the news. However, the inclusion of a female defendant added an atypical element and seemingly inevitably led to a focus on Knox's sexuality, thereby increasing the newsworthiness of the crime (Gonzalez, 2014) and opening the door to salacious reporting and commentary. Goulandris and McLaughlin (2016: 30) noted that Knox as the alleged sexually motivated female killer with very good looks was something so rare that it was 'ripe for newsworthy "gold" status'. This might also help to explain why Sollecito and Guede's names quickly dwindled into the background (Simkin, 2014) as Knox's gained increasing prominence, celebrity and notoriety.

Two tabloid journalists in particular reported the investigation and the trial to international audiences, Nick Pisa (*The Daily Mail*) and Barbie Latza Nadeau (*The Daily Beast*), while, overall, millions of people read or heard about Knox and Sollecito as the case unfolded (Gonzalez, 2014), even after their conviction, acquittal, reconviction and final acquittal. In the five years from arrest to appeal, social media had grown exponentially and Facebook pages were dedicated to seeking justice and the exoneration of Knox and Sollecito (Gies and Bortoluzzi, 2016). Although the commentary on social media was intense, interest in the case has lessened significantly in the last few years, although there are still Facebook pages dedicated to the case such as 'Amanda guilty or innocent Knox' and the 'Amanda Knox and Raffaele Sollecito Discussion Page'. Additionally, several 'true crime' books have been written about the case (Sarzanini, 2008; Dempsey, 2010; Nadeau, 2010; Follain, 2011; Waterbury, 2011; Burleigh, 2012; Kercher, 2012; Hodges, 2015; Harrington, 2017; Bremner, 2021). In this regard, it is interesting to note that Durham et al (1995) found that cases involving female offenders and victims, middle- or upper-class victims, rapes, romantic triangles and murders committed with a knife are over-represented in the true crime literature compared to their prevalence in official crime statistics. Thus, the prosecution's presentation of Kercher's murder as that of a young White woman murdered by another White, middle-class woman with a knife and involving a sexual attack by two accomplices had many of the ingredients that could be turned into a highly marketable true crime book.

Finally, Knox added her own book to the true crime literature with the publication of *Waiting to be Heard* in 2015. The title indicated very clearly that Knox wished to give her side of the story and it was a bid to repair the image of her character which had been subject to much scrutiny, some of it very critical, since the crime had occurred. It was a defence not only of her innocence but also of her persona, for all constructions of her guilt went beyond her alleged involvement in the murder to make sense of the crime by building a profile of her sexuality. She had been 'framed' for the crime, not in the legal sense of having been fraudulently placed at the scene, but in the sociological sense of having been portrayed in a way which she, and her supporters, disputed. It is this struggle over her public image – the construction of her guilt and innocence outside of the courts – which is the central focus of our chapter.

Framing Amanda Knox

The concept of 'frames' was originally developed by sociologist Erving Goffman (1974) to describe the way in which individuals organise and present information in order to give it meaning. His concept resonates with the earlier constructionist view of 'reality' which, in Burke's (1935: 70) effective and influential expression, holds that 'Every way of seeing is also a way of not seeing'. In a later and widely cited definition, Entman emphasised that framing involves the twin processes of selection and salience:

> To frame is *to select some aspects of a perceived reality and make them more salient in a communicating text, in such a way as to promote a particular problem definition, causal interpretation, moral evaluation, and/or treatment recommendation* for the item described. (Entman, 1993: 52, italics in original)

Frames work by highlighting some pieces of information and omitting others in order to increase the salience of what is included. This means making the information more noticeable, meaningful and memorable to audiences. Increased salience means that the reader or listener is more likely to retain the information. Salience may be achieved through repetition or by associating the text with concepts that are culturally familiar to the reader.

Even without these requisites, a text may still become salient to the receiver if it mirrors their belief systems (Entman, 1993).

Much work using the concept of framing has looked at its role in the presentation of political issues, such as climate change (for example, Levine and Kline, 2017) or racism (for example, Clark et al, 2018). However, framing also occurs in the presentation of individuals. For example, Entman and Gross (2008) analysed the media framing of the accuser in a case of alleged group rape in the US, showing that earlier reports tended to describe her as a 'mother' and a 'student' while later reports more often described her as a 'stripper' and a 'dancer'. Neither of these descriptions was inaccurate but each communicated very different frames about her identity, character and sexuality. As Entman and Gross (2008: 116) observed, the labels of 'stripper' and 'dancer' were likely to have undermined sympathy for the accuser 'particularly in light of the consistent references to her having been heavily intoxicated on that night'. It is this kind of framing that we examine in the Amanda Knox case.

An endlessly recycled video clip from 2 November 2007, showing Knox and Sollecito embracing and briefly kissing as they waited outside the house after Kercher had been found, was used to prompt initial suspicions about their involvement in the crime. A still photograph taken from the video of Knox and Sollecito kissing appeared in the Italian press alongside an article that indicated Kercher had died in a sex game gone wrong (Burleigh, 2012). Referring to Knox as 'untidy', Nadeau (2010: 56) wrote that a police officer said that contrary to Knox's report that she had showered that morning, she smelled of body odour and that she 'smelled like sex'. This seems to give the impression that as well as being obsessed with sex, Knox was also unhygienic – an assertion that was persistently made in the wider media based on reports from friends of Kercher. The photograph was to become notorious and underpinned the story of an unlikely killer who had manipulated two men into forcing Kercher into a sex game, which ultimately resulted in Knox wielding the knife as she delivered the *coup de grâce* to silence her victim (Vogt, 2014). Subsequently, reporters began to delve into Knox's background and behaviour.

Working for the *Daily Mail*, Pisa found that Knox's nickname on her Myspace page was 'Foxy Knoxy', something that was interpreted as self-proclaimed seductive sexuality, and which featured in more than one headline about the case. Knox (2015) later explained that she had earned the nickname as a child for her fox-like qualities on the soccer pitch. Reporters were also able to obtain photographs of Knox and Sollecito in the days before their arrest. For example, the *Mail Online* reported that 'New pictures reveal the day after Meredith Kercher was found dead, murder suspects Amanda Knox and her Italian boyfriend went shopping for lingerie and discussed having "wild sex"' (*Mail Online*, 2007). 'The day after' signalled the tone of the story, one of calculating individuals able to behave as if nothing had happened. The term 'lingerie' is a sexualised form of reference to 'underwear', and 'wild sex' suggested that the couple had a propensity for sexual deviance. Knox subsequently explained that she had been unable to enter her flat after the discovery of Kercher's body and needed to buy underwear. She also refuted the claim that she had discussed 'wild sex' with Sollecito. Even a year after the reports about shopping for underwear, *The Sun* proclaimed that 'Knox had no pants on in jail', the article indicating that she had shocked other inmates because she was 'KNICKERLESS' (*The Sun*, 31 October 2008, cited in Simkin, 2014: 3).

After her arrest, Knox was held in Capanne prison while awaiting the trial that took place some 14 months later. She kept a diary which, unbeknown to her, would be leaked to the media, most probably to Pisa of the *Daily Mail* (York, 2016). The *Mail Online* (Jones, 2008) reported that:

> The handwriting is meticulously neat, though it seems to belong to a conscientious first-form pupil rather than an expensively educated university undergraduate.
> The tone veers wildly from page to page.
> At times, it is vulgar and vain to the point of narcissism; at others, it is pathetically self-pitying, as though the author regards herself as a cruelly wronged Shakespearean heroine.

Significantly, the *Mail* focused on her thoughts about sex:

> The diary, which Knox began the day she entered prison, details her many lovers and her fears that she may have contracted a sexually transmitted disease. (Pisa, 2008a)

> Foxy Knoxy claims female cell mate begs her for sex 'because I'm so pretty'. (Pisa, 2008b)

> Secret diary reveals Foxy Knoxy was 'always thinking about sex'. (Mail Foreign Service, 2008)

Italian crime journalist Fiorenza Sarzanini's (2008) book about Knox also contained excerpts from her journal. Sarzanini wrote that Knox had compiled a list of things to do before she left Italy including visiting a sex shop to buy condoms. According to the *Daily Mail* (Mail Foreign Service, 2008) the book details the men whom Knox had had sex with and reported Sarzanini as writing in the book 'It's as if you [Knox] were always hunting men. You list your conquests as if you were displaying them like trophies'. Similarly, Nadeau (2010) referred to the list of seven sexual partners that Knox wrote in her diary, describing her as promiscuous. Knox (2015) later explained that, soon after arriving at Capanne, a prison doctor told her that she might be HIV positive, only to be told a month later that she was not. In the interim, she wrote down the list of her previous sexual partners in a bid to discover whom she might have contracted the disease from. Four of them related to when she was in the US and the other three when she was in Italy. However, the press reported that Knox had sex with all seven partners during her six-week stay in Italy before being arrested. Nadeau commented that Knox managed to 'bed a Greek, an Albanian, and an Italian' (2010: 31) during her short time in Perugia, implying a promiscuity that transcended nationalities. Additionally, she did not even describe Knox's short relationship with Sollecito as monogamous. Finally, Nadeau reported that Knox had a pink 'Rampant Rabbit' vibrator which was visible to everyone in the shared bathroom at the Perugian flat. She interpreted this as a public display of sexuality, as though 'Knox were brandishing it as a symbol of her sexual power over Meredith' (30).

To the image of a sex-obsessed and promiscuous female were added dimensions of domination and a possible propensity for violence. Nadeau (2010) referred to a Facebook posting in which Knox wrote 'I don't get embarrassed and therefore have very few social inhibitions' (29) and thought that one of her Myspace entries revealed a 'darker, more enigmatic personality' (80). Seal (2010: 38) explained that women accused of killing with men are often portrayed either as under the influence of their partners or 'cunning, dominant women who are able to make men do their bidding' and this means that such a woman is 'ultimately unknowable'. The narrative of the dominant woman was evident in some of Nadeau's book in which she offered her observations of Knox and Sollecito in court. She wrote that Sollecito declared in court that he was not Knox's 'dog on a leash' and then observed that 'minutes later, he would be staring and smiling at her across the table' (Nadeau, 2010: 129). She later criticised Sollecito for appearing as though he was 'mesmerised' (137) by the crime-scene photographs of Kercher's body. However, her book generally portrays Sollecito in a more favourable light compared to Knox. The joint trial, Nadeau postulated, was a problem for Sollecito and his family because Knox was 'extra baggage' (146). Burleigh (2012) also observed the more favourable perception of Sollecito, quoting Chief Prosecutor Giuliano Mignini who said that 'she is culpable for corrupting her Italian boyfriend: for involving in such a serious episode il giovane [young] Sollecito' (203), reflecting Seal's argument about the way in which an accused murderess may be framed and subsequently perceived.

Less central to the coverage of the case, but perhaps no less relevant, was the publication of a photograph of Knox taken while visiting a museum en route to Perugia. She was shown sitting behind an old machine gun cheerfully laughing as if she enjoyed the role play as a dispenser of lethal violence. Nadeau (2010) reported comments from Kercher's British friends in Perugia to support and sustain the perception of Knox's increasingly troubling character. Her 'dangerousness' was constructed through a narrative about her housemates becoming increasingly wary of her, particularly because she was 'bringing home a parade of strangers' (31). They feared that her guests might rape or rob them. As Nadeau observed, an image of Knox as a 'vixen with dark impulses' (82) was becoming well established among the Italian and British public.

Relatedly, a photograph of the bathroom Knox and Kercher shared was published in the British tabloids. Soon after the murder was discovered, the police had sprayed the bathroom with a substance called phenolphthalein, which turns pink within a minute if it detects blood. The substance did not immediately react all over the bathroom, but over time it turns everything pink whether blood is present or not. According to Burleigh (2012), the chemical was left for six weeks until every inch of the walls and sink had turned red. When the media published the photograph, without explanation, of what looked like a blood-smeared bathroom, it gave the impression that Knox was claiming she had showered there on the morning of 2 November when it was heavily spattered with blood (Burleigh, 2012).

Overall, in some of the news reports and commentaries and some of the true crime literature Knox was framed as someone who might have an 'angel face' (Nadeau, 2010: 8) but who was at the same time a 'she-devil, a diabolical person focused on sex, drugs and alcohol' (Gonzalez 2014: 77). Gonzalez (2014) argued that she was cast as a 'trickster archetype' who was deceptive and manipulative, but also as a 'seductress–goddess stereotype' who was obsessed with sex. She was nothing short of a 'witch', and Meredith Kercher had died as a result of a satanic sex orgy (Timeline: Amanda Knox case, 2011 cited in Freyenberger, 2013). We see here how the allegation of Knox's guilt went beyond a simple claim that she participated in the murder, to build a character profile that would fit with a perceived deviation from the patriarchal norms governing female sexuality.[3] She was not only thought to be legally guilty; she was also a deviant woman.

Entman and Gross (2008) reported that news media tend to rely on accounts of the crime and its suspects purveyed by the police and the prosecution, which means that many stories about a case are cast in a frame that points to the guilt of the accused. Additionally, the defence team may have few resources with which to counter the dominant narratives. Thus, reporting may not live up to the journalistic ideal of neutrality, particularly when it comes to editorials, opinion columns and talk shows. Nevertheless, in a detailed analysis of the 'Duke Lacrosse Case',[4] they found that, although the prosecutor made 'vivid assertions' of the suspects' guilt, quite a lot of reporting was neutral and some of it supported their innocence, particularly after DNA evidence had not conclusively linked them to the alleged crime (Entman and Gross, 2008: 123). The same situation held for Amanda Knox.

Freyenberger (2013) conducted a content analysis of 500 articles which mentioned Amanda Knox and had been published (in English) in 'major world newspapers'. She found that negative mentions of Knox, implying her guilt, were much less frequent than neutral or positive mentions, the latter implying her innocence. However, even though comparatively infrequent everywhere, negative mentions of Knox were significantly more likely to appear in articles published in the UK and Ireland. It is important to note that the 'major world newspapers' may not have included tabloids such as the *Daily Mail*, and that articles published in Italy were also not included. Thus, the balance and nature of the positive and negative comments would undoubtedly have looked different in a different sample of articles. Nevertheless, Freyenberger's study is interesting in that it reported mixed findings regarding positive and negative portrayals of Knox, which were not entirely dissimilar to Entman and Gross's (2008) findings on the frequency of positive and negative portrayals of the defendants in the Duke Lacrosse case.

Similarly, social media sites appear to have been split between those that supported Knox's claim of innocence and those that argued that she was guilty. For example, the Facebook page 'Amanda guilty or innocent Knox' showed many derogatory comments about Knox with one particularly inflammatory photograph of Kercher alongside the caption 'Knox you killed me'. Other Facebook pages framed Knox as a victim of a miscarriage of justice. For example, the page 'Amanda Knox and Raffaele Sollecito' at the time of writing has 7,085 likes, 'Free Amanda Knox' has 8,026 likes, and the 'Amanda Knox and Raffaele Sollecito Defense' has 4,799 members. Finally, the true crime literature also reveals a divided field, with Sarzanini (2008), Nadeau (2010) and Hodges (2015) arguing for Knox's guilt and Burleigh (2012), Waterbury (2011) and Knox herself (2015) arguing for her innocence. The title of Burleigh's book, *The Fatal Gift of Beauty*, reflects the way in which Knox's innocence is framed in the case: that she was a victim of a foreign legal system and a culture endemic with preconceptions about young American women. Burleigh highlighted the cultural misunderstandings of Knox's behaviour, for example the acceptability in the US of women being openly sexually active; behaviours which may be foreign to Italian culture (Fegitz, 2020). Other true crime accounts of the case scrutinise the media portrayal (see Dempsey, 2010; Waterbury, 2011; and Bremner, 2021). Follain (2011) dissected the evidence and interviewed several of the key characters involved in the case in order to construct a frame for Knox's innocence.

We see all of these developments as evidence of a long-running debate, now winding down, in the 'court of public opinion' about Knox's guilt or innocence and, inextricably related with that, about her character. Indeed, Knox's family saw this as a battle that needed to be won, hiring a public relations specialist just three days after her arrest in order to advise on a presentational strategy which would counter the accusations and claims of the prosecution (Nelson, 2014). Later on, webpages were set up to argue that Knox and Sollecito's convictions were a miscarriage of justice;[5] however, damaging headlines persisted, for example 'I'm proud of my one-night stands and drug use says Foxy Knoxy' (Eccles, 2013). Brown (2012) noted that reporting of crime can create 'flash mobs' on social media (people rapidly coming together in large numbers in virtual space), generating opinions that are not necessarily based on fact. Additionally, these comments can go viral in just a matter of hours.

There is little information on the impact of news reports and social media posts on public opinion about the case, largely because it would be very difficult to track the effects. Individual opinions were likely to have changed over time, as the case moved between convictions and acquittals, as the public relations campaign developed on behalf of Knox, and as the earlier true crime literature arguing for her guilt was balanced by later books, including her own, arguing for her innocence. Additionally, opinions were likely to have varied by country, particularly in those vicariously involved through the nationalities of the victim and the defendants – the UK, the US and Italy. For example, after the appeals court reinstated the guilty verdicts for both Knox and Sollecito in 2014, a YouGov survey indicated that 51 per cent of the British public thought Knox was probably guilty and only 13 per cent thought she had been wrongly convicted. However, American participants in the survey were reluctant to choose a side: 29 per cent thought Knox probably murdered Kercher and 21 per cent thought she was probably innocent (YouGov, 2014). Perhaps the British public were more likely to consider Knox guilty because the victim was British. Similarly, perhaps the American public were less likely to pick a side because the defendant was American. Given that the case and trial were located in Italy, it would also have been interesting to see Italian opinions about the case.

Exercise 2:

1. Do you think you would be able to confidently participate in a survey such as that conducted by YouGov in relation to Amanda Knox?
2. If so, why?
3. If not, why?
4. What factors might have influenced the public's judgement that Amanda Knox was guilty?

The influence of media content on its consumers' attitudes, beliefs and behaviour has been extensively researched and hotly debated (Birkbeck,

2014). It is clear that there is no simple causal connection running from content to its effects on consumers, and any link is crucially mediated by social and psychological variables. Consumers are not simply passive recipients of media content; they interact with it in a variety of ways – 'purposefully, accidentally, attentively, distractedly, passionately, apathetically, and so on' (Birkbeck, 2014: 5) – and use it to construct their own understandings of what is happening. Crucially, they may search for, or give more salience to, information which supports their pre-existing beliefs. Christiansen (2011: 153) made a similar observation about the reception of frames, arguing that the interpretation of meaning is very personal: 'As pointed out by Goffman, every person brings a unique and distinct set of values and beliefs into every social interaction'. These arguments counsel against the use of simplistic models of cause and effect when thinking about the role of the media in the court of public opinion.

In relation to crimes and trials, one factor which may affect the selection and reception of media content is prejudice, discussed by American legal scholar Neil Vidmar (2002). Vidmar drew on the American Heritage Dictionary definition of prejudice as 'an adverse judgment or opinion formed beforehand or without knowledge or examination of the facts' (2002: 4).[6] It is not clear here whether the adverse judgement is in relation to the prosecution or defence case, but it is best to think of prejudice as being either positive or negative in relation to the defendant. Positive prejudice is sympathetic or supportive; negative prejudice is critical and hostile. Vidmar identified four sources of prejudice that can affect people's opinions about a case. *Interest prejudice* arises from a person's direct or indirect interest in the outcome of the trial; thus, in the Kercher murder case the victim's family and friends, together with the families and friends of Knox, Sollecito and Guede, could have been respectively affected by negative and positive interest prejudice. *Specific prejudice* refers to 'attitudes or beliefs about specific issues in the case' (Vidmar, 2002: 77), which can be held by anyone who reads or hears about it. For example, framing Knox as a sex-obsessed she-devil could be seen as a very negative form of specific prejudice, which was countered by the positive portrayal of her as a victim of a miscarriage of justice, based partly on a very negative specific prejudice towards the Italian police and prosecutor (Annunziato, 2011). Vidmar defined *generic prejudice* as the transfer of 'pre-existing prejudicial attitudes, beliefs, or stereotypes about categories of persons to the trial setting. The stereotyping may involve the plaintiff or defendant, the victim/complainant, or witnesses' (2002: 78). Examples from the Kercher murder case would be the negative perception of young American females among segments of the Italian (and perhaps British) public, the positive perception of the victim as an exchange student, and a negative perception of the Italian courts among some US citizens. Finally, *conformity prejudice* exists when the person 'perceives that there is such strong community reaction in favor of a particular outcome of a trial that he or she is likely to be influenced in reaching a verdict consistent with the perceived community feelings rather than an impartial evaluation of the trial evidence' (Vidmar, 2002: 81–2). Here, we might think of a possible strong reaction among Italians, particularly in Perugia, in favour of Knox's conviction. Conversely, in the US there might have been a strong reaction favouring acquittal in Knox's home city of Seattle (Annunziato, 2011).

While Vidmar conducted surveys of citizens, considered as potential jurors, to measure these kinds of prejudice in relation to criminal trials in the US, no such information exists for the Kercher murder case, in the US, the UK or in Italy. Nevertheless, we see that there is ample possibility that such prejudices may have existed and influenced the way in which people viewed the case. That such prejudices could be positive or negative and that opinions about Knox's and Sollecito's guilt were not uniform (as revealed by the YouGov survey) suggests that there was and still is, to use legal parlance, a 'hung jury' in the court of public opinion and that as the case fades from view no definitive decision will be reached. Given this, it is worth asking why the conflicting frames and the debates they generated were so important. One answer is that, as shown by many of the cases we review in this book, there is a considerable public appetite for consuming and commenting on particular crimes and trials. A second explanation is that Knox was not only defending her innocence but also her character. Even with her final acquittal, a case such as this had a permanent impact on her personal and professional life: on the one hand turning her into a celebrity, but on the other leading her to feel that 'I exist only through the lens of Meredith's murder in some people's minds. They forget that I'm a human being with my own life and my own experiences' (Preskey, 2021). Finally, there were undoubtedly attempts by both the prosecution and the defence to use the media to recruit public opinion in support of their position and possibly influence the outcome of the trial and appeals.

In the US, Watson (2002) charted the rise in the use of media statements and press conferences among criminal defence lawyers in high-profile cases during the 1990s.[7] There was a shift, partly supported by changes in regulations, away from an occupational culture that advocated silence in the media to one that views media communication as useful, perhaps even obligatory. Such has been the shift that some now wonder whether defence lawyers should routinely include a clause about their media appearances in the contracts with clients (Watson, 2002) and whether public relations consultants can be included in the attorney-client privilege (Levine, 2015). The arguments supporting this change in practice are several (Watson, 2002; Hooker and Lange, 2003; Levine, 2015). First, under their duty to inform the public, police and prosecutors routinely provide the media with information about cases, obviously portraying the defendant as guilty. It is therefore important to counter this one-sided version of events with an outline of the defence's case. Second, because of the public's tendency to equate arrest and prosecution with guilt, the defendant's reputation may be severely damaged even if acquitted (as Knox claimed in the aftermath of her final acquittal). Thus, defendants should have the right, through their lawyers and public relations consultants, to give the public a different view. Third, if, as many people believe, judges and jurors are influenced by what they see or hear in the media, then it is important that both the prosecution and defence have access to them. In a sense, in high-profile cases there needs to be a 'trial in the media' (Watson, 2002: 97) that runs alongside the trial in the court. This certainly happened in relation to Amanda Knox and some other cases discussed in this book. A key question that emerges is whether lawyers are correct in their belief that media content can influence the verdicts of judges and jurors.

Media coverage of trials and its influence on verdicts

News and social media reports about a case as it develops are often called 'pretrial publicity', but publicity continues during the trial and sometimes for long afterwards. Such coverage can be a threat to the unbiased decision-making that the law demands of jurors and judges because media sources may relay information that is false, or present and interpret information with a view to establishing the defendant's guilt or innocence. Information circulating in the media must not be confused with evidence that is introduced during a trial, even where the two overlap, and the ideal model of justice is one in which adjudicators are completely insulated from extraneous information, or at the very least are able to make a clear separation between information in the media and evidence in court.[8] Many countries attempt to limit the circulation of information about a case in the news media in order to reduce this source of bias, such as in the UK through the Contempt of Court Act (1981) and the 2020 American Bar Association's (ABA) *Model Rules of Professional Conduct*. Nevertheless, this type of control is fairly lax and may allow quite a wide margin of operability for lawyers (Sprack, 2002).

Summarising US research on the effects of media coverage, Devine et al (2001) argued that ferocious reporting produces inadmissible material and, in turn, influences prospective jurors long before they sit in the jury box. Although they pointed out that it is difficult to measure the effects of publicity about the trial with real juries, studies have been undertaken with mock jurors. These involve participants reviewing transcripts or listening to recordings of cases with and without accompanying media accounts and then deciding on the guilt or innocence of the accused and recommending sentences. The findings support the view that publicised confessions are especially influential on jurors and that biased news is more influential if it is the sole source of information (Devine et al, 2001). Similarly, in a meta-analysis of studies concerning pretrial publicity, Steblay et al (1999) reported that exposure to negative pretrial publicity leads to a modest increase in judgments of guilt. More recently, Ruva and Coy (2020) reported similar findings: both positive and negative publicity about a defendant can lead to a greater probability of acquittal or conviction, respectively. However, findings from mock jurors should be interpreted with caution because of the artificiality of the publicity presented and the lack of variation in the types of media used (Devine et al, 2001). Devine et al also argued that there are short and unrealistic time lags between exposure to the publicity and the rendering of verdicts in an artificial situation. Additionally, they pointed out the difference between deciding the verdict in the laboratory setting and doing so in an actual courtroom. Nevertheless, findings such as these raise doubts about jurors' ability to follow the instruction to ignore everything that they have seen or heard about the case in the media.

In accordance with the Italian Code of Criminal Procedure, the adjudicators in the trial of Knox and Sollecito were two professional judges and six lay judges randomly selected from electoral lists (Mirabella, 2012). One of the judges, Giancarlo Massei, acted as president of the court and it was the task of this jury of eight to decide on the verdicts, which did not need to be unanimous but only a majority vote for either conviction or acquittal. By law, the verdict had to be delivered in a written document setting out a review of the evidence and the reasons for the decision to convict or acquit. For the Knox/Sollecito trial, what became known as the 'Massei Report' ran to nearly 400 pages.[9] Very much like the verdict in the Oscar Pistorius case (see Chapter 10), this document was set out as a reasoned review and evaluation of the evidence. The focus was exclusively on the evidence presented at the trial with no attention to information circulating in the media sources and it is therefore impossible to detect any direct influence of the latter on the decisions that were reached. The first appeal was similarly heard by two professional judges, led by Claudio Pratillo Hellmann, and six lay judges who likewise delivered a written opinion on the case, this time running to 95 pages.[10] Once again, there was no mention of media sources; everything focused on the evidence presented at the trial and the trial court's evaluation of it. If the media *did* have any influence on the decisions taken by the trial and appeals courts (and the courts that heard the third and fourth appeals), we note that it most probably would not involve reports or social media activity circulating internationally in English but reports within Italy itself. Additionally, the media would have to be posited as exerting an indirect effect on the decisions reached: the argument would be that the information gleaned by judges and jurors from the Italian media may have predisposed them to think that Knox and Sollecito were either guilty or innocent and that they developed their reasonings about the evidence to support their initial opinion. It would be tempting to suggest that specific, generic and conformity prejudice of a negative type influenced the verdict of the trial court, but why did they not influence the first appeals court in the same way? Perhaps it is more plausible to see the different and conflicting verdicts through a lens that looks at the politics of the Italian judiciary and of the international relations between Italy and the US. That, at least, was the interpretation of some observers. For example, Longhini (2014) noted that at the time there were tensions between the Italian prime minister Silvio Berlusconi and Italy's prosecutors and judges. Berlusconi and members of his party were trying to restrict the powers of prosecutors who also run the investigation of crimes (just as lead prosecutor Mignini in the Knox and Sollecito case also led the murder investigation). At the same time, however, prosecutors were trying to secure convictions against Berlusconi for various different offences. As Longhini speculated, perhaps the Italian Supreme Court was influenced by the ongoing political tensions with Berlusconi in their decision to reinstate Knox and Sollecito's convictions (although the Supreme Court also later definitively acquitted Knox and Sollecito in 2015). Furthermore, Donadio and Povoledo (2011) suggested that the American media circus around the case was humiliating for Italy, which was portrayed as a politically unstable country with 'amateur police officers'. The Italian judicial system was criticised once again when, in 2019, 18-year-old Christian Natale Hjorth, from California, was arrested in Rome for the murder of an Italian police officer. Following his confession to the police, a photograph was circulated in the global media of Hjorth handcuffed and blindfolded at a Roman police station. The US news media immediately made links between the treatment of Hjorth and Knox (Borrione, 2020). Here the role of the media as a conduit for political tussles must be acknowledged.

Conclusion

Like some of the other defendants discussed in this book, in addition to her legal trial (and appeals) Amanda Knox was subject to a trial in the media. It was an adversarial affair, particularly in social media, some parts of the tabloid press, and true crime programmes and books, with sometimes fierce disagreements between those who argued for her guilt and others who argued for her innocence. Only news organisations and reports seeking to live up to the journalistic ideals of neutrality and balance relayed information that did not imply a verdict. This trial in the media was almost as important to Knox as her legal trial because those who claimed that she was guilty did not simply argue that she had participated in the crime, but framed her as a sex-obsessed, deviant and potentially violent woman. She and her supporters fought back with a claim of innocence, a frame of the healthy, normal, American young woman who was the victim of biased Italian police and prosecutorial officials. We have seen that there was no resolution of these conflicting accounts in the court of public opinion: commentators and survey respondents were divided in their verdicts. Although these differences fade as time moves on, they never disappear, and Knox's work to defend her reputation will be necessary for as long as the case is held in public memory.

We have seen that prejudice may play a significant role in the way in which people select and interpret media content, such that the different opinions about Knox may be partly, even if unconsciously, fuelled by it. However, what may be observable in studies of citizens or mock jurors is not easily demonstrated when trial and appeal verdicts are written out, often very lengthily, as reasoned evaluations of the evidence, which happened in the judgments regarding Knox and Sollecito. It is problematic to assume that media content was uniformly negative or positive in relation to Knox and too simplistic to view the media as exerting a strong influence on the legal opinions that were expressed. At the most, media content may have created perceptions in the judges and jurors that led them to form an opinion about her guilt or innocence and which underpinned the reasoning set out in their formal documents.

Knox's initial conviction may also be partly explained by other factors that we discuss in this book. First, her confession during police interrogation that she had been in the flat while Lumumba murdered Kercher, although soon retracted, could have influenced the jurors' perception of her guilt. The confession was not admissible in the criminal trial because of the manner in which it was procured: Knox was not accompanied by a lawyer and nor was it recorded. Nonetheless, it followed her into the trial because Lumumba sued her for defamation and in Italy criminal and civil cases are heard together by the same jury (Mirabella, 2012). Thus, the defamation case against Knox for falsely implicating Lumumba was presented alongside the murder charge. Therefore, if the jurors had not heard about Knox's confession from pretrial publicity, they certainly heard about it during the trial itself. In Chapter 8, we examined the role of false confessions in the construction of guilt and innocence. Kassin (2012) argued that false confessions can corrupt other evidence from lay witnesses to forensic experts because of the influence of the confession. So much so, Kassin noted, that other evidence gathered following the interrogation is understood in the context of the confession and in turn, supports the confession.

Second, the social geometry of the case (see Chapter 6) could have contributed to its outcomes. When arrested, Knox had only been in Perugia for six weeks and hardly spoke Italian (during her police interrogation an interpreter was necessary). Although an international student at the university, she was a foreigner, on the margins of Italian society. Apart from Sollecito, there was no one that she could turn to locally for support, including finding a lawyer, because her family were all in Seattle. More importantly, perhaps, was the perception that she was deviant. For example, during the trial Carlo Pacelli, lawyer for Lumumba, told the court:

> You've heard the stories about her hygiene, about how messy she is. Well she is unclean on the outside because she is dirty on the inside. Who is the real Amanda Knox? Is she the one we see before us here, all angelic? Or is she really a she-devil focused on sex, drugs, and alcohol, living life on the edge? She is the Luciferina – she-devil. (Nadeau, 2010: 125)

Black's theory of the behaviour of law would predict that someone located at these intersecting points in social space is more likely to be convicted. Knox and her supporters' battles to redeem her reputation can be seen as an attempt to relocate her from a deviant to a conventional location, while by the time of her first appeal she was dressing more formally and could also speak Italian. Could this have had any influence on her first acquittal?

Social geometry may also explain why one of the other defendants in this case, Rudy Guede, was quickly tried and convicted. As a first-generation immigrant with a minor criminal record he was located towards the margins of Italian society, without the social capital that Sollecito had by virtue of coming from a middle-class professional family and that Knox and her supporters were able to mobilise as the case developed. A social geometry lens prompts important questions about the processes leading the Italian authorities to prosecute him separately.

Recommended reading

Gies and Bortoluzzi's (2016) edited book *Transmedia Crime Stories: The Trial of Amanda Knox and Raffaele Sollecito in the Globalised Media Sphere* is entirely dedicated to analysing the media representation of Amanda Knox from a variety of disciplinary perspectives and includes an examination of the narratives constructing both her guilt and innocence. Simkin's (2014) book *Cultural Constructions of the Femme Fatale: From Pandora's Box to Amanda Knox* is particularly useful for understanding the long history of the beautiful but lethal woman (the femme fatale) as she is portrayed in the media and how perceptions of such women are shaped. Burleigh's (2012) true crime book *The Fatal Gift of Beauty: The Trials of Amanda Knox* offers a more balanced account of the case than the others available. However, Knox's own book *Waiting to be Heard* (2015) provides the most detail and insight into not only the case but the media treatment and portrayal she experienced over the years.

Notes

1 Amanda Knox, cited by Preskey (2021).
2 Knox received an additional year for the separate charge of falsely implicating Lumumba in the murder.
3 In Chapter 4, we also mentioned a similar construction of deviance in relation to Rose West.
4 In 2006, three White members of the Duke University men's lacrosse team were accused of rape by Crystal Mangum, a Black student that the men had hired as a stripper for a party they were hosting. The prevailing narrative was that the case was another example of racist, sexist and privileged behaviour of elite White men. However, because of the lack of evidence and the accuser changing her story several times, the charges were eventually dropped (Wiedeman, 2017).
5 There are websites dedicated to raising awareness about Knox and Sollecito's case, for example www.injusticeinperugia.org and www.amandaknoxcase.com
6 Vidmar noted that this definition had been used by the presiding judge in the trial of Timothy McVeigh (discussed in Chapter 5).
7 Watson's article uses the O.J. Simpson case (see Chapter 6) as one of its examples.
8 In the US, juries are sometimes 'sequestered' (in a hotel) for the duration of the trial in order to isolate them from media reports, as happened in the Simpson case described in Chapter 6.
9 A copy in English is available at: http://themurderofmeredithkercher.com/The_Massei_Report_(English)
10 A copy in English is available at: http://themurderofmeredithkercher.com/The_Hellmann_Sentencing_Report_(English)

Afterword

Every so often, a trial comes along that attracts a great deal of public attention. Various factors appear to contribute to this explosion into the public domain: the violence – sometimes horrendous or shocking – with which the crimes were committed (for example, James Hanratty, Timothy McVeigh, Peter Sutcliffe, Rosemary West), the celebrity status of defendants and victims (for example, Oscar Pistorius, Michael Jackson, O.J. Simpson), or puzzles about the crime (for example, Casey Anthony, H.H. Crippen, Brendan Dassey, Amanda Knox). In this book, we have examined 11 such cases to help illuminate some of the processes which, according to sociologists, psychologists, criminologists and legal scholars, are involved in the construction of guilt and innocence. To the extent that these researchers' findings are valid, they should also be applicable to new cases that will certainly emerge in the future.

Of course, the law does not stand still and, indeed, may react to research findings by changing its practice. For example, more attention might be paid to the way in which vulnerable defendants are handled during the investigatory process; experts may be called to a trial to counter popular beliefs about the markers of credibility and reliability for people who take the stand; and courts may instruct jurors to put aside their notions of common sense or to 'switch' a key social or demographic characteristic of the defendant and test their assumptions about the 'reasonable person'. However, the influence of research on constructions of guilt and innocence looks to vary by jurisdiction, for example with more attention paid to it in the US than the UK. Furthermore, research itself has found that judges and jurors may ignore, or have a difficult time applying, the results of studies which are relevant to the adjudicatory process. We would not expect, therefore, that the processes we have described in this book will change rapidly in the immediate future.

Readers who take an avid interest in high-profile trials are therefore encouraged to follow them with an eye to the sorts of process that we have been exploring in this book. As stated in our introduction, the objective would be to *explain* or *predict* trial outcomes based on what we already know about the construction of guilt and innocence. Of course, there is often a natural tendency to want to judge the case, as is evidenced by the large number of verdicts for high-profile cases that emerge in the court of public opinion. When we have presented these cases to students they have frequently asked for our own opinions about the defendant's guilt or innocence. Rather than giving verdicts, we have encouraged students to apply some of the research findings in arriving at their own judgements, just as many researchers would like judges and jurors to do. Yet, while acknowledging that judges and jurors *must* arrive at a verdict, our objective in this book has also been to underline the contingent nature of those verdicts, for they depend on the particular ways in which the processes we describe play out in a specific case. The contingency is best illustrated by introducing counterfactuals referring to things that did not happen in a case, but which might have done. What would have happened if, for example:

- Casey Anthony had taken the stand and the prosecution had been able to question her credibility?
- Hanratty had not changed his alibi midway through the trial?
- Crippen had secured the services of Marshall Hall and the defence that he proposed of an accidental overdose given to Belle Elmore?
- Rose West had not denied knowledge of the murders but claimed that she was also a victim of abuse by Fred West?
- Timothy McVeigh had developed an excuse rather than a justification for his act?
- O.J. Simpson had relied on a public defender rather than hiring an expensive legal team?
- Michael Jackson's alleged victims belonged to other celebrity families?
- Brendan Dassey had been assisted by a lawyer during his interviews with the police?
- Peter Sutcliffe had mentioned hearing voices from God in his very first interview with the police?
- Oscar Pistorius's victim was a young Black male?
- Amanda Knox had flown back to the US on the day after Meredith Kercher's body was discovered?

These counterfactuals, and many others that could be thought of, help us to see very clearly that 'the truth' is not *found*; it is *made*.

Finally, although we have focused on very high profile cases in this book, the processes for constructing guilt and innocence are equally evident in every criminal case, serious or trivial, including where charges are dropped or the case is resolved through a guilty plea. Indeed, many of those processes are also present whenever someone's behaviour is subject to questioning or scrutiny, whether it be in a disciplinary hearing at school or work, or even a quick parental inquiry about a child's suspected wrongdoing. Thus, at some point or other each of us has had to construct our own guilt or innocence, or judge the guilt or innocence of others.

References

2015 Florida Statutes (2015) *782.04 Murder*. Available from: http://www. leg.state.fl.us/statutes/index.cfm?App_mode=Display_Statute&Search_ String=&URL=0700-0799/0782/Sections/0782.04.html

Abramowitz, M. and Black, D. (2010) 'How law behaves: an interview with Donald Black', *International Journal of Law Crime and Justice*, 38(1): 37–47.

Ahluwalia, P. and Rafferty, A. (2017) 'Defences available for women defendants who are victims/survivors of domestic abuse: briefing note prepared for the summit held by the Prison Reform Trust in London on Tuesday 17th October 2017', London: The Criminal Bar Association of England and Wales. Available from: http://www.prisonreformtrust.org. uk/Portals/0/Documents/CBA%20domestic%20violence%20briefing.pdf

Alderden, M.A. and Ullman, S.E. (2012) 'Creating a more complete and current picture: examining police and prosecutor decision-making when processing sexual assault cases', *Violence Against Women*, 18(5): 525–51.

Allnutt, S., Samuels, A. and O'Driscoll, C. (2007) 'The insanity defence: from wild beasts to M'Naghten', *Australasian Psychiatry*, 15(4): 292–8.

Alvarez, A. (1997) 'Adjusting to genocide: the techniques of neutralization and the Holocaust', *Social Science History*, 21(2): 139–78.

Amsterdam, A.G. and Hertz, R. (1992) 'An analysis of closing arguments to a jury', *New York Law School Law Review*, 37: 55–122.

Anderson, S.D. and Hewitt, J. (2002) 'The effect of competency restoration training on defendants with mental retardation found not competent to proceed', *Law and Human Behavior*, 26(3): 343–51.

Anderson, T., Schum, D. and Twining, W. (2005) *Analysis of Evidence*, 2nd edn, Cambridge: Cambridge University Press.

Annunziato, S. (2011) 'The Amanda Knox case: the representation of Italy in American media coverage', *Historical Journal of Film, Radio and Television*, 31(1): 61–78.

APA (American Psychiatric Association) (2013) *Diagnostic and Statistical Manual of Mental Disorders*, 5th edn, Washington, DC: APA.

Appelbaum, P.S. and Scurich, N. (2014) 'Impact of behavioral genetic evidence on the adjudication of criminal behavior', *Journal of the American Academy of Psychiatry and the Law*, 42(1): 91–100.

Appelbaum, P.S., Scurich, N. and Raad, R. (2015) 'Effects of behavioral genetic evidence on perceptions of criminal responsibility and appropriate punishment', *Psychology, Public Policy, and Law*, 21(2): 134–44.

Appellant Brief (2019) 'In the State of Wisconsin Court of Appeals, District 33', *State of Wisconsin v. Steven A. Avery*, Case No. 2017 AP002288. Available from: https://static1.squarespace.com/static/55203379e4b08b1328203a7d/t/5da62b030e2e901684b44b43/1571171077900/Updated+Avery+Doc.pdf

Areni, C.S. and Sparks, J.R. (2005) 'Language, power and persuasion', *Psychology & Marketing*, 22(6): 507–25.

Ashforth, B.E. and Anand, V. (2003) 'The normalization of corruption in organizations', *Research in Organizational Behavior*, 25: 1–52.

Ashton, J. (2011) 'Casey Anthony trial, prosecution closing statements', YouTube, 3 July. Available from: https://www.youtube.com/watch?v=wTtnTdZkfdo

Ashton, J. (2012) *Imperfect Justice: Prosecuting Casey Anthony*, New York: HarperCollins.

Associated Press (2005) 'Robert Blake found liable for wife's death', *Today Celebrities*, 18 November. Available from: https://web.archive.org/web/20151231021956/http://www.today.com/id/10099963/ns/today-today_entertainment/t/robert-blake-found-liable-wifes-death/

Atchison, M. and Keyes, D. (1996) 'Why Johnny Lee Wilson went to prison', in D.S. Connery (ed) *Convicting the Innocent: The Story of a Murder, a False Confession, and the Struggle to Free a 'Wrong Man'*, Cambridge, MA: Brookline, pp 118–26.

ATF (Bureau of Alcohol, Tobacco, Firearms and Explosives) (2019) 'Brady Law'. Available from: https://www.atf.gov/rules-and-regulations/brady-law

ATF (Bureau of Alcohol, Tobacco, Firearms and Explosives) (2020) 'National Firearms Act'. Available from: https://www.atf.gov/rules-and-regulations/national-firearms-act

Avakame, E.F., Fyfe, J.F. and Mccoy, C. (1999) '"Did you call the police? What did they do?" An empirical assessment of Black's theory of mobilization of law', *Justice Quarterly*, 16(4): 765–92.

Bachrach, S.J. (2016) 'Individualized Education Programs (IEPs)'. Available from: https://kidshealth.org/en/parents/iep.html

Baez, J. (2011) 'Closing arguments of lead defence attorney to Casey Anthony, part 1', YouTube, 3 July. Available from: https://www.youtube.com/watch?v=muVATnlDh_8

Baez, J. and Golenbock, P. (2013) *Presumed Guilty: Casey Anthony – The Inside Story*, Dallas: BenBella Books.

Bajwa, A. (2014) 'Young defendant not guilty of murder by reason of insanity', *Garden Court Chambers*, 1 October. Available from: https://www.gardencourtchambers.co.uk/news/young-defendant-not-guilty-of-murder-by-reason-of-insanity

Bandura, A., Barbaranelli, C., Caprara, G.V. and Pastorelli, C. (1996) 'Mechanisms of moral disengagement in the exercise of moral agency', *Journal of Personality and Social Psychology*, 71(2): 364–74.

Banerjee, S.C., Hay, J.L. and Greene, K. (2012) 'College students' cognitive rationalizations for tanning bed use: an exploratory study', *Archives of Dermatology*, 148(6): 761–2.

Barriga, A.Q. and Gibbs, J.C. (1996) 'Measuring cognitive distortion in antisocial youth: development and preliminary validation of the "how I think" questionnaire', *Aggressive Behavior*, 22(5): 333–43.

BBC (2010) 'Hanratty family in new appeal against murder conviction', *BBC*, 30 December. Available from: https://www.bbc.co.uk/news/uk-12092185

Beichner, D. and Spohn C. (2005) 'Prosecutorial charging decisions in sexual assault cases: examining the impact of a specialized prosecution unit', *Criminal Justice Policy Review*, 16(4): 461–98.

Beichner, D. and Spohn, C. (2012) 'Modeling the effects of victim behavior and moral character on prosecutors' charging decisions in sexual assault cases', *Violence and Victims*, 27(1): 3–24.

Bennett, W.L. and Feldman, M.S. (1981) *Reconstructing Reality in the Courtroom: Justice and Judgement in American Culture*, New Brunswick: Rutgers University Press.

Benoit, W.L. and Hanczor, R.S. (1994) 'The Tonya Harding controversy: an analysis of image restoration strategies', *Communication Quarterly*, 42(4): 416–33.

Benson, M.L. (1985) 'Denying the guilty mind: accounting for involvement in white-collar crime', *Criminology*, 23(4): 583–607.

Berlo, D.K., Lemert, J.B. and Mertz, R.J. (1969) 'Dimensions for evaluating the acceptability of message sources', *Public Opinion Quarterly*, 33(4): 563–76.

Berman, G.L., Narby, D.J. and Cutler, B.L. (1995) 'Effects of inconsistent eyewitness statements on mock-jurors' evaluations of the eyewitness, perceptions of defendant culpability and verdicts', *Law and Human Behavior*, 19(1): 79–88.

Berryessa, C., Coppola, F. and Salvato, G. (2020) 'The potential effect of neurobiological evidence on the adjudication of criminal responsibility of psychopathic defendants in involuntary manslaughter cases', *Psychology, Crime & Law*, 27(2): 140–58.

Bex, F.J. (2011) *Arguments, Stories and Criminal Evidence: A Formal Hybrid Theory*, Law and Philosophy Library 92, Dordrecht: Springer.

Bilton, M. (2012) *Wicked Beyond Belief: The Hunt for the Yorkshire Ripper*, updated edn, London: HarperPress.

Biography.com Editors (2020) 'Michael Jackson biography', *A&E Television Networks*. Available from: https://www.biography.com/musician/michael-jackson#citation

Birkbeck, C.H. (2014) *Media Representations of Crime and Criminal Justice*, Oxford Handbooks Online, DOI: 10.1093/oxfordhb/9780199935383.013.15

Birmingham Live (2012) 'From the archives: suicide in Birmingham saw Fred West cheat justice', *Birmingham Live*, 24 October. Available from: https://www.birminghammail.co.uk/news/local-news/from-the-archives-suicide-in-birmingham-saw-fred-148650

Black, D. (1976) *The Behavior of Law*, New York: Academic Press.

Black, D. (1979) 'Common sense in the sociology of law', *American Sociological Review*, 44(1): 18–27.

Black, D. (1993) *The Social Structure of Right and Wrong*, San Diego: Academic Press.

Black, D. (2002) 'The geometry of law: an interview with Donald Black', *International Journal of the Sociology of Law*, 30(2): 101–29.

Black, D. and Baumgartner, M.P. (1983) 'Toward a theory of the third party', in K.O. Boyum and L. Mather (eds) *Empirical Theories About Courts*, New York: Longman, pp 84–114.

Blankenship, K.L. and Holtgraves, T. (2005) 'The role of different markers of linguistic powerlessness in persuasion', *Journal of Language and Social Psychology*, 24(1): 3–24.

Blankenship, K.L. and Craig, T.Y. (2007) 'Language and persuasion: tag questions as powerless speech or as interpreted in context', *Journal of Experimental Social Psychology*, 43(1): 112–18.

Blom-Cooper, L. (1963) *The A6 Murder: Regina v. James Hanratty – The Semblance of Truth*, Harmondsworth: Penguin.

Blumenthal, J.A. (1993) 'A wipe of the hands, a lick of the lips: the validity of demeanor evidence in assessing witness credibility', *Nebraska Law Review*, 72(4): 1157–204.

Blumstein, P.W., Groves Carssow, K., Hall, J., Hawkins, B., Hoffman, R., Ishem, E., Plamer Maurer, C., Spens, D., Taylor, J. and Zimmerman, D.L. (1974) 'The honoring of accounts', *American Sociological Review*, 39(4): 551–66.

Bodenhausen, G.V. (1988) 'Stereotypic biases in social decision making and memory: testing process models of stereotype use', *Journal of Personality and Social Psychology*, 55(5): 726–37.

Bohner, G., Reinhard, M.A., Rutz, S., Sturm, S., Kerschbaum, B. and Effler, D. (1998) 'Rape myths as neutralizing cognitions: evidence for a causal impact of anti-victim attitudes on men's self-reported likelihood of raping', *European Journal of Social Psychology*, 28(2): 257–68.

Bond, C.F., Jr and DePaulo, B.M. (2006) 'Accuracy of deception judgments', *Personality and Social Psychology Review*, 10(3): 214–34.

Bond, C.F., Jr and DePaulo, B.M. (2008) 'Individual differences in judging deception: accuracy and bias', *Psychological Bulletin*, 134(4): 477–92.

Borg, M.J. and Parker, K.F. (2001) 'Mobilizing law in urban areas: the social structure of homicide clearance rates', *Law and Society Review*, 35(2): 435–66.

Borrione, F. (2020) 'The Amanda Knox trials and perceptions of Italy in the American media', *Italian American Review*, 10(2): 148–70.

Bosco, J. (1996) *A Problem of Evidence: How the Prosecution Freed O.J. Simpson*, New York: William Morrow.

Bothwell, R. and Jalil, M. (1992) 'The credibility of nervous witnesses', *Journal of Social Behavior and Personality*, 7(4): 581–6.

Bowker, A. (1949) *Behind the Bar: Clerk to the Late Sir Edward Marshall Hall and to Sir Norman Birkett*, London: Staples Press.

Bowling, B. and Phillips, C. (2002) *Racism, Crime and Justice*, Harlow: Longman.

Branson-Potts, H. (2015) 'After Oklahoma City bombing, McVeigh's arrest almost went unnoticed', *Los Angeles Times*, 19 April. Available from: https://www.latimes.com/nation/la-na-oklahoma-city-bombing-20150419-story.html

Bremner, A. (2021) *Amanda Knox and Justice in the Age of Judgement*, New York: Skyhorse.

Brewer, N. and Burke, A. (2002) 'Effects of testimonial inconsistencies and eyewitness confidence on mock-juror judgments', *Law and Human Behavior*, 26(3): 353–64.

Brewer, N. and Hupfeld, R.M. (2004) 'Effects of testimonial inconsistencies and witness group identity on mock-juror judgments', *Journal of Applied Social Psychology*, 34(3): 493–513.

Brewer, N., Potter, R., Fisher, R., Bond, N. and Luszcz, M (1999) 'Beliefs and data on the relationship between consistency and accuracy of eyewitness testimony', *Applied Cognitive Psychology*, 13(4): 297–313.

Brönimann, R., Herlihy, J., Müller, J. and Ehlert, U. (2013) 'Do testimonies of traumatic events differ depending on the interviewer?', *European Journal of Psychology Applied to Legal Context*, 5(1): 97–121.

Brown, K.R. (2012) 'Somebody poisoned the jury pool: social media's effect on jury impartiality', *Texas Wesleyan Law Review*, 19(3): 809–35.

Brown, P. (2019) 'Unfitness to plead in England and Wales: historical development and contemporary dilemmas', *Medicine, Science and the Law*, 59(3): 187–96.

Bruner, J. (1990) *Acts of Meaning*, London: Harvard University Press.

Bruner, J. (2002) *Making Stories: Law, Literature, Life*, Cambridge, MA: Harvard University Press.

Buckleton, J. (2005) 'Population genetic models', in J. Buckleton, C.M. Triggs and S.J. Walsh (eds) *Forensic DNA Evidence Interpretation*, 2nd edn, London: CRC Press, pp 87–118.

Bugliosi, V. (1996) *Outrage: The Five Reasons Why O.J. Simpson Got Away with Murder*, London: W.W. Norton.

Burgin, R. and Flynn, A. (2021) 'Women's behavior as implied consent: male "reasonableness" in Australian rape law', *Criminology & Criminal Justice*, 21(3): 334–52.

Burleigh, N. (2012) *The Fatal Gift of Beauty: The Trials of Amanda Knox*, New York: Broadway Paperbacks.

Burn, G. (2019) *Somebody's Husband, Somebody's Son: The Story of the Yorkshire Ripper*, London: Faber and Faber.

Burney, I. and Pemberton, N. (2011) 'Bruised witness: Bernard Spilsbury and the performance of early twentieth-century English forensic pathology', *Medical History*, 55(1): 41–60.

Burns, R.P. (1999) *A Theory of the Trial*, Princeton: Princeton University Press.

Burns, S. (2011) *The Central Park Five: A Chronicle of a City Wilding*, New York: Alfred A. Knopf.

Bybee, J. and Zigler, E. (1992) 'Is outerdirectedness employed in a harmful or beneficial manner by students with and without mental retardation?', *American Journal on Mental Retardation*, 96(5): 512–21.

Byers, B., Crider, B.W. and Biggers, G.K. (1999) 'Bias crime motivation: a study of hate crime and offender neutralization techniques used against the Amish', *Journal of Contemporary Criminal Justice*, 15(1): 78–96.

Byers, B.D. and Crider, B.W. (2002) 'Hate crimes against the Amish: a qualitative analysis of bias motivation using routine activities theory', *Deviant Behavior*, 23(2): 115–48.

Campbell, B.A., Menaker, T.A. and King, W.R. (2015) 'The determination of victim credibility by adult and juvenile sexual assault investigators', *Journal of Criminal Justice*, 43(1): 29–39.

Candel, I., Merckelbach, H., Loyen, S. and Reyskens, H. (2005) '"I hit the shift-key and then the computer crashed": children and false admissions', *Personality and Individual Differences*, 38(6): 1381–7.

Cantone, J.A., Martinez, L.N., Willis-Esqueda, C. and Miller, T. (2019) 'Sounding guilty: how accent bias affects juror judgments of culpability', *Journal of Ethnicity in Criminal Justice*, 17(3): 228–53.

Card, R. and English, J. (2017) *Police Law*, 15th edn, Oxford: Oxford University Press.

Carlin, J. (2014) *Chase Your Shadow: The Trials of Oscar Pistorius*, London: Atlantic Books.

Caso, L., Palena, N., Vrij, A. and Gnisci, A. (2019a) 'Observers' performance at evaluating truthfulness when provided with comparable truth or small talk baselines', *Psychiatry, Psychology and Law*, 26(4): 571–9.

Caso, L., Palena, N., Carlessi, E. and Vrij, A. (2019b) 'Police accuracy in truth/lie detection when judging baseline interviews', *Psychiatry, Psychology and Law*, 26(6): 841–50.

Celebrity Net Worth (nd) 'Michael Jackson net worth', *Celebrity Net Worth*. Available from: https://www.celebritynetworth.com/richest-celebrities/singers/michael-jackson-net-worth/

Chamberlain, J., Miller, M.K. and Jehle, A. (2006) 'Celebrities in the courtroom: legal responses, psychological theory and empirical research', *Vanderbilt Journal of Entertainment and Technology Law*, 8(3): 551–72.

Chan, J.C.K. and McDermott, K.B. (2006) 'Remembering pragmatic inferences', *Applied Cognitive Psychology*, 20(5): 633–9.

Christiansen, J. (2011) 'Framing theory', in The Editors of Salem Press (eds) *Sociology Reference Guide: Theories of Social Movements*, Pasadena: Salem Press, pp 145–55.

Cirincione, C., Steadman, H.J. and McGreevy, M.A. (1995) 'Rates of insanity acquittals and the factors associated with successful insanity pleas', *Bulletin of the American Academy of Psychiatry and the Law*, 23(3): 399–409.

Clare, I. and Gudjonsson, G.H. (1995) 'The vulnerability of suspects with intellectual disabilities during police interviews: a review and experimental study of decision-making', *Journal of Applied Research in Intellectual Disabilities*, 8(2): 110–28.

Clark, A.D., Dantzler, P.A. and Nickels, A.E. (2018) 'Black Lives Matter: (re) framing the next wave of Black liberation', *Research in Social Movements, Conflicts and Change, Vol. 42*, Bingley: Emerald Publishing, pp 145–72.

Clark, C. and Tate, T. (2015) *Yorkshire Ripper: The Secret Murders*, London: John Blake.

Clark, M. (1995) Prosecution closing statement, 26 September. Available from: https://simpson.walraven.org/sep26.html. The transcript is an unofficial record; however, you can also access the closing statements on YouTube.

Clarkson, C.M.V. (2005) *Understanding Criminal Law*, 4th edn, London: Sweet & Maxwell.

Clay-Warner, J. and McMahon-Howard, J. (2009) 'Rape reporting: "classic rape" and the behavior of law', *Violence and Victims*, 24(6): 723–43.

Cloud, J. (2011) 'How the Casey Anthony murder trial became the social-media trial of the century', *Time*, 16 June. Available from: http://content.time.com/time/nation/article/0,8599,2077969,00.html

Cloud, M., Shepherd, G.B., Barkoff, A.N. and Shur, J.V. (2002) 'Words without meaning: the Constitution, confessions, and mentally retarded suspects', *University of Chicago Law Review*, 69(2): 495–624.

Cochran, J. (1995a) Defence closing statement, 27 September. Available from: https://simpson.walraven.org/sep27.html. The transcript is an unofficial record; however, you can also access the closing statements on YouTube.

Cochran, J. (1995b) Defence closing statement, 28 September. Available from: https://simpson.walraven.org/sep28.html. The transcript is an unofficial record; however, you can also access the closing statements on YouTube.

Cohen, A.K. (1955) *Delinquent Boys*, New York: Free Press.

Coleman, J.W. (2005) *The Criminal Elite: Understanding White-Collar Crime*, New York: Worth Publishers.

Colon, K.M., Kavanaugh, P.R., Hummer, D. and Ahlin, E.M. (2018) 'The impact of race and extra-legal factors in charging defendants with serious sexual assault: findings from a five-year study of one Pennsylvania court jurisdiction', *Journal of Ethnicity in Criminal Justice*, 16(2): 99–116.

Colwell, K., Hiscock-Anisman, C., Memon, A., Colwell, L., Taylor, L. and Woods, D. (2009) 'Training in assessment criteria indicative of deception to improve credibility judgments', *Journal of Forensic Psychology Practice*, 9(3): 199–207.

Connell, N. (2005) *Walter Dew: The Man Who Caught Crippen*, Stroud: History Press.

Conner, K. (2006) 'Factors in a successful use of the insanity defence', *Internet Journal of Criminology*. Available from: https://docs.wixstatic.com/ugd/b93dd4_f8014a86cec7488191d1f698b35c454f.pdf

Cooney, M. (1994) 'Evidence as partisanship', *Law and Society Review*, 28(4): 833–58.

Copes, H., Kerley, K.R., Mason, K.A. and Van Wyk, J. (2001) 'Reporting behavior of fraud victims and Black's theory of law: an empirical assessment', *Justice Quarterly*, 18(2): 342–63.

Cornell Law School, Legal Information Institute (nd) 'Diminished capacity'. Available from: https://www.law.cornell.edu/wex/diminished_capacity

Corsini, R.J. (2002) *The Dictionary of Psychology*, London: Routledge.

Cotterill, J. (ed) (2003) *Language and Power in Court: A Linguistic Analysis of the O.J. Simpson Trial*, Basingstoke: Palgrave Macmillan.

Court of Assizes of Appeal of Perugia (2012) *Sentence of the Court of Assizes of Appeal of Perugia (presided over by Dr. Claudio Pratillo Hellmann) in the murder of Meredith Kercher*. Available in English from: http://themurderofmeredithkercher.com/PDF/pmf_hellmann_report_translation_draft.pdf

CPS (Crown Prosecution Service) (2019) 'Homicide: murder and manslaughter, legal guidance, violent crime', updated on 18 March. Available from: https://www.cps.gov.uk/legal-guidance/homicide-murder-and-manslaughter

Cronbach, L.J. (1942) 'Studies of acquiescence as a factor in the true-false test', *Journal of Educational Psychology*, 33(6): 401–15.

Cronbach, L.J. (1950) 'Further evidence on response sets and test design', *Educational and Psychological Measurement*, 10(1): 3–31.

Crosby, K. (2017) 'Keeping women off the jury in 1920s England and Wales', *Legal Studies*, 37(4): 695–717.

Cuevas-Nazario, M. and Karas, B. (2010) 'Judge takes himself off Anthony case', *CNN*, 20 April. Available from: http://edition.cnn.com/2010/CRIME/04/19/casey.anthony.judge.quits/index.html

Dall'Osto, R., Meyer, B. and Luczak, J. (2019) 'What does it take to obtain a criminal pardon in Wisconsin?', *Gimbel, Reilly, Guerin and Brown LLP*, 22 November. Available from: https://www.grgblaw.com/wisconsin-trial-lawyers/what-does-it-take-to-obtain-a-criminal-pardon-in-wisconsin

Darden, C. (1995a) Prosecution closing statement, 26 September. Available from: https://simpson.walraven.org/sep26.html. The transcript is an unofficial record; however, you can also access the closing statements on YouTube.

Darden, C. (1995b) Prosecution closing statement, 27 September. Available from: https://simpson.walraven.org/sep27.html. The transcript is an unofficial record; however, you can also access the closing statements on YouTube.

Davies, M. (2015) *Davies, Croall and Tyrer's Criminal Justice*, 5th edn, Harlow: Pearson Education.

Davies, M. and Rogers, P. (2009) 'Perceptions of blame and credibility toward victims of childhood sexual abuse: differences across victim age, victim-perpetrator relationship, and respondent gender in a depicted case', *Journal of Child Sexual Abuse*, 18(1): 78–92.

Davies, N. (1981) 'Psychiatrist concedes he could be wrong about Sutcliffe insanity', *The Guardian*, 15 May. Available from: https://www.nickdavies.net/1981/05/15/3505/

Davies, N. and Rusbridger, A. (1981a) 'Sutcliffe speaks of God, his girlfriend, and his mission to murder', *The Guardian*, 12 May. Available from: https://www.nickdavies.net/1981/05/12/sutcliffe-speaks-of-god-his-girlfriend-and-his-mission-to-murder/?catid=138

Davies, N. and Rusbridger, A. (1981b) 'Sutcliffe tells court there is nothing wrong with him', *The Guardian*, 13 May. Available from: https://www.nickdavies.net/1981/05/13/sutcliffe-tells-court-there-is-nothing-wrong-with-him/

Davies, N. and Rusbridger, A. (1981c) 'Sutcliffe "felt righteous" as he killed for God', *The Guardian*, 14 May. Available from: https://www.nickdavies.net/1981/05/14/sutcliffe-felt-righteous-as-he-killed-for-god/

Davis, M. (2005) 'Jackson counts the cost of freedom', *BBC News*, 15 June. Available from: http://news.bbc.co.uk/2/hi/entertainment/4094082.stm

Dawson, M. (2003) 'The cost of "lost" intimacy: the effect of relationship state on criminal justice decision making', *British Journal of Criminology*, 43(4): 689–709.

Dear, W.C. (2014) *O.J. Is Innocent and I Can Prove It: The Shocking Truth about the Murders of Nicole Brown Simpson and Ron Goldman*, New York: Skyhorse.

Defence's Heads of Arguments (2014) 'The State and Oscar Leonard Carl Pistorius, Heads of Argument'. Available from: https://juror13lw.files. wordpress.com/2014/08/defense-heads-of-argument.pdf

DeFreitas, K.D. and Hucker, S.J. (2015) 'Forensic psychiatry and forensic psychology: criminal responsibility', in J. Payne-James and R.W. Byard (eds) *Encyclopedia of Forensic and Legal Medicine*, 2nd edn, Amsterdam: Elsevier, pp 574–8.

DeLisi, M., Umphress, Z.R. and Vaughn, M.G. (2009) 'The criminology of the amygdala', *Criminal Justice and Behavior*, 36(11): 1241–52.

Demos, M. and Ricciardi, L. (dirs) (2015) *Making a Murderer*, TV series, Netflix.

Dempsey, C. (2010) *Murder in Italy: Amanda Knox, Meredith Kercher and the Murder Trial that Shocked the World*, New York: Berkley Books.

den Boer, M. (1995) 'Anchored narratives', *International Journal for the Semiotics of Law*, 8(3): 327–34.

Denault, V. and Dunbar, N.E. (2019) 'Credibility assessment and deception detection in courtrooms: hazards and challenges for scholars and legal practitioners', in T. Docan-Morgan (ed) *The Palgrave Handbook of Deceptive Communication*, Cham: Palgrave Macmillan, pp 915–36.

Department of Health (2001) *Valuing People: A New Strategy for Learning Disability for the 21st Century*. Available from: https://www.gov.uk/ government/publications/valuing-people-a-new-strategy-for-learning-disability-for-the-21st-century

DePaulo, B.M., Lindsay, J.L., Malone, B.E., Muhlenbruck, L., Charlton, K. and Cooper, H. (2003) 'Cues to deception', *Psychological Bulletin*, 129(1): 74–118.

Dershowitz, A. (1996) 'Life is not a dramatic narrative', in P. Brooks and P. Gewirtz (eds) *Law's Stories*, London: Yale University Press, pp 99–105.

Dershowitz, A. (nd) *Christopher Darden OJ Simpson Attorney Alan Dershowitz*. Formerly available from: https://www.youtube.com/watch?v= 5neoa4IqK6c&t=2s&pbjreload=10

Devine, D.J. (2012) *Jury Decision Making: The State of the Science*, New York: New York University Press.

Devine, D.J. and Caughlin, D.E. (2014) 'Do they matter? A meta-analytic investigation of individual characteristics and guilt judgments', *Psychology, Public Policy, and Law*, 20(2): 109–34.

Devine, D.J., Clayton, L.D., Dunford, B.B. and Pryce, J. (2001) 'Jury decision making: 45 years of empirical research on deliberating groups', *Psychology, Public Policy and Law*, 7(3): 622–727.

Dimond, D. (2005) *Be Careful Who You Love: Inside the Michael Jackson Case*, New York: Atria Books.

Dix, A. (2015) 'Ethos in sports: an Aristotelian examination focused on source credibility and the modern day athlete', *Sport Science Review*, 24(5/6): 267–84.

Dixon, J.A. and Mahoney, B. (2004) 'The effect of accent evaluation and evidence on a suspect's perceived guilt and criminality', *Journal of Social Psychology*, 144(1): 63–73.

Dixon, J.A., Mahoney, B. and Cocks, R. (2002) 'Accents of guilt? Effects of regional accent, race, and crime type on attributions of guilt', *Journal of Language and Social Psychology*, 21(2): 162–8.

DJILP (Denver Journal of International Law & Policy) (2014) 'Oscar Pistorius verdict: judicial criticism and uncertain sentencing', 6 October. Available from: https://djilp.org/oscar-pistorius-verdict-judicial-criticism-and-uncertain-sentencing/

Donadio, R. and Povoledo, E. (2011) 'As Amanda Knox heads home, the debate is just getting started', *The New York Times*, 4 October. Available from: https://www.nytimes.com/2011/10/05/world/europe/amanda-knox-freed-after-appeal-in-italian-court.html

Dong, Y., Hu, S. and Zhu, J. (2018) 'From source credibility to risk perception: how and when climate information matters to action', *Resources, Conservation and Recycling*, 136: 410–17.

Doyle, D.P. and Luckenbill, D.F. (1991) 'Mobilizing law in response to collective problems: a test of Black's theory of law', *Law and Society Review*, 25(1): 103–16.

Drane-Burdick, L. (2011) 'Casey Anthony Trial: Prosecution Rebuttal', YouTube, 4 July. Available from: https://www.youtube.com/watch?v=ajpyHokxmdM

Drizin, S. (2018) 'Words and words only' (Episode 2), *Making a Murderer*, Season 2, directed by M. Demos and L. Ricciardi, Netflix.

Drizin, S.A. and Colgan, B. (2004) 'Tales from the juvenile confession front: a guide to how standard police interrogation tactics can produce coerced and false confessions from juvenile suspects', in G.D. Lassiter (ed) *Interrogations, Confessions, and Entrapment*, New York: Kluwer Academic/Plenum, pp 127–62.

Drizin, S.A. and Leo, R.A. (2004) 'The problem of false confessions in the post-DNA world', *North Carolina Law Review*, 82(3): 891–1007.

Drummond Ayres, B., Jr (1994) '"Absolutely" not guilty, a confident Simpson says', *The New York Times*, 23 July. Available from: https://www.nytimes.com/1994/07/23/us/absolutely-not-guilty-a-confident-simpson-says.html

Durham, A., III, Elrod, H.P. and Kinkade, P.T. (1995) 'Images of crime and justice: murder and the "true crime" genre', *Journal of Criminal Justice*, 23(2): 143–52.

Eades, D. (2008) 'Telling and retelling your story in court: questions, assumptions and intercultural implications', *Current Issues in Criminal Justice*, 20(2): 209–30.

Eccles, L. (2013) 'I'm so proud of my one-night stands and drug use says Foxy Knoxy', *The Mail Online*, 28 April. Available from: https://www.dailymail.co.uk/news/article-2316338/Amanda-Knox-book-Im-proud-night-stands-drug-use-says-Foxy-Knoxy.html

Eliason, S.L. and Dodder, R.A. (1999) 'Techniques of neutralization used by deer poachers in the western United States', *Deviant Behavior*, 20(3): 233–52.

Elliott, C. and Quinn, F. (2016) *Criminal Law*, 11th edition, London: Pearson.

Ellis, J.W. and Luckasson, R.A. (1985) 'Mentally retarded criminal defendants', *George Washington Law Review*, 53: 414.

Ellison, L. and Munro, V.E. (2009) 'Turning mirrors into windows: assessing the impact of (mock) juror education in rape trials', *British Journal of Criminology*, 49(3): 363–83.

Ellison, L. and Munro, V.E. (2010) 'A stranger in the bushes, or an elephant in the room? Critical reflections upon received rape myth wisdom in the context of a mock jury study', *New Criminal Law Review*, 13(4): 781–801.

Emmelman, D.S. (1994) 'The effect of social class on the adjudication of criminal cases: class-linked behavior tendencies, common sense, and the interpretive procedures of court-appointed defense attorneys', *Symbolic Interaction*, 17(1): 1–20.

England and Wales Court of Appeal (Criminal Division) Decisions. Neutral Citation Number: [2002] 2 Cr App R30. Crim 1141. England and Wales Court of Appeal. Available from: http://www.bailii.org/ew/cases/EWCA/Crim/2002/1141.html

Enticott, G.P. (2011) 'Techniques of neutralising wildlife crime in rural England and Wales', *Journal of Rural Studies*, 27(2): 200–8.

Entman, R.M. (1993) 'Framing: toward clarification of a fractured paradigm', *Journal of Communication*, 43(4): 51–8.

Entman, R.M. and Gross, K.A. (2008) 'Race to judgment: stereotyping media and criminal defendants', *Law and Contemporary Problems*, 71(4): 93–133.

Evening Standard (2007) 'New pictures reveal the day after Meredith Kercher was found dead, murder suspects Amanda Knox and her Italian boyfriend went shopping for lingerie and discussed having "wild sex"', *The Mail Online*, 24 November. Available from: https://www.dailymail.co.uk/news/article-495966/Pictures-moment-Foxy-Knoxy-went-shopping-sexy-lingerie-day-Merediths-murder.html

Everington, C. and Fulero, S.M. (1999) 'Competence to confess: measuring understanding and suggestibility of defendants with mental retardation', *Mental Retardation*, 37(3): 212–20.

Fegitz, E. (2020) 'The phallic girl goes to Italy: Amanda Knox, post-feminism and phallicism between the national and international spheres', *European Journal of Women's Studies*. Ahead of print: https://doi.org/10.1177/1350506820945346

Fenwick, P. (1990) 'Automatism, medicine and the law', *Psychological Medicine Monograph Supplement*, 17: 1–27.

Finkel, N.J. and Handel, S.F. (1989) 'How jurors construe "insanity"', *Law and Human Behavior*, 13(1): 41–59.

Finlay, W.M.L. and Lyons, E. (2002) 'Acquiescence in interviews with people who have mental retardation', *Mental Retardation*, 40(1): 14–29.

Firth, Paul (former District Judge) (2016) Personal communication.

Fisher, R.P., Brewer, N. and Mitchell, G. (2009) 'The relation between consistency and accuracy of eyewitness testimony: legal versus cognitive explanations', in R. Bull, T. Valentine and T. Williamson (eds) *Handbook of Psychology of Investigative Interviewing: Current Developments and Future Directions*, Chichester: Wiley-Blackwell, pp 121–36.

Follain, J. (2011) *A Death in Italy: The Definitive Account of the Amanda Knox Case*, New York: St. Martin's Press.

Foot, P. (1971) *Who Killed Hanratty?* London: Jonathan Cape.

Forbes Africa (2013) 'Oscar's lost millions: when South African athlete Oscar Pistorius shot his girlfriend, Reeva Steenkamp, on Valentine's Day, his sponsors distanced themselves', *Forbes Africa*, 1 April. Available from: https://www.forbesafrica.com/sport/2013/04/01/oscars-lost-millions/

Forell, C. (2010) 'What's reasonable: self-defense and mistake in criminal and tort law', *Lewis & Clark Law Review*, 14(4): 1401–34.

Freedman, J. (2021) 'Kathleen Zellner links Steven Avery's nephew Bobby Dassey to Teresa Halbach's disappearance', *Tyla*, 13 April. Available from: https://www.tyla.com/news/tv-and-film-steven-avery-new-evidence-witness-kathleen-zellner-bobby-dassey-update-20210413

Frenda, S.J., Berkowitz, S.R., Loftus, E.F. and Fenn, K.M. (2016) 'Sleep deprivation and false confessions', *Proceedings of the National Academy of Sciences of the United States of America*, 113(8): 2047–50.

Freyenberger, D. (2013) 'Amanda Knox: A Content Analysis of Media Framing in Newspapers Around the World', MA thesis, East Tennessee State University. Available from: http://dc.etsu.edu/etd/1117

Friedland, S.I. (1989) 'On common sense and the evaluation of witness credibility', *Case Western Reserve Law Review*, 40(1): 165–225.

Friedman, R.D. (1991) 'Character impeachment evidence: psychoBayesian (!?) analysis and a proposed overhaul', *UCLA Law Review*, 38: 637–97.

Fritsche, I. (2002) 'Account strategies for the violation of social norms: integration and extension of sociological and social psychological typologies', *Journal for the Theory of Social Behaviour*, 32(4): 371–94.

Frohmann, L. (1991) 'Discrediting victims' allegations of sexual assault: prosecutorial accounts of case rejections', *Social Problems*, 38(2): 213–26.

Frohmann, L. (1997) 'Convictability and discordant locales: reproducing race, class, and gender ideologies in prosecutorial decision making', *Law & Society Review*, 31(3): 531–56.

Fulero, S. and Everington, C. (1995) 'Assessing competency to waive Miranda rights in defendants with mental retardation', *Law and Human Behavior*, 19(5): 533–43.

Fulero, S.M. and Everington, C. (2004) 'Mental retardation, competency to waive Miranda rights, and false confessions', in G.D. Lassiter (ed) *Interrogations, Confessions, and Entrapment*, New York: Kluwer Academic / Plenum, pp 163–79.

Fulkerson, A. and Bruns, D. (2014) 'Defenses, excuses and rationalizations of perpetrators of sex offenses against children', *Journal of International Criminal Justice Research*, 1: 1–23.

Furneaux, R. (2006) 'Harry K. Thaw (New York, 1907–8)', in R. Wilkes (ed) *The Mammoth Book of Famous Trials*, London: Robinson, pp 405–46

Furno-Lamude, D. (1999) 'The media spectacle and the O.J. Simpson case', in J. Shuetz and L.S. Lilley (1999) *The O.J. Simpson Trials: Rhetoric, Media, and the Law*, Carbondale: Southern Illinois University Press, pp 19–35.

Gadzhiyeva, N.M. and Sager, K.L. (2017) 'Maximizing the persuasiveness of a salesperson: an exploratory study of the effects of nonverbal immediacy and language power on the extent of persuasion', *Revista de Psicología del Trabajo y de las Organizaciones*, 33(2): 83–93.

Gallini, B. (2019) 'The interrogations of Brendan Dassey', *Marquette Law Review*, 102(3): 777–838.

Ganer, P.M. (1999) 'The credibility of O.J. Simpson: "If the shoe fits…"', in J. Schuetz, and L.S. Lilley (eds) *The O.J. Simpson Trials: Rhetoric, Media, and the Law*, Carbondale: Southern Illinois University Press, pp 78–99.

Geiger, G.J. (2004) Persuasive Strategies and Closing Arguments in a Trial Setting: A Pilot Study, MA thesis, University of Hawai'i. Available from: https://scholarspace.manoa.hawaii.edu/bitstream/handle/10125/11513/uhm_ma_3165_r.pdf

Geiger-Oneto, S. and Phillips, S. (2003) 'Driving while Black: the role of race, sex, and social status', *Journal of Ethnicity in Criminal Justice*, 1(2): 1–25.

Gellerman, S.W. (2003) 'Why corporations can't control chicanery', *Business Horizons*, 46(3): 17–24.

George, W.H. and Martínez, L.J. (2002) 'Victim blaming in rape: effects of victim and perpetrator race, type of rape, and participant racism', *Psychology of Women Quarterly*, 26(2): 110–19.

Geva, A. (2006) 'A typology of moral problems in business: a framework for ethical management', *Journal of Business Ethics*, 69(2): 133–47.

Ghetti, S., Goodman, G., Eisen, M., Qin, J. and Davis, S. (2002) 'Consistency in children's reports of sexual and physical abuse', *Child Abuse & Neglect*, 26(9): 977–95.

Gies, L. and Bortoluzzi, M. (2016) 'Introduction: transmedia crime stories', in L. Gies and M. Bortoluzzi (eds) *Transmedia Crime Stories: The Trial of Amanda Knox and Raffaele Sollecito in the Globalised Media Sphere*, London: Palgrave Macmillan, pp 1–14.

Gill, P. (2016) 'Analysis and implications of the miscarriages of justice of Amanda Knox and Raffaele Sollecito', *Forensic Science International: Genetics*, 23: 9–18.

Glissan, J.L. (1991) *Cross-Examination: Practice and Procedure*, Sydney: Butterworths.

Goatley, L.S. (2019) *Understanding Fred and Rose West*, Kibworth: Book Guild.

Goffman, E. (1974) *Frame Analysis: An Essay on the Organization of Experience*, Cambridge, MA: Harvard University Press.

Goffman, E. (2009) *Relations in Public: Microstudies of the Public Order*, New Brunswick: Transaction.

Goldman, F. and Goldman, K. (2007) *If I Did It: Confessions of the Killer*, New York: Beaufort Books.

Goldstein, N.E.S., Oberlander Condie, L., Kalbeitzer, R., Osman, D. and Geier, J.L. (2003) 'Juvenile offenders' Miranda rights comprehension and self-reported likelihood of offering false confessions', *Assessment*, 10(4): 359–69.

Golladay, K. (2017) 'Reporting behaviors of identity theft victims: an empirical test of Black's theory of law', *Journal of Financial Crime*, 24(1): 101–17.

Gonzalez, M. (2014) 'Innocent blood on manicured hands: how the media has brought the new Roxie Harts and Velma Kellys to center stage', *University of Denver Sports and Entertainment Law Journal*, 16: 56–88.

Gottfredson, M.R. and Hindelang, M.J. (1979) 'A study of *The Behavior of Law*', *American Sociological Review*, 44(1): 3–18.

Goulandris, A. and McLaughlin, E. (2016) 'What's in a name? The UK newspapers' fabrication and commodification of Foxy Knoxy', in L. Gies and M. Bortoluzzi (eds) *Transmedia Crime Stories: The Trial of Amanda Knox and Raffaele Sollecito in the Globalised Media Sphere*, London: Palgrave Macmillan, pp 17–46.

Gould, P. (2000) 'James Hanratty: close to a final verdict?', *BBC News*, 17 October. Available from: http://news.bbc.co.uk/1/hi/uk/977517.stm

Greene E. and Cahill B.S. (2012) 'Effects of neuroimaging evidence on mock juror decision making', *Behavioral Sciences & the Law*, 30(3): 280–96.

Griesbach, M. (2014) *The Innocent Killer: A Wrongful Conviction and Its Astonishing Aftermath*, London: Windmill Books.

Griew, E. (1988) 'The future of diminished responsibility', *Criminal Law Review*, 75: 79–80.

Griffin, L.K. (2013) 'Narrative, truth, and trial', *The Georgetown Law Journal*, 101(2): 281–335.

Grisso, T. (1981) *Juveniles' Waiver of Rights: Legal and Psychological Competence*, New York: Plenum.

Grisso, T., Steinberg, L., Woolard, J., Cauffman, E., Scott, E., Graham, S., Lexcen, F., Reppucci, N.D. and Schwartz, R. (2003) 'Juveniles' competence to stand trial: a comparison of adolescents' and adults' capacities as trial defendants', *Law and Human Behavior*, 27(4): 333–63.

Gross, S.R., Jacoby, K., Matheson, D.J., Montgomery, N. and Patil, S. (2005) 'Exonerations in the United States, 1989 through 2003', *Journal of Criminal Law and Criminology*, 95(2): 523–60.

Grossi, L.M. and Green, D. (2017) 'An international perspective on criminal responsibility and mental illness', *Practice Innovations*, 2(1): 2–12.

Gudjonsson, G.H. (1984) 'A new scale of interrogative suggestibility', *Personality and Individual Differences*, 5(3): 303–14.

Gudjonsson, G.H. (2003) *The Psychology of Interrogations and Confessions: A Handbook*, Chichester: Wiley.

Gudjonsson, G.H. (2018) *The Psychology of False Confessions: Forty Years of Science and Practice*, Chichester: Wiley.

Gudjonsson, G.H. and Mackeith, J.A.C. (1994) 'Learning disability and the Police and Criminal Evidence Act of 1984: Protection during investigative interviewing – a video-recorded false confession to double murder', *Journal of Forensic Psychiatry*, 5(1): 35–49.

Gudjonsson, G.H., Sigurdsson, J.F., Asgeirsdottir, B.B. and Sigfusdottir, I.D. (2006) 'Custodial interrogation, false confession, and individual differences: a national study among Icelandic youth', *Personality and Individual Differences*, 41(1): 49–59.

Gudjonsson, G.H., Sigurdsson, J.F. and Sigfusdottir, I.D. (2009) 'Interrogations and false confessions among adolescents in seven countries in Europe: what background and psychological factors best discriminate between false confessors and non-false confessors?', *Psychology, Crime & Law*, 15(8): 711–28.

Gulayets, M. (2016) 'Exploring differences between successful and unsuccessful mental disorder defences', *Canadian Journal of Criminology and Criminal Justice*, 58(2): 161–93.

Gumbel, A. and Charles, R.G. (2013) *Oklahoma City: What the Investigation Missed and Why It Still Matters*, New York: William Morrow and Company.

Gurley, J.R. and Marcus, D.K. (2008) 'The effects of neuroimaging and brain injury on insanity defenses', *Behavioral Sciences and the Law*, 26(1): 85–97.

Gutman, M. and Thom, L. (2014) 'Pistorius' housekeeper was inside home during shooting', *ABC News*, 6 May. Available from: https://abcnews.go.com/International/pistorius-housekeeper-inside-home-shooting/story?id=23602899

Hagerty, J. (2019) 'Wisconsin pardon board denies Brendan Dassey's clemency application', *The Rock River Times*, 20 December. Available from: http://rockrivertimes.com/2019/12/20/wisconsin-pardon-board-denies-brendan-dasseys-clemency-application/

Hahn, D.A. and Cummins, R.G. (2014) 'Effects of attractiveness, gender, and athlete-reporter congruence on perceived credibility of sport reporters', *International Journal of Sport Communication*, 7(1): 34–47.

Hale, B. and Pisa, N. (2007) '"Foxy Knoxy": I heard Meredith scream then … covered my ears', *The Mail Online*, 8 November. Available from: http://www.dailymail.co.uk/news/article-491608/Foxy-Knoxy-I-heard-Meredith-scream--covered-ears.html

Hanratty v Regina (2002) *England and Wales Court of Appeal (Criminal Division)*, 10 May. Available from: https://www.casemine.com/judgement/uk/5a8ff7b460d03e7f57eb15a5

Hantler, S.B., Schwartz, V.E. and Goldberg, P.S. (2004) 'Extending the privilege to litigation communications specialists in the Age of Trial by Media', *CommLaw Conspectus: Journal of Communications Law and Policy*, 13(1): 7–34.

Harrington, R. (2017) *Amanda: What Really Happened in Perugia – The True Story of Amanda Knox and the Murder of Meredith Kercher*, independently published.

Harris, L.C. and Daunt, K.L. (2011) 'Deviant customer behaviour: a study of techniques of neutralisation', *Journal of Marketing Management*, 27(7/8): 834–53.

Harris, R.J. and Monaco, G.E. (1978) 'Psychology of pragmatic implication: information processing between the lines', *Journal of Experimental Psychology: General*, 107(1): 1–22.

Harrison, Y. and Horne, J.A. (2000) 'The impact of sleep deprivation on decision making: a review', *Journal of Experimental Psychology: Applied*, 6(3): 236–49.

Hart, H.L.A. (2008) *Punishment and Responsibility: Essays in the Philosophy of Law*, 2nd edn, Oxford: Oxford University Press.

Hastie, R. (1980) 'Memory for behavioural information that confirms or contradicts a personality impression', in R. Hastie, T.M. Ostrom, E.B. Ebbesen, R.S. Wyer, Jr, D.L. Hamilton and D.E. Carlston (eds) *Person Memory: The Cognitive Basis of Social Perception*, Hillsdale: Erlbaum, pp 155–78.

Hauch, V., Blandón-Gitlin, I., Masip, J. and Sporer, S.L. (2015) 'Are computers effective lie detectors? A meta-analysis of linguistic cues to deception', *Personality and Social Psychology Review*, 19(4): 307–42.

Hazani, M. (1991) 'The universal applicability of the theory of neutralization: German youth coming to terms with the Holocaust', *Crime, Law and Social Change*, 15(2): 135–49.

Helm, R.K., Ceci, S.J. and Burd, K.A. (2016) 'Unpacking insanity defence standards: an experimental study of rationality and control tests in criminal law', *The European Journal of Psychology Applied to Legal Context*, 8(2): 63–8.

Helmore, E. (1995) 'The Dogg has his day in court', *The Independent*, 25 November. Available from: https://www.independent.co.uk/arts-entertainment/the-dogg-has-his-day-in-court-1583507.html

Heltsley, M. and Calhoun, T.C. (2003) 'The good mother: neutralization techniques used by pageant mothers', *Deviant Behavior*, 24(2): 81–100.

Henkel, L.A., Coffman, A.J. and Dailey, E.M. (2008) 'A survey of people's attitudes and beliefs about false confessions', *Behavioral Sciences and the Law*, 26(5): 555–84.

Hernandez, E. (2021) 'Where is Casey Anthony now? See what she has been up to since the death of her daughter Caylee', *InTouch*, 24 May.

High Court, Gauteng Division (2014a) *State v Pistorius* (CC113/2013) [2014] ZAGPPHC 793 (12 September 2014).

High Court, Gauteng Division (2014b) *State v Pistorius* (CC113/2013) *Sentence* (21 October 2014).

Hildebrand-Edgar, N. and Ehrlich, S. (2017) '"She was quite capable of asserting herself": powerful speech styles and assessments of credibility in a sexual assault trial', *Language and Law*, 4(2): 89–107.

Hilton, D.J. (1995) 'The social context of reasoning: conversational inference and rational judgment', *Psychological Bulletin*, 118(2): 248–71.

HLN After Dark (2013) 'Is the "Blade Runner" Pistorius' story the truth?', HLN TV, broadcast 20 August. Available from: https://www.youtube.com/watch?v=BBJxm0U7ScQ

Hodges, A.G. (2015) *As Done Unto You: The Secret Confession of Amanda Knox*, Birmingham, AL: Village House.

Hollinger, R.C. (1991) 'Neutralizing in the workplace: an empirical analysis of property theft and production deviance', *Deviant Behavior*, 12(2): 169–202.

Hollway, W. (1981) '"I just wanted to kill a woman." Why? The Ripper and male sexuality', *Feminist Review*, 9(1): 33–40.

Holtfreter, K. (2008) 'The effects of legal and extra-legal characteristics on organizational victim decision-making', *Crime Law and Social Change*, 50(4): art 307, https://doi.org/10.1007/s10611-008-9139-z

Home Office (2020) *Crime Outcomes in England and Wales 2019–2020.* Available from: https://assets.publishing.service.gov.uk/government/uploads/system/uploads/attachment_data/file/901028/crime-outcomes-1920-hosb1720.pdf

Hooker, M. and Lange, E. (2003) 'Limiting extrajudicial speech in high-profile cases: the duty of the prosecutor and defense attorney in their pre-trial communications with the media', *Georgetown Journal of Legal Ethics*, 16(4): 655–74.

Horney, J. and Spohn, C. (1996) 'The influence of blame and believability factors on the processing of simple versus aggravated rape cases', *Criminology*, 34(2): 135–62.

Hosman, L.A. and Siltanen, S.A. (1994) 'The attributional and evaluative consequences of powerful and powerless speech styles: an examination of the "control over others" and "control of self" explanations', *Language and Communication*, 14(3): 287–98.

Hosman, L.A. and Siltanen, S.A. (2006) 'Powerful and powerless language forms: their consequences for impression formation, attributions of control of self and control of others, cognitive responses, and message memory', *Journal of Language and Social Psychology*, 25(1): 33–46.

Hosman, L.A. and Siltanen, S.A. (2011) 'Hedges, tag questions, message processing, and persuasion', *Journal of Language and Social Psychology*, 30(3): 341–9.

Hovland, C.I., Janis, I.L. and Kelley, H.H. (1953) *Communication and Persuasion*, New Haven: Yale University Press.

Howard, R.C. and Clark, C.R. (1985) 'When courts and experts disagree: discordance between insanity recommendations and adjudications', *Law and Human Behavior*, 9(4): 385–95.

Imwinkelried, E.J. (1985) 'Demeanor impeachment: law and tactics', *American Journal of Trial Advocacy*, 9(2): 183–236.

Inbau, F.E., Reid, J.E., Buckley, J.P. and Jayne, B.C. (2001) *Criminal Interrogation and Confessions*, Gaithersburg: Aspen.

Inbau, F.E., Reid, J.E., Buckley, J.P. and Jayne, B.C. (2013) *Criminal Interrogation and Confessions*, 5th edn, Burlington: Jones and Bartlett Learning.

Inflation Tool (2021) 'Value of 1969 British pounds today'. Available from: https://www.inflationtool.com/british-pound/1969-to-present-value

Injustice Anywhere (nd) 'The contradictions of shopkeeper Marco Quintavalle'. Available from: http://www.amandaknoxcase.com/marco-quintavalle/

Innes, B.M. (2007) 'Speaking up in court: repair and powerless language in New Zealand courtrooms', *International Journal of Speech, Language and the Law*, 11(1): 163–5.

Innes, M. (2014) *Signal Crimes: Social Reactions to Crime, Disorder and Control*, Oxford: Oxford University Press.

Innocence Project (2019) 'DNA exonerations in the United States'. Available from: https://www.innocenceproject.org/dna-exonerations-in-the-united-states/

Innocence Project (2021) 'Ronald Cotton, time served: 10 years'. Available from: https://innocenceproject.org/cases/ronald-cotton/

Interrogation of Brendan Dassey (2006a) At Mishicot High School, 27 February, Calumet County Sheriff's Department, Complaint number: 05-0157-955. Transcript available from: http://www.stevenaverycase.org/wp-content/uploads/2016/02/Brendan-Dassey-Interview-at-School-Transcript-2006Feb27_text.pdf

Interrogation of Brendan Dassey (2006b) At Manitowoc County Sheriff's Department, 1 March, Calumet County Sheriff's Department. Complaint number: 05-0157-955. Transcript available from: http://www.stevenaverycase.org/wp-content/uploads/2016/02/Brendan-Dassey-Interview-Transcript-2006Mar01_text.pdf

Interrogation of Brendan Dassey (2006c) At Sheboygan County Sheriff's Department, 13 May, Calumet County Sheriff's Department. Complaint number: 05-0157-955. Transcript available from: https://jenniferjslate.files.wordpress.com/2019/03/interviewtranscript_5.13.06.pdf

Janofsky, J.S., Vandewalle, M.B. and Rappeport, J.R. (1989) 'Defendants pleading insanity: an analysis of outcome', *The Bulletin of the American Academy of Psychiatry and the Law*, 17(2): 203–11.

Jellema, H. (2020) 'The reasonable doubt standard as inference to the best explanation', *Synthese*, https://doi.org/10.1007/s11229-020-02743-8

Jesilow, P., Pontell, H.N. and Geis, G. (1993) *Prescription for Profit: How Doctors Defraud Medicaid*, Berkeley: University of California Press.

John E. Reid and Associates, Inc. (n.d.) 'Behavior symptom analysis: assessing a subject's credibility' [audio]. Available from: https://web.archive.org/web/20200113103458/http://www.reid.com/newmedia/bsa.html

Jones, D. (2008) 'I got 23 fan letters from guys today: Foxy Knoxy's disturbing diary', *Daily Mail*, 28 June. Available from: http://www.dailymail.co.uk/femail/article-1030042/I-got-23-fan-letters-guys-today-Foxy-Knoxys-disturbing-diary.html

Jones, D.W. (2019) *Understanding Criminal Behaviour: Psychosocial Perspectives on Criminality and Violence*, 2nd edn, Abingdon: Routledge.

Jones, S. (1997) 'Opening statement of defense attorney Steven Jones in the Timothy McVeigh trial', *Famous Trials*, 24 April. Available from: https://famous-trials.com/oklacity/722-defenseopen

Josephson, J.R. (2000) 'On the proof dynamics of inference to the best explanation', *Cardozo Law Review*, 22: 1621–43.

Jules, S.J. and McQuiston, D. (2013) 'Speech style and occupational status affect assessments of eyewitness testimony', *Journal of Applied Social Psychology*, 43(4): 741–8.

Justia (2018) 'The criminal defense of necessity'. Available from: https://www.justia.com/criminal/defenses/necessity/

Justice, J. (1964) *Murder vs. Murder: The British Legal System and the A.6 Murder Case*, Paris: Olympia Press.

Kaiser, K.A., O'Neal, E.N. and Spohn, C. (2017) '"Victim refuses to cooperate": a focal concerns analysis of victim cooperation in sexual assault cases', *Victims & Offenders*, 12(2): 297–322.

Kalven, H. and Zeisel, H. (1966) *The American Jury*, Boston, MA: Little, Brown.

Kaptein, M. and van Helvoort, M. (2019) 'A model of neutralization techniques', *Deviant Behavior*, 40(10): 1260–85.

Kardashian, R. (1996) Barbara Walters 1996 interview with Robert Kardashian, YouTube. Available from: https://www.youtube.com/watch?v=jcKJy4zDiaU&t=632s

Kassin, S.M. (2002) 'False confessions and the jogger case', *New York Times*, 1 November, p A31. Available from: https://www.nytimes.com/2002/11/01/opinion/false-confessions-and-the-jogger-case.html

Kassin, S.M. (2012) 'Why confessions trump innocence', *American Psychologist*, 67(6): 431–45.

Kassin, S.M. (2017) 'False confessions', *WIREs Cognitive Science*, e1439: 1–11.

Kassin, S.M. and Wrightsman, L.S. (1985) 'Confession evidence', in S.M. Kassin and L.S. Wrightsman (eds) *The Psychology of Evidence and Trial Procedure*, Beverly Hills: Sage, pp 67–94.

Kassin, S.M. and McNall, K. (1991) 'Police interrogations and confessions: communicating promises and threats by pragmatic implication', *Law and Human Behavior*, 15(3): 233–51.

Kassin, S.M. and Kiechel, K.L. (1996) 'The social psychology of false confessions: compliance, internalization, and confabulation', *Psychological Science*, 7(3): 125–8.

Kassin, S.M. and Gudjonsson, G.H. (2004) 'The psychology of confession evidence: a review of the literature and issues', *Psychological Science in the Public Interest*, 5(2): 33–67.

Kassin, S.M., Leo, R.A., Meissner, C.A., Richman, K.D., Colwell, L.H., Leach, A.M. and La Fon, D. (2007) 'Police interviewing and interrogation: a self-report survey of police practices and beliefs', *Law and Human Behavior*, 31(4): 381–400.

Kassin, S.M., Drizin, S.A., Grisso, T., Gudjonsson, G.H., Leo, R.A. and Redlich, A.D. (2010) 'Police-induced confessions, risk factors and recommendations: looking ahead', *Law and Human Behavior*, 34(1): 49–52.

Kassin, S.M., Redlich, A.D., Alceste, F. and Luke, T.J. (2018) 'On the general acceptance of confessions research: opinions of the scientific community', *American Psychologist*, 73(1): 63–80.

Katz, J. (1988) *Seductions of Crime: Moral and Sensual Attractions in Doing Evil*, New York: Basic Books.

Keegan, K. (2013) 'The true man and the battered woman: prospects for gender-neutral narratives in self-defense doctrines', *Hastings Law Journal*, 65(1): 259–83.

Kennefick, L. (2011) 'Introducing a new diminished responsibility defence for England and Wales', *The Modern Law Review*, 74(5): 750–66.

Kercher, J. (2012) *Meredith: Our Daughter's Murder and the Heartbreaking Quest for the Truth*, London: Hodder & Stoughton.

Kerper, J. (1997) 'Killing him softly with his words: the art and ethics of impeachment with prior statements', *American Journal of Trial Advocacy*, 21(1): 81–112.

Kerstetter, W.A. (1990) 'Gateway to justice: police and prosecutorial response to sexual assaults against women', *Journal of Criminal Law and Criminology*, 81(2): 267–313.

Klaver, J.R., Lee, Z. and Rose, V.G. (2008) 'Effects of personality, interrogation techniques and plausibility in an experimental false confession paradigm', *Legal and Criminological Psychology*, 13(1): 71–88.

Knight, J.L., Giuliano, T.A. and Sanchez-Ross, M.G. (2001) 'Famous or infamous? The influence of celebrity status and race on perceptions of responsibility for rape', *Basic and Applied Social Psychology*, 23(3): 183–90.

Knowles, J.B. (2015) 'The abolition of the death penalty in the United Kingdom: how it happened and why it still matters', London: The Death Penalty Project. Available from: https://www.deathpenaltyproject.org/wp-content/uploads/2017/12/DPP-50-Years-on-pp1-68-1.pdf

Knox, A. (2015) *Waiting to be Heard*, New York: Harper.

Kövecses, Z. (2000) *Metaphor and Emotion: Language, Culture, and Body in Human Feeling*, Cambridge: Cambridge University Press.

Kraus, M.W. and Mendes, W.B. (2014) 'Sartorial symbols of social class elicit class-consistent behavioral and physiological responses: a dyadic approach', *Journal of Experimental Psychology: General*, 143(6): 2330–40.

Krix, A.C., Sauerland, M., Lorei, C. and Rispens, I. (2015) 'Consistency across repeated eyewitness interviews: contrasting police detectives' beliefs with actual eyewitness performance', *PLOS ONE*, 10(2): e0118641. Available from: https://doi.org/10.1371/journal.pone.0118641

Kruttschnitt, C. (1980) 'Social status and sentences of female offenders', *Law and Society Review*, 15(2): 247–66.

Kuo, S.Y., Cuvelier, S.J., Sheu, C.J. and Chang, K.M. (2012) 'Crime reporting behavior and Black's *Behavior of Law*', *International Sociology*, 27(1): 51–71.

LaDuke, C., Locklair, B. and Heilbrun, K. (2018) 'Neuroscientific, neuropsychological, and psychological evidence comparably impact legal decision making: implications for experts and legal practitioners', *Journal of Forensic Psychology Research and Practice*, 18(2): 114–42.

LaFree, G.D. (1981) 'Official reactions to social problems: police decisions in sexual assault cases', *Social Problems*, 28(5): 582–94.

Lakoff, G. and Johnson, M. (1980) *Metaphors We Live By*, Chicago: University of Chicago Press.

Lakoff, R.T. (1975) *Language and Woman's Place*, New York: Harper & Row.

Langa, M., Kirsten, A., Bowman, B., Eagle, G. and Kiguwa, P. (2020) 'Black masculinities on trial *in absentia*: the case of Oscar Pistorius in South Africa', *Men and Masculinities*, 23(3/4): 499–515.

Laudan, L. (2006) *Truth, Error, and Criminal Law: An Essay in Legal Epistemology*, New York: Cambridge University Press.

Lazzaro, T. (2011) 'Casey Anthony trial: day 2, part 2 of 2 – Casey's ex-boyfriend', 25 May, YouTube. Available from: https://www.youtube.com/watch?v=6X_WNz9OiHk

Leaving Neverland: Michael Jackson and Me (2019) Documentary, Channel 4, broadcast 6 and 7 March. Available from: https://www.channel4.com/programmes/leaving-neverland-michael-jackson-and-me

Lee, C. (2003) *Murder and the Reasonable Man: Passion and Fear in the Criminal Courtroom*, New York: New York University Press.

Leo, R.A. (2008) *Police Interrogation and American Justice*, Cambridge, MA: Harvard University Press.

Leo, R.A. (2009) 'False confessions: causes, consequences, and implications', *Journal of the American Academy of Psychiatry and the Law*, 37(3): 332–43.

Leo, R.A. and Liu, B.S. (2009) 'What do potential jurors know about police interrogation techniques and false confessions?', *Behavioral Sciences and Law*, 27(3): 381–99.

Leverick, F. (2020) 'What do we know about rape myths and juror decision making?', *The International Journal of Evidence & Proof*, 24(3): 255–79.

Levi, K. (1981) 'Becoming a hit man: neutralization in a very deviant career', *Journal of Contemporary Ethnography*, 10(1): 47–63.

Levine, A. and Kline, R. (2017) 'A new approach for evaluating climate change communication', *Climactic Change*, 142(1/2): 301–9.

Levine, M. (2015) 'The competing roles of an attorney in high-profile case: trying a case inside and outside the courtroom', *Georgetown Journal of Legal Ethics*, 28(3): 683–702.

Li, D.K. (2009) 'Phil Spector faces the music', *New York Post*, 13 April. Available from: https://nypost.com/2009/04/13/phil-spector-faces-the-music/

Liddick, D. (2013) 'Techniques of neutralization and animal rights activists', *Deviant Behavior*, 34(8): 618–34.

Lilley, L.S. (1999) 'Opening statements: lasting impressions', in J. Shuetz, and L.S. Lilley (eds) *The O.J. Simpson Trials: Rhetoric, Media, and the Law*, Carbondale: Southern Illinois University Press, pp 36–57.

Linder, D.O. (nd) 'The Oklahoma City bombing and the trial of Timothy McVeigh: an account', *Famous Trials*. Available from: https://famous-trials.com/oklacity/730-home

Lindsay, R., Lim, R., Marando, L. and Cully, D. (1986) 'Mock-juror evaluations of eyewitness testimony: a test of metamemory hypotheses', *Journal of Applied Social Psychology*, 16(5): 447–59.

Lippman, M. (2013) *Criminal Evidence*, Thousand Oaks: Sage.

Litwin, K.J. (2004) 'A multilevel multivariate analysis of factors affecting homicide clearances', *Journal of Research in Crime and Delinquency*, 41(4): 327–51.

Llewellyn, N. and Whittle, A. (2019) 'Lies, defeasibility and morality-in-action: the interactional architecture of false claims in sales, telemarketing and debt collection work', *Human Relations*, 72(4): 834–58.

Loeterman, B. (1997) 'What Jennifer saw', *Frontline*, 25 February. Available from: https://www.pbs.org/wgbh/pages/frontline/shows/dna/etc/script.html

Longhini, D. (2014) 'Was Amanda Knox a political pawn in Italian politics?', *CBS News*, 7 February. Available from: https://www.cbsnews.com/news/was-amanda-knox-a-political-pawn-in-italian-politics/

Lonsway, K.A. and Fitzgerald, L.F. (1994) 'Rape myths. In review', *Psychology of Women Quarterly*, 18(2): 133–64.

Lonsway, K.A., Welch, S. and Fitzgerald, L. (2001) 'Police training in sexual assault response process, outcomes, and elements of change', *Criminal Justice and Behaviour*, 28(6): 695–730.

Mackay, R. and Mitchell, B.J. (2003) 'Provoking diminished responsibility: two pleas merging into one?', *Criminal Law Review*, November: 745–59.

Madigan, N. and Newman, M. (2003) 'Michael Jackson's ranch is raided', *New York Times*, 18 November. Available from: https://www.nytimes.com/2003/11/18/national/michael-jacksons-ranch-is-raided.html

Mail Foreign Service (2008) 'Secret diary reveals Foxy Knoxy was always thinking about sex', *The Mail Online*, 30 November. Available at: http://www.dailymail.co.uk/news/article-1090608/Secret-diary-reveals-Foxy-Knoxy-thinking-sex.html

Malcolm, J. (1999) *The Crime of Sheila McGough*, New York: Vintage.

Malvern, J. (2014) 'Separated twin is now living a full life, says judge', *The Times*, 4 October. Available from: https://www.thetimes.co.uk/article/separated-twin-is-now-living-a-full-life-says-judge-66b3qf8cvww

Mann, S., Vrij, A. and Bull, R. (2002) 'Suspects, lies, and videotape: an analysis of authentic high-stake liars', *Law and Human Behavior*, 26(3): 365–76.

Maresca, F. (2011) 'Lawyer for falsely accused barman brands Amanda Knox a "she-devil" in court', *The Telegraph*, 26 September. Available from: https://web.archive.org/web/20120106123345/http://www.telegraph.co.uk/news/worldnews/europe/italy/8789979/Lawyer-for-falsely-accused-barman-brands-Amanda-Knox-a-she-devil-in-court.html

Marjoribanks, E. (1929) *The Life of Sir Edward Marshall Hall*, New York: Macmillan.

Martin, J.H., Van Wijk, C.H. and Bowden, W.J. (2019) 'Diving, cannabis use, and techniques of neutralisation: exploring how divers rationalise cannabis use', *International Maritime Health*, 70(2): 88–94.

Martin, S., Kish-Gephart, J.J. and Detert, J.R. (2014) 'Blind forces: ethical infrastructures and moral disengagement in organizations', *Organizational Psychology Review*, 4(4): 295–325.

Maruna, S. and Copes, H. (2005) 'What have we learned from five decades of neutralization research?', *Crime and Justice*, 32: 221–320.

Masters, B. (1997) *'She Must Have Known': The Trial of Rosemary West*, London: Transworld.

Matoesian, G. (1997) '"You were interested in him as a person?" Rhythms of domination in the Kennedy Smith rape trial', *Law and Social Inquiry*, 22(1): 55–93.

Mauet, T.A. (2017) *Trial Techniques and Trials*, New York: Wolters Kluwer.

McAdams, D.P. (1985) *Power, Intimacy and the Life Story: Personological Inquiries into Identity*, New York: Guildford.

McAdams, D.P. (1993) *The Stories We Live By: Personal Myths and the Making of the Self*, New York: W. Morrow.

McConville, M., Hodgson, J., Bridges, L. and Pavlovic, A. (1994) *Standing Accused: The Organisation and Practices of Criminal Defence Lawyers in Britain*, Oxford: Clarendon Press.

McDonell-Parry, A. (2019) 'Michael Jackson child sexual abuse allegations: a timeline', *Rolling Stone*, 29 January. Available from: https://www.rollingstone.com/culture/culture-features/michael-jackson-child-sexual-abuse-allegations-timeline-785746/

McGlynn, R.P. and Dreilinger, E.A. (1981) 'Mock juror judgment and the insanity plea: effects of incrimination and insanity information', *Journal of Applied Social Psychology*, 11(2): 166–80.

McSwiggan, S., Elger, B. and Appelbaum, P. (2017) 'The forensic use of behavioral genetics in criminal proceedings: case of the MAOA-L genotype', *International Journal of Law and Psychiatry*, 50: 17–23.

Meissner, C.A., Redlich, A.D., Michael, S.W., Evans, J.R., Camilletti, C.R., Bhatt, S. and Brandon, S. (2014) 'Accusatorial and information-gathering interrogation methods and their effects on true and false confessions: a meta-analytic review', *Journal of Experimental Criminology*, 10(4): 459–86.

Mesereau Law Group (2020) Available from: http://mesereaulaw.com/

Mesereau, T. (2005a) Defence opening statement, 28 February. Available from: https://www.themichaeljacksoninnocentproject.com/blog/022805.txt

Mesereau, T. (2005b) Cross examination of June Chandler, 11 April. Available from: http://www.reflectionsonthedance.com/04-11-05_FINAL__Jones_Brown_Swindler___June_Chandler_.txt

Mesereau, T. (2005c) Cross examination of Janet Arvizo, 15 April. Available from: http://www.reflectionsonthedance.com/04-15-05_FINAL__Janet_Arvizo_Cross_.txt

Mesereau, T. (2005d) Defence closing statement, 2 June. Available from: https://www.themichaeljacksoninnocentproject.com/blog/060205.txt

Mesereau, T. (2005e) Defence closing statement, 3 June. Available from: https://www.themichaeljacksoninnocentproject.com/blog/060305.txt

Mesereau, T. (2013) 'Wade Robson allegation', *NBC Today*, 16 May. Available from: https://www.youtube.com/watch?v=ayMOt6zypT4

Michel, L. and Herbeck, D. (2001) *American Terrorist: Timothy McVeigh and the Oklahoma City Bombing*, New York: Harper Collins.

Miller, A. (2010) 'Inherent (gender) unreasonableness of the concept of reasonableness in the context of manslaughter committed in the heat of passion', *William and Mary Journal of Women and the Law*, 17(1): 249–75.

Miller, J. and Schwartz, M.D. (1995) 'Rape myths and violence against street prostitutes', *Deviant Behavior*, 16(1): 1–23.

Miller, L. (2001) *Shadows of Deadman's Hill: A New Analysis of the A6 Murder*, London: Zoilus Press.

Millstein, S. (2016) 'Why did John Mark Karr confess to killing JonBenet Ramsey? His false confession was a strange turn of events', *Bustle*, 7 September. Available from: https://www.bustle.com/articles/182309-why-did-john-mark-karr-confess-to-killing-jonbenet-ramsey-his-false-confession-was-a-strange

Milmo, C. (2014) 'Court of Appeal upholds guilt of A6 killer Hanratty', *The Independent*, 1 March. Available from: https://www.independent.co.uk/news/uk/crime/court-appeal-upholds-guilt-a6-killer-hanratty-9161840.html

Mindthoff, A., Evans, J.R., Perez, G., Woestehoff, S.A., Olaguez, A.P., Klemfuss, J.Z., Normile, C.J., Scherr, K.C., Carlucci, M.E., Carol, R.N., Meissner, C.A., Michael, S.W., Russano, M.B., Stocks, E.L., Vallano, J.P. and Woody, W.D. (2018) 'A survey of potential jurors' perceptions of interrogations and confessions', *Psychology, Public Policy, and Law*, 24(4): 430–48.

Minor, W.W. (1981) 'Techniques of neutralization: a reconceptualization and empirical examination', *Journal of Research in Crime and Delinquency*, 18(2): 295–318.

Minzner, M. (2008) 'Detecting lies using demeanor, bias, and context', *Cardozo Law Review*, 29(6): 2557–82.

Mirabella, J.G. (2012) 'Scales of justice: assessing Italian criminal procedure through the Amanda Knox trial', *Boston University International Law Journal*, 30: 229–60.

Moles, R.N. and Sangha, B. (2002) *R. v. James Hanratty (deceased)* [2002] EWCA Crim 1141. Available from: http://netk.net.au/UK/HanrattyJudgment.asp

Moran, M. (2010) 'The reasonable person: a conceptual biography in comparative perspective', *Lewis & Clark Law Review*, 14(4): 1233–83.

Moran, R. (2019) 'Casey Anthony and the social media trial', *Women Leading Change: Case Studies on Women, Gender and Feminism*, 4(1).

Morash, M. (2006) *Understanding Gender, Crime and Justice*, Thousand Oaks: Sage.

Morgenstein, M. (2013) 'Two of four Casey Anthony convictions thrown out; she vows to "keep fighting"', *CNN*, 26 January.

Morrison, B.R., Porter, L.L. and Fraser, I.H. (2007) 'The role of demeanour in assessing the credibility of witnesses', *The Advocates Quarterly*, 33(1): 170–92.

Morse, S.J. (1999) 'Craziness and criminal responsibility', *Behavioral Sciences and the Law*, 17(2): 147–64.

Mowle, E.N., Edens, J.F., Clark, J.W. and Sörman, K. (2016) 'Effects of mental health and neuroscience evidence on juror perceptions of a criminal defendant: the moderating role of political orientation', *Behavioral Sciences and the Law*, 34(6): 726–41.

Munday, R. (1981) 'The Royal Commission on Criminal Procedure', *The Cambridge Law Journal*, 40(2): 193–8.

Murphy, P. and Glover, R. (2009) *Murphy on Evidence*, 12th edn, Oxford: Oxford University Press.

Murphy, P.R. and Dacin, M.T. (2011) 'Psychological pathways to fraud: understanding and preventing fraud in organizations', *Journal of Business Ethics*, 101(4): 601–18.

Myers, M.A. (1980) 'Predicting the behavior of law: a test of two models', *Law & Society Review*, 14(4): 835–57.

Nadeau, B.L. (2010) *Angel Face: The True Story of Student Killer Amanda Knox*, New York: Beast Books.

National Prosecution Authority (2016) 'National Prosecuting Authority to appeal Oscar Pistorius's sentence', *South African Government*, 21 July. Available from: https://www.gov.za/speeches/npa-decision-appeal-sentence-oscar-pistorius-21-jul-2016-0000#

NDTV (2011) 'Casey Anthony cleared of murdering young daughter', *NDTV*, 6 July. Available from: http://www.ndtv.com/world-news/casey-anthony-cleared-of-murdering-young-daughter-460524

Nelson, S. (2014) 'Was Amanda Knox innocent, or did she just have good PR?', *The Huffington Post UK*, 22 August. Available from: https://www.huffingtonpost.co.uk/selene-nelson/amanda-knox-pr_b_5694432.html

Nirider, L. (2019) Northwest Pritzker School of Law, Bluhm Legal Clinic, Centre on Wrongful Convictions [tweet], 20 December. Available from: https://twitter.com/lauranirider/status/1179381970213785600

Nirider, L. and Drizin, S. (2018) 'A Legal Miracle' (episode 3), *Making a Murderer*, directed by Moira Demos and Laura Ricciardi, Netflix.

Nirider, L., Drizin, S.A., Dvorak, R.J. and Waxman, S.P. (2019) Petition for Executive Clemency, before the Wisconsin Pardon Advisory Board, advising the Honorable Governor Tony Evers, 2 October. Available at http://www.law.northwestern.edu/legalclinic/wrongfulconvictionsyouth/documents/brendan-dassey-petition-for-executive-clemency.pdf

Nobles, R. and Schiff, D. (2000) *Understanding Miscarriages of Justice: The Law, the Media and the Inevitability of Crisis*, Oxford: Oxford University Press.

Nusbaum, D.J. (2002) 'Craziest reform of them all: a critical analysis of the constitutional implications of "abolishing" the insanity defense', *Cornell Law Review*, 87(6): 1509–72.

O'Barr, W.M. (1982) *Linguistic Evidence: Language, Power, and Strategy in the Courtroom*, London: Academic Press.

O'Connell, M. (2017) *Delusions of Innocence: The Tragic Case of Stefan Kiszko*, Hook: Waterside Press.

O'Connell, M.J., Garmoe, W. and Goldstein, N.E.S. (2005) '*Miranda* comprehension in adults with mental retardation and the effects of feedback style on suggestibility', *Law and Human Behavior*, 29(3): 359–69.

O'Donohue, W., Smith, V. and Schewe, P. (1998) 'The credibility of child sexual abuse allegations: perpetrator gender and subject occupational status', *Sexual Abuse*, 10(1): 17–24.

O'Grady, R.L. and Matthews-Creech, N. (nd) 'Why children don't tell', *LACASA Center*. Available from: https://lacasacenter.org/why-child-abuse-victims-dont-tell/

O'Neal, E.N. (2017) '"Victim is not credible": the influence of rape culture on police perceptions of sexual assault complainants', *Justice Quarterly*, 36(1): 127–60.

O'Neal, E.N. and Hayes, B.E. (2020) '"A rape is a rape, regardless of what the victim was doing at the time": detective views on how "problematic" victims affect sexual assault case processing', *Criminal Justice Review*, 45(1): 26–44.

O'Neill, H. (2001) 'The perfect witness', *The Washington Post*, 4 March. Available from: http://www.washingtonpost.com/archive/lifestyle/2001/03/04/the-perfect-witness/a7fa0461-c15c-4237-86db-52ab5069fbea

O'Regan, D. (2017) 'Eying the body: the impact of classical rules for demeanor credibility, bias, and the need to blind legal decision makers', *Pace Law Review*, 37(2): 379–454.

Oeberst, A. (2012) 'If anything else comes to mind ... better keep it to yourself? Delayed recall is discrediting – unjustifiably', *Law and Human Behavior*, 36(4): 266–74.

Ofshe, R.J. and Leo, R.A. (1997) 'The social psychology of police interrogation: the theory and classification of true and false confessions', *Studies in Law, Politics, and Society*, 16: 189–251.

Ognibene, S. and Binnie, I. (2015) '"Glaring errors" led court to annul Knox murder conviction', *Reuters*, 7 September. Available from: http://www.reuters.com/article/us-italy-knox-motivations-idUSKCN0R71V320150907

Ohanian, R. (1990) 'Construction and validation of a scale to measure celebrity endorsers' perceived expertise, trustworthiness, and attractiveness', *Journal of Advertising*, 19(3): 39–52.

Ohayon, M.M., Crocker, A., Bernard St-Onge, A. and Caulet, M. (1998) 'Fitness, responsibility, and judicially ordered assessments', *Canadian Journal of Psychiatry*, 43(5): 491–5.

Owen-Kostelnik, J., Reppucci, N.D. and Meyer, J.R. (2006) 'Testimony and interrogation of minors: assumptions about maturity and morality', *American Psychologist*, 61(4): 286–304.

Oxford Reference (2021) 'Similar-fact evidence'. Available from: https://www.oxfordreference.com/view/10.1093/oi/authority.20110803100506670

Packer, I.K. (1987) 'Homicide and the insanity defense: A comparison of sane and insane murderers', *Behavioral Sciences and the Law*, 5(1): 25–35.

Palena, N., Caso, L., Vrij, A. and Orthey, R. (2018) 'Detecting deception through small talk and comparable truth baselines', *Journal of Investigative Psychology and Offender Profiling*, 15(2): 124–32.

Pardieck, A. (2006) 'Differ or die: prevailing in an era of rampant anti-plaintiff bias', *The Jury Expert*, 18(6): 1–6.

Pardo, M.S. and Allen, R.J. (2008) 'Juridical proof and the best explanation', *Law and Philosophy*, 27(3): 223–68.

Parton, S.R., Siltanen, S.A., Hosman, L.A. and Langenderfer, J. (2002) 'Employment interview outcomes and speech style effects', *Journal of Language and Social Psychology*, 21(2): 144–61.

Paus, T. (2009) 'Brain development', in R. Lerner and L. Steinberg (eds) *Handbook of Adolescent Psychology, Vol. 1: Individual Bases of Adolescent Development*, 3rd edn, Hoboken: Wiley, pp 95–115.

Pennington, N. and Hastie, R. (1986) 'Evidence evaluation in complex decision making', *Journal of Personality and Social Psychology*, 51(2): 242–58.

Pennington, N. and Hastie, R. (1988) 'Explanation-based decision making: effects of memory structure on judgment', *Journal of Experimental Psychology: Learning, Memory, and Cognition*, 14(3): 521–33.

Pennington, N. and Hastie, R. (1991) 'A cognitive theory of juror decision making: the story model', *Cardozo Law Review*, 13(2): 519–57.

Pennington, N. and Hastie, R. (1992) 'Explaining the evidence: tests of the story model for juror decision making', *Journal of Personality and Social Psychology*, 62(2): 189–206.

Pérez-Sales, P. (2017) *Psychological Torture: Definition, Evaluation and Measurement*, Abingdon: Routledge.

Perlin, M.L. (1990) 'Psychodynamics and the insanity defense: "ordinary common sense" and heuristic reasoning', *Nebraska Law Review*, 69(1): 3–70.

Perlman, N.B., Ericson, K.I., Esses, V.M. and Isaacs, B. (1994) 'The developmentally handicapped witness: competency as a function of question format', *Law and Human Behavior*, 18(2): 171–87.

Perry, B., Jr (2011) 'Jury instructions in the Casey Anthony trial', 4 July. Available from: https://web.archive.org/web/20160219235414/http://insession.blogs.cnn.com/2011/07/04/jury-instructions-in-the-casey-anthony-trial/

Perry, B., Jr (2013) 'Casey Anthony judge felt "shock, disbelief" at verdict', YouTube, 6 May. Available from: https://www.youtube.com/watch?v=q6wPvdLPv6Q

Pershing, J.L. (2003) 'To snitch or not to snitch? Applying the concept of neutralization techniques to the enforcement of occupational misconduct', *Sociological Perspectives*, 46(2): 149–78.

Perske, R. (1994) 'Thoughts on the police interrogation of individuals with mental retardation', *Mental Retardation*, 32(5): 377–80.

Persons, W.R. (2005) 'Preparing and delivering the defense closing argument', *The Practical Litigator*, 16(3): 55–61. Available from: http://files.ali-cle.org/thumbs/datastorage/lacidoirep/articles/PLIT_PLIT0505-PERSONS_thumb.pdf

Peters, E. (1996) *Torture*, expanded edn, Philadelphia: University of Pennsylvania Press.

Phelps, K. (2016) 'The role of *error in objecto* in South African criminal law: an opportunity for re-evaluation presented by *State v Pistorius*', *Journal of Criminal Law*, 80(1): 45–63.

Phillips, S. (2009) 'Status disparities in the capital of capital punishment', *Law and Society Review*, 43(4): 807–38.

Piacentini, M., Chatzidakis, A. and Banister, E. (2012) 'Making sense of drinking: the role of techniques of neutralisation and counter-neutralisation in negotiating alcohol consumption', *Sociology of Health & Illness*, 34(6): 841–57.

Pickel, K.L. (1998) 'The effects of motive information and crime unusualness on jurors' judgments in insanity cases', *Law and Human Behavior*, 22(5): 571–84.

Pisa, N. (2008a) 'Foxy Knoxy protests innocence and details her many lovers – and her fanmail – in prison diary', *The Mail Online*, 25 June. Available from: http://www.dailymail.co.uk/news/article-1029136/Foxy-Knoxy-protests-innocence-details-lovers--fan-mail--prison-diary.html

Pisa, N. (2008b) 'Foxy Knoxy claims female cell mate begs her for sex "because I'm so pretty"', *The Mail Online*, 24 October. Available from: http://www.dailymail.co.uk/news/article-1080204/Foxy-Knoxy-claims-female-cell-mate-begs-sex-Im-pretty.html

Pistorius Testimony (2014) Available from: https://s3-eu-west-1.amazonaws.com/pmb-portals/behind-the-door/downloads/transcripts/Oscar+Pistorius.pdf

Polgreen, L. and Cowell, A. (2013) 'Pistorius is granted bail in killing of girlfriend', *New York Times*, 22 February. Available from: https://www.nytimes.com/2013/02/23/world/africa/oscar-pistorius-bail-hearing.html

Pornpitakpan, C. (2004) 'The persuasiveness of source credibility: a critical review of five decades' evidence', *Journal of Applied Social Psychology*, 34(2): 243–81.

Portes, A. (1998) 'Social capital: its origins and applications in modern sociology', *Annual Review of Sociology*, 24: 1–24.

Pospisil, L.J. (1971) *Anthropology of Law: A Comparative Theory*, New York: HRAF Press.

Potter, R. and Brewer, N. (1999) 'Perceptions of witness behaviour–accuracy relationships held by police, lawyers and mock-jurors', *Psychiatry, Psychology and Law*, 6(1): 97–103.

Prakken, H. (2018) 'A new use case for argumentation support tools: supporting discussions of Bayesian analyses of complex criminal cases', *Artificial Intelligence and Law*, 28(1): 27–49.

Preskey, N. (2021) '"I am a human being": Amanda Knox on life after her wrongful conviction for Meredith Kercher's murder', *The Independent*, 24 January. Available from: https://www.independent.co.uk/life-style/amanda-knox-campaign-podcast-meredith-kercher-b1791874.html

Pryor, B. and Buchanan, R.W. (1984) 'The effects of a defendant's demeanor on juror perceptions of credibility and guilt', *Journal of Communication*, 34(3): 92–9.

Ramos, N.C. and McCullick, B.A. (2015) 'Elementary students' construct of physical education teacher credibility', *Journal of Teaching in Physical Education*, 34(4): 560–75.

Redlich, A.D. (2007) 'Double jeopardy in the interrogation room: young age and mental illness', *American Psychologist*, 62(6): 609–11.

Redlich, A.D. and Goodman, G.S. (2003) 'Taking responsibility for an act not committed: the influence of age and suggestibility', *Law and Human Behavior*, 27(2): 141–56.

Redlich, A.D., Silverman, M., Chen, J. and Steiner, H. (2004) 'The police interrogation of children and adolescents', in G.D. Lassiter (ed) *Interrogations, Confessions, and Entrapment*, New York: Kluwer Academic/ Plenum, pp 107–25.

Remmel, R., Glenn, A.L. and Cox, J. (2019) 'Biological evidence regarding psychopathy does not affect mock jury sentencing', *Journal of Personality Disorders*, 33(2): 164–84.

Rendell, J., Huss, M. and Jensen, M. (2010) 'Expert testimony and the effects of a biological approach, psychopathy, and juror attitudes in cases of insanity', *Behavioral Sciences & the Law*, 28(3): 411–25.

Ridgeway, C. and Walker, H. (1995) 'Status structures', in K.S. Cook, G.A. Fine and J. House (eds) *Sociological Perspectives on Social Psychology*, Boston: Allyn and Bacon, pp 281–310.

Rieke, R.D. and Sillars, M.O. (2001) *Argumentation and Critical Decision Making*, 5th edn, New York: Longman.

Rieke, R.D. and Stutman, R.K. (1995) *Communication in Legal Advocacy*, Columbia: University of South Carolina Press.

Riordan, C.A., Marlin, N.A. and Kellogg, R.T. (1983) 'The effectiveness of accounts following transgression', *Social Psychological Quarterly*, 46(3): 213–19.

Roberts, C.F. and Golding, S.L. (1991) 'The social construction of criminal responsibility and insanity', *Law and Human Behavior*, 15(4): 349–76.

Roberts, C.F., Golding, S.L. and Fincham, F.D. (1987) 'Implicit theories of criminal responsibility: decision making and the insanity defense', *Law and Human Behavior*, 11(3): 207–32.

Robinson, G. (2021) 'Making a murderer: Kathleen Zellner gives update in Steven Avery's ongoing murder appeal', *Tyla*, 19 November. Available from: https://www.tyla.com/tv-and-film/steven-avery-appeal-denied-kathleen-zellner-making-a-murderer-netflix-20211119

Robinson, S.L. and Kraatz, M.S. (1998) 'Constructing the reality of normative behavior: the use of neutralization strategies by organizational deviants', in R.W. Griffin, A. O'Leary-Kelly and J.M. Collins (eds) *Dysfunctional Behavior in Organizations: Violent and Deviant Behavior*, Stamford: JAI Press, pp 203–20.

Robson, W. (2013) 'Wade Robson allegation', *NBC Today*, 15 May. Available from: https://www.youtube.com/watch?v=ayMOt6zypT4

Rodriguez, L., Agtarap, S., Boals, A., Kearns, N.T. and Bedford, L. (2018) 'Making a biased jury decision: using the Steven Avery murder case to investigate potential influences in jury decision-making', *Psychology of Popular Media Culture*, 8(4): 429–36.

Rofé, Y. (1984) 'Stress and affiliation: a utility theory', *Psychological Review*, 91(2): 235–50.

Rogers, H., Fox, S. and Herlihy, J. (2015) 'The importance of looking credible: the impact of the behavioural sequelae of post-traumatic stress disorder on the credibility of asylum seekers', *Psychology, Crime & Law*, 21(2): 139–55.

Romano, L. and Kenworthy, T. (1997) 'McVeigh guilty on all 11 counts', *The Washington Post*, 3 June. Available from: https://www.washingtonpost.com/wp-srv/national/longterm/oklahoma/stories/guilty2.htm

Rorty, R. (1989) *Contingency, Irony, and Solidarity*, New York: Cambridge University Press.

Rose, V.M. and Randall, S.C. (1982) 'The impact of investigator perceptions of victim legitimacy on the processing or rape/sexual assault cases', *Symbolic Interaction*, 5(1): 23–36.

Rothstein, M.A. (1999) 'The impact of behavioral genetics on the law and the courts', *Judicature*, 83(3): 116–23.

Rumbelow, D. (2013) *The Complete Jack the Ripper*, London: Virgin.

Russano, M.B., Meissner, C.A., Narchet, F.M. and Kassin, S.M. (2005) 'Investigating true and false confessions within a novel experimental paradigm', *Psychological Science*, 16(6): 481–6.

Ruva, C.L. and Coy, A.E. (2020) 'Your bias is rubbing off on me: the impact of pretrial publicity and jury type on guilt decisions, trial evidence interpretation, and impression formation', *Psychology, Public Policy, and Law*, 26(1): 22–35.

Sanbonmatsu, D.M., Mazur, D., Pfeiffer, B., Kardes, F.R. and Posavac, S.S. (2012) 'The less the public knows the better? The effects of increased knowledge on celebrity evaluations', *Basic and Applied Social Psychology*, 34(6): 499–507.

Sarzanini, F. (2008) *Amanda e gli altri: Vite perdute intorno al delitto di Perugia* [Amanda and the Others: Lives Lost Around the Perugia Crime], Milan: Bompiani.

Schachter, S. (1959) *The Psychology of Affiliation: Experimental Studies of the Sources of Gregariousness*, Stanford: Stanford University Press.

Scheck, B. (1995) Defence closing statement, 28 September. Available from: http://simpson.walraven.org/sep28.html The transcript is an unofficial record; however, you can also access the closing statements on YouTube.

Scherr, K.C., Redlich, A.D. and Kassin, S.M. (2020) 'Cumulative disadvantage: a psychological framework for understanding how innocence can lead to confession, wrongful conviction, and beyond', *Perspectives on Psychological Science*, 15(2): 353–83.

Schlenker, B.R. (1980) *Impression Management: The Self-Concept, Social Identity, and Interpersonal Relations*, Monterey: Brookes/Cole.

Schönbach, P. (1990) *Account Episodes: The Management or Escalation of Conflict*, Cambridge: Cambridge University Press.

Schooler, C. (2013) 'Social class and social status', *Oxford Bibliographies in Psychology*. Available from: https://www.oxfordbibliographies.com/view/document/obo-9780199828340/obo-9780199828340-0085.xml

Schuetz, J. (1999a) 'Introduction: telelitgation and its challenges to trial discourse', in J. Shuetz and L.S. Lilley (eds) *The O.J. Simpson Trials: Rhetoric, Media, and the Law*, Carbondale: Southern Illinois University Press, pp 1–18.

Schuetz, J. (1999b) 'Detective Mark Fuhrman: the race card', in J. Shuetz and L.S. Lilley (eds) *The O.J. Simpson Trials: Rhetoric, Media, and the Law*, Carbondale: Southern Illinois University Press, pp 58–77.

Schuetz, J. (1999c) 'Final summation: narratives in contrast', in J. Schuetz and L.S. Lilley (eds) *The O.J. Simpson Trials: Rhetoric, Media, and the Law*, Carbondale: Southern Illinois University Press, pp 100–21.

Schuetz, J. and Lilley, L.S. (eds) (1999) *The O.J. Simpson Trials: Rhetoric, Media, and the Law*, Carbondale: Southern Illinois University Press.

Schuetz, J.E. and Snedaker, K.H. (1988) *Communication and Litigation: Case Studies of Famous Trials*, Carbondale: Southern Illinois University Press.

Schuller, R.A. and Stewart, A. (2000) 'Police responses to sexual assault complaints: the role of perpetrator/complainant intoxication', *Law and Human Behavior*, 24(5): 535–51.

Schum, D.A. and Martin, A.W. (1982) 'Formal and empirical research on cascaded inference in jurisprudence', *Law & Society Review*, 17(1): 105–52.

Schweitzer, D.A. (1970) 'The effect of presentation on source evaluation', *Quarterly Journal of Speech*, 56(1): 33–9.

Schweitzer, N.J. and Saks, M.J. (2011) 'Neuroimage evidence and the insanity defense', *Behavioral Sciences & the Law*, 29(4): 592–607.

Scott, M.B. and Lyman, S.M. (1968) 'Accounts', *American Sociological Review*, 33(1): 46–62.

Seal, L. (2010) 'Women, murder and narratives of femininity', in R. Roberts (ed) *Debating ... Bad Language in Criminal Justice*, Criminal Justice Matters: Violence of the British State, 82, London: Centre for Crime and Justice Studies. Available from: http://www.crimeandjustice.org.uk/publications/cjm/article/debating...-bad-language-criminal-justice

Secord, P. (1958) 'Facial features and inference processes in interpersonal perception', in R. Tagiuri and L. Petrullo (eds) *Person Perception and Interpersonal Behavior*, Stanford: Stanford University Press, pp 300–15.

Shan, Y. (2016) 'How credible are online product reviews? The effects of self-generated and system-generated cues on source credibility evaluation', *Computers in Human Behavior*, 55(B): 633–41.

Shapiro, D.L. (1991) 'The effects of explanations on negative reactions to deceit', *Administrative Science Quarterly*, 36(4): 614–30.

Shaw, J. and Bashir, M. (2003) *Living with Michael Jackson*, broadcast 3 February on ITV, UK.

Shaw, J.A. and Budd, E.C. (1982) 'Determinants of acquiescence and naysaying of mentally retarded persons', *American Journal of Mental Deficiency*, 87(1): 108–10.

Shaw, L. (2011) 'Casey Anthony trial turned into media frenzy', *Reuters*, 6 July. Available from: https://www.reuters.com/article/us-casey-idUSTRE7650HY20110706

Shigihara, A.M. (2013) 'It's only stealing a little a lot: techniques of neutralization for theft among restaurant workers', *Deviant Behavior*, 34(6): 494–512.

Shoemaker, D.J., South, D.R. and Lowe, J. (1973) 'Facial stereotypes of deviants and judgments of guilt or innocence', *Social Forces*, 51(4): 427–33.

Shover, N. and Bryant, K.M. (1993) 'Theoretical explanations of corporate crime', in M.B. Blankenship (ed) *Understanding Corporate Criminality*, New York: Garland, pp 141–76.

Sigelman, C.K., Budd, E.C., Spanhel, C.L. and Schoenrock, C.J. (1981) 'When in doubt, say yes: acquiescence in interviews with mentally retarded persons', *Mental Retardation*, 19(2): 53–8.

Sigelman, C.K., Winer, J.L. and Schoenrock, C.J. (1982) 'The responsiveness of mentally retarded persons to questions', *Education and Training in Mental Retardation*, 17(2): 120–4.

Simkin, S. (2014) *Cultural Constructions of the Femme Fatale: From Pandora's Box to Amanda Knox*, Basingstoke: Palgrave Macmillan.

Simon, D.R. and Eitzen, D.S. (1993) *Elite Deviance*, 4th edn, Boston: Allyn and Bacon.

Simon, M. (2015) 'Knox trial: both sides say the truth is in the evidence', *CNN*, 26 March. Available from: https://edition.cnn.com/2014/01/31/world/amanda-knox-evidence/

Simpson, O.J. (2006) *If I Did It*, New York: Regan Books/HarperCollins.

Skeem, J.L. and Golding, S. (2001) 'Describing jurors' personal conceptions of insanity and their relationship to case judgments', *Psychology, Public Policy, and Law*, 7(3): 561–621.

Skolnick, P. and Shaw, J.I. (1997) 'The O.J. Simpson criminal trial verdict: racism or status shield?', *Journal of Social Issues*, 53(3): 503–16.

Sky News (2014) 'Oscar Pistorius describes night he shot Reeva Steenkamp dead', YouTube, 14 May. Available from: https://www.youtube.com/watch?v=JHqKytF8kGk

Smith, D. (2014) 'Oscar Pistorius prosecutors granted right to appeal against verdict', *The Guardian*, 10 December. Available from: https://www.theguardian.com/world/2014/dec/10/oscar-pistorius-prosectors-granted-right-appeal-verdict

Smith, D.J. (2005) *Supper with the Crippens*, London: Orion.

Smith, J. (2013) *Misogynies*, London: Westbourne Press.

Snyman, C.R. (2004) 'The two reasons for the existence of private defence and their effect on the rules relating to the defence in South Africa', *South African Journal of Criminal Justice*, 17(2): 178–92.

Sounes, H. (1995) *Fred and Rose*, London: Little, Brown Book Group.

Spears, J.W. and Spohn, C.C. (1997) 'The effect of evidence factors and victim characteristics on prosecutors' charging decisions in sexual assault cases', *Justice Quarterly*, 14(3): 501–24.

Spencer, K., Mansaray, J. and Peplow, G. (2021) 'R Kelly convicted: everybody knew the allegations – so why has it taken 30 years to get justice', *Sky News*, 29 September. Available from: https://news.sky.com/story/r-kelly-convicted-everybody-knew-the-allegations-so-why-has-it-taken-30-years-to-get-justice-12420062

Spohn, C. and Tellis, K. (2014) *Policing and Prosecuting Sexual Assault: Inside the Criminal Justice System*, Boulder: Lynne Rienner.

Spohn, C., Beichner, D. and Davis-Frenzel, E. (2001) 'Prosecutorial justifications for sexual assault case rejection: guarding the "Gateway to Justice"', *Social Problems*, 48(2): 206–35.

Sprack, J. (2002) 'Publicity surrounding the trial', in M. McConville and G. Wilson (eds) *The Handbook of the Criminal Justice Process*, Oxford: Oxford University Press, pp 221–36.

St. Johnston, T.E. (1966) 'Judges' rules and police interrogation in England today', *Journal of Criminal Law and Criminology*, 57(1): 85–92.

Stanko, E.A. (1981–82) 'The impact of victim assessment on prosecutors' screening decisions: the case of the New York County District Attorney's Office', *Law and Society Review*, 16(2): 225–40.

State's Heads of Arguments (2014) 'The State versus Oscar Leonard Carl Pistorius, State's Heads of Argument'. Available from: https://juror13lw.files.wordpress.com/2014/08/oscar-pistorius-heads-of-argument.pdf

Steadman, H.J., Keitner, L., Braff, J. and Arvanites, T.M. (1983) 'Factors associated with a successful insanity plea', *American Journal of Psychiatry*, 140(4): 401–5.

Steblay, N.M., Besirevic, J. Fulero, S.M. and Jimenez-Lorente, B. (1999) 'The effects of pretrial publicity on juror verdicts: a meta-analytic review', *Law and Human Behavior*, 23(2): 219–35.

Stewart, M.W. and Byrne, C. (2000) 'Genocide, political violence, and the neutralization of evil'. Paper presented at the American Sociological Association Annual Meeting, Washington, DC.

Stone, A.A. (1993) 'Murder with no apparent motive', *Journal of Psychiatry & Law*, 21(2): 175–89.

Storrs, E. (2004) ' "Our scapegoat": an exploration of media representations of Myra Hindley and Rosemary West', *Theology & Sexuality*, 11(1): 9–28.

Strickland, S. (2012) 'Full interview: former Casey judge talks verdict, jury', *WESH 2 News*, 3 July. Available from: https://www.youtube.com/watch?v=PNH6iiQrbvQ

Strömwall, L. and Granhag, P.A. (2003) 'How to detect deception? Arresting the beliefs of police officers, prosecutors and judges', *Psychology, Crime & Law*, 9(1): 19–36.

Suckle-Nelson, J.A., Colwell, K., Hiscock-Anisman, C., Florence, S., Youschak, K.E. and Duarte, A. (2010) 'Assessment criteria indicative of deception (ACID): replication and gender differences', *The Open Criminology Journal*, 3: 23–30. Available from: https://benthamopen.com/contents/pdf/TOCRIJ/TOCRIJ-3-23.pdf

Summers, C. (2005) 'Remembering "trial of the century"', *BBC News*, 22 November. Available from: http://news.bbc.co.uk/1/hi/uk/4447478.stm

Supreme Court of Appeal (2015) *Director of Public Prosecutions, Gauteng v Pistorius* (96/2015) [2015] ZASCA 204 (3 December 2015).

Supreme Court of Appeal (2017) *The Director of Public Prosecutions, Gauteng v Oscar Leonard Carl Pistorius* (950/2016) [2017] ZASCA 158 (24 November 2017).

Sweetingham, L. (2005) 'Actor Robert Blake acquitted of his wife's murder', *CNN*, 29 March. Available from: https://edition.cnn.com/2005/LAW/03/17/ctv.blake/

Sykes, G. and Matza, D. (1957) 'Techniques of neutralization: a theory of delinquency', *American Sociological Review*, 22(6): 664–70.

Symons, J. (2001) *Horatio Bottomley*, Looe: House of Stratus.

Tabb, K., Lebowitz, M.S. and Appelbaum, P.S. (2019) 'Behavioral genetics and attributions of moral responsibility', *Behavior Genetics*, 49(2): 128–35.

Tanford, J.A. (1983) *The Trial Process, Law, Tactics and Ethics*, 1st edn, Charlottesville: The Michie Company.

Tarm, M. (2019) 'R. Kelly was acquitted in 2008: here's why the current case against him may be stronger', *Global News*, 22 February. Available from: https://globalnews.ca/news/4990839/r-kelly-acquitted-2008-current-case/

Tennant, E.E. (2001) *The Future of the Diminished Responsibility Defence to Murder*, Chichester: Barry Rose.

Terblanche, S. and Mackenzie, G. (2008) 'Mandatory sentences in South Africa: lessons for Australia?', *The Australian and New Zealand Journal of Criminology*, 41(3): 402–20.

Testa, M. and Friedman, S.H. (2012) 'Diminished capacity', *Journal of the American Academy of Psychiatry and the Law*, 40(4): 567–9.

Thalji, J. (2011) 'Evidence "wasn't there"', *Tampa Bay Times*, 7 July.

Thalji, J. and LaPeter, L. (2011) 'Casey Anthony juror No. 2 says the jury wanted to find her guilty, but the evidence "wasn't there"', *Tampa Bay Times*, 6 July. Available from: https://web.archive.org/web/20170808205453/http://www.tampabay.com/news/courts/casey-anthony-juror-2-says-the-jury-wanted-to-find-her-guilty-but-the/1179177

The American Bar Association (2020) *Model Rules of Professional Conduct*. Available from: https://www.americanbar.org/groups/professional_responsibility/publications/model_rules_of_professional_conduct/model_rules_of_professional_conduct_table_of_contents/

The Fargo Forum (1910) 'Leneve girl is silent', 3 August. Available from: https://www.gastearsivi.com/en/gazete/fargo_forum/1910-08-03/1

The Guardian (2016) 'Yorkshire Ripper Peter Sutcliffe "moved back to jail"', 25 August. Available from: https://www.theguardian.com/uk-news/2016/aug/25/yorkshire-ripper-peter-sutcliffe-moved-back-to-jail

The State and Oscar Leonard Carl Pistorius (2014) Judgment. Available from: http://www.saflii.org/za/cases/ZAGPPHC/2014/793.pdf

The Telegraph (2018) 'Rose West launches new bid for release as friends say she doesn't want to die in prison', 30 December. Available from: https://www.telegraph.co.uk/news/2018/12/30/rose-west-launches-new-bid-release-friends-say-doesnt-want-die/

The Washington Post (1981) 'Psychiatrist's view of Sutcliffe', 14 May. Available from: https://www.washingtonpost.com/archive/politics/1981/05/14/psychiatrists-view-of-sutcliffe/04617aa3-7481-4a39-91f7-e3fb60d31e18/

Thomas, J. (1996) 'Oklahoma Bombing case to be moved to Colorado', *New York Times*, 21 February. Available from: https://www.nytimes.com/1996/02/21/us/oklahoma-bombing-case-to-be-moved-to-colorado.html

Timony, J.P. (2000) 'Demeanor credibility', *Catholic University Law Review*, 49(4): 903–43.

Toobin, J. (1996) *The Run of His Life: The People v. O.J. Simpson*, New York: Random House [republished in 2016 as *The People v. O.J. Simpson: The Run of His Life*].

Topping, A. (2020) 'Peter Sutcliffe, Yorkshire Ripper, dies aged 74', 13 November. Available from: https://www.theguardian.com/uk-news/2020/nov/13/yorkshire-ripper-peter-sutcliffe-dies-aged-74

Torry, Z.D. and Billick, S.B. (2010) 'Overlapping universe: understanding legal insanity and psychosis', *Psychiatric Quarterly*, 81(3): 253–62.

Transcript of Preliminary Hearing (1995) 'Grand Jury indictment of Timothy McVeigh and Terry Nichols', *Famous Trials*, 27 April. Available from: https://www.famous-trials.com/oklacity/734-indictment

Trocchio, S. (2015) 'Miranda rights', in W.G. Jennings (ed) *The Encyclopedia of Crime and Punishment, Vol. 2*, Chichester: Wiley Blackwell, pp 883–6.

Tsimploulis, G., Niveau, G., Eytan, A., Giannakopoulos, P. and Sentissi, O. (2018) 'Schizophrenia and criminal responsibility: a systematic review', *Journal of Nervous and Mental Disease*, 206(5): 370–7.

Uchino, B.N., Cacioppo, J.T. and Kiecolt-Glaser, J.K. (1996) 'The relationship between social support and physiological processes: a review with emphasis on underlying mechanisms and implications for health', *Psychological Bulletin*, 119(3): 488–531.

van Koppen, P. (2011) *Overtuigend bewijs: Indammen van rechterlijke dwalingen* [Convincing Evidence: Reducing the Number of Miscarriages of Justice], Amsterdam: Nieuw Amsterdam.

van Zyl Smit, D. and Isakow, N.M. (1985) 'Assessors and criminal justice', *South African Journal on Human Rights*, 1(3): 218–35.

Vidmar, N. (2002) 'Case studies of pre- and midtrial prejudice in criminal and civil litigation', *Law and Human Behavior*, 26(1): 77–105.

Viljoen, J.L., Klaver, J. and Roesch, R. (2005) 'Legal decisions of preadolescent and adolescent defendants: predictors of confessions, pleas, communication with attorneys, and appeals', *Law and Human Behaviour*, 29(3): 253–77.

Viljoen, J.L., Zapf, P.A. and Roesch, R. (2007) 'Adjudicative competence and comprehension of Miranda rights in adolescent defendants: a comparison of legal standards', *Behavioral Sciences & the Law*, 25(1): 1–19.

Vogt, A. (2014) 'Amanda Knox wielded the knife that killed Meredith, says judge', *The Week*, 29 April. Available from: http://www.theweek.co.uk/amanda-knox/58324/amanda-knox-wielded-the-knife-that-killed-meredith-says-judge

Vrij, A. (1995) 'Behavioral correlates of deception in a simulated police interview', *Journal of Psychology: Interdisciplinary and Applied*, 129(1): 15–28.

Vrij, A. (2000) *Detecting Lies and Deceit: The Psychology of Lying and the Implications for Professional Practice*, Chichester: Wiley.

Vrij, A. (2008) *Detecting Lies and Deceit: Pitfalls and Opportunities*, Chichester: Wiley.

Vrij, A. (2014) 'Interviewing to detect deception', *European Psychologist*, 19(3): 184–94.

Vrij, A. (2018) 'Verbal lie detection tools from an applied perspective', in J.P. Rosenfeld (ed) *Detecting Concealed Information and Deception: Recent Developments*, London: Academic Press, pp 297–327.

Vrij, A. and Fisher, R.P. (2016) 'Which lie detection tools are ready for use in the criminal justice system?', *Journal of Applied Research in Memory and Cognition*, 5(3): 302–7.

Vrij, A., Fisher, R.P. and Blank, H. (2017) 'A cognitive approach to lie detection: a meta-analysis', *Legal and Criminological Psychology*, 22(1): 1–21.

Wagenaar, W.A. (1995) 'Anchored narratives: a theory of judicial reasoning and its consequences', in G. Davies, S. Lloyd-Bostock, M. McCurran and C. Wilson (eds) *Psychology, Law, and Criminal Justice: International Developments in Research and Practice*, Berlin: De Gruyter, pp 267–85.

Wagenaar, W.A., van Koppen, P.J. and Crombag, H.F.M. (1993) *Anchored Narratives: The Psychology of Criminal Evidence*, New York: St. Martin's Press.

Wardrup, M. (2009) 'Michael Jackson: events that led to child abuse trial', *The Telegraph*, 26 June. Available from: https://www.telegraph.co.uk/culture/music/michael-jackson/5643915/Michael-Jackson-events-that-led-to-child-abuse-trial.html

Warren, J.I., Murrie, D.C., Chauhan, P., Dietz, P.E. and Morris, J. (2004) 'Opinion formation in evaluating sanity at the time of the offense: an examination of 5175 pre-trial evaluations', *Behavioral Sciences & the Law*, 22(2): 171–86.

Waterbury, M.C. (2011) *The Monster of Perugia: The Framing of Amanda Knox*, np: Perception Development.

Watson, J.C. (2002) 'Litigation public relations: the lawyers' duty to balance news coverage of their clients', *Communication Law and Policy*, 7(1): 77–103.

Waxman, S.P. (2020) 'Innocent juvenile confessions', *Journal of Criminal Law and Criminology*, 110(1): 1–8.

Wei, R. and Lo, V. (2021) *News in Their Pockets: A Cross-City Comparative Study of Mobile News Consumption in Asia*, New York: Oxford University Press.

Weir, B. (2020) Child Sexual Abuse and the Australian Roman Catholic Church: Using Techniques of Neutralisation to Examine Institutional Responses to Clergy-Perpetrated Child Sexual Abuse, PhD thesis, School of Justice, Faculty of Law, Queensland University of Technology. Available from: https://eprints.qut.edu.au/177244/

Weiss, K.J., Gutman, A.R. and Berrettini, W.H. (2020) 'Invoking behavioural genetics in criminal mitigation: what can experts reasonably say?' *SM Journal of Forensic Research and Criminology*, 4: 7 doi: https://dx.doi.org/10.36876/smjfrc945423.

Wellborn, O.G., III (1990) 'Demeanor', *Cornell Law Review*, 76(5): 1075–105.

Wentz, E. and Keimig, K. (2019) 'Arrest and referral decisions in sexual assault cases: the influence of police discretion on case attrition', *Social Sciences*, 8(6): art 180. Available from: https://www.mdpi.com/2076-0760/8/6/180

Wesson, M. (2006) '"Particular intentions": the Hillmon case and the Supreme Court', *Law & Literature*, 18(3): 343–402.

West, M. (with McKay, N.) (2018) *Love as Always, Mum xxx: The True and Terrible Story of Surviving a Childhood with Fred and Rose West*, London: Seven Dials.

White, S. (1985) 'The insanity defense in England and Wales since 1843', *The Annals of the American Academy of Political and Social Science*, 477(1): 43–57.

Wiedeman, R. (2017) 'The Duke Lacrosse scandal and the birth of the Alt-Right', *Intelligencer*, 14 April. Available from: https://nymag.com/intelligencer/2017/04/the-duke-lacrosse-scandal-and-the-birth-of-the-alt-right.html

Wigmore, J.H. (1931) *The Principles of Judicial Proof or the Process of Proof as Given by Logic, Psychology, and General Experience, and Illustrated in Judicial Trials*, 2nd edn, Boston: Little, Brown.

Wigmore, J.H. (1970) *Evidence in Trials at Common Law, Vol. 3A*, revised by J.H. Chadbourn, Boston: Little, Brown [first published 1904].

Williamson, T. (2006) 'Towards greater professionalism: minimizing miscarriages of justice', in T. Williamson (ed) *Investigative Interviewing: Rights, Research, Regulation*, Cullompton: Willan, pp 147–66.

Willmott, D., Boduszek, D., Debowska, A. and Woodfield, R. (2018) 'Introduction and validation of the Juror Decision Scale (JDS): an empirical investigation of the story model', *Journal of Criminal Justice*, 57: 26–34.

Wilson, A.N. (2006) 'Rose West', in R. Wilkes (ed) *The Mammoth Book of Famous Trials*, New York: Carroll & Graf, pp 497–515.

Winkel, F.W. and Koppelaar, L. (1991) 'Rape victims' style of self-presentation and secondary victimization by the environment: an experiment', *Journal of Interpersonal Violence*, 6(1): 29–40.

Winter, J. (2004) 'The role of gender in judicial decision-making: similar fact evidence, the Rose West trial and beyond', *International Journal of Evidence & Proof*, 8(1): 31–46.

Wise, A. (2009) 'Amanda Knox trial told her DNA mixed with victim's blood', *ABC News*, 22 May. Available from: http://abcnews.go.com/International/story?id=7656872

Wixted, J.T., Mickes, L. and Fisher, R.P. (2018) 'Rethinking the reliability of eyewitness memory', *Perspectives on Psychological Science*, 13(3): 324–35.

Woestehoff, S.A. and Meissner, C.A. (2016) 'Juror sensitivity to false confession risk factors: dispositional vs. situational attributions for a confession', *Law and Human Behavior*, 40(5): 564–79.

Woffinden, B. (1997) *Hanratty: The Final Verdict*, London: Macmillan.

Wolf, S. and Bugaj, A.M. (1990) 'The social impact of courtroom witnesses', *Social Behaviour*, 5(1): 1–13.

Wong, S.K. (2010) 'Crime clearance rates in Canadian municipalities: a test of Donald Black's theory of law', *International Journal of Law Crime and Justice*, 38(1): 17–36.

Wong, M., Goodboy, A.K., Murtagh, M.P., Hackney, A.A. and McCutcheon, L.E. (2010) 'Are celebrities charged with murder likely to be acquitted?', *North American Journal of Psychology*, 12(3): 625–36.

Woodrow, J.C. (2012) *Rose West: The Making of a Monster*, London: Hodder & Stoughton.

Woody, W.D., Forrest, K.D. and Yendra, S. (2014) 'Comparing the effects of explicit and implicit false-evidence ploys on mock jurors' verdicts, sentencing recommendations, and perceptions of police interrogation', *Psychology, Crime and Law*, 20(6): 603–17.

Wykes, M. (1998) 'A family affair: the British press, sex and the Wests', in C. Carter, G. Branston and S. Allan (eds) *News, Gender and Power*, London: Routledge, pp 233–47.

Yallop, D.A. (1981) *Deliver Us from Evil*, London: Macdonald Futura.

York, C. (2016) 'Nick Pisa Twitter criticism slams journalist for "Amanda Knox" documentary appearance', *Huffington Post*, 4 October. Available from: https://www.huffingtonpost.co.uk/entry/nick-pisa-journalist_uk_57f35d9ce4b038eb7459b571

YouGov (2014) 'Brits think Knox is guilty, Americans not so sure', 5 February. Available from: https://yougov.co.uk/topics/politics/articles-reports/2014/02/05/brits-knox-guilty-americans-not-sure

Young, F. (1920) *The Trial of Hawley Harvey Crippen*, Edinburgh: William Hodge.

YouTube Clip (2008) 'George and Cindy Anthony clash with protestors again – Sept 18 – Caylee Marie Anthony', 19 September. Available from: https://www.youtube.com/watch?v=lQHi-6NdltQ

YouTube Documentary (2016) 20/20 'Amanda Knox: Guilty Again'. Available from: https://www.youtube.com/watch?v=0A7Vd5NneLk

Zellner, K. (2018) 'A Legal Miracle' (episode 3), *Making a Murderer*, directed by Moira Demos and Laura Ricciardi, Netflix.

Zellner, K. (2021) @zellnerlaw, Twitter, 19 November. Available from: https://twitter.com/ZellnerLaw/status/1461666547022405639

Zha, X., Yang, H., Yan, Y., Liu, K. and Huang, C. (2018) 'Exploring the effect of social media information quality, source credibility and reputation on informational fit-to-task: moderating role of focused immersion', *Computers in Human Behavior*, 79: 227–37.

Zonen, R. (2005a) Cross examination of Macaulay Culkin, 11 May. Available from: http://www.reflectionsonthedance.com/05-11-05__Marcus_VNrman_McCauly___Outtake_.txt

Zonen, R. (2005b) Prosecution closing statement, 3 June. Available from: https://www.themichaeljacksoninnocentproject.com/blog/060305.txt

Zuraidah, A. (2009) 'Powerless language for powerful communication: delineating influence in group decision making', *International Journal of Learning*, 16(10): 509–20.

Case law

Broome v Perkins [1987] Crim LR 271

R v Ahluwalia [1992] 96 Cr APP R 133 Court of Appeal

R v Byrne [1960] 2 QB 396

R v Campbell [1987] 84 Cr App R 255

R v Gittens [1984] 79 Cr App R 272

R v Martin [2002] 2 WLR 1

R c. Martin [2017] QCCS 193 (CanLII)

R c. Pinard [2014] QCCQ 5630 (CanLII)

R v Reynolds 1988

Re A (conjoined twins) [2001] 2 WLR 480

State v Neutzel [1980] 606 P.2d 920

Acts of Parliament

Contempt of Court Act 1981

Coroners and Justice Act 2009

Criminal Procedure (Insanity and Unfitness to Plead) Act 1991

Homicide Act 1957

Murder (Abolition of Death Penalty) Act 1965

Police and Criminal Evidence Act 1984

Trial of Lunatics Act 1883

US Legislation

2005 Wisconsin Act 60

Brady Handgun Violence Protection Act 1993

Index

References to endnotes show both the
page number and the note number (231n3).